This is the first comprehensive study of how different ethical traditions deal with the central moral problems of international affairs. Using the organizing concept of a tradition, it shows that ethics offers many different languages for moral debate rather than a set of unified doctrines.

Each chapter describes the central concepts, premises, vocabulary and history of a particular tradition and explains how that tradition has dealt with a set of recurring ethical issues in international relations. Such issues include national self-determination, the use of force in armed intervention or nuclear deterrence, and global distributive justice.

Written by leading specialists in the USA and UK, *Traditions of International Ethics* treats the subject of international ethics in an encyclopedic way, allowing readers to identify internal tensions within, as well as points of agreement and disagreement between, a wide variety of traditions. It is an invaluable source that students and specialists of international affairs, moral philosophers and theologians will consult for information on the full range of reflection on international ethics.

CAMBRIDGE STUDIES IN INTERNATIONAL RELATIONS: 17

TRADITIONS OF INTERNATIONAL ETHICS

Cambridge Studies in International Relations is a joint initiative of Cambridge University Press and the British International Studies Association (BISA). The series will include a wide range of material, from undergraduate textbooks and surveys to research-based monographs and collaborative volumes. The aim of the series is to publish the best new scholarship in International Studies from Europe, North America and the rest of the world.

CAMBRIDGE STUDIES IN INTERNATIONAL RELATIONS

TRADITIONS OF INTERNATIONAL ETHICS

edited by

TERRY NARDIN

Professor of Political Science, University of Wisconsin–Milwaukee

and

DAVID R. MAPEL

Associate Professor of Political Science, University of Colorado at Boulder

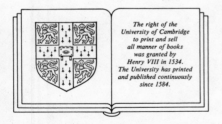

The right of the
University of Cambridge
to print and sell
all manner of books
was granted by
Henry VIII in 1534.
The University has printed
and published continuously
since 1584.

CAMBRIDGE UNIVERSITY PRESS
Cambridge   New York   Port Chester
Melbourne   Sydney

Published by the Press Syndicate of the University of Cambridge
The Pitt Building, Trumpington Street, Cambridge CB2 1RP
40 West 20th Street, New York, NY 10011–4211, USA
10 Stamford Road, Oakleigh, Victoria 3166, Australia

First published 1992

Printed in Great Britain at the University Press, Cambridge

A catalogue record
for this book is
available from the
British Library

Library of Congress cataloguing in publication data

Traditions of international ethics/edited by Terry Nardin and David R. Mapel.
    p.   cm. – (Cambridge studies in international relations: 17)
Includes index.
ISBN 0 521 40458 4
1. International relations – Moral and ethical aspects.
2. International law.
I. Nardin, Terry, 1942– .
II. Mapel, David, 1952– .
III. Series.
JX1255.T69   1992
172'.4 –dc20   91–8136   CIP

ISBN 0 521 40458 4 hardback

CE

CONTENTS

CONTRIBUTORS

Joseph Boyle is Professor of Philosophy at St. Michael's College, University of Toronto and past president (1989) of the American Catholic Philosophical Association. He is the author (with John Finnis and Germain Grisez) of *Nuclear Deterrence, Morality and Realism* (1987) and has authored and co-authored books and articles on ethical theory, applied ethics, and Thomistic interpretation.

Chris Brown is Lecturer in Politics and International Relations at the University of Kent at Canterbury. He has published articles on international relations theory, Marxism and international relations, and development and dependency in the *Review of International Studies*, *Millennium*, and other journals.

Michael G. Cartwright is Assistant Professor of Philosophy and Religious Studies at Allegheny College. He is the author of *Practices, Politics and Performance: Toward an Ecclesial Hermeneutic for Christian Ethics* (1991) and of several articles on biblical hermeneutics and the use of Scripture in Christian ethics.

Thomas Donaldson is a professor at Georgetown University, where he holds appointments in the School of Business, the Department of Philosophy, and the Kennedy Institute for Ethics. He is also a Senior Fellow of the Olsson Center for Ethics at the Darden School of the University of Virginia. His books include *Corporations and Morality* (1982) and *The Ethics of International Business* (1989).

Jack Donnelly is Associate Professor of Political Science at the University of North Carolina at Chapel Hill. He is the author of *The Concept of Human Rights* (1985), *Universal Human Rights in Theory and Practice* (1989), and articles on the theory and practice of human rights.

Anthony Ellis is Professor of Philosophy at Virginia Commonwealth University. He was formerly Senior Lecturer and Chairman of the Department of Moral Philosophy at the University of St. Andrews, Scotland, and Academic Director of the St. Andrews Centre for Philosophy and Public Affairs. He has published articles on ethics in a number of journals, and is the editor of *Ethics and International Relations* (1986).

Steven Forde is Assistant Professor of Political Science at the University of North Texas. His work covers the history of political philosophy and includes a book on Thucydides, *The Ambition to Rule: Alcibiades and the Politics of Imperialism in Thucydides* (1989).

Murray Forsyth is Professor of Politics at the University of Leicester, where he is Director of the Centre for Federal Studies. He was educated at Balliol College, Oxford, and the College of Europe, Bruges. His publications include *Unions of States: the Theory and Practice of Confederation* (1981) and *Reason and Revolution: the Political Thought of the Abbé Sieyes* (1987).

Dorothy V. Jones is a diplomatic historian working on issues of international peace and security. She has been a visiting scholar in the Department of History, the University of Chicago, and is currently a research associate of the Newberry Library in Chicago. She is the author of *License for Empire* (1982), *Splendid Encounters: the Thought and Conduct of Diplomacy* (1984), and *Code of Peace: Ethics and Security in the World of the Warlord States* (1991). Her work on this chapter was supported by a John D. and Catherine T. MacArthur Foundation Fellowship in International Peace and Security, in a program administered by the Social Science Research Council.

David R. Mapel is Associate Professor of Political Science at the University of Colorado at Boulder. He is the author of *Social Justice Reconsidered* (1989) and has published articles in *The Journal of Politics*, *Political Theory*, *Polity*, and other journals. His research interests include contemporary Anglo-American political philosophy and international ethics.

Terry Nardin is Professor of Political Science at the University of Wisconsin–Milwaukee. He has been a Rockefeller Foundation Humanities Fellow and is the author of *Law, Morality, and the Relations of States* (1983). He is a member of the Board of Directors of the Ethikon

Institute of Los Angeles and chair of the Institute's Standing Committee on Intersocietal Relations.

Michael Joseph Smith is Associate Professor of Government and International Relations at the University of Virginia in Charlottesville, where he teaches international relations and political theory. He is the author of *Realist Thought from Weber to Kissinger* (1987).

R. J. Vincent was Montague Burton Professor of International Relations at the London School of Economics at the time of his death in November 1990. He had also taught at the Australian National University, Keele, Princeton, and Oxford. His books include *Nonintervention and International Order* (1974) and *Human Rights and International Relations* (1986).

PREFACE

There are many discussions of ethics and international affairs written from within a particular tradition like political realism or natural law. There are also many books and articles that deal with particular international issues, like military intervention or global justice. But there is no general work that teachers, students, and others interested in international affairs can consult to orient themselves to the full diversity of the major traditions of inquiry and debate concerning the ethics of international relations. The contributors to this book have worked together with the hope that a comprehensive and systematic study of how these ethical traditions approach the basic questions of international relations would help to clarify the disagreements and misunderstandings that characterize current discussions of international ethics.

While no volume short of an encyclopedia could cover the entire range of ethical thinking about international affairs, most of the important voices in the continuing debate on this subject are represented here. The most obvious omissions are the traditions of Islamic, Chinese, and other non-Western civilizations. We did not attempt to examine these partly because the debate about international ethics for many years has been so decisively shaped by Western ideas, partly because we were afraid to take on a task so obviously beyond our abilities. The result is a gap which we hope others will be able to fill in coming years.

Our aim was to produce a basic reference work on international ethics, rather than a collection of individual essays. To achieve this aim we have chosen to adopt a descriptive stance and to consider the central concepts, vocabulary, and premises of the major traditions that have shaped current discussions of the subject. Furthermore, in order to strengthen the unity of the volume, the chapters have been written to a common set of standards.

Each chapter addresses the following guiding questions: (1) How does the tradition understand and connect the ideas of individual good, the common good, the state, and the international community? (2) How does the tradition understand the relation between principles and consequences? (3) How does the tradition establish the validity of its principles? And (4) How does the tradition understand the international environment, and what are the ethical implications of that understanding?

Each chapter also considers the history of its tradition and draws from a common pool of examples in discussing how the tradition handles particular issues of normative judgment. The individual chapters have been extensively cross-referenced so that the reader can pursue particular themes that are treated in more than one place, and each of the substantive chapters concludes with a bibliographic essay. Finally, the editors have provided an introductory chapter on the idea of tradition in the study of international ethics and a conclusion that explores relationships among the traditions.

The volume grows out of a working group on international ethics assembled and coordinated by Terry Nardin at the invitation of International Studies Association Past President Harold Guetzkow. With generous support from the Carnegie Council on Ethics and International Affairs, the working group was able to meet twice a year during a three-year period beginning in 1987 to discuss the research of its members and to revise contributions to the present volume in response to criticism from the group as a whole. Robert J. Myers, President of the Carnegie Council, and Joel Rosenthal, who directs its Education and Studies Program, provided valuable guidance while permitting us complete scholarly independence. We are also indebted to Bruce Nichols, formerly of the Carnegie Council, who helped launch the project, and to Philip Valera, President of the Ethikon Institute of Los Angeles, who developed the model of comparative analysis of ethical traditions, using a common set of questions, on which the present volume is based.

During its final stages the project was guided by an editorial committee comprising the editors, Bruce Nichols, and Michael Joseph Smith. In addition to providing the initial impetus, Harold Guetzkow supplied detailed criticism of all the chapters. All the contributors offered useful suggestions about other chapters, as did working group members Alberto R. Coll, Russell Hardin, Robert C. Johansen, and Moorhead Wright. We are grateful to friends and colleagues who commented on particular chapters, including David A. Duquette, Gordon Graham, Glenn Holland, Brad Hooker, Rhoda Howard, L. Gregory Jones, David Lumsdaine, Howard Tamashiro, Robert W. Tucker, Todd Whitmore, and students and faculty in the

Program on International Politics, Economics, and Security at the University of Chicago. We also wish to thank Holly Arrow for her editorial work on the typescript and Jack Donnelly for preparing the index.

1 ETHICAL TRADITIONS IN INTERNATIONAL AFFAIRS

TERRY NARDIN

Ethical concerns have always been part of international affairs. "I will grant the Ammonites no reprieve, because in their greed for land they invaded the ploughlands of Gilead," the Lord says in Amos 1:13, and his anger is perfectly intelligible to us. There are times when such judgments are out of fashion, but disdain for them is never permanent. Current judgments of the rights and wrongs of foreign policy are affected by past efforts to articulate the legitimate claims of political communities, to lay down rules for civilized diplomacy, to distinguish just and unjust wars, and to establish procedures for the peaceful settlement of international disputes. Even the issue of distributive justice, though new to the international agenda, has a long history in political thought. When we argue about international affairs we draw directly or indirectly on established traditions of ethical discourse.

The premise of this volume is that our understanding of the ethical dimension of international affairs would be enlarged by a better understanding of the traditions of conduct and inquiry that shape debate in this field. What are these traditions? How do they understand the proper ends and means of foreign policy and the moral basis of international order? What can we learn by comparing them? Can we identify areas of convergence? What differences persist both within and between traditions? By asking questions like these, we focus attention on the intellectual heritage that underlies our arguments about the ethics of international relations.

The moralist may want to reclaim a forgotten or corrupted tradition in order to use it, while the historian can be satisfied with nothing more (or less) ambitious than a better understanding of the past. In neither case, however, is the heritage to be recovered something we must regard with uncritical deference. One can be interested in a tradition without being a traditionalist. Ethical traditions are traditions of argument, not uniform and unchanging doctrines. This is as true of the traditions of inquiry that shape moral philosophy – like utilitarianism or natural law – as it is of the practical traditions of moral judgment

1

and public debate – such as liberal internationalism, political realism, or international law. While each tradition shapes ethical debate in different ways, all make room for a wide range of opinions. Each reveals internal tensions as well as differences with other traditions.

The following chapters explore a number of ethical traditions that have been important in international affairs. My aim in this introduction is to consider certain issues raised by the effort to identify and investigate these traditions. I will discuss what an ethical tradition is, the criteria by which one tradition may be distinguished from another, and the implications of approaching international ethics through the idea of tradition. I will defend the thesis that in making ethical judgments, we make use of the resources of inherited traditions of judgment – that ethical judgment is in one way or another judgment within a tradition. And I will consider the most common objections to approaching ethics through the idea of tradition: that relying on the idea of tradition is necessarily relativist or conservative.

Ethical judgment and ethical inquiry

We usually think of ethics as a branch of philosophy, but other eras and civilizations have treated ethical concerns as an aspect of law or theology. Medieval thought, for example, did not make the sharp distinctions Westerners later established between ethics, law, and religion, and such distinctions are still alien to Islam. In seventeenth-century Europe, ethical books were often manuals of religious casuistry; a century later, readers in search of ethical guidance could turn to the epistolary novel. We must not confuse the narrow understanding of ethics that prevails in modern Western societies with the full range of ethical concerns. And we should be particularly careful to avoid defining ethics as moral philosophy.

Moral philosophy is systematic. Philosophers want to put the precepts of received morality into some sort of consistent order. They interpret morality as a system of general principles and try to discover a rational foundation for this system. Ethics, in the hands of the philosopher, turns into ethical theory. To some extent this is the unavoidable consequence of thinking methodically about ethical experience, and the present volume offers many examples of this process at work. But it is nevertheless an error to think that an ethical outlook or tradition is, in essence, a theoretical system of general principles. Like the law, ethics involves principles, but it also involves the interpretation and application of these principles by particular persons in particular circumstances. Philosophers are not, of course,

2

unaware of this; on the contrary, the point is central to the arguments of Aristotle, Aquinas, Kant, and many other moral philosophers. But it is in the nature of philosophy to be more interested in the general than in the particular, and so it is not surprising that ethics often becomes a search for moral principles rather than a study of how such principles are applied in particular cases.[1] Nor is it surprising that philosophers are seldom interested in describing and classifying ethical traditions, as a linguist or ethnographer might classify languages or cultures. The contributors to this volume are concerned with the sort of philosophical analysis just mentioned, but they are also concerned with the historical circumstances and characteristics of the traditions they examine.

Ethical traditions are resilient but not immutable practices that are constantly modified in use. To think ethically is to move back and forth between the general and the particular – to draw upon general principles in reaching particular judgments and decisions and, at the same time, to revise those principles in the light of the particular circumstances in which they are used. Ethics involves principles but it also involves interpretation, choice, and action. And this points toward the importance of judgment in interpreting principles and in choosing and acting on the basis of these interpretations. Let us therefore consider what is involved in making an ethical judgment, without assuming that focusing on judgment is the only approach to the subject of ethics.

What does it mean to call a judgment "ethical?" Why speak of "ethical judgments" rather than, say "moral judgments?" It is probably pointless to demand that these expressions be consistently distinguished, partly because the words "ethics" and "morality" are in fact used in many different ways, often as synonyms, and partly because philosophers, like parliamentarians or diplomats, fear that the resolution of substantive issues will be determined by the vocabulary in which the issues are framed. For the sake of clarity, however, I will mostly use "ethics" to refer to a wide range of considerations affecting choice and action and "moral" for the more limited realm defined by rules of proper conduct. In many contexts, "morality" is in fact the narrower term, for, unlike "ethics," it refers to a distinct institution, one that "demands a sharp boundary for itself" (Williams 1985, 7). The institution of morality is particularly concerned with duties that arise from the rules or precepts that constitute it, whereas

---

[1] For an argument that the analysis of cases is fundamental to ethics, see Jonsen and Toulmin (1988). Fullinwider (1988) argues the advantages of the case approach for teaching ethics.

the ethical realm also includes a concern with ideals and ends that go beyond these duties, and especially with the outcomes of action. This concern with outcomes, which is forward-looking, pulls against morality's concern with existing rules and duties. By adopting an inclusive definition of "ethics" I mean to include within the range of ethical concerns much that is important in politics and international affairs that would not, in my definition, count as moral.

If the domain of ethics is so large, it is not surprising that no ethical theory is able, for long, to sustain its claim to provide a comprehensive account of this domain. One should be particularly suspicious of efforts to define ethical judgments as judgments that balance all the various kinds of considerations – moral, prudential, utilitarian, legal, religious, aesthetic, and so on – that might bear on practical choice. According to this approach, a sound ethical judgment is one that reflects the most comprehensive view we can manage regarding our practical choices, as if there were only one such view. Fewer questions are begged by the suggestion, adopted here, that ethics includes many different kinds of concerns and that these concerns are not necessarily reconcilable.

If we adopt this inclusive conception, then ethics is not limited to judging acts to be morally right or wrong. Some ethical judgments are "moral" in the restricted sense that they involve the application of principles of right conduct, but others are concerned with acts as desirable or undesirable according to the outcomes they produce, or as virtuous or vicious according to the character they display. All these judgments can be either prospective or retrospective, and can be made from the perspective of the agent or the spectator. And, as the various chapters of this volume make clear, one can judge policies, institutions, and ways of life, as well as individual actions and character.

Furthermore, ethics is not limited to making judgments. We not only make ethical judgments, we try to understand them. So another kind of activity that is part of ethics involves studying various kinds of ethical judgment and the considerations underlying them. If we do this, we are engaged in ethical inquiry rather than in ethical evaluation. We are engaged with ethics as a branch of knowledge. We are not doing only "moral philosophy," however, both because ethics is concerned with other things besides morality, and because it pursues these concerns by a variety of methods, of which philosophy is only one. We can study the moral practices of particular communities or civilizations, and thus set out to write a history or ethnography of morals. Or we can study moral beliefs in relation to factors like age, gender, or social class, thereby becoming sociologists of morals. Some

4

disciplines are particularly concerned with the rationality of ethical judgments (economics, philosophy, political theory), others with their authority (jurisprudence, moral theology).

There is a strong tendency in some of these disciplines to challenge the view that ethical judgment involves interpretation. One of the advantages of the idea of tradition in the study of ethics is that it focuses attention on the interpretive dimension of ethical judgment. This is salutary, for judgment does indeed entail interpretation. The arguments supporting this claim are straightforward. First, in judging one necessarily applies standards of judgment and this application involves interpretation. Second, in making ethical judgments we judge conduct, and conduct is meaningful. It exhibits intelligence and embodies intention and choice. Intention and choice in turn presuppose a conception by the agent of the act to be performed and of the ends sought in choosing and acting, as well as a social context within which these choices are made and have consequences. In other words, conduct involves concepts and concepts have meaning. And meaning implies interpretation.

Although the metaphor can be pushed too far, in some respects human conduct is indeed like a text: it must be interpreted to be understood and it can be interpreted in different ways. Like biblical hermeneutics, jurisprudence, literary criticism, and other disciplines concerned with textual interpretation, ethics resists reduction to a single theory or method. In all the interpretive fields, we need to pay close attention to our "text" (whether it is the words on a page or the actions and practices of real people), but we cannot decode that text in a way that is authoritative in all contexts. Even in a given context it is often hard to agree for long what authoritative decoding would mean: interpretations are regularly challenged and often modified if not overthrown. We should realize that, in ethics as in literature, asking different questions will produce different answers and that it makes sense to ask as many questions as seem relevant to us. We don't have to be critical purists, either as judges of conduct or as readers of narratives. We can be eclectic, and we can be individual. We should know when the questions we ask reflect personal concerns, but that need not stop us from asking them.

In ethics and political theory, and perhaps in literature too, this kind of talk invites the charge of "relativism." Although no reading of a text is unchallengeable, and every text worth thinking about will probably continue to generate new readings, this does not mean that all readings are equally good. Likewise, although actions can be interpreted and evaluated in many different ways, it does not follow that

5

judgment is completely subjective. On the contrary, the clash of different judgments raises rather than banishes the question of their relative merits. Disagreement invites inquiry into the claims for each position and, indeed, where conduct is at issue, demands it. In both literature and ethics, judgment is linked to rational inquiry within the traditions of interpretation and debate that give shape to literary and ethical experience.

Ethical tradition

Let us look more closely at the idea of an ethical tradition. The word "tradition" comes from the vocabulary of law. It once referred to the act of handing over – delivering, transferring – a material thing to another person. The idea of relaying or communicating nonmaterial things like stories, beliefs, and customs is a generalization of this more limited legal concept. And what can be handed over can also be handed down from generation to generation. If tradition is the process of handing down then, by extension, a tradition is the thing handed down, the belief or custom transmitted from one generation to another. And this leads us to the conception of a tradition as a long-established practice possessing something like the force of law, a practice that is authoritative precisely because of its status as a tradition.

More needs to be said about two aspects of the idea of tradition. First, we need to consider the defining attributes of tradition. What does it mean to call a practice a "tradition"? Are all practices traditional? If not, what makes a particular practice traditional? And, second, what is the relation between tradition and judgment? Is ethical judgment necessarily a matter of tradition? Are all ethical perspectives to be understood as traditions, or would it be more accurate to say that some are traditional, while others are not traditional or even antitraditional? The first set of questions is discussed in the remainder of this section, the second later in the chapter.

The ordinary understanding of tradition as an inheritance has been summed up by Martin Krygier as involving the authoritative presence of a continuously transmitted past. There are three elements in this definition. The first is that tradition looks to the past: "the contents of every tradition have, or are believed by its participants to have, originated some considerable time in the past." The second element is the authority within some community of an inherited practice or belief: its traditionality "consists in its *present* authority and significance." And, finally, there is the element of continuity in transmission:

a tradition "must have been, or be thought have have been, passed down over intervening generations" (Krygier 1986, 240).

Notice that the definition emphasizes subjectivity: a practice can be traditional within a community if members of that community believe it to be an ancient and continuously practiced inheritance, and if its present devotees acknowledge its authority. It allows possibilities that would be excluded by a more objective definition of tradition stressing the actual antiquity and continuity of a belief or custom. As Eric Hobsbawm has suggested, "'traditions' which appear or claim to be old are often quite recent in origin and sometimes invented" (Hobsbawm and Ranger 1983, 1). This raises the possibility of "invented tradition" – practices revived or even fabricated, that have emerged rapidly or have even been formally instituted, to which ancient origin and continuous transmission have been mistakenly or disingenuously attributed.

The concept of invented tradition is particularly important for the study of nationalist movements, which often encourage the construction of a past to fit currently favored political conceptions and programs (Hobsbawm and Ranger 1983, 13; Kedourie 1970). Historical criticism has repeatedly revealed the traditions of nations to be fictional. But there is probably an element of invention in every tradition that draws authority from its past, for such traditions characteristically legitimize change by minimizing it. At the same time they may exaggerate the discontinuity between the foundation of the tradition – Moses coming down from the mountain, or Romulus slaying Remus – and what is thought to have come before. By finding precedent in the past for new doctrines and practices, the tradition assimilates them to conventional opinion and reconciles them with other, more slowly changing elements in the tradition. For devotees of a tradition the discovery that an ancient rite or doctrine is in fact a recent innovation can be shattering: many a nineteenth-century Christian lost faith as historical investigations undermined one after another of the traditions of Christianity, while today the Maoris must assimilate the news that their legends were largely invented by European anthropologists (Wilford 1990).

The dogmatic elements of tradition are the most vulnerable to rational criticism. The identification of tradition with the unquestioned authority of inherited beliefs – which can lead to the refusal to question such beliefs and to the persecution of those who challenge them – is certainly connected with the low esteem in which both tradition and authority have been held since the Enlightenment. A tendency to see an opposition between dogmatic religion and

7

enquiring science, between obscurantism and enlightenment, and between repression and liberation, is part of our own inheritance today. But such thinking reflects a limited and simplistic conception of tradition, for at least two reasons.

First, authority of belief is only one kind of authority a tradition may have. It is important in religion, but there are other areas of life, such as law, in which it may play hardly any role at all. In modern societies, the authority of the law is a matter of procedure, not belief. The idea of civil or positive law becomes important in societies marked by deep religious and ideological disagreement. Where they exist, shared beliefs may bind the members of a community together. But where there is disagreement, social unity must rest on something else, even if it is something as unsatisfying as allowing those whose beliefs are disagreeable to live by them. The authority of civil law is required where the authority of once-shared beliefs has come into question, and is indeed the only sort of authority on which a liberal or pluralist order can be established (Friedman 1973, 1989). In short, while some traditions rest on dogma or the authority of a body of shared beliefs, others rest on the authority of a common framework of laws and procedures.

Second, the criticism of tradition as inherently dogmatic overlooks another important distinction by regarding all knowledge as information that can be reduced to a set of propositions. This kind of knowledge – "technical knowledge" – is not an embodiment of tradition but, on the contrary, its antithesis. The kind of knowledge inherent in tradition is knowledge one acquires by being apprenticed in a trade or serving as an intern in a hospital or congressional office. Here one learns not facts and doctrines but rather how things are done and how to behave. A person who knows the trade or discipline is one who has absorbed its traditions and made them his own. Those who really know a tradition are not, however, necessarily uncritical. On the contrary, only the person who has acquired an intimate firsthand working knowledge of a tradition is really in a position to criticize it; the outsider will have only a dim notion of what it is all about. The effective reform of a tradition is most likely to come from those who have been educated in it.

"Enlightened" criticism of traditions as repositories of ignorance and prejudice is not, however, entirely misconceived. The mistake is in thinking that the evil is inseparable from tradition itself, and that it can only be purged by rejecting all tradition. As historian of Christianity Jaroslav Pelikan has cogently argued, what must be rejected is not tradition as such but the ideology of traditionalism, according to

8

which a tradition becomes an end in itself requiring "an idolatrous submission" to the authority it asserts. But we must also reject the rationalist view that general truths can be entirely isolated from the particular traditions in which they are embedded. For a tradition is not merely an accidental and distorted expression of truths knowable in ways that are independent of the historical manner in which they came to be known. A tradition, properly understood, can show us "the way that we who are its heirs must follow if we are to go beyond it ... to a universal truth that is available only in a particular embodiment." There is no need to accept the choice, on which so many debates about tradition seem to insist, between the universal and the particular, the rational and the historical. "A living tradition," Pelikan argues, "must be both" (1984, 55–57).

Common morality and international law

The interplay between the rational structure of a tradition and its historical embodiments is nicely illustrated by the debate over whether there exists a universal or common morality and, if so, what its principles are. If "common morality" is a tradition, it is one identified at a fairly high level of generality for, as the substantive chapters of this volume demonstrate, the idea of common morality has received a variety of interpretations. It is, in other words, an abstraction from an immensely complicated accumulation of historically specific ideas and practices. Furthermore, it is an inherently controversial abstraction, for any tradition or family of traditions can be reconstructed in different ways depending on the questions, controversies, periods, or texts the interpreter thinks most important. And yet it is only by abstracting, by articulating recurrent patterns and continuities, that anything resembling a "tradition" can be identified at all.

Following Alan Donagan (1977, 1–9), I will use the expression "common morality" to refer to a point of view that was first articulated by the Stoics, became an important element in Jewish and Christian ethics, and is central to the great syntheses of Aquinas and Kant. The most significant philosophical interpretations of common morality, those of natural law and the Kantian tradition, understand it to be an ethic transcending the moral practices of particular communities. This ethic is sometimes called, simply, "morality," a name to which it lays claim by virtue of its superior rationality and universality. Its defining characteristic is that it depends neither on custom nor on divine authority, but on reason. Its principles must therefore be distinguished

9

from what Jews or Christians assert to be "moral," much of which is concerned with defining a full Jewish or Christian life, as they understand it. Common morality is the part of these communal moralities that applies to everyone. It is a universal code – "the moral law" or "natural law" – whose principles apply to human beings as rational creatures and is known to them through the exercise of reason.

This code has a complex structure that is not yet fully understood. But an account like Donagan's conveys its main lines and spirit. The precepts of common morality may be divided into those that concern the permissibility of acts considered objectively (right or wrong acts) and those that concern the subjective spirit in which a person acts (what a person may or may not be held responsible for). Intentions make a difference. Duties to oneself (such as the prohibition of self-injury) may be distinguished from duties to others (such as the precepts forbidding lying or cruelty). All the precepts of common morality are united by a fundamental principle, often identified as "the golden rule," which Kant formulates as the principle that one should always act so as to treat other human beings as an end and never as a means. This is by no means a self-evident principle, and both moralists and philosophers devote much effort to interpreting it.

Theorists of common morality assign great importance to the distinction between negative prohibitions and positive commands, though this distinction has more to do with the kinds of conduct governed by each than whether the duty is expressed negatively or positively. Our negative duties stem from the golden rule: we must not act in ways that treat human beings as objects, for example by enslaving them. On any interpretation of common morality, there are going to be a fair number of "thou shalt nots." Positive duties, in contrast, have to do with promoting good rather than avoiding harm. We ought to develop our own capacities and we ought to act so as to increase other people's well-being, insofar as we can do this without disproportionate difficulty and without violating any moral prohibitions. These qualifications are critical. We have a duty to act, if we reasonably can, in ways that have good consequences, but we must not use morally impermissible means in doing so. The prohibitions of common morality are absolute; the acts they forbid are wrong even if they are done for the sake of a good end. One must avoid acting wrongly, whatever the consequences.

The reason for putting limits on our duty to promote good is clear. Without such limits there would be no end to our duties to help others or promote other kinds of good outcomes.[2] We would lose our identi-

---

[2] On this principle and its international implications see Fishkin (1986).

ties as individuals guided by our own freely chosen ends and become mere instruments for the promotion of a necessarily impoverished set of human goods. And we would be unable to avoid inconsistency between the precepts of negative and positive duty if we could achieve good ends through morally forbidden actions. To permit good outcomes to be produced by morally impermissible means would be to tolerate violation of the fundamental principle of respect. Hence St. Paul's principle (Romans 3:7–8) that evil is not to be done that good may come of it.[3] This prohibition limits the application of another principle, sometimes called "the principle of least evil," which is of fundamental importance to political realism and other outcome-oriented ethical theories. In such theories the principle of least evil guides not only the choice among ends but also the choice between promoting a good and respecting a prohibition, because the interests protected by the prohibition are understood to be a good to be balanced against other goods. In common morality, however, the principle of least evil applies only to the choice among ends, not to the choice between promoting an end and respecting a prohibition.

The theory of common morality is often criticized for excluding reasoning about consequences. But it should be clear from the foregoing account that this criticism is based on a misunderstanding. Common morality, by requiring us to take our own development as persons seriously and by encouraging beneficence toward other persons, gives such reasoning a place within a more inclusive structure of constraining principles. It is therefore a mistake to say that common morality leaves no room for measuring and comparing different goods, for cost-benefit analysis, or for other forms of reasoning about consequences. Common morality limits such reasoning but it does not exclude it. What it does exclude is consequentialism, the doctrine that the consequences of an act, rather than its relation to principles of conduct, determine its rightness or wrongness, and that such principles have, at best, instrumental value in helping to secure morally desirable ends.

A related criticism is that common morality is unequal to the complexity of public affairs because it is a morality of formal and rigid rules. This, however, seems to be based on a misconception concerning the nature of rules and their place in moral reasoning. Rules are an abstraction from, not the essence of, moral conduct. The latter goes on within a complex framework of principles, precepts, standards, customs, habits, sentiments, and other considerations affecting

---

[3] Daube's (1965) discussion of the parallel principle in Jewish law has much significance for international ethics.

choice and action. These considerations can be expressed as rules only at the price of simplification. It is hard even for a grammarian to formulate rules that capture the complexity of linguistic usage. Moralists face an analogous difficulty. Because morality involves judgment in terms of moral considerations expressed as rules, interpreting what these rules mean in the particular circumstances of action is at the core of moral reasoning: moral reasoning is interpretive, not computational.

Common morality applies to international relations as well as to everyday life. But, as Chapters 6, 7, and 13 on natural law, Kantian ethics, and biblical argument demonstrate, there are different views on how it applies. One understanding of the tradition holds that the moral principles governing individual conduct apply with little modification to public and international affairs. A contrary tendency emphasizes the special principles governing international relations: treaties must be observed, diplomatic immunity respected, aggression resisted, and war crimes punished. Once called "the law of nations" and more recently labeled "the morality of states," these principles represent an interpretation of common morality in the circumstances of international affairs, one reflected most prominently, if incompletely, in the tradition of international law.

It may seem odd to speak of international law as an ethical tradition. If so, the problem cannot be that international law does not constitute a tradition. Like all law, it is explicitly traditional in its reliance on precedent. What seems problematic is the claim that international law is an *ethical* tradition. We are used to thinking of law as one thing and morality as another. Law is an institution about which we make ethical judgments, not itself a source of such judgments.

Yet if we consider law in light of the definitions of ethical judgment with which we began, it is hard to find any grounds except stipulative ones for concluding that legal judgments are not ethical. Law involves the application of principles to conduct. Like morality, it is concerned with duties and obligations. The topics covered in textbooks on international law do not differ greatly from those discussed in the literature on international ethics. Questions concerning treaties, diplomacy, and the use of force can be looked at from the lawyer's perspective as well as from the perspective of the realist, the Kantian moralist, or the utilitarian. For all these reasons, international law belongs on any short list of traditions of ethical judgment in international affairs.

Nonetheless, a number of doubts have been raised about international law that, if valid, would undermine its status as an independent ethical tradition possessing its own internal coherence. Some of these resemble the criticisms leveled against common morality and, indeed, the two traditions are combined as a target in the realist attacks of Kennan and others on "legalism-moralism." As the realists emphasized, politics has to do with the pursuit of interests and is therefore primarily concerned with results, whereas law, like common morality, imposes limits on that pursuit. Many are impatient with what appears to be the unrealistic and impractical character of legal as well as moral judgment, and are tempted to assimilate both into a more comprehensive ethic of consequences.

Other doubts about international law focus on its unique and problematic character as a system of law. Every student of international affairs has encountered the view that international law is "not really law" because it lacks effective institutions for making and applying laws, and that it is therefore of negligible importance in international affairs. Stated in a less extreme way, these observations are in fact well founded. Significant areas of foreign policy are excluded from judicial examination by such devices as the act of state doctrine, the principle of sovereign immunity, domestic jurisdiction clauses and self-judging reservations in treaties, and judicial deference to the executive on so-called "political questions." Furthermore, cases involving international law are often settled in national courts, or in international tribunals composed of representatives from various states; this undermines the credibility of the reasoning behind many international law decisions. As a result, few international disputes are adjudicated, while those that are may appear to have been decided politically rather than on the basis of international law.

Because adjudication is the chief method by which legal systems establish the precedents that transform adversarial interpretations of law into a coherent tradition, the paucity and inconsistency of judicial precedents in international law results in a high degree of uncertainty. Controversies about the application of international law cannot be authoritatively and consistently resolved in the absence of reliable procedures for ruling on particular disputes, and for enforcing these rulings. Despite these difficulties, however, international law remains an important source of principles for judging the conduct of states. Indeed, its defects increase the resemblance between international law and the other ethical traditions we have considered, which rely even less on authoritative interpretation.

But moralists are likely to criticize international law from a different angle. Those who see it from the perspective of common morality, for example, think the real problem with international law lies in the ethical defects it reveals when judged by the standards of common morality. The existence of alternative standards raises the question of which standard should prevail in cases of disagreement. Some critics argue that international law is justified only to the extent that it contributes to the pursuit of important national or international goals, while others regard it as an imperfect reflection of a more important "higher law" whose duties take precedence over those of positive law. Most of these traditions, while conceding that international law can be a valuable means for realizing ethical ends, sometimes justify disregard for the law where it interferes with achieving those ends.

That each of these traditions should insist on the priority of its own standards is not surprising. But it appears that international law must also insist on its own priority. If it does not, it risks becoming the instrument of whatever ends are held to be superior to it. If law is regarded as a means for achieving such ends, and therefore as subordinate to the demands of prudence or morality, it can be a short step to holding that undesirable or immoral laws are not legally binding. To insist that its authority is dependent on extra-legal grounds is to challenge the autonomy and integrity of the legal tradition.

International law provides a tradition of debate not about which rules are advantageous or morally justified in the circumstances of international relations, but about which rules are valid and binding as law. International law can answer this question consistently and authoritatively only insofar as the interpretation of its rules rests on its own procedures and not on the judgments of statesmen or philosophers regarding the moral validity of these rules or the desirability of their consequences.

Ethical judgment as judgment within a tradition

Let us turn now to our second main question, which concerns the relation between tradition and judgment, and in particular the relation between ethical tradition and ethical judgment. Is ethical judgment necessarily traditional in the sense that it involves the application of ideas that have been handed down over time and are authoritative for those who use them? Some ethical perspectives, like the biblical traditions of Christianity or precedent-oriented international law, are traditional in this sense, but it would seem that others are not. A central claim of political realism, for example, is that political decisions should be made on the basis of prudential reason, not received tradition. This does not mean that the realist does not value tradition. But realists see tradition as a value to be preserved by prudent policy rather than as a guide to the making of policy for, as the realist points out, those with too much respect for Christian morality or the rule of law may be overthrown by less scrupulous enemies. It will help illuminate the idea of tradition to examine the antitraditional arguments of realism, Marxism, and utilitarianism more closely.

Is realism a tradition of international ethics? As the discussions of classical and modern realism by Steven Forde (Chapter 4) and Jack Donnelly (Chapter 5) illustrate, the label "political realism" has been applied to a wide range of ideas. But a common thread running through all the realist literature is the rejection of traditional morality. Realism seems to be a reaction against tradition in at least two ways. First, it repudiates traditional morality as an adequate guide to political action. Second, realism appeals to "reason of state" rather than to the authority of an inherited body of laws or moral precepts. Its outlook is deliberately antitraditional.

The first of these antitraditional elements, the attack on morality, can reflect the skeptical judgment that moral arguments rationalize self-interest and are therefore inherently hypocritical. But though it is doubtless true that many realists have been moral skeptics, skepticism is not an essential part of the realist position. A more significant feature of realism, as an ethical outlook, is the pessimistic judgment that, sound or unsound, moral arguments have little force in foreign affairs. But it is only the more vulgar forms of realism that insist on amorality as an everyday approach to foreign policy. What, at a minimum, realism does require is that public officials be prepared to override the constraints of ordinary law and morality in the kind of emergency that puts a state in danger of foreign conquest. When a state's independence is threatened, foreign policy is constrained by necessity – and necessity knows no law.

Realism thus relies on the distinction between ordinary and extraordinary situations and on the concept of necessity. Statecraft is properly regulated by morality and law up to the point at which necessity intervenes and attention to consequences starts to outweigh deference to ordinary morality. Realists often disagree, however, about when that point has been reached.

Realists also disagree about the relation between morality and prudence. The realist argument that ordinary morality must yield to necessity generates different conclusions depending on whether this argument is thought to have moral or merely prudential force. As a moral argument, realism amounts to a claim that the reasons for overriding the constraints of ordinary morality in emergency situations are themselves moral. There is, in other words, a higher law that legitimizes bowing to the necessities of national survival, one that requires that these ordinary constraints be set aside when the state is

15

threatened with catastrophe (Strauss 1953, 160; Morgenthau 1973, 10). In short, this kind of realism moralizes prudence by arguing that policies required to protect national independence are morally justified.

Other realists reject such efforts to reconcile ordinary morality with political expediency. Instead of appealing to higher law or moral ends, they follow Machiavelli in arguing that if they are to protect the community, public officials must often act in ways that not only seem, but really are, immoral. Prudence simply overrides morality. This strand of realist ethics draws a sharp distinction between prudential and moral considerations and resists justifying the pursuit of national interests in moral terms. It may be desirable to violate ordinary morality to preserve the political community, but it is not just. The argument here is instrumental rather than moral: if we take preservation of the political community to be the supremely important good, then there will be times when prudence rather than morality must guide foreign policy. It is in this spirit that Michael Walzer (1977, 255–63) defends British bombing raids on German cities in the supreme emergency created by the Nazi conquest of the Netherlands and France as necessary murder – that is, as indispensable for Britain to remain independent, but not "just," given the meaning of that word in ordinary moral discourse. Walzer, though not usually classed as a realist, here invokes the classic argument of reason of state.

The writings of Walzer and others who have tried to articulate an ethic of foreign policy that gives weight to both ordinary morality and prudence illustrate the difficulty of finding room for traditional principles within an essentially consequence-oriented framework. For if moral principles can be overridden for the sake of consequences, then the latter are fundamental. As Alan Donagan has argued, in any system of moral principles that contains a consequentialist escape clause for extreme situations, "whatever validity ordinary morality has, it has conditionally, within the scope of a more embracing consequentialist system" (1977, 184).

I hope I have said enough to suggest not only that realism can go beyond moral skepticism to embrace a definite ethical outlook, but that this outlook has both principles and a history. Its practitioners argue about the relative importance of rules and consequences, and each has articulated his own version of a morality of rules with an escape clause for emergencies. Each is participating in an ongoing debate about where to draw the line, how to define an emergency, and other perennial topics of realist discourse. All draw upon the concepts and principles – necessity, security, vital interests, prudence, responsibility – that define a particular tradition of ethical judgment, regardless of whether or not they think of themselves, or are thought of by others, as "political realists." What they are rejecting is not tradition as such but the principles of alternative ethical traditions.

Another ethical perspective that appears to have little use for tradition is Marxism, at least in some of its important variants. For, like certain versions of realism (especially the recent movement in international relations sometimes labeled "neorealism," discussed by Jack Donnelly in Chapter 5), Marxism emphasizes the scientific rather than the traditional basis of defensible policy-making. There are truths about society and history, about the structure of the state and the international system, that determine what is and is not politically possible. Traditions are ideologies – they reflect the realities of economics and power but do little to determine these realities. Rational policy-making must be based on the criticism of ideology and the development of objective social theory. And what is true of realism and Marxism is also true of utilitarianism and other forms of consequentialist ethics: all challenge the authority of traditional morality and law and offer new, ostensibly more rational and objective methods of ethical reasoning. This is true even of the kind of utilitarian argument that tries to show that utility and ordinary morality are substantially equivalent for, according to this argument, ordinary morality is obligatory only insofar as it is supported by utility; it has no independent authority.

Suspicion of tradition is not limited to the rationalist philosophies of Bentham and Marx, or to the doctrine of reason of state, however. Those who look for moral guidance in revelation, and study Scripture for evidence of what has been revealed, may choose to give more weight to conscience than to the tradition of a church. Natural law appeals to reason, not authority. Liberal societies may presume that one need accept only such tradition as can be shown on independent grounds to be reasonable. And moral philosophers in particular are professionally committed to discovering rules that are binding not because they are authoritative but because they are reasonable.

On reflection, however, these antitraditional ethical perspectives can themselves be seen to be traditional, at least in some ways. First, those who employ the ideas and vocabulary of political realism, Marxism, utilitarianism, Christianity, and other ethical perspectives have disagreed and continue to disagree among themselves about what prudence, science, logic, or revelation require, and their ongoing arguments have gradually constituted new traditions of debate. It is thus, Pelikan suggests, that the antitraditionalism of the Reformation

17

itself turned into a tradition: "after four centuries of saying . . . that 'the Bible only is the religion of Protestants,' Protestants have, in this principle, nothing less than a full-blown tradition" (1984, 11). Alasdair MacIntyre (1988, 10, 335, 349) makes a similar point, arguing that liberalism, which began by rejecting the authority of tradition in the name of rational principles has, through its inability to reach agreement on those principles, grown into yet another tradition of moral argumentation.

Second, as the analogy between ethical and literary judgment suggests, all argument presupposes interpretation, which in turn implies a community of interpreters for whom the activity of interpreting literary, legal, or other texts has a point. Therefore, it is not just the oral epics of Homer that are traditional, but all literature. Not only customary and common law but also black-letter statutes are part of legal tradition, since they too depend on the vocabulary, procedures, and tacit assumptions of the legal community – in short, on tradition (Krygier 1988, 27–28). Neither in literature nor in law is it possible to escape "the tradition out of which the text speaks" (Gadamer 1975, 262). The same may be said of ethical discourse. In each case we encounter the discourse of a community of critics and judges, a community constituted by its inherited traditions of interpretation and criticism.[4]

Yet, as Joseph Boyle points out in Chapter 6, a philosophical tradition like natural law is in essence a tradition of inquiry into morality, not itself a tradition of moral practice. It might therefore be objected that it is one thing to claim that everyday ethical discourse is traditional, quite another to claim that traditions of moral philosophy are traditional in the same sense. The discussions of philosophers are premised on a determination to challenge rather than to defer to received ideas. But these discussions also presuppose agreed vocabularies and methodologies that may be thought of as authoritative, for without them it is hard to see how any sort of inquiry could proceed. While some of the necessary agreement comes at a fundamental level and is shared across philosophical traditions, these traditions are also defined and guided by more specific vocabularies and methodological commitments. No inquiry can question everything at once, and therefore every inquiry is in some ways traditional because in questioning some things the questioner must take others, however provisionally, for granted. In short, insofar as they make tacit assumptions, employ shared vocabularies, and structure debate around

[4] Among those who have considered the ethical significance of the idea of an interpretive community are White (1984) and Walzer (1987).

certain recurrent problems, even moral philosophers – those most rational of all beings – are marked by the traditions within which they work.

Traditions as languages of ethical judgment

Focussing on the traditional character of ethical discourse has many implications for the study of international ethics. For one thing, it reminds us that arguments about international affairs, like ethical and political arguments generally, have a history. Accordingly, the study of international ethics must be, at least in part, historical. The idea of tradition encourages us to ask what kinds of arguments were characteristic of particular communities at particular moments. It also suggests the importance of looking at the concepts or "languages" employed by particular kinds of argumentation. And because conceptual languages change through time, in some cases becoming transformed into new languages, the study of tradition leads naturally to the study of conceptual change.[5]

In the study of political thought a concern with political language and conceptual change has recently been pressed so far that the idea of tradition has come to seem inadequate to historians interested in discerning the subtleties that differentiate particular discursive communities. It is worth considering briefly why this might be so, and why the idea of tradition might nevertheless be preferred to that of language in the study of political and ethical discourse.

Thinking requires concepts and concepts are a matter of language: this seems to be the chain of reasoning that has led historians of political thought away from the idea of tradition toward a reliance on "language" as an organizing metaphor for their studies (Pocock 1968). This reasoning suggests that the historian should investigate modes or styles of political discourse – the idioms or rhetorics used within particular communities of discourse. While some idioms use characteristic metaphors and technical vocabularies that signal the presence of a particular language, more often there is a confusion of vocabularies, a subtlety of discourse, and an individuality of style that makes what is going on less easy to identify. This complexity requires us to be sensitive both to the diversity of political styles or vocabularies

---

[5] Examples of this approach to the study of ethics and political theory are provided by MacIntyre (1966), Pagden (1987), Tully (1988), and Ball, Farr, and Hanson (1989). We should also include here the work now being done in many fields under the banner of postmodernism. Though the historical study of languages of discourse has not yet had much impact in the field of international relations, there is a growing postmodernist literature that may be sampled in Der Derian and Shapiro (1989).

and to the ways in which they influence one another. Political languages are not mutually exclusive, often coexisting not only within the same community but within the same text. Political texts are characteristically "polyglot" and can be read as examples of more than one language (Pocock 1985, 9).

While all of this might well be true of both traditions and languages, the language metaphor highlights the manner rather than the content of ethical arguments. The historian J. G. A. Pocock, for example, argues that the study of political language is the study of "the languages in which utterances were performed," not "the utterances which were performed in them" (Pagden 1987, 21). A language of argument and the arguments it is used to make are not, however, completely independent or easily separated. Insofar as the two can be distinguished, it is probably true that more attention needs to be paid to language. But to conclude that the historian should study the languages of political discourse to the exclusion of substantive arguments is surely to go too far, even where we are able to distinguish the language of an argument from its propositional content. Those who want to understand how ethical debate has been shaped by the traditions upon which it draws will want to study both the substance and the style of the arguments in these debates. The concept of tradition facilitates this study because it includes both languages of argument and particular arguments that have been (or might be) made in these languages.

Another doubt about the idea of tradition is that, by directing attention to the past and casting doubt on the idea of tradition-independent reason, it implicitly endorses a conservative attitude. If an ethical tradition is even in part a language of argument, this fear is unfounded. The existence of a tradition does not preclude disagreement and criticism. On the contrary, disagreement is inherent in any tradition of ethical discourse, for there can be no interpretation of the tradition without disagreement. All discourse presumes the existence of at least some shared ideas, but these ideas are never beyond interpretation and criticism. Ethical traditions can provide the basis for penetrating, even radical, social criticism.

Because discourse goes on between as well as within traditions, ethical traditions are seldom entirely independent of one another. Despite the efforts of each tradition to articulate an autonomous and consistent outlook, the traditions we explore in this book are not independent, mutually exclusive ethical systems. They are interdependent, overlapping, and historically entangled perspectives on a common body of experience. As the following chapters repeatedly illustrate, each has evolved its own characteristic outlook in dialogue with other perspectives and cannot really be understood except as a response to them. So intimate are the connections and oppositions among these traditions that they might almost be said to constitute a single tradition – a tradition of disagreement and debate over the relative importance of principles and consequences, of reason and authority, of unwritten custom and written law, and of different visions of the common good.

The concluding chapter (Chapter 14) considers this larger debate among the traditions, and the reader may wish to turn to it for an overview of the main points of agreement and disagreement. The aim of the present chapter has been to introduce the concept of tradition and to suggest its importance for international ethics. Ethical traditions shape the particular controversies over right and wrong that have always been a central feature of international relations. If we want to understand international affairs, we must understand these traditions.

References

Ball, Terence, James Farr, and Russell L. Hanson, eds. 1989. *Political Innovation and Conceptual Change*. Cambridge: Cambridge University Press.

Daube, David. 1965. *Collaboration with Tyranny in Rabbinic Law*. Oxford: Oxford University Press.

Der Derian, James and Michael J. Shapiro, eds. 1989. *International/Intertextual Relations: Post Modern Readings of World Politics*. Lexington, Ma.: Lexington Books.

Donagan, Alan. 1977. *The Theory of Morality*. Chicago: University of Chicago Press.

Fishkin, James. 1986. "Theories of Justice and International Relations: The Limits of Liberal Theory." In Anthony Ellis, ed., *Ethics and International Relations*. Manchester: Manchester University Press, 1–12.

Friedman, Richard B. 1973. "On the Concept of Authority in Political Philosophy." In Richard E. Flathman, ed., *Concepts in Social and Political Philosophy*. New York: Macmillan, 121–46.

1989. "Oakeshott on the Authority of Law." *Ratio Juris*, 2:27–40.

Fullinwider, Robert. 1988. "Learning Morality." *QQ-Report from the Institute for Philosophy and Public Policy*, 8, no. 2:12–15.

Gadamer, Hans-Georg. 1975. *Truth and Method*. New York: Seabury Press.

Hobsbawm, Eric and Terence Ranger, eds. 1983. *The Invention of Tradition*. Cambridge: Cambridge University Press.

Jonsen, Albert R. and Stephen Toulmin. 1988. *The Abuse of Casuistry: A History of Moral Reasoning*. Berkeley: University of California Press.

Kedourie, Elie. 1970. *Nationalism in Asia and Africa*. New York: New American Library.

Krygier, Martin. 1986. "Law as Tradition." *Law and Philosophy*, 5:237–62.
  1988. "The Traditionality of Statutes." *Ratio Juris*, 1:20–39.
MacIntyre, Alasdair. 1966. *A Short History of Ethics*. New York: Macmillan.
  1988. *Whose Justice? Which Rationality?* Notre Dame: University of Notre Dame Press.
Morgenthau, Hans J. 1973. *Politics Among Nations*, 5th edn. New York: Knopf.
Pagden, Anthony, ed. 1987. *The Languages of Political Theory in Early Modern Europe*. Cambridge: Cambridge University Press.
Pelikan, Jaroslav. 1984. *The Vindication of Tradition*. New Haven: Yale University Press.
Pocock, J. G. A. 1968. "Time, Institutions and Action: An Essay on Traditions and Their Understanding." In Preston King and B. C. Parekh, eds., *Politics and Experience*. Cambridge: Cambridge University Press, 209–37.
  1985. "Introduction: The State of the Art." In J. G. A Pocock, *Virtue, Commerce, and History*. Cambridge: Cambridge University Press, 1–34.
Strauss, Leo. 1953. *Natural Right and History*. Chicago: University of Chicago Press.
Tully, James, ed. 1988. *Meaning and Context: Quentin Skinner and his Critics*. Princeton: Princeton University Press.
Walzer, Michael. 1977. *Just and Unjust Wars*. New York: Basic Books.
  1987. *Interpretation and Social Criticism*, Cambridge, Ma.: Harvard University Press.
White, James Boyd. 1984. *When Words Lose Their Meaning: Constitutions and Reconstitutions of Language, Character, and Community*. Chicago: University of Chicago Press.
Wilford, John Noble. 1990. "Anthropology Seen as Father of Maori Lore." *New York Times*, February 20.
Williams, Bernard. 1985. *Ethics and the Limits of Philosophy*. Cambridge, Ma.: Harvard University Press.

2 THE TRADITION OF INTERNATIONAL LAW

MURRAY FORSYTH

"And law was brought into the world for nothing else, but to limit the natural liberty of particular men, in such manner, as they might not hurt, but assist one another, and join together against a common enemy." Hobbes's words (1960, 175) remind us forcibly that a body politic or a "state," whatever else it may be, is a unity organized to protect its members against a real or a potential external enemy. Whatever form a body politic may take, whether it be a tribe or clan, a "city state," a composite feudal system, a "church state," or a modern sovereign state, the capacity to engage in an armed contest with adversaries, reflected in a fundamental inner division of labor between military and other occupations, remains a constant characteristic.

Before this is labeled as an uncompromisingly "realist" viewpoint, however, it must be added that another characteristic is equally constant, namely the endeavor of states to introduce some kind of order or regularity into their external relations, to prevent them from being merely a succession of violent encounters. History reveals a primordial effort by political units to establish formal boundary lines between a state of war, or of hostility towards other units, and a state of peace or friendship. It reveals a ubiquitous effort to endow with special status the envoys and messengers who enable communication to take place between political units in time of peace or war, and a similar effort to give special sanctity to treaties and pacts between such units. The nature of these forms and modalities varies according to the structure and unity of the bodies concerned, and also according to the religious, ethnic, and cultural factors that create links and affinities between them, or which deepen and accentuate their political separation. Despite their immense variation, the overall tendency is unmistakable, and gives the lie to any undiluted doctrine of "realism."

Taken in its broadest sense "international law" embraces all these multifarious forms and procedures. It corresponds to Montesquieu's idea when he wrote that "all nations have a *droit des gens*; even the

23

Iroquois, who eat their prisoners, have one" (1951, 237). "Nation" or *"gens"* here means simply a politically organized group, and "law" or *"droit"* a host of practices both crude and sophisticated. But international law can also be taken to mean a specific kind of practice that emerged in history amongst a particular species of body politic. It refers here to the complex of rules that were developed by the "sovereign states" of Europe from the period of the Reformation and Renaissance onwards, which blossomed into what is sometimes referred to as "classic" international law in the nineteenth century, and which, although challenged and remodeled in the period after 1918, is still discernible in the international law of today. The implication of this usage is that, while there may have been intimations of international law at other times and periods, the essential doctrines originated in Europe during the sixteenth and seventeenth centuries.

It is with international law in this more restricted sense that this chapter will be concerned, and in particular with the period of foundation and growth that lasted until 1914. What were the leading features of the law that developed at this time? What changes did it undergo in the course of development? To what extent can it be called the application of ethics to international relations? These are the questions that will guide the inquiry.

Origins of the tradition

Inevitably one is faced at the outset with the problem of origin. When precisely did the new system of law emerge? Clearly it was largely the result of new ideas emerging to cope with new facts and, of these new facts, the most important was the succession of civil wars and revolts that convulsed Christendom in the wake of the Reformation and gave the period between the Treaty of Cateau-Cambrésis in 1559 and the Peace of Westphalia in 1648 its particular character. The hallmark of these wars and revolts was that they were simultaneously religious and political in nature, that is to say they were both struggles for power and struggles to promote the "truth" and, like all conflicts of this nature, they were fought with peculiar ferocity. They also tended to be simultaneously domestic and international, with religious loyalties and animosities cutting across political boundaries. "In former times," wrote a Catholic firebrand in 1565, "friend and enemy divided according to the boundaries of countries and kingdoms ... Now the division must be between Catholics and heretics. A Catholic prince must have the Catholics of all lands as his friends in the same way that heretic princes have all heretics as their friends, be they their vassals or those of another" (Platzhoff 1968, 10). It was scarcely surprising that this long series of bitter "ideological" struggles – the French wars of religion, the revolt of the Netherlands, the Thirty Years War, the English civil wars – should provoke men to think afresh not only about the bases of domestic order but also about the bases of international order. Here is the main root of the new tradition.

Yet, paradoxically, the change can also be seen in part as an adjustment of the facts to older theories. To take a prime example, the idea that a legitimate "state of war" only existed when it was declared by those who "recognized no superior" was by no means foreign to the later Middle Ages. Bartolus, in particular, had propagated this idea well before the Reformation. The difficulty was that in the complex political world of that time, with its intricate feudal gradations and its parallel spiritual and temporal authorities, the identity of those who "recognized no superior" was not easy to discern. It was only when powerful territorial governments with standing armies at their disposal emerged out of the post-Reformation maelstrom of religious civil war that this old doctrine could take on a precise meaning.

With this reminder that the relationship between ideas and the concrete evolution of political institutions is not a simple one, we will focus on the new ideas about the international world that surfaced during the sixteenth and seventeenth centuries. Clearly, any assessment of the relative significance of particular thinkers as "founders" depends on what one judges to be the main features of the international law that developed over the years up to 1914. At root this law was the external correlate of the idea of the sovereign territorial state. The concept of sovereignty expressed a determination to restrain the imperatives of individual moral conscience, anchored in religious belief, and to accord priority instead to the requirements of peaceful coexistence within a given political space. It was the assertion of a legal and secular standpoint, in the face of a moral and religious one, which had the effect of "privatizing" and "neutralizing" the latter.

The new international law that evolved up to 1914 was an assertion of precisely the same standpoint. It sought to rein back moral and religious imperatives in the international arena in favor of the requirements of ordered coexistence. To say that it gave precedence to "order" over "justice" begs the question whether the two concepts can be pitted against one another in this way. Hedley Bull clearly believed that they were indeed antitheses (1977). However it may be argued that, while order may or may not be just, justice is always a form of order. For this reason it seems truer to say not that the new international law abandoned justice in favor of order but rather that it redefined the just order. Such an order no longer meant conformity to the rules of God's kingdom established – or about to be established – here on earth. Rather, it meant the order necessitated by the natural contrarieties of human wills here on earth. More precisely it meant an order that acknowledged the freedom inherent in each sovereign state and that was designed to reconcile these freedoms with one another, without abolishing them. It was a law of coordination, not of subordination, and its norms tended to be formal and procedural.

If this is accepted as the focus of international law then the problem of identifying its origin becomes a little easier. The claim of the great Spanish writers of the sixteenth and seventeenth centuries – Vitoria and Suarez in particular – to be the "founders" of international law, a claim advanced with particular vigor by James Brown Scott in the 1930s, becomes difficult if not impossible to sustain. The Dominican Vitoria wrote expressly as a theologian concerned with matters of conscience. The Jesuit Suarez was engaged quite openly in the struggle of the Catholic church to defeat the Reformation. These men were sophisticated latter-day protagonists of the "old" moral and religious viewpoint rather than pioneers of the "new" secular and legal one (for a discussion of how these writers contributed to the natural law tradition, see "A tradition of 'natural law' ethics identified," Chapter 6).

The claims of Grotius also seem difficult to substantiate, despite his undoubted impact on his contemporaries. The clearest and most influential part of his work on *The Law of War and Peace*, his appeal for "moderation" in warfare contained in Book III, expressly appeals to "internal" or moral justice, and not to legal principles (1964, 716–82). Grotius wrote as much as a pious Christian, seeking to recall the princes and peoples of Christendom to the pure and uncontested doctrines of the early church, as he did as a jurist. His discussion of the law of nature and the law of nations, which relies so heavily on examples drawn from the Bible and from classical antiquity, seems to miss, rather than to grasp, the significance and implications of the doctrine of sovereignty. Undoubtedly he opened up a host of problems, but he lacked the method to resolve them. (For further discussion of the tensions in Grotius's writings, see "The Bible and the traditions: Protestant arguments," Chapter 13.) In what Wight called the "baroque thickets" (1977, 127) of his work, the curious and the persistent can find support for a variety of arguments; it is significant that he was taken up after 1918, by writers such as Vollenhoven and Lauterpacht, not as a progenitor of the "classic" system of international law but rather as the protagonist of a system that was opposed to it (Bull 1966).

Those writers who have drawn attention to the contribution made by Jean Bodin and Alberico Gentili to the emergence of international law – writers such as Holland in the nineteenth century (1874) and Gardot (1934) and Schmitt (1950) in more recent times – seem to be on the surest ground. The ideas of Bodin and Gentili complement one another in a highly instructive manner. The two men were contemporaries, Bodin producing his classic work on *The Commonwealth* in 1576, and Gentili his pathbreaking study of *The Law of War* in 1598. Both had the religious-cum-political struggles of the time before their eyes. Bodin concentrated for the most part on the internal meaning and implications of sovereignty, while Gentili focused on its external implications. Gentili clearly admired Bodin, referring to him repeatedly in his later writings as "learned prince" (Molen 1968, 227). Both men were lawyers, not theologians. Gentili, in a blunt phrase that has become famous, told the latter to mind their own business: "Let the theologians keep silent about matters outside their province" (1964, 57). Both men were also specialists in Roman Law, following in the same tradition that had been established by Baldus and Bartolus in the Middle Ages, a tradition that looked at the texts of classical antiquity for their practical, legal value and not merely as subjects of historical or antiquarian investigation. In the language of the day they were protagonists of the "Italian way," the *mos italicus*, not of the *mos gallicus*.

Perhaps most important of all, both men had broken with the "old faith" without moving into the camp of militant Protestantism. Bodin is probably best described as a theist, who prudently aligned himself with the Catholic League for some years, but who at heart belonged to no particular confession or sect. Gentili was a Protestant, but a persecuted rather than a persecuting one. Both men placed a high premium on unity of religious belief within the state but did not believe that such unity should be maintained by force. Where there were profound religious differences they advocated toleration. As Gentili wrote:

> Since the laws of religion do not properly exist between man and man, therefore no man's rights are violated by a difference in religion, nor is it lawful to make war because of religion. Religion is a relationship with God. Its laws are divine, that is, between God and man; they are not human, namely between man and man. Therefore a man cannot complain of being wronged because others differ from him in religion. (1964, 41)

Bodin would have agreed with this. His doctrine of sovereignty endowed the state with a unity, autonomy, and status – in a word with a personality – that the medieval "state" conspicuously lacked. The

27

latter was what Figgis called a "loosely compacted union" (1956, 17), in which a categorical distinction between public and private, sovereignty and property, law and custom, war and rebellion, and internal and external relationships was not made. Bodin's relentless insistence on the qualitative difference between a sovereign power and all other institutions, corporations, or associations, and his equally relentless insistence that sovereignty was the mainspring of the state (regardless of the form of government), transformed a "loosely compacted" agglomeration into a genuine unity, an aggregate into a *magna persona*. Moreover, he asserted that the quality of sovereignty, which was the essence of a commonwealth, made the smallest commonwealth equal in kind to the largest – made Ragusa, as he said, equal to the empire of the Turks (Bodin 1967, 8). Here we can see the modern doctrine of the equality of states, expressed in perhaps its earliest form.

At the same time, Bodin showed himself fully aware of the degree to which unequal power relationships between states – manifested in treaties of protection and guarantee and so on – were or were not compatible with the equal sovereign status of those who were parties to them. He realized, and indeed he took great pains to demonstrate, that there came a point at which the realities of power, or material inequality, cut across and extinguished the status of formal equality. But Bodin – rightly in my view – did not believe that this situation "at the margin" rendered the notion of equal status nugatory.

It was precisely Bodin's sovereign *magnae personae* that were to become the subjects of the new international law. The authors of the great textbooks on international law produced in the eighteenth and nineteenth centuries begin, almost without exception, by repeating in miniature the same analytical process that Bodin undertook in his great work on the *Republic*. They attempt to distinguish and define the political bodies that can truly be called sovereign, because these bodies, and these alone, are the subjects of the law they wish to expound.

International law in its early stages, as elaborated by a writer like Gentili, was not superimposed upon sovereign states as an external barrier but was rather the reasoned extrapolation of the consequences of sovereignty for the mutual adjustment of states. The "law of nature," with which the law of nations was equated by writer after writer from Gentili's time up until that of Vattel, was the organizing concept for this work of logical extrapolation. For Roman lawyers, like Bodin and Gentili, it stood ready to hand as a familiar non-theological reference point.

War was the area in which it was most urgent to extrapolate the rules. The "right of war" remained one of the great primary subdivisions of all the great books on international law up to 1914. As the titles of Gentili's and Grotius's works indicate, it originally took pride of place, but in the following centuries a more or less standard pattern of exposition emerged: first, a discussion of the subjects of international law, to which we have already referred; then a discussion of the rights and duties of these subjects in time of peace; and finally a discussion of their rights and duties in time of war. The rights and duties of neutrality, which began to be discussed systematically in the eighteenth century, were sometimes incorporated into the section on war and sometimes given separate treatment after it.

There was thus no doubt in the minds of international lawyers during this period that the law which they expounded was the law of peace *and* war, and not *just* the law of peace. Nor was there any doubt that this law was essentially the sum of rights that a state might claim for itself and its nationals from other states, plus the duties that in consequence it must observe towards them (Brierly 1944, 5). As these words suggest, this close identity of international law with the mutual definition of states' rights did not mean that individual rights were ignored. On the contrary, the increasing recognition accorded during the eighteenth and nineteenth centuries to the rights of the individual within the state, or the growing tendency already implicit in Bodin's doctrine to equate the "true" state not merely with the attribute of sovereignty, but with protection of the individual rights of life, liberty, and property, inevitably spilled out into the international sphere and made states more solicitous about these matters in their external dealings with one another. The progressive "humanization" of the international rules regarding prisoners of war, the taking of booty, military occupation, the treatment of the civilian population, and the treatment of aliens, as well as more dramatic moves such as the abolition of the slave trade, reflect this development. As we shall see, it also brought with it a sharpening of the distinction between states that respected individual rights and those that did not.

The new international law was not without its critics and opponents. From Gentili's time up until 1914, a succession of writers argued that the problem of war and peace between states could only be resolved by *union*, that is to say by some kind of federal or confederal arrangement, and not by mere rules of *coexistence*. Sully, Penn, the Abbé St. Pierre (whose plan was examined by Rousseau), and Kant, are probably the best known of these writers, but the numerous "peace societies" that were founded in Europe and America from the end of the Napoleonic wars onward carried forward this tradition, and spawned innumerable schemes for federal union. Students of the theory of international relations have devoted much attention to this tradition of ideas, and it is understandable that in the period since the Second World War, when the preconditions for the formation of some kind of federal construct in Europe have become far more apparent, that the idea of union (Forsyth 1981) should come to the forefront. Yet the idea of union never represented the mainstream either of international thought or of international action during the period up to 1914. It stood on the periphery. The international lawyers, by contrast, *were* very much in the mainstream of thought and practice. Some may have been unrealistic, others muddled and unreadable but, in the mass, they both reflected and influenced the practice of interstate relations. Even Treitschke, who can scarcely be accused of harboring illusions about the realities of power politics, could write at the end of the nineteenth century:

> The greatest triumph of the science of international law lies in the field that is considered by fools to be purely and simply a barbaric one; in the law of war. We seldom find brutal contraventions of this law in modern times. It is, on the whole, the outstanding beauty of international law, that here, unmistakably, a continual progress is shown, and that, through the *universalis consensus* alone, a series of principles of international law has developed so firmly, that we can say to-day that they stand as securely as any legal axiom in the private code of any State. (1914, 124)

The right of war

Let us look more closely at the specific area to which Treitschke referred. Gentili's thoughts on the right of war provide a useful indication of the way international law developed on this crucial theme. It is sometimes suggested that the change from medieval to modern was synonymous with a shift of emphasis from the *jus ad bellum* to the *jus in bello*. There is a grain of truth in this, but the generalization can be misleading because it was immensely important in the early modern period to determine *who* had the right to make war. Sovereignty itself was the right of war and peace, or the *jus belli*, and the theorists of sovereignty all insisted that the essence of sovereignty was that it could not be divided. It followed that all the subjects of a sovereign power were stripped of the right of war and had to submit all their disputes to peaceful arbitration. Hence a rightful state of war could only exist externally, between sovereign, public entities. Gentili stated the underlying logic succinctly:

30

There cannot be judicial processes between supreme sovereigns or free peoples unless they themselves consent, since they acknowledge no judge or superior. Consequently, they only are supreme and they alone merit the title of public, while all others are inferior and are rated as private individuals. The sovereign has no earthly judge, for one over whom another holds a superior position is not a sovereign ... Therefore it was inevitable that the decision between sovereigns should be made by arms. (1964, 15)

For Gentili a genuine or authentic war was emphatically a public contest waged by public or sovereign authority for a public cause. From this the definition of a genuine or "just" enemy – *justus hostis* – followed. "He is an enemy who has a state, a senate, a treasury, united and harmonious citizens, and some basis for a treaty of peace, should matters so shape themselves." Hence brigands, pirates and rebels were not authentic enemies. "For the word *hostis*, 'enemy,' while it implies equality, like the word 'war,' ... is sometimes extended to those who are not equal, namely to pirates, proscribed persons, and rebels; nevertheless it cannot confer the rights due to enemies, properly so called, and the privileges of regular warfare" (1964, 25).

The significance of Gentili's restriction of the concept of "war" and the concept of "enemy" is heightened by a glance back at the medieval situation. In the late Middle Ages (Keen 1965, 104–9) there were, if we exclude the truce, at least three possible conditions or states of war. First was what the lawyers called Roman war, which was typically war waged on the authority of the church against heretics or infidels, and of which the Crusades were a classic example. It was war to the death, or *guerre mortelle*, in which there was no equality of status between the opponents, and in which the conquered were slain or enslaved. It was the crusading mentality inherent in this kind of war, which can be traced back to Augustine, that broke out with renewed intensity in the religious and political struggles of the sixteenth and seventeenth centuries – we need think only of Cromwell in Ireland. This mentality can even be detected, paradoxical and unlikely as it sounds, in John Locke's theory of war, according to which one side was inevitably a criminal "aggressor" and the "cause" of a war, and the other side was peaceloving and punitive. As in the medieval system, Locke gave the righteous victor unlimited power to dispose of the vanquished, including the right of enslavement. Conversely, victory by the unrighteous side, even when the defeated come to terms with the victor, created no obligations whatsoever, either for present or future generations.

A second type of war in the late Middle Ages was public or open war

31

between Christian princes who acknowledged no superior. In this the men might take spoil, and captured enemies had the right to ransom themselves. Finally, there was feudal or covered war (*guerre couverte*), waged between the members of the feudal nobility and opened by formal acts of defiance, in which men could wound and kill without blame, but could not burn or take spoil.

Gentili's doctrine clearly refuses the title or status of "war" to the first and third of these types of contest, and grants it only to the second, which it elevates to a new level of conceptual clarity. What needs to be particularly stressed is his insistence on the equal status and rights of enemies in an authentic or "just" war. He breaks firmly with the notion that justice in relation to war is an absolute concept, that is to say a quality or virtue possessed exclusively and necessarily by only one side in the contest. Justice for Gentili is a due or proper relationship between the participants in the contest. He does also specify just causes for going to war (necessity, expedience, and honor) and it might seem as if he is here bringing in the old absolute concept of justice once again. But, in fact, when he discusses just causes he means basically permissible or allowable causes, and does not imply that only one side will be fighting for such a permissible or allowable cause.

This is really the crux. Gentili did not believe that men could penetrate to the "purest and truest form of justice" and perceive in any dispute, before it was concluded, on which side justice lay. We, he wrote, "for the most part are unacquainted with that truth. *Therefore we aim at justice as it appears from man's standpoint*" (1964, 31, italics added). He makes a typical analogy between a legal and an armed contest and then discusses some implications for justice:

> If it is doubtful on which side justice is, and if each side aims at justice, neither can be called unjust ... Those who contend in the litigation of the Forum justly, that is to say, on a plausible ground, either as defendants or plaintiffs, and lose their case and the verdict, are not judged guilty of injustice. And yet the oath regarding false accusation is taken by both parties. Why should the decision be different in this kind of dispute and in a contest of arms? ... Although it may sometimes happen ... that injustice is clearly evident on one of the two sides, nevertheless this ought not to affect the general principle, and prevent the laws of war from applying to both parties. For laws are not based upon rare instances and adapted to them ... Therefore no change must be made in this law of the enemy and of war; for it is impartial to both sides, just as in the contests of the Forum the law is impartial towards each of the litigants, until sentence has been pronounced in favour of one or

32

other of them. But if the unjust man gain the victory, neither in a contention in arms nor in the strife carried on in the garb of peace is there any help for it. Yet it is not the law which is at fault, but the execution of the law. (1964, 32–33)

The final outcome of the "armed litigation" of war may thus not coincide with the demands of justice, but then (we may add) there is no guarantee that the final decision of the supreme arbiter or sovereign in relation to the "peaceful litigation" within the state will coincide with the demands of justice either. Bodin and Gentili agreed that (1) we need the sovereign to make a final decision – just or unjust – *within* the state, for otherwise there would be no area of guaranteed peace; and (2) we must abide by the final outcome of a regularly or fairly conducted trial of strength *outside* the state, for we have no infallible means of determining *a priori* where justice lies in a fundamental dispute between sovereign equals.

This "agnostic" position reflected the general attitude towards war and its regulation adopted by international lawyers in the three centuries that followed Gentili's death, and the gradual elaboration of the rights and duties of "neutrality" grew naturally and logically out of it. The aim was to contain and limit war, not to abolish it. The underlying principle was restated with characteristic incisiveness by W. E. Hall at the end of the nineteenth century. "International law has . . . no alternative but to accept war, independently of the justice of its origin, as a relation which the parties to it may set up if they choose, and to busy itself only in regulating the effects of the relation. Hence both parties to every war are regarded as being in an identical legal position, and consequently as being possessed of equal rights" (1880, 82). It is sometimes suggested that the development of this approach marked the end of the "just-war tradition" which only reemerged in the course of the twentieth century, but this again seems to be an oversimplification. It was not that the idea of the "just war" ended, but that the meaning of the term altered. A just war became a war "in due form" (to use Vattel's phrase), one waged by sovereigns according to certain rules. Obviously this new approach faced its own problems. One had to identify, for example, the point in a civil war at which mere "rebels" grew to such a level of strength and organization that they qualified as genuine "belligerents," and became entitled to be recognized by outside states as at least claimants for recognition as sovereign entities. One had to reconcile – to take another extremely thorny and prolonged problem – the right to wage war at sea, which involved by its very nature the imposition of economic sanctions on the enemy state, with the rights of neutral powers to use the "open sea" to trade freely with whom they wished.

We have concentrated here on the right of war, but it is necessary to refer, if only briefly, to the rights of states in times of peace as well. Of the rights discussed and defined by international lawyers under this head perhaps the most important was the right of state possession with regard to land and sea. After a long struggle it was finally agreed that the sea could not be the object of appropriation by particular states, except in the case of "territorial waters." After an equally long struggle the notion of "effective occupation" came to displace "discovery" and "papal dispensation" as the legitimating principle for the acquisition of unoccupied territories. Another important right in peacetime was that of legation, or the rights of the authorized representatives of states in one another's territories. The familiar notion or fiction of the exterritoriality of embassies developed in this context. Lawyers also discussed the right of the state over the subjects of another state present on its territory, and the establishment of rules regarding such matters as extradition, asylum, and naturalization. Finally, discussion of the right of intervention was usually expanded to examine how far the maintenance of the "balance of power" justified armed action by one state against another. Not surprisingly, some writers, such as James Lorimer in the nineteenth century, thought that the right of intervention was an adjunct of the right of war and not of rights in time of peace.

The evolution of international law

It is time now to look more directly at the evolution of international law that took place during this long period. What were the main turning points? Grewe (1988) distinguishes between a "Spanish epoch" that lasted until 1648, a "French epoch" that lasted from 1648 to 1815, and an "English epoch" that lasted from 1815 to 1919. Nussbaum (1947) treats each century separately and in turn. In the present context it is perhaps sufficient to draw attention to the most important turning point, which took place at the end of the eighteenth and the beginning of the nineteenth centuries, not, however, because of the impact of the French Revolution, important as this was. The Revolution represented an interruption of the growth of international law rather than a transformation of it. It signified the reemergence of the crusading spirit that international law had sought to restrain, though this time the crusade was for philosophical rather than for religious ideals. Like the Reformation, the Revolution produced a counter-crusade in the form of the Holy Alliance. This ideological antithesis harkened back to the sixteenth century and pointed forward to the twentieth and, although it stirred up intense debate on the right of intervention, it did not exert a lasting effect on the development of international law from 1815 to 1914. Nor, strange as it may seem, did the powerful idea of national self-determination. In the course of the nineteenth century, certain Italian jurists sought to make it the basis of a new international law, but they met with little success. Doubtless the strong countercurrent of imperialism was largely responsible for this. It was not until after the First World War that the principle of national self-determination became an influential international norm, and not until the end of the Second World War that it was formally recognized as a general norm (Brownlie 1970).

The change that took place at the end of the eighteenth century was partly one of method. Before Vattel published his classic text on *The Law of Nations* (1758), most of the leading publicists had seen either an identity or a very close connection between what they termed the law of nations and the law of nature. In other words they were intent on demonstrating what the "nature" or "reason" of things indicated were the proper modes of state conduct. This is not to say that they were all austere, deductive, stringently philosophical reasoners. In fact, only Hobbes, Pufendorf, and perhaps Wolff can be said to fall into that category. The others tended, when trying to define what the law of nature prescribed, to fall back on the cumbersome procedure of accumulating testimonies from the writers of all ages.

Soon after Vattel's work appeared, a profound change of approach began. It can be dated most conveniently from J. J. Moser's *Essay on the most recent European Law of Nations*, which appeared between 1777 and 1780, though a slightly later German writer, G. F. von Martens, undoubtedly made a greater contribution to the transformation. A quotation from one of the few early British writers who adopted the new approach may help to give a general idea of its character. "Rejecting therefore," wrote Robert Ward in 1795, "the laws of Nature and Reason (as the sole foundation of the law of Nations) because we do not conceive them powerful or fixed enough to bear the fabric that is erected upon them; we conclude that what is commonly called the law of nations, is not the law of *all* nations, but only such sets or classes of them as are united together by similar religions, and systems of morality" (1795, I, 127).

As Ward's words indicate, there were two sides to the new approach. On the one hand there was a growing sense that it was no longer appropriate or adequate to deduce the law of nations from the abstract dictates of "nature" or "reason." It was necessary instead to start from how existing states actually regulated their dealings with one another, whether this took the form of express treaties and pacts, or merely modes of interaction habitually practiced and accepted. One had to begin, not from the natural, but from the "positive." The task of the science of the law of nations was to sift through the mass of treaties and practices that had arisen between the states of the modern world to find the most general, uniform, and persistent norms that were articulated or presupposed in them, for these norms *were* the law of nations. In this way, it was argued, the science of international law would not only become more concrete and empirical, it would also become more practical. Its practitioners would become of greater service to diplomats and statesmen.

Linked to this change was a heightened realization of the unique nature of the rules of international behavior that had evolved in Europe during the previous two centuries. It became increasingly clear to observers that no single, uniform law of nations was observed throughout the world; there was a specific system of "European public law," which had spread to a few other parts of the globe (the United States being the most obvious example), but elsewhere forms of international behavior bore only a limited resemblance to it. This change was reflected in the titles of leading works on the law of nations produced between Moser's *Essay* and the middle of the nineteenth century. Works by Martens, Schmalz, Klüber, and Heffter, for example, all referred expressly to the "European" law of nations.

Running parallel with this was a further innovation that can tentatively be said to have begun about the time of the Congress of Vienna. This was the practice of equating the "European law of nations" with the law of "civilized" nations, or simply of "civilization." This term, redolent of the Enlightenment, signified that the European law of nations had come to be viewed not only as different from others, but as higher, more advanced – the embodiment of "progress." The notion of civilization provided the European states with a criterion, a standard by which to ascertain which of the states outside their own circle (with which they were coming into ever increasing contact) were eligible for admission to the full rights and privileges of international law. Those that did not meet the standard were by definition "barbarous" or semi-barbarous. Their existence might well be recognized by civilized states, but it would not be the full recognition that was implied in membership of the club of civilized states. This meant in turn that the right of civilized states to intervene in the affairs of barbarous states was far wider than their right to intervene in one another's affairs. Civilization thus provided a criterion for both inclusion and intervention. To see it (and the other changes that took place concomitantly) purely as an ostracizing exercise – as C. H. Alexandrowicz has tended to do in his writings (1967, 1973) – is to distort its double-edged character.

As Gong (1984) has shown, the precise meaning of the standard of civilization was not clearly articulated until the end of the nineteenth century, although it had been invoked earlier. Essentially it meant two things. To be entitled to recognition as a full member of the international community a political unit had to possess a government that (1) was sufficiently stable and institutionalized for it to enter into binding international commitments and (2) was able to guarantee certain basic individual rights, in particular life, liberty, and property, especially for foreigners. A true state, or a true subject of international law, not only had to possess sovereign power over its land and people but had to be a "liberal" state as well.

In the latter half of the nineteenth century references to Europe in the titles of the leading works on the law of nations decline and the usage preferred by English and US writers, namely "international law" – a term invented by Bentham – comes to predominate. Always, however, it is made plain that it is the international law of civilized nations that is meant. Partly, of course, the change can be attributed to the increasing number of non-European powers accepted into the inner circle of the system, a number that expanded dramatically in the two decades preceding the First World War. At the first peace conference at the Hague in 1899 twenty-six states were represented, while at the second, in 1907, there were forty-four, including eighteen from Latin America.

It is not possible here to explore in detail the reasons for the major changes that took place at the end of the eighteenth and the beginning of the nineteenth centuries in the way international law was conceived. A few observations must suffice. First, it is important not to exaggerate the contrast between the "natural-law" approach and the "positive" approach that succeeded to it. Those who turned to natural law did so largely because they sought a firm point outside the religious disputes of their age on which to lay the foundations of a new order. With the Peace of Westphalia and the Peace of the Pyrenees, this new order started to emerge as an historical reality, and Europe began to be bound together as a society by a thickening network of treaties. These treaties in turn began to be codified and published, starting with Leibniz's *Diplomatic Code* of 1693 and continuing with massive compilations by writers such as Bernard, Dumont, Rousset, and Mably. It seems almost inevitable in retrospect that this abundant material should suggest, sooner or later, an alternative approach to the law of nations, one that would base itself on existing usages. This new approach did not so much contradict the earlier one as complement it. The philosophical or quasi-philosophical natural-law theorists were concerned with the substructure and foundations, the presuppositions of the law of nations; the new empirical school were concerned with the superstructure, the positive law that implemented the basic principles.

This leads to a second observation. Many of the exponents of the new approach tacitly accepted at least a part of the old. It is true that some, like Moser, dissociated the law of nations entirely from the law of nature, and some, like Oppenheim, denied the very existence of natural law. But this was not the practice of the majority, and even those who denied any connection between the two laws were rarely content simply to chronicle what states had actually agreed on amongst themselves, but explicitly adduced "reason" as a criterion for assessing the significance and validity of pacts and usages. An aura of natural law still hung around the writings of many of the empirical school throughout the nineteenth century and beyond.

It is also important not to equate the positive approach described here with the positive approach of Bentham and his followers, of whom (in the field of international law) John Austin was by far the most significant. Austin's basic assumption was that law, for the purposes of jurisprudence, consisted of the command of a determinate human superior, either individual or collective, who had the power to impose sanctions in case of disobedience. So-called human laws that did not meet this criterion were relegated to the sphere of morality, while God's law belonged to the sphere of religion. International law – ironically in view of Bentham's coinage of the term – was thus not properly law at all but "positive morality." It consisted merely of "opinions or sentiments current among nations generally" (1971, 142). (For additional discussion of Bentham and Austin on international law see "Benthamite politics and foreign policy," Chapter 8.) This thesis was emphatically not accepted by mainstream writers on international law before 1914 either in England or elsewhere. Many English writers took pains to refute the Austinian position and to demonstrate that international law, while not emanating from a superior armed with sanctions, was a genuine form of law. In other words, those who focussed on the actual practice of states in order to deduce the norms of international law were not legal positivists in the sense in which this term is generally used today and in which it is discussed by Joseph Boyle in Chapter 6.

The prolonged destruction and suffering of the First World War provoked a profound reaction against the tradition of international law which has been described here. For many, a law consisting of norms reciprocally recognized by sovereign states, a law that expressly acknowledged the right of war and sought solely to regulate its exercise, had come to seem inadequate. The attempt was made to create a new system in which international law was to stand over and above the sovereign state, and collective action was to be taken against those who were guilty of aggression. International law was thus to be made into law in the Benthamite or Austinian sense, the command of a determinate superior with the power to compel obedience. Unfortunately the political implications of such an immense transformation were not fully grasped. States were not in reality prepared to discard a system of coexistence and replace it with a form of federal union. The older rules, developed so painstakingly from the age of Gentili onwards, have proved more enduring than the idealists of the League of Nations imagined.

Suggested reading

The number of readily available books on the overall historical development of international law is surprisingly small. The full history of the subject has still to be written. All the more valuable, therefore, is Arthur Nussbaum's *A Concise History of the Law of Nations* (1947). It is a careful, lucid and well-documented survey. The historical articles by Wolfgang Preiser, Stephan Verosta, and Hans-Ulrich Scupin in Installment 7 of the *Encyclopaedia of Public International Law*, edited by R. Bernhardt (Amsterdam: Elsevier, 1984), are also very useful, and include extensive bibliographies. The title of J. H. W. Verzijl's massive *International Law in Historical Perspective* 10 vols. (Leiden: A. W. Sijthoff, 1968–1978) is slightly misleading insofar as it contains a mixture of analytical, descriptive, and historical studies of different aspects of international law. Geoffrey Best's *Humanity in Warfare: the Modern History of the International Law of Armed Conflicts* (London: Methuen, 1983) is an excellent study of a central theme. The historical evolution of international law provides the starting point of Terry Nardin's sensitive analysis of *Law, Morality, and the Relations of States* (Princeton: Princeton University Press, 1983).

There have been innumerable studies of particular aspects of the development of the law of nations. Mention may be made here of the wealth of material contained in the *Recueil des Cours*, published by the Académie de Droit International at the Hague from 1923 onwards. The main texts of the great writers on international law between the sixteenth and eighteenth centuries are available in English in the series *The Classics of International Law*, edited by James Brown Scott and published under the auspices of the Carnegie Endowment for International Peace, Washington. They were republished by Oceana Publications in 1964.

For readers of German, two important books deserve to be mentioned. Wilhelm G. Grewe's *Epochen der Völkerrechtgeschichte* (1988) is particularly valuable because it links the evolution of the doctrines of international law to the evolution of political reality. Carl Schmitt's *Der Nomos der Erde im Völkerrecht des Jus Publicum Europaeum* (Cologne: Greven, 1950, now handled by Duncker and Humblot, Berlin) is a characteristically brilliant and stimulating survey that has been unjustly neglected outside Germany.

References

Alexandrowicz, C. H. 1967. *An Introduction to the History of the Law of Nations in the East Indies.* Oxford: Oxford University Press.

1973. *The European-African Confrontation.* Leiden: A. W. Sijthoff.

Austin, John. 1971. *The Province of Jurisprudence Determined.* Introduced by H. L. A. Hart. London: Weidenfeld and Nicolson.

Bodin, Jean. 1967. *Six Books of the Commonwealth.* Oxford: Basil Blackwell.

Brierly, J. L. 1944. *The Outlook for International Law.* Oxford: Clarendon.

Brownlie, Ian. 1970. "An Essay in the History of the Principle of Self-Determination." In *Grotian Society Papers 1968*, ed. C. H. Alexandrowicz. The Hague: M. Nijhoff, 90–99.

Bull, Hedley. 1966. "The Grotian Conception of International Society." In *Diplomatic Investigations*, ed. Herbert Butterfield and Martin Wight. London: George Allen and Unwin, 51–73.

1977. *The Anarchical Society.* London: Macmillan.

Figgis, John Neville. 1956. *Studies of Political Thought from Gerson to Grotius.* Cambridge: Cambridge University Press.

Forsyth, Murray. 1981. *Unions of States: the Theory and Practice of Confederation.* Leicester: Leicester University Press.

Gardot, André. 1934. "Jean Bodin: sa place parmi les fondateurs du droit international." In *Recueil des Cours* of the Académie de Droit International, vol. 50, 545–747. Paris: Sirey.

Gentili, Alberico. 1964. *De Jure Belli Libri Tres.* Trans. John C. Rolfe. New York: Oceana.

Gong, Gerrit W. 1984. *The Standard of "Civilization" in International Society.* Oxford: Clarendon.

Grewe, Wilhelm G. 1988. *Epochen der Völkerrechtsgeschichte.* 2nd edn. Baden-Baden: Nomos.

Grotius, Hugo. 1964. *De Jure Belli ac Pacis Libri Tres.* Trans. Francis W. Kelsey. New York: Oceana.

Hall, W. E. 1880. *A Treatise on International Law.* Reprint. London: Oxford University Press, 1924.

Hobbes, Thomas. 1960. *Leviathan.* Ed. Michael Oakeshott. Oxford: Basil Blackwell.

Holland, T. E. 1874. *An Inaugural Lecture on Albericus Gentilis.* London.

Keen, M. H. 1965. *The Laws of War in the Late Middle Ages.* London: Routledge and Kegan Paul.

Molen, Gesina van der. 1968. *Alberico Gentili and the Development of International Law.* Leiden: A. W. Sijthoff.

Montesquieu. 1951. *Oeuvres complètes*, vol. 2. Paris: Gallimard.

Nussbaum, Arthur. 1947. *A Concise History of the Law of Nations*. New York: Macmillan.

Platzhoff, Walter. 1968. *Geschichte des Europäischen Staatensystems 1559–1660*. Munich: Oldenbourg.

Schmitt, Carl. 1950. *Der Nomos der Erde im Völkerrecht des Jus Publicum Europaeum*. Cologne: Greven.

Treitschke, Heinrich von. 1914. *Selections from the Lectures on Politics*. Trans. Adam L. Gowans. London: Gowans and Gray.

Ward, Robert. 1795. *An Enquiry into the Foundation and History of the Law of Nations in Europe*. 2 vols. London.

Wight, Martin. 1977. *Systems of States*. Ed. Hedley Bull. Leicester: Leicester University Press.

3 THE DECLARATORY TRADITION IN MODERN INTERNATIONAL LAW

DOROTHY V. JONES

In recent times, the states of the international system have taken an increasingly active role in articulating and shaping a declaratory tradition in international law. They have always been involved, of course, in creating the whole body of the law, both written and customary. The nature and extent of their involvement has, however, changed in the modern period, a change that can be dated from about the end of the First World War. In the past, as Murray Forsyth shows in Chapter 2, international law has been the product of a complex interaction between theory and practice, with the states' actions providing the body of practice on which jurists, political theorists, and moral philosophers have reflected. These reflections and comments have, in turn, affected the practice of states by influencing the conceptions of leaders and policymakers as to what actions were possible and proper. In this process, states have generally been content to pursue their national goals and let others articulate the principles on which they were acting or were supposed to act.

After the First World War this situation changed, and it has been changing at an increasing rate ever since. Through their political leaders, foreign-service officers, and delegates to international bodies, the states have begun to reflect upon their own behavior, and have become major contributors to the explication of international law. In conference after conference, and in numerous treaties, conventions, declarations, charters, covenants, and the like, the states have, through their official representatives, set down principles to guide their own behavior and to provide standards by which that behavior can be judged. This sustained effort has created a body of reflections and rules that is closer to moral philosophy than it is to positive law. In this chapter, the many philosophical statements that have been incorporated into various international instruments are taken as expressions of the declaratory element that is such a prominent feature of modern international law.

Some comparisons of international instruments will illustrate the

42

point. There is, for example, a difference not just of degree but of kind between Article 1 of the 1947 peace treaty between the Allies and Italy, and Article 5h of the 1948 Charter of the Organization of American States. Article 1 of the 1947 treaty reads, "The frontiers of Italy shall, subject to the modifications set out in Articles 2, 3, 4, 11 and 22, be those which existed on January 1, 1938."[1] Article 5h of the 1948 Charter says, "Social justice and social security are bases of lasting peace."[2] The first article deals with specific territorial arrangements incident to establishing peace. The second article deals with peace in a totally different way. It sets out certain general conditions, and declares that they are necessary to secure peace on a lasting basis.

A comparison between the Geneva Protocol of 1924 and the Kellogg–Briand Pact of 1928 brings out this difference strongly. Both the protocol and the pact were concerned with restraining the use of force in the international system. The protocol's approach to this goal was instrumental. It linked arbitration procedures, security concerns, and the reduction of armaments into one comprehensive plan. The approach in the Kellogg–Briand Pact was declaratory. Through state renunciation of war as an instrument of national policy, the use of force was declared to be unacceptable. The Geneva Protocol (which eventually failed of adoption) took a principle regarding the use of force and attempted to give it institutional form and a means of application. The Kellogg–Briand Pact (which was agreed to and acclaimed by most of the world states) took the same principle and elevated it into an absolute rule.

The pact is a model of the declaratory form that the states have used with increasing frequency since 1928, and especially since the Second World War. They have rung many changes on this basic form, and they have not always – as they did in the pact – let a rule or a principle stand alone with no provision for either execution or for interpretation in the light of specific circumstances. Still, there is more assertion than action in this ethical tradition, so much so that we might ask: why bother with it at all? If we want to learn about international norms, we will look at what the states do, not at what they say.

But it is precisely in this declaratory strand that the states have spelled out what international law means to them, and what they think it ought to be. Further, through these various declarations, they have sketched a picture of the way that they think the *world* ought to

---

[1] *United Nations Treaty Series* (*UNTS*) 49: 128. A double system of citation has been employed in Chapter 3 to enable the reader to locate the relevant portions of the documents cited, as well as the works of individual authors.
[2] *UNTS* 119: 54.

be and, in so doing, have opened themselves to the possibility that they will be taken seriously enough that there will be attempts to hold them to their word. And, as we shall see, this is what is happening in certain areas where the states have been most explicit about the shape of the world-to-be.

This chapter focusses on discerning and defining the declaratory tradition in modern international law and identifying what role it plays there. The role is an important one. State reflections upon their own behavior form a core of explicit principles and rules that provides stability and continuity throughout the various changes in the tradition's external forms. These reflections rely on the thought of the jurists and philosophers that Forsyth describes in Chapter 2, but that thought has been further shaped by the turbulent political processes of the international system. The ideas set down in the declaratory strand are tough and tested, and have been remarkably consistent over time.

Consistency, then, has been one aspect of the role played by the declaratory element. Reflection looks inward, to the law itself in its manifold expressions. When states look outward to the world, rather than inward to the law, a different aspect appears. There, the many assertions of universal principles and rules can act – and have been acting – as a stimulus for change. The changes cut both ways: the world may change to conform more closely to the law, and the law may change to become more responsive to the needs of the world. The subject of this chapter is thus a moving target, at once vital and elusive, that shifts even as it is brought within the range of description and analysis.

Fundamental principles

At the core of the declaratory tradition in modern international law is a set of nine fundamental principles that constitute a summary of state reflection upon proper action in the international sphere. (Two additional, less widely accepted principles – creation of an equitable international economic order and protection of the environment – will be discussed separately.)

The nine basic principles are:

1. The sovereign equality of states,
2. The territorial integrity and political independence of states,
3. Equal rights and self-determination of peoples,
4. Nonintervention in the internal affairs of states,
5. Peaceful settlement of disputes between states,

6. No threat or use of force,
7. Fulfillment in good faith of international obligations,
8. Cooperation with other states,
9. Respect for human rights and fundamental freedoms.

All nine principles can be found in the United Nations Charter, but the authors of that document did not create them. The principles summarize years of thought about the proper relations between sovereign entities. That thought was formalized by jurists and philosophers in the period discussed by Forsyth, and then institutionalized by the states themselves in the modern period. The UN Charter is only one example of an international instrument in which the principles can be found. Throughout all the changes of the international scene, states have asserted some or all of these principles in international instruments that range in date from 1919 to the present, and in kind from the Covenant of the League of Nations to the Vienna convention on the Law of Treaties.[3] It is from these many efforts to work out international standards of behavior that this list has been compiled.

These basic principles rest on a broad base of state support that cuts across the barriers of time, culture, and circumstance. For example, in 1937 US Secretary of State Cordell Hull set out what he called fundamental principles of international policy, and invited the comments of other states. Hull's list was longer and more diffuse than later formulations – this was eight years before there was an attempt at standardization – but it included five of the nine basic principles noted above: equality, nonintervention, peaceful settlement, no use of force, and fulfillment of obligations. Sixty of the world's states responded to Hull's request with statements of agreement.[4]

In 1955 the leaders of the independent Asian and African states who gathered at Bandung, Indonesia, had probably never heard of Hull's list, and they specifically rejected the Western tradition of thought on which it rested. Instead they looked to Asian and African traditions for guidance in articulating ten principles which, in their view, ought to underlie the "friendly cooperation" that was their ideal for the international system. Yet the same five principles that Hull included show up again in the 1955 Bandung Final Communiqué, constituting half of the Afro-Asian proposals to promote "world peace and cooperation" – in a world far different from that of 1937.[5]

---

[3] Arts. 1, 2, 55, 62.1–2, United Nations (UN) Charter; preamble, arts. 10, 11–15, 17, 22, 23, Covenant of the League of Nations; preamble, art. 26, Vienna Convention (Brownlie 1983, 350, 361).

[4] US Department of State (1954, 1:699–700).

[5] Pt. G.3, 4, 7, 8, 10, Bandung Final Communiqué (Kahin 1956, 83–85).

Support for the nine basic principles is an issue we will return to later. The examples above indicate support for at least some of the nine principles; they also illustrate an important fact about the principles and thus about international law itself. The law is and can be universal because the conditions that formed and shaped it have become or are becoming universal.

The conditions are those of an international system created by the institutions and interactions of sovereign states. The states are politically independent, territorially based, and protective of their independence, their territory, and their sovereign prerogatives. In the maintenance and strengthening of modern international law, these conditions are more important than the cultural tradition or ideological persuasion of any of the states, and it helps to explain why the states that have entered the system since the Second World War have made so little change either in the system or in its basic principles. As Tom J. Farer has noted, the new states have "generally found them useful," and so they have been retained (1988, 25). The new states' major contribution lies elsewhere, as will be clear in the discussion of the two auxiliary principles below.

Contours of the tradition

The list of fundamental principles articulated by the states makes it possible to depict in considerable detail the contours of the declaratory tradition. Most obviously, it is state-centered. The basic political community is understood to be the nation-state, a political entity that is the focus of eight out of the nine principles. Numbers one through three focus on the protection, definition, and creation of states. Numbers four through seven deal with restraints upon state actions. The eighth principle speaks of cooperation between states. Only the ninth principle shifts the focus from states to human beings, and even there the admonition of respect for human rights and fundamental freedoms could be seen as laying a positive duty upon the states.

In this declaratory tradition, the concept of the state has received sustained and careful attention, from the League of Nations stipulation of "fully self-governing" as a requirement for membership, through the efforts of the United Nations to end South Africa's administration of the former German colony of South-West Africa and bring the territory to full independence as the sovereign state of Namibia.[6] As a logical extension of this emphasis on states, the

[6] Art. 1, League Covenant. For Namibia, see UN Resolution 435/78, UN Security Council, *Resolutions and Decisions, 1978*, 13, and "The United States and Angola, 1974–88: A Chronology," [US] *Department of State Bulletin* 89 (Feb. 1989): 16–23.

international community is conceived in state-centered terms. It is a community of sovereign states that interact with one another through traditional channels of diplomacy and trade, supplemented by regional and international institutions, under self-imposed rules and regulations derived from agreed-upon principles.

As this summary makes clear, relations between states in the international community are to be peaceful relations. Peace is the desired norm. That it is also rarely attained can be presumed by the number of principles devoted to restraining bellicose tendencies or demanding good behavior. States are not to use or threaten to use force. They are to settle disputes peacefully. And – in case the point is still not understood – they are not to intervene in each other's affairs. Further, they are not to break or ignore their pledged word but are to carry out in good faith their obligations as members of the international community.

These principles, particularly those regarding force, peaceful settlement, and nonintervention, are universally endorsed in the international system. They have been exemplified in numerous resolutions, declarations, treaties, and conventions. Early attempts to give them institutional form range from the Locarno arbitration agreements of 1925 through the well-known renunication of war in the Kellogg–Briand Pact of 1928 to the lesser-known Saavedra–Lamas Anti-War Treaty of 1933. They were restated in the UN Charter, and then given expanded treatment by a twenty-six member special UN committee (later enlarged to thirty-one members) that was formed in 1964 to bring the principles and rules of the charter under review. As a result of the review, a new declaration was adopted by the General Assembly in 1970 with the support of all the voting blocs: African, Asian, Latin American, socialist, and the developed states.[7] It was entitled the Declaration on Principles of International Law concerning Friendly Relations and Co-operation among States in accordance with the Charter of the United Nations.

Even this declaration has not satisfied the desire of the states to draw out the implications of the principles that are to assure peaceful relations in the community of states. In 1987, as the culmination of a ten-year effort, the UN General Assembly adopted a Declaration on

[7] Locarno arbitration treaties, *League of Nations Treaty Series* (*LTS*) 54: 293–301, 305–13, 317–25, 329–39, 343–51; General Treaty for Renunciation of War . . . (Kellogg–Briand Treaty, 1928), *LTS* 94: 57–64; Anti-War Treaty of Nonaggression and Conciliation (Saavendra–Lamas Treaty, 1933), *LTS* 163: 395–413; arts. 1, 2, UN Charter; UN Special Committee Reports (1964–1970): UN General Assembly, *Official Records*, 19th session (1964), A/5746; 21st sess. (1966), A/6230; 22nd sess. (1967), A/6799; 23rd sess. (1968), A/7326; 24th sess. (1969), A/7619; 25th sess. (1970), A/8018; support of voting blocs: 25th sess. (1970), A/8082.

the Enhancement of the Effectiveness of the Principle of Refraining from the Threat of Force in International Relations. In this expression of their "deep concern at the continued existence of situations of conflict and tension," the states considered a broad range of ideas on settling conflicts, and brought them under the single rubric of the enhancement of the effectiveness of the no-force principle. They covered subjects as diverse as terrorism, UN peace-keeping operations, the Security Council's obligations, and the functions of the UN secretary-general. As for the principle itself, they affirmed it in the strongest possible terms, stating that the obligation to refrain from the threat of or use of force "is universal in character and is binding, regardless of each State's political, economic, social or cultural system or relations of alliance. No consideration of whatever nature may be invoked to warrant resorting to the threat or use of force in violation of the Charter."[8]

The basic principles discussed so far are based on the states' experiences in an international environment that they have created through the steady pursuit of their own self-interest. The principles reflect that competitive, potentially hostile setting. The assertions of rights and equality, the restraints on force and intervention, and the admonitions to peaceful settlement and good faith are, in a very real sense, based on fear – fear of what can happen in such an environment, fear of what did happen in the First and Second World Wars.

These principles are old in concept. They constitute what H. L. A. Hart has called the "common requirements of law and morality," a set of mutual forbearances for "the minimum purpose of survival" (1961, 189, 190). The nine principles have been developed over the centuries by sovereign entities of many different forms and lineages for many different reasons related to their immediate circumstances. The circumstances have changed, but the principles remain and, in the twentieth century, they have taken on new meaning and urgency. As the states themselves noted in the 1987 Declaration of Enhancement, "In the present world situation in which nuclear weapons exist there is no reasonable alternative to peaceful relations."[9]

A large part of this tradition, however, is not fearful but full of hope. It looks not to the past, but to the future. In this part of the tradition, the states have set out their conception of the common good. The first characteristic, the condition on which all else depends is, of course, peace. The raison d'être of the League of Nations was "to promote international co-operation and to achieve international

8 *International Legal Materials (ILM)* 27 (1988): 1674, 1676.   9 *ILM* 27 (1988): 1675.

peace and security," and the first purpose of the United Nations is "to maintain international peace and security."[10]

These are only the most obvious statements of the goal that is, in the states' own testimony, the reason for most of the institutions and international instruments through which this ethical tradition has been expressed. Even the 1933 Convention on the Rights and Duties of States, one of the most extreme assertions of state autonomy, gave at least token recognition to this overriding purpose by stating that "The primary interest of states is the conservation of peace."[11] The 1981 African Charter of Human and Peoples' Rights takes the leveling and universalizing tendencies of the years since 1933 to their logical extreme: "All peoples shall have the right to national and international peace and security."[12] The goal of peace that the League was to achieve, the states were to conserve, and the United Nations was to maintain has become a right for "all peoples" to assert. Against what or whom is a point on which the tradition is silent.

The tradition is not silent on the details of the common good. These details are found chiefly in the international instruments that are derived from or that express the ninth principle: respect for human rights and fundamental freedoms. Here a life of peace, freedom, and prosperity for all is set out as a model of the way that the world ought to be, and *would* be if conditions would only conform to the guidelines through which the states have spelled out their vision of the good life. The vision is articulated with a completeness that goes from cradle to grave, and a confidence that allows for no exceptions to the stipulations that define the states' ideal world.

Shall is one of the operative words in articulating the ideal, especially in the years since the Second World War. "The child shall enjoy special protection."[13] "Primary education shall be compulsory and available free to all."[14] "Women shall be entitled to hold public office."[15] "Everyone's right to life shall be protected by law."[16] "The States Parties shall take all effective measures to ensure that their ports, airfields and coasts are not used for the conveyance of

---

[10] Preamble, League Covenant; art. 1, UN Charter.

[11] Art. 10, Convention on the Rights and Duties of States (1933), in *The International Conferences of American States, First Supplement, 1933–1940* (Washington: Carnegie Endowment for International Peace, 1940), 122.

[12] Art. 23.1, 1981 African Charter of Human and Peoples' Rights (Sieghart 1985, 236).

[13] Principle 2, 1959 Declaration of the Rights of the Child (Brownlie 1981, 109).

[14] Art. 13.2a, 1966 International Covenant on Economic, Social, and Cultural Rights (Brownlie 1981, 123).

[15] Art. III, 1953 Convention on the Political Rights of Women (Brownlie 1981, 91).

[16] Art. 2.1, 1950 Convention for the Protection of Human Rights and Fundamental Freedoms (Brownlie 1981, 243).

slaves."[17] "The family shall be the natural unit and basis of society."[18] "Everyone shall have the right to live in a healthy environment."[19]

There is legal precedent for this use of the word *shall*, but, given the subject matter of these instruments and, in most cases, the lack of any enforcement authority, the word takes on a different meaning than that of an obligation to be defined through judicial or administrative review. Instead, it becomes the strongest possible assertion of the conditions that the states think ought to obtain in their ideal world.

From these examples it can be seen that *rights* is another key word in this tradition. In modern international law, rights language is used both for states, as in the 1933 Convention on the Rights and Duties of States, and for individuals, as in the 1948 Universal Declaration of Human Rights. In theory, these two need not be regarded as antithetical since state rights can be understood to derive ultimately from a doctrine of individual rights. The practical effect is, however, quite different. When applied to states, rights language, even when modified by duties, enlarges the power of the state and emphasizes its autonomy. When applied to individuals, rights language limits the power of the state and enlarges, not its autonomy, but its areas of responsibility. (For a discussion of the different ways in which individual and state rights have been related, see "Rights in a plan of world politics," Chapter 12.)

Finally, the states are in the process of defining two other principles that may one day be added to the basic set. Because they have not yet attained the acceptance of the nine principles listed above, they are treated here as auxiliaries.

1.   Creation of an equitable international economic order,
2.   Protection of the environment.

The first of these principles is at the heart of the North/South dialogue discussed by R. J. Vincent in Chapter 12. The new states have put this principle on the agenda of international concerns in a way, and to an extent, that markedly differentiates the present from the past. Free trade was the principle that guided pre-Second World War concerns about the international economy. The principle was expressed in a single article of the League Covenant in which members

[17] Art. 3.2b, 1956 Supplementary Convention on the Abolition of Slavery ... (Brownlie 1981, 46).
[18] Art. 18.1, 1981 African Charter of Human and Peoples' Rights (Sieghart 1985, 235).
[19] Art. 11.1, Additional Protocol to the American Convention on Human Rights ... (1988), *ILM* 28 (1989): 165.

agreed to "make provision to secure and maintain ... equitable treatment for the commerce of all Members of the League,"[20] a statement so brief that it gives little idea of the importance this principle would assume in the many international efforts to restore a free flow of goods and capital in the interwar years.

After the Second World War, the emphasis changed from a free *flow* of goods and capital to a *transfer* of goods and capital. The transfer was to be from the developed states to the less developed states – in effect, from the established states to the newly independent states that began to enter the international system in significant numbers after the Second World War. The demands of the new states rested on a concept of equity that went beyond the ideal of equal access embodied in the principle of free trade. For the new states, equity was a matter of distributive justice. Both within and without the bodies and conferences of the United Nations, the new states made call after call for a new economic order. They sought legitimacy for their demands by linking them to principles that were already accepted by the international community.

As the new states put it in the 1974 Charter of Economic Rights and Duties of States (which was largely their creation), "Economic as well as political and other relations among States shall be governed, *inter alia*, by the following principles." They then set out the nine basic principles and added six more, including "Remedying of injustices which have been brought about by force and which deprive a nation of the natural means necessary for its normal development."[21] How the remedying is to be done is, of course, the point at issue. Differences over that very point keep this auxiliary principle from universal acceptance and, at the same time, keep it in the forefront of international concerns.

Since the Second World War, protection of the environment has also entered the arena of legitimate international concern. There were hints of this concern in the prewar period, but the relevant actions expressed economic or sporting interests as much as care for the environment. There is a dramatic difference between prewar efforts to protect migratory water fowl and fur-bearing seals and the assertion of the 1972 Declaration of the United Nations Conference on the Human Environment (the Stockholm Declaration) that "The protection and improvement of the human environment is a major issue which affects

[20] Art. 23, League Covenant.
[21] Ch. 1, 1.i, 1974 Charter of Economic Right and Duties of States (Brownlie 1983, 238, 239).

the well-being of peoples and economic development throughout the world."[22]

The wording of this assertion reflects the conflicts that surfaced at Stockholm between environmental protection and the new states' aspirations for rapid economic development. The whole document, with its twenty-six principles "for the protection and improvement of the human environment," is a compromise between these contending points of view. The main achievement of the conference was, however, not the Stockholm Declaration, important though it is in providing a philosophical grounding and standards for action. As Lynton Caldwell has said, the conference "legitimized environmental policy as a universal concern among nations, and so created a place for environmental issues on many national agendas where they had been previously unrecognized" (1984, 19).

Recognition is not acceptance, of course, and the definition and placing of this auxiliary principle in the international system is still very much in process.

Contradictions and comparisons

The contradictions within the declaratory tradition in international law can be traced to the fact that several lines of ethical thought have been brought together in the tradition, with no systematic attempt to reconcile the differences between them. One line of thought focusses on the manifold uses and definitions of sovereignty. It derives from the long struggle of nation-states to establish themselves as independent political entities, and to define the rights and relationships of an existence separate from the dominion of church or empire. From this line of thought arises an abiding concern with the rights and duties of states, and an insistence on assertions of equality. The 1975 Final Act of the Conference on Security and Cooperation in Europe (CSCE) sums this up in one sentence: "The participating States will respect each other's sovereign equality and individuality as well as all the rights inherent in and encompassed by its sovereignty, including in particular the right of every State to juridical equality, to territorial integrity and to freedom and political independence."[23]

Another line of ethical thought can be traced to the social justice concerns of the late nineteenth and early twentieth centuries, when

[22] I.2, 1972 Declaration of the United Nations Conference on the Human Environment (Henkin et al. 1987, 633).
[23] Principle I, *Final Act, Conference on Security and Co-operation in Europe (CSCE)* (Helsinki, 1975), 4.

the social effects of industrialization began to receive widespread attention. In modern international law, action on these concerns was, in the early years, channelled largely through the International Labour Organization (ILO), whose charter was included in the Versailles Peace Treaty of 1919. The principle that provided the rationale for the many subsequent international instruments dealing with working conditions and labor rights was included in the ILO Charter as a guiding principle of "special and urgent importance," namely "that labour should not be regarded merely as a commodity or article of commerce."[24] The social justice component of this ethical tradition has gradually evolved from an emphasis on curbing employers' abuses (such as excessive hours of work or unsafe working conditions) to an emphasis on the obligation of states to provide for the well-being of workers and to achieve social justice in general. "It is the duty of the states to provide measures of social security and welfare for the benefit of workers," reads one article of the 1948 Inter-American Charter of Social Guarantees.[25] The 1961 European Social Charter exemplifies the expansion of the social justice component of this ethical tradition with its detailed lists of rights and principles that the signatory states are to attain "to improve the standard of living and to promote the social well-being of both their urban and rural populations."[26]

Since the end of the Second World War, the concept of social justice in this tradition has been under pressure to include the entire international economic system and the states' role in and responsibility for that system. Abundant institutional responses to that pressure range from those with global scope such as the International Bank for Reconstruction and Development (the World Bank) and the United Nations Conference on Trade and Development (UNCTAD) to regional organizations such as the Association of Southeast Asian Nations (ASEAN) and the European Free Trade Association (EFTA). Management of economic relations to provide some measure of control and predictability is, of course, one of the major purposes of these groups, but ideas of equity are also involved. Currently, as noted earlier, the states hold widely different concepts of economic equity and of the actions needed to achieve it. These differences help account for the cool reception by the developed states of the Charter of Economic Rights and Duties of States, but at a high level of generality, few of them would quarrel with the charter's statement of "the need to

[24] Art. 427, Versailles Peace Treaty (Parry 1981, 225:385).
[25] Art. 28, Inter-American Charter of Social Guarantees, in *Final Act of the Ninth International Conference of American States* (Washington, DC: Pan American Union, 1948), 36.
[26] Preamble, 1961 European Social Charter (Harris 1984, 312).

establish and maintain a just and equitable economic and social order."[27]

A third line of ethical thought that the states have worked into the declaratory tradition focusses on the inherent rights of individuals. Human rights as a philosophical construct is discussed at the beginning of Chapter 12. The emphasis here is on the tensions that the human rights focus helps to create within the declaratory tradition in international law. In past centuries, the rights of individuals were asserted against the authority of popes, lords, emperors, and kings. In the modern period they are asserted against the authority of the state itself. Individual rights are set up as barriers against a too great extension of that authority into areas where, it is claimed, the state's writ does not apply. This is done by making these rights independent of any enabling legislation that the states might enact to secure or protect them. The 1948 American Declaration of the Rights and Duties of Man puts this succinctly: "The American States have on repeated occasions recognized that the essential rights of man are not derived from the fact that he is a national of a certain state, but are based upon attributes of his human personality."[28] This same presumption underlies the 1948 Universal Declaration of Human Rights and the 1950 European Convention on Human Rights, and it is made explicit in the two International Human Rights Covenants of 1966, the 1969 American Convention on Human Rights and the 1988 Additional Protocol, the 1975 CSCE Final Act, and the 1981 African Charter on Human and Peoples' Rights.[29]

These three lines of ethical thought, focussing on sovereignty, social justice, and inherent human rights, coexist somewhat uneasily within modern international law. Their differences set up tensions that can be contained or even ignored until the circumstances of time, place, and event bring them into the open. Take, for example, the tension between the principle of nonintervention and the principle of respect for human rights and fundamental freedoms. (This tension is also discussed in "Liberal internationalism: the problem of intervention," Chapter 10.) On the one hand, the states uniformly insist on the right of each state "freely to choose and develop its political, social, economic and cultural systems as well as its right to determine its laws

[27] Preamble, 1974 Charter of the Economic Rights and Duties of States (Brownlie 1983, 237).
[28] Preamble, American Declaration of the Rights and Duties of Man (1948), in *Final Act of the Ninth International Conference of American States* (1948), 38.
[29] For the 1948 Universal Declaration, the 1950 European Convention, the two 1966 International Covenants, and the 1969 American Convention, see Brownlie (1981). The 1988 Additional Protocol is in *ILM* 28 (1989), and the African Charter is in Sieghart (1985).

and regulations," as the CSCE Final Act puts it.[30] In the 1987 Declaration on the Enhancement of the No-Force Principle, the states reaffirmed "the inalienable right of every State to choose its political, economic, and social and cultural system without interference in any form by another State."[31] On the other hand, states have set at least theoretical limits to that freedom through such instruments as the Universal Declaration, the 1948 Convention on the Prevention and Punishment of the Crime of Genocide, and the 1965 Convention on the Elimination of all Forms of Racial Discrimination.[32]

It is in the application of these principles that the tensions become apparent. The states have repeatedly affirmed that there are international standards of human rights behavior, but they are not sure how or when the standards should be applied. Present practice indicates selective condemnation of human rights abuses. Until recently, South Africa was almost always singled out for condemnation. In most other cases, international criticism was deflected by a quick retreat behind the principle of nonintervention.

Another tension is evident in the states' attitude toward the use of force. Their frequent recourse to force provides abundant empirical underpinning for the realist traditions discussed in Chapters 4 and 5. Yet the states themselves, when setting out the principles that are to govern their relationships, simply outlaw force entirely. Understanding here requires that we look beyond the list of principles to the institutional structure on which it rests. In the Covenant of the League of Nations and again in the UN Charter, the states preserved the ancient right of self defense, and added the modern duty of collective action against aggression. This is the assumed but unstated background for the principles that address the problem of force in international affairs.

To these two acceptable uses of force – self defense and collective action against aggression – a third must be added. Since the Second World War the states have frequently affirmed a modern version of the old argument that war against injustice is a justified war. In the words of the 1987 declaration mentioned earlier, "peoples under colonial and racist regimes" must be allowed to struggle and to seek and receive support in order to secure their "right to self-determination, freedom and independence."[33]

There are significant differences between the declaratory tradition

[30] Principle I, *Final Act, CSCE* (1975), 4.
[31] Preamble, Annex to the Declaration (1987), in *ILM* 27 (1988): 1675.
[32] The Universal Declaration and the Genocide and Racial Discrimination Conventions can be found in Brownlie (1981).
[33] *ILM* 27 (1988): 1679.

and the other traditions discussed in this book. Where the others bring certain approaches or insights to bear on an issue such as nonintervention, this tradition simply asserts it as a fundamental – and therefore non-negotiable – principle. In other traditions, nonintervention can be examined as a question and its consequences can be discussed. In this ethical tradition, such matters as nonintervention and sovereign equality are not questions at all. They are the point from which discussion starts, but the discussion is directed toward amplification and development, not modification. There is no hint that the under-lying principles might be withdrawn or replaced. It is only when the principles are placed in the context of the whole tradition of inter-national law and played off against each other that modifications and shadings can be seen. Then the flat assertions appear more nearly in the round, and connections can be made from them to the real life situations that they address.

Much in this tradition could be analyzed in the Kantian terms set out by Thomas Donaldson in Chapter 7, especially if we were to accept Kant's doctrine of states as moral persons subject to universal rights and duties (for discussion of this doctrine, see "Kantian internation-alism," Chapter 7). The states conceive of themselves as inherently valuable entities. They have universalized the principles of their tradition, saying that the principles apply to all situations. From those principles the states have drawn a multitude of universal rules: "Every State has the duty . . .; States shall fulfill . . .; no State may use or encourage to use . . .; States shall take effective measures."[34]

This kind of analysis, however, imposes on the international law tradition an intellectual rigor and tidiness that is foreign to it. And even if we tried to analyze this tradition with this sort of rigor, many others have argued that these supposedly exceptionless rules must admit of exception (for this objection to Article 2(4) of the UN Charter see "The Kantian-deontological approach to international affairs," Chapter 7). In any case, this tradition was not devised by philosophers but by leaders of states who picked and chose from the rich storehouse of thought that is suggested by this volume. The method of selection has been unsystematic, but the outcome is impressively consistent. Over and over the states have declared that they are chiefly concerned with the requirements of what might be called a "just peace." Their efforts at definition and elaboration have, since the First World War, made the "just peace" component an increasingly important one in modern international law. So far as the declaratory strand of the law is concerned, the purpose of the whole ethical endeavor is to secure

[34] Sec. I.1, I.6, I.8, II.18, Annex to the Declaration (1987), in *ILM* 27 (1988): 1676, 1677.

peace based on justice, and, in the words of the UN Charter, "to save succeeding generations from the scourge of war."[35]

Law, morality, and international affairs

Our final tasks are to look at the relationship of this tradition to some general concepts of law and then to sum up the discussion by asking what difference the tradition makes to international affairs. Without a tradition of international law, how might the behavior of states differ? The answer can only be speculative, of course, but the exercise is a useful way of taking a fresh look at the tradition's strengths and weaknesses. Before we proceed, the relationship between this ethical tradition and some broader concepts of law deserves our attention.

Many scholars have sought to explain the ultimate obligatory power of law by demonstrating the connection between law and morality. In his essay "Modern Ethics and the Law," Felix Cohen notes that despite every attempt to derive legal rules solely from logic or science, "the law has never been wholly freed from an avowed moral basis" (1960, 27). And Charles de Visscher warns against overemphasizing the separation of legal and ethical categories. The separation, he says, "must not be pushed to the point of completely separating law from the primary moral notions to which all the normative disciplines are attached as to a common stem" (1959, 58).

Even H. L. A. Hart, whose writings express the positivist view that law is neither more nor less than what a legitimate authority says it is, does not sever all connection between law and morality. On the contrary, he points out that the development of law in all times and places has been "profoundly influenced" by the conventional morality and ideals of certain social groups and also "by forms of enlightened moral criticism urged by individuals, whose moral horizon has transcended the morality currently accepted" (1961, 181). (For further discussion of the relation between morality and law, see "Common morality and international law," Chapter 1, and "The evolution of international law," Chapter 2.)

Modern international law is a special case in the search for the connections between morality and law, just as it is a special case in the search for a satisfactory definition of law. For the purposes of this discussion, the much-debated question of whether or not international law is truly law is beside the point. What is of interest here is

---

[35] Preamble, UN Charter.

the ethical element, which is one of the most prominent characteristics of modern international law. This element is so prominent that there is no need to postulate morality as an ultimate source for international law, or to attach both law and ethics to primary moral notions as to a common parental stem. The preambular portions of dozens of international instruments and the abundant lists of principles and rules derived from those principles are all the evidence that is needed. These portions of modern international law are strongly philosophical, and are much concerned with the "oughts" of the international system. When they are abstracted from the routine business of the system, the connections between them and their internal consistency over the years is obvious. Abstracted in this fashion, they can be studied as an explicit ethical tradition.

Finally, what difference does it make that such a tradition exists and that the states have been active in its articulation? Obviously, the tradition is not effectively binding on the states, despite their frequent attempts to give it obligatory force by saying that the fundamental principles that underlie the tradition are principles of law. The principles enjoin or call for certain kinds of state behavior, but the appeal is almost always to conscience, not to courts. What then, is the value of this ethical tradition?

Most importantly, it provides standards by which the conduct of states can be judged. These standards have not been imposed from the outside. They have been set out and accepted by the states themselves. Moreover, since the mid-1960s, formulation of the tradition has resulted from the efforts and interaction of states of different political systems, ideological commitments, cultural heritages, and levels of economic development. If ever an ethical tradition could be called universal in the sense of encompassing the many varieties of states and peoples on the globe today, this one can.

The weaknesses of the tradition are also obvious. Some spring from the difficulties inherent in any attempt to work out standards and rules for the conduct of affairs. Some spring from the tendency of the states to excuse themselves from the very rules they have themselves devised. But there are also possibilities that are not at first apparent and that may take years to work out. One of the tradition's chief characteristics is its dynamism. It is in a continuous process of change, and one way it is changing is in the use of the fundamental principles at its core. The use of these principles as guides for state behavior and as standards by which to judge that behavior has already been mentioned, but such abstract statements are little more than indicators of potential. It is when the abstractions are translated into actual procedures that the possibilities in this ethical tradition are brought more clearly into view.

During the early years of the modern period, the model for using these standards was primarily judicial. In 1920 the Permanent Court of Justice was formed, to be followed in 1946 by the International Court of Justice.This effort to establish legal institutions for interpretation and judgment at the international level was based on the pattern of Western domestic legal systems. Transferred into the very different international environment, where there was no single source of authority, the judicial model was pressed into new shapes of advice and arbitration without ever losing the domestic ideal of strict adjudication. In the 1980s that was still a potent ideal, expressed most effectively in the judicial procedures and institutions established under the 1950 [European] Convention for the Protection of Human Rights and Fundamental Freedoms. A less effective expression is found in the institutions established under the 1969 American Convention on Human Rights.

Institutionalized review of compliance is another way that the principles of this ethical tradition are being used in the latter half of the twentieth century. The model is the Helsinki or CSCE process, in which reviews take place on a regular basis. Meetings are set on an agreed-upon schedule, not just when some difficulty occurs that cannot be handled through routine diplomatic channels. Thus after the signing of the CSCE Final Act by thirty-five nations in Helsinki in 1975, there were full-scale follow-up meetings in Belgrade in 1977 and in Madrid in 1980. This review model is evolving toward smaller, more frequent meetings with specialized areas of review such as human rights (1989, 1990, 1991), the environment (1989), and peaceful settlement of disputes (1991). The ten principles agreed upon by the states that signed the Final Act of the CSCE include the nine fundamental principles discussed above.[36]

A third use of these principles that also stems from the CSCE Final Act is the formation of citizen groups in the signatory nations to monitor their own state's compliance with the principles. The focus of the several Helsinki Watch Groups has been on compliance with provisions of "Basket III" of the Final Act, "Co-operation in Humanitarian and Other Fields." This set of actions and goals is based on the principle of respect for human rights and fundamental freedoms.

From these examples, it can be seen that this ethical tradition is continuing to change in response to the needs of a changing international system and to changing perceptions of that system. If the

[36] Principles I–II. IV–X, *Final Act, CSCE* (1975), 4–8.

changes continue in the direction they have started, the tradition will increasingly become a tool that is used and shaped not only by the states of the international system, but also by the people whose interests, according to one of the tradition's most basic tenets, the states are presumed to represent.

Suggested reading

Murray Forsyth's comment in the bibliography to Chapter 2 about the scarcity of books on the overall historical development of international law applies with special force to the period since the First World War. Arthur Nussbaum's *A Concise History of the Law of Nations* (New York: Macmillan, 1947) is particularly weak on the twentieth century, even in the revised edition of 1954. Readers wishing to pursue the subject in the modern period might begin with J. L. Brierly, *The Law of Nations* (6th edn., Oxford: Clarendon Press, 1963), keeping in mind that Brierly writes from within the tradition that is analyzed in this chapter.

The arguments for and against classifying international law as law are well summarized by Gidon Gottlieb in "The Nature of International Law: Toward a Second Concept of Law," in *The Future of the International Legal Order*, vol. 4, *The Structure of the International Environment*, ed. Cyril E. Black and Richard A. Falk (Princeton NJ: Princeton University Press, 1972), 331–83. Gottlieb does not merely summarize. He proposes a definition of law that offers a way out of the intellectual impasse created by posing the question in yes/no terms. Extensive notes make this article a useful review of the literature to the time of publication.

As Forsyth notes, Terry Nardin's *Law, Morality, and the Relations of States* (Princeton NJ: Princeton University Press, 1983) takes the evolution of international law as the starting point for his analysis, an analysis that provides a much needed bridge from the discussion of law to the discussion of ethics. Two older works are also useful in this respect. Part I of Edmond Cahn's *The Moral Decision* (1955; Bloomington IN: Indiana University Press, 1981) explores the relationship between law and morals. Cahn's subject is US domestic law, but the quality of his thought sheds light on the relationship in any setting. Felix Cohen is another scholar whose thought is illuminating. He sets out the difficulties in applying general principles to specific cases with unequalled clarity and brevity in his "Casuistry" (Cohen 1960, 14–16).

The George Kennan article (1985/86) recommended by Jack Donnelly in the bibliography to Chapter 5 should be read in tandem with Paul Nitze's "The Recovery of Ethics," in *Moral Dimensions of American Foreign Policy*, ed. Kenneth W. Thompson (New Brunswick NJ: Transaction Books, 1984), 51–73. The fact that Nitze's realist credentials are as impeccable as Kennan's lends particular interest to this plea for an ethical framework to give relevance to the analysis of foreign policy.

One of the best of the many arguments for international economic equity is made by José Figueres, former president of Costa Rica. His "Some Economic Foundations of Human Rights" was published in 1968 as an official UN

THE DECLARATORY TRADITION

Document. It is more easily available in Ian Brownlie, ed., *Basic Documents on Human Rights* (1981, 472–88).

References

Brownlie, Ian, ed. 1981. *Basic Documents on Human Rights*. Oxford: Clarendon Press.

1983. *Basic Documents in International Law*. Oxford: Clarendon Press.

Caldwell, Lynton Keith. 1984. *International Environmental Policy*. Durham NC: Duke University Press.

Cohen, Felix. 1960. *The Legal Conscience: Selected Papers of Felix S. Cohen*. New Haven, CT: Yale University Press.

Farer, Tom J. 1988. "International Law: The Critics Are Wrong." *Foreign Policy* 71: 22–45.

Harris, David. 1984. *The European Social Charter*. Charlottesville VA: University of Virginia Press.

Hart, H. L. A. 1961. *The Concept of Law*. Oxford: Clarendon Press.

Henkin, Louis, et al. 1987. *Basic Documents Supplement to International Law Cases and Materials*. St. Paul, MN: West Publishing Co.

Kahin, George McTurnan. 1956. *The Asian–African Conference*. Ithaca, NY: Cornell University Press.

Parry, Clive, ed. 1981. *Consolidated Treaty Series*. Dobbs Ferry, NY: Oceana Publications.

Sieghart, Paul. 1985. *The Lawful Rights of Mankind*. Oxford: Oxford University Press.

US Department of State. 1954. *Foreign Relations of the United States, 1937*. Washington, DC: Department of State.

Visscher, Charles de. 1959. *Theory and Reality in Public International Law*. Princeton, NJ: Princeton University Press.

4 CLASSICAL REALISM

STEVEN FORDE

"Realism" is probably the second oldest perspective we have on the place of ethics in international politics. The oldest, of course, is the patriotic moralism that sees a simple struggle between right and wrong in international affairs, with one's own community infallibly in the right. Realism appears against this background as a skepticism concerning the relevance of moral categories to the relations among states. The realist tradition in Western thought dates to ancient Greece, particularly to the writing of the historian and political thinker Thucydides. The "classical realism" that is the subject of this chapter is a tradition that begins with Thucydides and extends through Machiavelli to the early social contract theorists Hobbes, Spinoza, and Rousseau. Though this tradition has been immensely powerful, it is to some extent an artificial construct – these thinkers did not by and large think of themselves as adherents to a tradition, but as innovators. Nevertheless, as we shall see, they share a fundamental perspective that puts them on the same side of the important questions of ethics and international politics.

The essence of international realism is its belief in the primacy of self-interest over moral principle, of necessity and therefore *as of right*, in international politics. This can mean either that self-interest confers a positive right of some kind, as when the "national interest" is seen as a moral principle, or that morality is wholly inapplicable to international politics. In the second understanding, states have a "right" to pursue their self-interest only in the sense that they have no duty to do otherwise. Realists, as we shall see in this chapter and the next, may take either position, or some position in between (see also the discussion of realism in "Ethical judgment as judgment within a tradition," Chapter 1). The classical realists differ from their successors in general in being more uncompromising in their realism. The classical realists tend as well to be more philosophical in their approach and orientation. They are engaged in a serious dialogue with moral philosophy, and are aware of the need to explain theoretically why moral principle does not apply to relations among states.

It is sometimes proposed that particular features are essential to realism, such as a belief in the primacy of the nation-state, or the principle that states behave rationally, or the balance of power. These views are advanced by some realists, but not by all. Thucydides and Machiavelli, for example, ascribe as much importance to individual actors (Alcibiades, Cesare Borgia) as to states, under the proper circumstances. Machiavelli had nothing but scorn for the balance-of-power advocates of his day and, for him at least, realism represents an attempt to improve on what he regards as the woefully defective rationality of modern Christian states. All realists do agree that the international environment is inherently anarchic, lacking any central, order-enforcing power. Since ethical restraints are not enforced in this environment, the argument holds, they lose their binding character. The realists often speak in terms of *necessity*: international conditions compel states to defend their interests by frequently immoral means, and this compulsion of self-defense dissolves moral duties.

The fact that the international system may at times be characterized by harmony and ethical behavior does not, in the realist view, change the matter. International harmony may be broken at any time, leaving states that continue to behave morally at a serious disadvantage, perhaps even threatening their existence. Whatever appearance international politics may wear at a given time, the reality behind it is the "jungle." The formulation that this view received in the early modern period was that the international environment is naturally or intrinsically a "state of war." As both Hobbes and Rousseau used this phrase, it implies not that states are perpetually assaulting each other on the field of battle, but that they are in a chronic state of opposition or conflict that may break out into battle at any time. No power prevents a resort to arms whenever states find it advantageous, and no power protects the victims of aggression except the victims themselves. If there is a "society of nations," it is not strong enough to overcome the state of war. If there is a common good among states, it is not significant enough to outweigh the conflicts of interest among them. No actual international institutions, or any reasonably to be expected, have the capacity to remedy this situation. States are left to fend for themselves in an environment that places them all at risk, and that especially jeopardizes those states that allow moral inhibitions to block the pursuit of their own interests.

These are the outlines of the realist position. As we shall see, realist authors differ among themselves on the interpretation and the

63

consequences of these precepts. Realists may attribute the anarchy of international politics to human nature, or to the nature of the international environment, though the classical realists tend to combine these explanations. One important difference among realists has to do with what we might call degrees of realism. The most thoroughgoing realist maintains that moral restraints have no validity in the arena of international politics and, moreover, that morality is a fraud or an illusion in all areas of human life. A more tempered realist holds that some moral strictures are applicable among states, but that these are far fewer and far weaker than those that apply in the domestic life of states. Moving further along this line, we eventually leave realism altogether. This chapter, which defines realism fairly rigorously, excludes some authors who have occasionally been put in the realist camp. Hugo Grotius is sometimes considered a realist, based on his state-centric perspective and his authorization of wars on purely legal rather than moral grounds, but Grotius is also one of the defenders of modern international law understood partly as a system of ethical restraints (for assessments of Grotius, see "Origins of the tradition," Chapter 2, and "The Bible and the traditions: Protestant arguments," Chapter 13). David Hume is an important advocate of the balance of power, but he also defends moral duties in international politics.[1] Even Kant's understanding of international morality has distinct realist elements (see "Kantian internationalism," Chapter 7, and "Classical contractarianism," Chapter 9). Our exploration of the realist argument will be confined to authors who adhere quite strictly to the precepts outlined above.

Machiavelli

Machiavelli develops the realist argument in its purest form, arguing that the nature of international politics absolves states of any moral duties whatsoever. He endorses imperialism, the unprovoked subjugation of weaker nations by stronger, without reservation and without limit. He develops a new and amoral basis for the political community, to conform with the necessities of international politics as he sees them, and to reflect his negative assessment of the status of moral principle altogether.[2] Machiavelli's political writings are manuals on how to thrive in a completely chaotic and immoral world.

---

[1] See Hume's essay, "Of the Balance of Power" (in Hume [1741], 332–41), but also Hume [1789] Book III, Part II, Section XI, "Of the Law of Nations," pp. 567–69.

[2] Not all interpreters regard Machiavelli to be this thorough a realist. Some have sought to make Machiavelli less "Machiavellian," usually by arguing that his commitment to republics is partially an ethical commitment. By treating Machiavelli as a complete

The distinctive features of Machiavelli's international realism are exhibited in Chapter 3 of *The Prince*, a chapter whose theme is imperialism.[3] Machiavelli praises the ancient Romans for pursuing a policy of universal imperialism, and holds them up as an example to be imitated by prudent states and princes (*The Prince*, 11–13). Their policy was justified, in Machiavelli's view, by the nature of the international environment: the Romans were compelled to conquer to forestall threats to their security. They entered Greece, for example, to preempt a future threat from king Antiochus of Syria, who was himself plotting to invade Greece. Neither the Greeks nor Antiochus threatened Roman security immediately; but "the Romans, seeing inconveniences from afar, always found remedies for them and never allowed them to continue so as to escape a war, because they knew that war may not be avoided but is deferred to the advantage of others" (12–13). Though war may seem remote at any given moment, it is inevitable, for threats are always forming on the horizon. A state faces only two choices: fighting at its own initiative or awaiting attack at a moment favored by the opponent.

It is easy to see that Machiavelli's argument destroys any possible distinction between "just" and "unjust" wars, or indeed between aggression and defense. Under the circumstances of international politics, according to Machiavelli, preemptive attack is justified, indeed required by prudent policy. The prudent state acts before its neighbors become a serious threat.[4] Indeed, a state is justified in intervening to establish its control over neighbors who by no means constitute a threat, as the Romans intervened in Greece, if those neighbors' weaknesses provide an opening for other powers who *will* constitute a threat. Proceeding on this principle, the Romans conquered ever widening circles of territory, until there was nothing left to threaten them. In Machiavelli's analysis, they conquered the world out of self-defense. They reacted rationally to a hostile environment that could reliably be neutralized only by the force of arms, ultimately only by universal imperialism.

What is important here is the realist logic that this argument reveals. Machiavelli's analysis of international politics overrides moral duties by extending the plea of self-defense to all states, and arguing that it

realist, I follow a more traditional line of interpretation. I also differ from some contemporary interpreters in believing that Machiavelli's *The Prince* and *Discourses* contain the same thoroughly realist teaching (I draw primarily on *The Prince* as the more succinct of the two). For other interpretations, see under "Suggested reading," this chapter.

3 Machiavelli, *The Prince*, pp. 7–16. The chapter bears the coy title, "Of Mixed Principalities."
4 See also Francis Bacon's essay "Of Empire," in Bacon 1890, 129–35.

justified even imperialism. In the chapter discussed above, Machiavelli insists on the *inevitability* of the events he describes – of their "natural and ordinary necessity," of their "universal causes," and of "the order of things" (*The Prince*, 8, 9, 11). The scientific certainty of these threats serves to overcome the moral compunctions against realism. Machiavelli casts himself in the role of a doctor (12), diagnosing the danger and prescribing the cure – preemptive attack. For Machiavelli, realism represents a new and scientific approach to politics. The promise of the Machiavellian science or art of politics is the conquest of fortune (see, for example, *The Prince*, Ch. 25): by acting on this true understanding of international politics, a state may escape the vagaries of chance. The Romans, recognizing the inevitability of foreign threats, left nothing to chance and attacked first. Obeying moral restraints – waiting until a threat is at one's borders, say – risks one's survival. Machiavelli argues that the moral rules simply do not correspond to "the order of things." Indeed, the natural order actually *punishes* those who attempt to play not by its rules but by moral rules instead.

International politics, in Machiavelli's view, is an independent realm, with laws of its own, and these laws of the political realm are dramatically different from the moral laws that some would apply to politics. The moral philosophers claim that politics is an activity intrinsically directed to moral goals – virtue or piety, or the greater good of mankind. Machiavelli discerns only one goal that is intrinsic to the political realm, and that is success measured as survival, longevity, or glory. This distinguishes Machiavelli's thought from what is called "political science" today, and from some contemporary versions of realism that derive from modern political science. Modern political science, like the Machiavellian variety, aspires to free itself from moral preconceptions and discover laws of political behavior. But it also refuses to condemn any particular view of the ends of politics, or "ideology." Machiavelli's science extends also to ends. For Machiavelli, survival (and the means to it, power) is the only *natural* goal of political action; pursuit of other goals is ruled out. The pursuit of other goals, especially moral or "ideological" goals, interferes with the primary goal.

The principles of international action can be known with such certainty, according to Machiavelli, because they are grounded both in human nature and in the structure of the international realm. That structure is radically conflictual and anarchic. Conflict and anarchy are inevitable because of natural scarcity and human ambition (*Discourses* 2.8). The ambition of republics and princes is an ineradicable part of the political equation for Machiavelli. In his discussion of imperialism, Machiavelli says matter-of-factly, "truly it is a very natural and ordinary thing to desire to acquire, and always, when men do it who can, they will be praised or not blamed" (*The Prince*, Ch. 3, 14). This outlook helps explain why foreign threats are inevitable, and therefore why preemptive attack is justified. It also provides an independent justification of imperial ambition, or the "desire to acquire," in its own right. This desire is both "natural and ordinary," and thus might properly be indulged apart from all defensive justifications for attack. Of course, under the influence of such ambition, the world becomes necessarily a place of scarcity – there can never be enough to go around if the unlimited human desire for more is both irrepressible and blameless. States can do nothing but adapt as prudently as possible to the circumstances. In Machiavelli's account, ambition and self-interest both overcome morality "as of right," but this only reflects his view that there is no "right" in the moral sense of the term.

It is a key part of Machiavelli's critique of international ethics that the moral approach to international politics prevents states and statesmen from responding adequately to this reality. Not only does moral action in international politics lead to failure, it tends to produce a greater measure of evil than would a purely realist course. Thus Machiavelli attacks Christianity for making the world prey to the wicked through its refusal to resist evil with evil (*Discourses*, II.2, 277–79). Christian morality is not strong enough to prevent states from indulging their ambitions – no morality is strong enough to suppress nature entirely – only strong enough to cause those ambitions to fail. The result is a chaos of never-ending, badly fought wars that probably generate more violence than a consistently realist system of states would. Machiavelli contrasts the actions of Cesare Borgia, who reduced his state to order with utter ruthlessness, with those of the Florentines, who, shrinking from cruelty, allowed such disorder to develop in one of their acquisitions that the place was "destroyed" (*The Prince*, Ch. 17, 65). Their virtue proved to be vice, because it did not correspond to political necessity. The same point is made by Machiavelli's famous dictum concerning "well-used cruelty": cruelty is well-used when it is carried out all at once, and does not have to be repeated (Ch. 8, 37–38). Following this course requires prudence, to see in the beginning exactly what cruelties must be committed, but it also requires over-coming the moral sense that recoils from such acts. As Machiavelli says in introducing these arguments, a prince must "learn to be able not to be good, and to use this and not use it according to necessity" (Ch. 15, 61).

Machiavelli's realism thus attempts to overcome moral inhibitions in the pursuit of self-interest. However, Machiavelli does not say that a prince or state must *always* be "not good." They must be so when "necessity" – the laws of political action – so dictates. This means that the prince's allegiance is to necessity rather than morality, but he should not be gratuitously immoral when such immorality would create unnecessary obstacles or cost him domestic support and the fame he desires (*The Prince*, Chs. 15–19). And, even then, Machiavelli's argument does not imply that a thoroughly moral policy is always doomed. The point is rather that to be both moral and successful, one must also be lucky – dependent on fortune. With luck, one may live in tranquil times, never encounter a truly formidable foe, or be surrounded by others who likewise behave morally. But fortune is fickle; in the long run it will betray you. This perspective is the perspective of the founders of Rome, or of any nation or dynasty, and it is only in this perspective that we can truly speak of the "necessity" of attacks on the state. In the short run, of course, everything is contingent.

A state's obligation to abide by treaties or agreements is an important issue in discussions of international ethics. Machiavelli's view of the matter is that since men "are wicked and do not observe faith with you, you also do not have to observe it with them." The realist logic is familiar – since moral obligations to you will not be honored, you may preemptively disregard obligations to others. A prudent prince "cannot observe faith, nor should he, when such observance turns against him, and the causes that made him promise have been eliminated" (Ch. 18, 69). Machiavelli does not say that treaties and other promises should not be made. What he dismisses is the notion that such agreements have an independently binding *moral* force. No state can, or should be expected to, abide by an agreement in contravention of its own interests. No such duty exists in international relations.

Machiavelli hopes to transform political action with his realist attack on international moralism, but he does not believe moralism itself will ever disappear. Moral convictions have great power, and moralism is so durable precisely because realism, at its full Machiavellian depth, is a remarkably cold and inhospitable view of the world. It liberates princes and states to pursue their ambitions without restraint, but it also decrees that one may be conquered or killed by an opponent without blame. It leaves people to fend for themselves, without aid from God or other human beings. The moral view makes the world seem more hospitable, and morality thus arises naturally enough as a form of wishful thinking (cf. *Discourses* I.2, 107). Moralists from the ancient to the contemporary world have tried to use the universality of moral belief, or the existence of a "common morality," as a sign that morality has some objective validity,[5] but Machiavelli rejects this argument. He is aware that moral beliefs are a permanent feature of the political landscape and even that they are politically necessary, and he doesn't expect his realism to become a popular doctrine. Princes and architects of foreign policy must violate ethical principles, but domestic order will always depend upon moral beliefs among citizens. Princes must somehow maintain moral beliefs in their followers, even as they violate them in practice (*The Prince*, Chs. 15, 18).

The Machiavellian prince strives to overcome this problem of realist statecraft by simple deceit or hypocrisy. For republican leaders, however, this task is obviously delicate, and realism poses special difficulties for popular or democratic regimes. This problem has bedeviled many modern realists, as discussed in the following chapter. In the *Discourses*, a work largely devoted to republican politics, Machiavelli argues on realist grounds that a republic like ancient Rome, with the power of its citizen armies and the prudence of its leaders, is the best form of polity. The participation of the plebs, or lower classes, was essential to Rome's power, but this required the more prudent, that is, realist, leaders to manipulate the people on certain occasions.[6] In Machiavelli's view, the Roman constitution established an antagonistic balance of power between these two factions rather than a *community* in the full and ethical sense elaborated by the earlier philosophic tradition, and this internal hostility helped make Rome powerful and guarantee its survival (cf. *Discourses* I.6–I.8). For Machiavelli, realism in the international arena is inseparable from moral skepticism that extends to the very foundations of political life.

Thucydides

Not many realists, classical or otherwise, share Machiavelli's extremism, particularly concerning the possibility for a genuine ethical basis for domestic community. On this point, Thucydides differs with Machiavelli in a way that has significant consequences for his attitude toward international ethics. With Thucydides we enter a

---

[5] Plato and Michael Walzer may serve as ancient and contemporary examples here. See Plato's *Republic* and Walzer 1977. For a discussion of the idea of a common morality, see also "Common morality and international law," Chapter 1.

[6] The depiction of Roman domestic politics I am summarizing here is spread throughout the first book of the *Discourses*. On the Roman use of religion for popular manipulation, see I.14; on electoral deceptions, I.48.

world in which realism competes with ethical concern in an irresolvable tension.

Thucydides' book, an account of the Peloponnesian War between Athens and Sparta, is also an exploration of the place of ethics in international politics. This exploration begins with a discussion of the causes of the Peloponnesian War, in Book One of his History.[7] In Thucydides's estimation, the war was "inevitable" (1.23), owing in part to causes that are universal. The Greek world was locked in a "bipolar" competition between Sparta and Athens. What made war inevitable was "the growth of Athenian power, which inspired fear in the Spartans and compelled them to go to war" (1.23). This view has important ethical consequences. First, although the Spartans were guilty of starting the war (1.87–88, 2.1–2), this was excusable: they were "compelled" to do what they did. Second, this compulsion stemmed not from imminent danger but from the less immediate threat that the growth of Athenian power posed to Sparta and its allies. The Spartans were justified in starting this war because of an unfavorable shift in the balance of power.

This kind of logic has traditionally made the "balance of power" part of the realist arsenal of ideas. The moral perspective, in contrast, would tend to focus not on this balance but on the treaty that was violated by the outbreak of war. The "thirty years' truce," like most if not all treaties, represented an attempt to create peace by sanctifying the status quo. Thucydides' analysis makes this treaty a dead letter halfway into its life, for reasons that Machiavelli would endorse. Treaties are not binding outside the common interests they reflect; as conditions change, they simply lose their relevance. The Spartans, unfortunately, did not share this realist insight. Thucydides remarks later that they fought poorly in the first part of the war because of a guilty belief that they had violated the treaty in starting it (7.18). They were unaware of the fact, implicit in Thucydides' analysis, that such moral considerations are superseded by compulsions derived from the balance of power. Thucydides' analysis systematically blocks taking a "just war" approach to the origins of the Peloponnesian War.

Some moralists might concede that the treaty was defunct, but blame the Athenians for undermining it, if not violating its letter (cf. 1.68, 118). The menacing growth of Athenian power, after all, was due to Athenian imperialism. Athenian imperialism, which stands behind

---

[7] Since Thucydides did not give his work any title that has come down to us, I will refer to it simply as the History, capitalized but not italicized, for convenience. In future I will cite Thucydides in the text wherever possible, in the standard form by book and chapter.

the moral dilemma of the beginning of this war, raises the most difficult issues of international ethics in Thucydides' History. The Athenians in Thucydides make the realist argument that imperialism is blameless, and the History largely backs up their claim. It also demonstrates, however, that the Athenians were blind to some serious problems with imperialist realism.

The realism of Thucydides' Athenians, like that of Machiavelli, is based on certain laws of political behavior. Invited to address a Spartan conclave before the war, the Athenians argue that imperialism is blameless because it is universal – the compulsions of fear, honor, and self-interest, they say (1.75, 76), drive all states with the requisite power to expand – making domination of the stronger an unalterable law of international politics. Justice has no place in relations among states of unequal power. The compulsion of fear corresponds to the "structural" argument for realism – that the insecurity of the international environment justifies states in expanding out of self-defense. What the Athenians say about this compulsion, however, indicates that they understand it in a much more limited sense than did Machiavelli. The Athenian motives of self-interest and honor, by contrast, are limitless, corresponding roughly to Machiavelli's notion of ambition as a root of empire. "Honor" as the Athenians use it, however, seems to give imperialism a nobler pedigree. Modern opinion is much more likely to ground imperialism in traits like "aggressiveness," paradoxically following Machiavelli's negative analysis of human motivation in order to condemn his realist conclusions. Thucydides' Athenians, to the contrary, insist that their empire is honorable (1.75–77, 2.39–40), and readers of Thucydides cannot help but give some credence to this Athenian attitude.

The fact that imperialism may stem from human impulses more generous than mere self-interest or lust for power complicates the moral issue, and Thucydides confronts this issue in the most famous expression of Thucydidean realism, the Melian Dialogue (5.85–113). The Athenians here reiterate their realist defense of empire, some sixteen years after their first statement, and some of the arguments they make are important to the realist tradition. The Athenians bring a force to the island of Melos to subdue it, but offer a dialogue with Melian representatives first. When the Melians complain that the presence of Athenian troops does not sit very well with the idea of a dialogue (5.86), the Athenians respond in effect that discussions of this type always take place within the context of relations of power. The relations of power, and consequently the wishes of the stronger, are the givens of this debate, not the issue to be contested (5.87).

71

The Melians, who can say nothing to this, attempt instead to move to the notion of a "common good" among nations. The common good is traditionally the basis of justice in the domestic politics of states, and arguments have been made, from Thucydides' day to this, that a common good also exists in international relations and has a similar moral force. The Melians say that fairness or equity between the weak and the strong is a principle that serves the common good, a principle that the Athenians should respect since they themselves may someday have need of it (5.90). The Athenians reply that great powers pursue only their interests, and do not terrorize their subjects gratuitously (5.91); if Athens were ever conquered Athenians would presumably have the good sense to submit to the inevitable domination of the stronger, without moralizing about the supposed "injustice" of it. Just so, the "common good" at this particular moment is for the Melians to submit to Athens without resistance, thus minimizing the suffering on both sides. As in the previous exchange, the Athenians insist on the primacy of the immediate situation defined by relations of power and consequently the desires of the powerful. Within that situation, the common good is so limited that it has, we might say, no moral content. The common good as the Melians construe it depends on a global and abstract perspective in which just or equal treatment is in the interest of all.

Acting on their convictions, the Melians defy the Athenians, and are defeated. The Athenians slaughter the adult men and sell the women and children into slavery. The terrible fate of the Melians underscores the realist arguments of the Athenians: in the immediate situation, power is more important than words, and the immediate situation in international politics takes precedence. In the immediate situation, justice only exists, if it exists, by grace of the powerful, and the weak rely upon it at their peril. Debating about the justice or injustice of acts of forceful intervention is simply beside the point.

Thucydides' History as a whole corroborates the Athenian argument concerning justice and power in international politics. The Athenians' assertion that the strong universally dominate the weak is supported by examples from the most ancient period (1.1–18) to contemporary communities such as Syracuse (4.61, 64; 6.33) and even the Spartans themselves. The Spartans, moralistic in rhetoric (1.86, 3.32) and guilt-ridden over having broken the treaty (7.18), are nonetheless not a counterexample to the Athenian claim that all powerful cities are expansionist. They manipulate many of their allies (1.19, 76), but more significantly they rule tyrannically over a vast population of Helot slaves, who are peoples conquered in old wars of expansion (1.101; cf. 4.80). Spartan imperialism is older, but not less real, than the Athenian variety. The Spartans too were unable to resist the compulsions of "fear, honor, and self-interest," until expansionism brought them to the limits of their power. Thucydides' realist view of Athenian imperialism, meanwhile, is sufficiently shown by his remark that Athens's subjects had only themselves to blame for their servitude, since they failed to do what they could to forestall the ambitions of Athens early on (1.99; cf. 1.69).

In other words, the Athenians are correct when they accuse the Spartans of hypocrisy for condemning their imperialism – the Spartans, indeed all states, pursue their own interests and declaim about justice only when it is to their advantage (1.76, 5.105). Realism, in this context, appears as an advance in intellectual and moral honesty. Thucydides also shows that realism, as a basis of foreign policy, can prove more gentle than moralism. Ideological or moral crusades can be much more cruel than policies based simply and frankly on the national interest, and moralism can blind states to their own injustices. This element of Spartan policy is demonstrated by the city's treatment of Plataea (3.52–68; see also 1.86, 3.32). The Athenians, with their frank realism, were capable at least of treating subjects and defeated enemies gently, as their handling of the Mytilenaeans shows (3.36–50).

The Athenians' realism, however, was also responsible for their slaughter of the Melians. Thucydides leads his readers to regard this as an act of barbarism – that is, as morally reprehensible in some sense – which points to the difference between his and Machiavelli's realism. The final chapter in Thucydides' account of realism is constituted by the portrait of Athenian barbarism on Melos, followed by the decay and defeat of Athens itself. Athens defeated itself in the war with Sparta, because the moral consensus on which its internal cohesion was based decayed during the twenty-seven years of the war (2.65). The city's frank realism ultimately led Athenians to believe that no moral restraints applied to them even as citizens, and private self-interest and factious strife eventually prevailed over the common good in the domestic life of the city (2.65).

This development tempers Thucydides' realism, without undoing it. Athens's ultimate fate does not alter the important truths about human nature and the relations of states that the Athenians discovered. The realism we are left with at the end of Thucydides' History, therefore, is almost a tragic one. Political communities are confronted with external necessities and driven by internal compulsions that impel them to violate moral principles in foreign affairs; yet, in doing so, they risk their integrity as communities which depend upon moral consensus. For Thucydides, moreover, the integrity of the community is not simply a matter of balancing material interests, as it is for Machiavelli. Rather, the attainment of moral community is intrinsically valuable, a measure of higher civilization. Thucydides' skepticism concerning moral restraints in international life, unlike Machiavelli's, does not extend to all of morality. The tension between the ethical achievement of political communities and realist necessity is thus ultimately irresolvable.

This tension between realism and domestic morality led Machiavelli's prince to rely on deception and led Machiavelli to abandon the ideal of ethical community. The Thucydidean leader, in contrast, would bow to necessity, disregarding justice in international politics when circumstances required. He would use hypocrisy at times to protect the community from the corrosion of international realism, though this would always be problematic for one who, unlike Machiavelli, believes in the communal ideal. Hence he would also strive to temper the realism of his policy, that is, to act ethically where circumstances permitted. This is an imperfect compromise, both theoretically and practically, but in Thucydides' view it is necessary.

The insolubility of this dilemma is one reason so few moral philosophers in the classical tradition dealt with problems of international ethics. Plato, for example, would have to be classed as a realist, but his remarks about international politics are very few. His response to the dilemma is essentially that the perfectly just regime would have to be isolated from international relations as much as possible. The regime of the *Republic* has no significant external relations (see also Aristotle's *Politics* 1324a–25b); but, if attacked, its response will be purely "Machiavellian," contracting alliances based on the prospect of plunder and seeking the internal subversion of the attacking state (*Republic* 422–23). Plato matter-of-factly founds the city on land stolen in war (373–4), and he fashions his "noble lie" in part to conceal the city's origin from its citizens (414–15). Plato's realism concerning international politics seems to be so routine that he regards international relations as simply a non-subject for moral philosophy. Morality can be perfected within the tight bounds of a well-crafted community, but can never extend farther, at least to any meaningful degree.[8]

---

[8] The *Republic* does contain some interesting passages on the importance of mitigating the harshness of war (469–71). These seem to be motivated in part by a "Thucydidean" concern with the corrupting potential of war, but more importantly by Plato's philosophic perspective, which transcends even the best city and is simply cosmopolitan. For Plato, this perspective can never form the civic consciousness of any actual community.

After the classical period of Greece, we encounter more thought on international ethics, in Rome and then increasingly in medieval Europe, but the increased attention given to international politics in moral or political theory serves for the most part only to draw it further away from realism. There are realist elements in the thought of Cicero, for example, but they exist within the framework of his more famous development of the notion of the natural law and the *jus gentium*.[9] Christian authors, of course, concentrated on the exegesis of a much stronger form of natural law, grounded in divine will. Of these, Saint Augustine incorporated the strongest realist elements into his thinking. Augustine was more concerned than other Christian writers with studying the ways of the pre-Christian world of politics and war; he was also influenced by a stronger sense of the corruption of human nature and of the "city of man" by original sin. Because this world is corrupt, for example, even just men will be forced to wage wars, and soldiers who obediently fight are not guilty of murder. But Augustine's remarks on international ethics specifically are quite few.[10]

Early modern realism: Hobbes, Spinoza, Rousseau

The most important classical realists after Machiavelli belong to the social contract school of the early modern period (see "Classical contractarianism," Chapter 9). Thomas Hobbes is both the founder of this school and a principal contributor to the realist tradition. Hobbes postulates a "state of nature" prior to the formation of society, which he says was a state of insecurity and war. To escape this condition, individuals contracted to form societies that enforce order domestically. The societies thus formed, however, remain in the state of nature among themselves, that is, the state of war. Hobbes's realism is defined by his argument concerning this state, and why it dissolves all moral duties in international relations.

The "state of war" Hobbes speaks of in international politics does not imply continual battle, but "the known disposition thereto, during all the time there is no assurance to the contrary" (*Leviathan* Ch. 13, 186). For Hobbes, this is simply a product of the anarchy of international relations and the competition it creates. In Hobbes's pivotal

---

[9] See especially *De Officiis*, 1.7, 1.11–13, 1.16; 3.5–6, 3.29. One must be wary of identifying the *ius gentium*, "law of nations," too closely with "international law," with which it was later associated. In its original Roman context the phrase signified only those moral principles that had been embraced by the domestic law of all peoples, hence a kind of common morality. As such however, it would have distinct implications for inter-state relations.

[10] For some of the more important remarks see Augustine [426], 1.21, 3.10, 4.15, 15.4, 19.7.

analysis of the psychology of individuals and states, conditions of anarchy lead them to fear the worst from their fellows, and to act accordingly. In the original state of nature, individuals would attack one another simply out of the natural fear that others posed a threat to their safety. Hobbes maintains that these actions were justified, though this means in reality that there is no justice among individuals in the state of nature. Inter-state relations remain in the natural condition of hostility and war, which likewise justifies states in defending their interests by any means they judge appropriate, by the same right that existed in the original state of nature (*Leviathan* Ch. 13; *De Cive* Chs. 1, 13). This extends even to expansion, which Hobbes says states indulge in "upon all pretences of danger," and, in fact, do so "justly" (*Leviathan* Ch. 17, 224).

Hobbes does not deny that there are objective ethical principles, or a "law of nature." Rather, like most realists, he argues that ethical principles are simply suspended under the conditions of international politics. Hobbes constructs a lengthy list of laws of nature, which are duties that apply to human beings in and out of the state of nature. These laws differ fundamentally from more traditional systems of natural law in that their foundation is self-interest. In essence, according to these laws, people have a "duty" only to preserve themselves (*De Cive* Ch. 2, 123; *Leviathan* Ch. 14, 184). Seeking peace is a corollary of this, as are, consequently, "duties" to be fair and forgiving; but the primacy of self-preservation dictates that individuals are required to take no significant risks to comply with them. Only a contract with a sovereign power to enforce obedience can remove just fear and give these duties real force. In the international realm, there is by definition no such power. Such compacts as states have among themselves may suffice for limited purposes; but they are incapable of lifting the fundamental state of war in international politics.

We might paradoxically say, therefore, that Hobbes accepts a universal code of ethics, but it is one that no state is morally bound to follow. And Hobbes sees no prospect of a compact to remedy this. In the original state of nature, conflict and insecurity were so immediately threatening that individuals were effectively driven into a social compact, but international conflict does not threaten individuals in the same way. And states themselves are not threatened as mortally by the state of war. Thus the formation of a supranational sovereignty never becomes imperative. In other respects, however, the international state of war is worse than the original state of nature. The equality characteristic of the original state does not obtain among nations, making security wholly relative, depending upon the strength of a particular nation's adversaries. Nations must therefore heed a fluctuating balance of forces, and arm in accordance with the circumstances. One of the few *duties* Hobbes is willing to give his sovereign is the duty to maintain adequate armaments, and he insists on the propriety of sovereigns doing whatever they can to undermine the power of other states, whether "by slight or force" (*De Cive* Ch. 13, 262). All of this can take place in what is ordinarily regarded as peacetime, but which Hobbes considers only "a breathing time" in the interminable state of war (260). Hobbes goes so far as to say a sovereign may, without injustice, inflict any harm whatsoever on "innocent" foreign persons in the pursuit of state interests, also in "peacetime" (*Leviathan* Ch. 28, 360). For only by compact can the state of war be terminated; and a state can have no binding compacts, in the Hobbesian sense of the word, with people who are not its subjects. The conditions of international politics preclude any real justice, or even simple humanity, among states.

Spinoza supplements Hobbes's contributions to the realist tradition in some important respects. He is somewhat more explicit than Hobbes on the subject of treaties, and considerably bolder in laying out the amoral basis of this type of contract theory. Spinoza agrees that society is formed by compact, that its sole end is to preserve itself and its members, and that the natural law that underlies both civil society and international relations essentially equates might with right. Spinoza explicitly states that, by nature, states or individuals have a "right" to whatever they have the power to obtain. The social compact, for example, pools individuals' power, and only in that way stakes their right to a piece of territory (*Political Treatise* 2.13, 2.15). Others with more power who desire the same territory will have greater right; a successful war of conquest sufficiently establishes their right. Moreover, Spinoza maintains that states, like individuals, are naturally enemies because of the contentious passions of human nature. There is, of course, no basis whatsoever for international justice in this view, which points much more strongly to imperialism than does the exposition of Hobbes. Spinoza admits the usefulness of treaties among states, and even suggests, unlike Hobbes, that allied states are no longer enemies (*Theologico-Political Treatise* Ch. 16, 208–9; *Political Treatise* 3.13–14). But treaties and alliances derive their force exclusively from the mutual interests they serve; when circumstances change, parties may unilaterally abrogate such agreements without injustice. For, as Spinoza says, the state has obligations only to its subjects and the advancement of their interests, and abiding by disadvantageous agreements would

77

be a violation of this trust (*Political Treatise* 3.14, 3.17; *Theologico-Political Treatise* Ch. 16).

Rousseau belongs to both the realist and contractarian traditions, but a difference in his basic philosophical principles makes his realism milder than that of Hobbes or Spinoza. Rousseau speaks much more affirmatively of natural moral duties; for him, such duties are grounded in compassion and a universal common good, as well as in simple self-preservation (*Second Discourse*, 95; *Political Economy*, 212). He takes a cosmopolitan perspective, and he visibly worries about war and injustice in international politics. In this he resembles Thucydides more than the other classical realists. Rousseau's view of the nature of the social contract and the psychology of states, along with the anarchy of the international environment, dictates his realism.

Rousseau follows other contractarians in grounding political justice in a compact. Though this compact, according to Rousseau, settles issues of property and individual rights in an authoritative way among citizens, these arrangements mean nothing to foreigners (*Social Contract* 1.9). A community's possession of its territory, respect for which is surely a threshold principle for any system of international justice, is of questionable legitimacy, at best, to outsiders. The soul of justice within society according to Rousseau is the "general will." This is what the community as a whole wills for itself, and as such it is an infallible guide to justice, domestically. However, this will may be blind to any notion of justice in foreign affairs. For this reason, Rousseau says, even the most just state, following its own general will, might engage in an unjust war (*Political Economy*, 212, 213). Imperfect states indulge in warfare for much more corrupt reasons as well, such as ambition and greed. Rousseau thus differs from the extreme realists Machiavelli, Hobbes, and Spinoza in recognizing "unjust" wars, but the practical result of this may be slight. Rousseau is ambivalent on the natural law that would distinguish between just and unjust wars. This law is based on a universal "general will," the law of nature, and grounded in human compassion, but these things become so thin when applied globally, according to Rousseau, that they lose all force. Existing codes of international morality consist mostly of mere conventions, based on the self-interest of the parties. And these are ineffective due to lack of sanctions (*Second Discourse*, 160; "That the State of War Arises from the Social State," 386).

Rousseau denies that human beings are naturally as contentious as Hobbes had argued. But he has at least as pessimistic a view of the prospects of justice in the relations of states, once states are formed. In one of his writings, Rousseau explains the existence of war by saying that nature itself decrees conflict, making the well-being of each incompatible with that of the rest ("Fragment on War," 380–81). This is but a more extreme statement of the view that the general wills of each society and of humanity as a whole are at odds. Rousseau, like Hobbes, argues that because the power of states is purely relative, they are forced into competition with one another. Moreover, the very interdependence of states aggravates this competition – no state can seek safety through separation, and any change becomes a shock to the system as a whole ("That the State of War Arises from the Social State," 383; "Perpetual Peace," 336). Quarrels are more likely to arise and to become violent. This contradicts the view, which was becoming widespread in Rousseau's day and remains popular today, that interdependence and commerce breed more hospitable international relations. Rousseau argues that commerce is never important enough to overcome perceived national interest, where the two conflict ("Judgment on the Project of Perpetual Peace," 349).

The European state system was the most highly developed international "society" of its day but, according to Rousseau, that only made it more prone to violent conflict. Its very ties serve as the occasion for endless disputes over trade, territory, armaments, or prestige. Similarly, its common history makes the disentanglement of rival claims of right impossible – Rousseau claims that even if all genuinely desired to act justly under these circumstances, war would still be the result ("Perpetual Peace," 337). Despite its relatively stable political balance, Rousseau insists that Europe is fundamentally in a state of war, which the treaties among its states do nothing to change. This lamentable situation exists *because* Europe forms an interdependent "society" of states, not in spite of it. It would be a mistake, Rousseau adds, to suppose that this condition will improve by the natural course of events. Only a contrivance like a European league, with enforcement powers, could remedy it. Such a league would be in the interests of all the parties, and would be perpetual once in existence; nevertheless, Rousseau says, it will never be established. States are too jealous of their sovereignty, and sovereigns too enamored of their foreign ambitions, ever to embrace it. Under actual conditions, acting in accordance with the international common good when others refuse to do so is harmful, and perhaps even immoral, considering the state's obligation to the safety of its members.

This suggestion, that the defense of the national interest is a moral duty, is shared by Hobbes, Spinoza, and Rousseau. The moral status they give, albeit ambivalently, to the national interest, puts them in a camp with Thucydides and against Machiavelli. For the classical contract theorists, the social contract (and the nation that it brings into being) is the primary, if not the sole, focus of moral legitimacy. Moral obligations, weak or inoperative in nature, are solidified only under contract, and only among fellow citizens. The state becomes the representative of the community in international politics, and as representative or fiduciary, its concerns run overwhelmingly – and legitimately – to the defense and advancement of its members' interests at the expense of broader moral duties. Thus while classic contract theory makes moral obligation more secure within society, it undermines obligations without. It is precisely owing to the weakness or incompleteness of justice in nature, after all, that the social contract comes into being in the first place. The natural weakness of justice remains, or is even exacerbated, in the relations among states.

Objections to realism

Perhaps we can better understand the realist position if we consider some of the objections other traditions make against it. One of the pillars of the realist position is its analysis of how states are compelled to respond to the anarchy of international relations. Other traditions argue that this anarchy is neither as extreme nor as threatening as the realists believe. Hence the extreme realist view, that international circumstances provide a blanket justification for states violating ethical principles, is unwarranted. Classical realists take the worst moments of crisis and war as epitomes of the international climate, something non-realists regard as tendentious. Under normal conditions, they argue, the costs or risks involved in moral action are not nearly as great as the realists claim, and the benefits of moral consensus and cooperation greater. In extreme situations states might indeed be compelled to violate moral principles, but this does not signify the collapse of the whole moral edifice. Morality, non-realists might say, is a system of rules capable of admitting exceptions of this kind, like the exceptions in personal ethics that are grounded in self-defense.

Non-realists point out that in the actual practice of states, a great deal of mutually beneficial cooperation takes place. This cooperation and the "interdependence" that goes with it have a self-sustaining character and tend to pacify international relations. Though in one sense anarchy remains – there is no sovereign enforcement of the rules – it is not sufficiently *lawless* to be fairly depicted as a latent "state of war." Peace, though sometimes fragile, nevertheless has a substantial reality in international politics. States that act in flagrant disregard of international standards, meanwhile, do not always fare well. Coalitions form against them to apply pressures that seem to be effective, short of war. Non-realists would point to the difficulties faced by regimes today labeled "terrorist." They would also point to the evolution of strategic doctrine in the Soviet Union, which discovered in the 1980s that a goal of superiority against all possible combinations of adversaries was overly provocative, and had to be scaled back to "sufficiency," though at a cost to the Machiavellian ideal of guaranteed security. Overall, non-realists would contend that very few states are as aggressive and dangerous as Machiavelli would have them be, and few exhibit the paranoid reactions to anarchy that Hobbes and other realists describe. Under actual conditions, it is misleading to say that states are "compelled" to abandon all restraints to protect themselves. It is usually appropriate at most to speak of certain *risks* states run in acting ethically, and the traditions of moral thought would hold that such risks are ordinarily small enough that states have a moral duty to take them. Of course, this presupposes the validity of moral principles to begin with, something that Machiavelli, at least, denies.

The argument between realists and non-realists is only partly an empirical one. Both sides agree that there are periods of relative stability and of relative instability in international politics. Realists argue that, even in periods of stability, the underlying reality of international anarchy makes that stability vulnerable and conditional. The anarchy of international politics is threatening enough to overcome moral obligation, rather than simply necessitating a series of exceptions to it. For example, the stability of the postwar world, and the hospitable environment it provides for ethical action, would be traced by realists to an unusually stable balance of power, rather than any ethical foundation. If that balance were seriously upset, stability and its opportunities for ethical action would vanish. As to the prospect of provoking opposition by pursuing *machtpolitik* too ruthlessly, Machiavelli, at least, takes the moral sensibilities of other states seriously enough to counsel princes to disguise their actions where possible. The fact that coalitions of states may apply sanctions in the name of their ethical, religious, or ideological principles would demonstrate to Machiavelli the power of sanctions, not the force of moral principle.

Another set of objections to the realist position tries to engage the moral issue more directly. One of these, based on the notion of either a natural or historically produced community of mankind, tries to argue that there is an implicit transnational contract that establishes duties across borders. Realists would charge that the alleged moral bond among all men is not corroborated by experience. Even Rousseau, who does speak of such a universal moral bond, concludes that other elements in human nature, as well as the nature of the international environment and the social contract itself, negate it in practice. Classic contractarians, as we have seen, consciously reject the notion of a purely implicit, universal contract (though some contemporary contractarians take the opposite view – see Classical contractarianism" and "Modern contractarianism," Chapter 9).

It has been urged by at least one critic that while realism is presented as the soundest basis for foreign policy, it fails to provide the motivation such a policy needs (Carr 1940, Ch. 6). This is based on the view that political society requires a moral ideal to drive it, which simple self-interest cannot provide. This issue is complex, inasmuch as defending national self-interest is ordinarily a legitimate moral mission from the citizen's point of view. It loses this moral veneer only when realism is pushed to extremes and national policy becomes blatantly immoral. For Thucydides, realism becomes self-destructive at this point, because it undermines the community, not because it fails to provide sufficient motivation. Machiavelli solves the problem by resorting to public deceptions and by removing morality from the foundation of the political community. Hobbes and Spinoza follow Machiavelli in reducing the basis of community to self-interest. The issue engaged here reaches to the deepest levels of political philosophy, dealing as it does with the basis and goals of political community. This objection to realism questions whether self-interest – the core of realism – is a viable basis of political and, indeed, human life. Perhaps the realism of even Machiavelli's prince fails due to the hollowness of power and fame in the bleak world of Machiavellian realism. Some classical realists, like Thucydides, agree that politics should be directed to a richer, ethical human good. The issue raised by realism is how that ethical good can be reconciled with the necessities of international politics and, indeed, whether it remains plausible in the face of a world characterized by immoral necessities.

Suggested reading

Though the secondary literature on each of the authors discussed in this chapter is vast, surprisingly little of it focusses on the international dimension of their thinking. An excellent essay that covers a broad historical range of thought on international ethics is Thomas Pangle's "The Moral Basis of National Security: Four Historical Perspectives" (in Klaus Knorr, ed., *Historical Dimensions of National Security Problems*, Lawrence, Kansas: University Press of Kansas 1976, pp. 307–372).

On the subject of Thucydides' international ethics, Clifford Orwin's "The Just and the Advantageous in Thucydides: The Case of the Mytilenean Debate" (*American Political Science Review* 78 (1984), 485–94) and "Justifying Empire: The Speech of the Athenians at Sparta and the Problem of Justice in Thucydides" (*Journal of Politics* 48 (1986), 72–85) are to be recommended. Useful general works on Thucydides that touch significantly on international ethics include Leo Strauss's *The City and Man*, Ch. 3 (Chicago: University of Chicago Press, 1964, reissued in 1977); W. Robert Connor's *Thucydides* (Princeton: Princeton University Press, 1984); and Steven Forde's *The Ambition to Rule: Alcibiades and the Politics of Imperialism in Thucydides* (Ithaca, New York: Cornell University Press, 1989).

Good general works on Machiavelli, touching only partly on his international ethics but demonstrating some of the variety of Machiavelli's interpretation, are Sheldon Wolin's *Politics and Vision: Continuity and Innovation in Western Political Thought* (Boston: Little, Brown, & Co., 1960); Leo Strauss's *Thoughts on Machiavelli* (Chicago: University of Chicago Press, 1958); J. G. A. Pocock's *The Machiavellian Moment: Florentine Political Thought and the Atlantic Republican Tradition* (Princeton: Princeton University Press, 1975); and Mark Hulliung's *Citizen Machiavelli* (Princeton: Princeton University Press, 1983).

The arguments of the early modern writers on international ethics are discussed by Kenneth Waltz in *Man, the State, and War: A Theoretical Analysis* (New York: Columbia University Press, 1959). Stanley Hoffmann's essay "Rousseau on War and Peace" is quite useful (in *The State of War: Essays on the Theory and Practice of International Politics*. New York: Frederick A. Praeger, 1965). The essays "Hobbes on International Relations" by David Gauthier (in Gauthier, *The Logic of Leviathan*. Oxford: Clarendon Press, 1969), and "Hobbes and the International Anarchy" by Hedley Bull (*Social Research* 48 [1981], 717–38) provide some useful insights on Hobbes's position.

References

Aristotle. (*c.* 330 B.C.) 1984. *The Politics*. Trans. Carnes Lord. Chicago: University of Chicago Press.

Augustine, Saint. (*c.* 426) 1972. *Concerning the City of God Against the Pagans*. Ed. David Knowles. Baltimore: Penguin Books.

Bacon, Francis. 1890. *The Essays, or Counsels, Civil and Moral, of Francis Bacon*. Ed. Samuel Harvey Reynolds. Oxford: Clarendon Press.

Carr, E. H. 1940. *The Twenty Years Crisis, 1919–1939*. London: Macmillan.

Hobbes, Thomas. (1642) 1972. *De Cive* (or *The Citizen: Philosophical Rudiments Concerning Government and Society*). In *Man and Citizen*, ed. Bernard Gert. Garden City, New York: Doubleday Anchor.

(1651) 1968. *Leviathan*. Ed. C. B. MacPherson. Baltimore: Penguin Books.

Hume, David. (1741) 1985. *Essays Moral, Political, and Literary*. Ed. Eugene F. Miller. Indianapolis: Liberty Classics.

(1789) 1968. *A Treatise of Human Nature*. Ed. L. A. Selby-Bigge. Oxford: Clarendon Press.

Machiavelli, Niccolo. (1513) 1985. *The Prince*. Trans. Harvey C. Mansfield, Jr. Chicago: University of Chicago Press.

(1532) 1976. *The Discourses*. Trans. Leslie J. Walker, S. J., ed. Bernard Crick. Baltimore: Penguin Books.

Plato. (*c*. 380 B.C.) 1968. *The Republic of Plato*. Trans. Allan Bloom. New York: Basic Books.

Rousseau, Jean-Jacques. (1755) 1964. *Second Discourse* ("Discourse on the Origin and Foundations of Inequality Among Men"). In *The First and Second Discourses*, Trans. Roger D. and Judith R. Masters; ed. Roger D. Masters. New York: Saint Martin's Press.

(1758) 1978. "Discourse on Political Economy." In *On the Social Contract, with Geneva Manuscript and Political Economy*, Trans. Judith R. Masters; ed. Roger D. Masters. New York: Saint Martin's Press.

(1762) 1978. "On the Social Contract." In *On the Social Contract, with Geneva Manuscript and Political Economy*, Trans. Judith R. Masters; ed. Roger D. Masters. New York: Saint Martin's Press.

(1756?) 1971. *Que l'état de guerre nait de l'état social* ("That the State of War Arises from the Social State"). In *Oeuvres complètes*, vol. 2. Paris: Editions du Seuil, 381–87.

(1756?) 1971. *Fragment sur la guerre* ("Fragment on War"). In *Oeuvres complètes*, vol. 2. Paris: Editions du Seuil, 379–81.

(1761) 1971. *Extrait de projet de paix perpetuelle de Monsieur l'Abbe de Saint-Pierre* ("Perpetual Peace"). In *Oeuvres complètes*, vol. 2. Paris: Editions du Seuil, 334–47.

(1782) 1971. *Jugement sur le projet de paix perpetuelle* ("Judgment on the Project of Perpetual Peace"). In *Oeuvres complètes*, vol. 2. Paris: Editions du Seuil, 348–52.

Spinoza, Benedict de. (1670) 1951. *A Theologico-Political Treatise*. In *A Theologico-Political Treatise and A Political Treatise*. Trans. R. H. M. Elwes. New York: Dover.

(1677?) 1951. *A Political Treatise*. In *A Theologico-Political Treatise and a Political Treatise*. Trans. R. H. M. Elwes. New York: Dover.

Thucydides. (*c*. 400 B.C.) 1972. *The Peloponnesian War*. Trans. Rex Warner. Baltimore: Penguin Books.

Walzer, Michael. 1977. *Just and Unjust Wars*. New York: Basic Books.

5 TWENTIETH-CENTURY REALISM

JACK DONNELLY

The preceding chapter explored the roots of the realist tradition. This chapter looks at the work of twentieth-century realists who typically have seen themselves as participants in a common theoretical enterprise that reaches back at least to Machiavelli (Carr 1946, 63–64; Meinecke 1957) or Thucydides (Morgenthau 1946, 42; Gilpin 1986, 304). Realists such as E. H. Carr and Hans Morgenthau played central roles in establishing international relations as an academic discipline in Britain and the United States. In recent years realism has reestablished its predominance in the academic study of international relations. Realist arguments also remain prevalent in contemporary policy debates. All of this, as well as the continuing relevance of the realist challenge to morality in foreign policy, makes these writers an essential subject for this volume.

Realist premises

Rather than focus on individual theorists, however, I will consider twentieth-century realists as a group, reflecting a distinctive school or style of analysis with four central premises. Realism stresses "the primacy in all political life of power and security" (Gilpin 1986, 305). This focus arises from an account of human nature that emphasizes self-interest and the egoistic passions and an account of international relations that emphasizes the constraints imposed by international anarchy. As a result realists typically argue that "universal moral principles cannot be applied to the actions of states" (Morgenthau 1954, 9). These realist premises concerning egoism, anarchy, power, and morality in international relations define the basic structure of the realist tradition of international ethics during the twentieth century.[1]

---

[1] For a variety of definitions of realism complementary to this one, see Carr 1946, 63 and Ch. 2; Morgenthau 1954, 4–13; Waltz 1979, 117; Vasquez 1983, 15–19, 26–30; Olson and Onuf 1985, 7; Keohane 1986a, 163; Gilpin 1986, 304–5; and Smith 1986, 219–21. These premises can also be applied to domestic politics, but here I will consider realism only as a theory of international relations.

Human nature and international anarchy

Human nature is the starting point for realism. And the core of human nature, for realists, lies in the egoistic passions, which incline men and women to evil. Indicative is an index entry in a collection of Herbert Butterfield's political writings (1979) that reads, in its entirety, "Human nature. *See* Cupidity; Evil; Sin."

Realists view human nature as constant, egoistic, and therefore inevitably inclined toward evil. As Machiavelli put it, the prudent legislator should assume that "all men are wicked and that they will always give vent to the malignity that is in their minds when opportunity offers" (*Discourses* I.3). Some realists take this as a descriptive statement. For example, Reinhold Neibuhr argues that "there is no level of human moral achievement in which there is not some corruption of inordinate self-love" (1944, 19). Many others contend only that there are enough egoists to make any other assumption too risky, expecially in international relations. All, however, give overriding emphasis to the egoistic passions and self-interest in (international) politics. As a result, conflict is seen as the normal state of affairs in international relations.

Almost all realists, however, recognize that people are also driven by other desires and goals, which reflect a more admirable side to human nature. For example, Niebuhr couples his harsh doctrine of original sin with an insistence that "individuals are not consistently egoistic" (1944, 123), and he calls for "an adequate view of human nature, which does justice to both the heights and depths of human life" (1934, 113). Morgenthau, likewise, argues not only that the aspiration for power is "an all-permeating fact which is of the very essence of human existence" (1962a, 312) but also that "to do justice and to receive it is an elemental aspiration of man" (1970, 61; compare Carr 1946, 145; Spykman 1942, 7; Thompson 1966, 4, 75).

Nonetheless, realists give primary emphasis to egoistic passions and "the tragic presence of evil in all political action" (Morgenthau 1946, 202). And because human egoism is ineradicable, they argue that "conflict is inevitable" (Niebuhr 1932, xv). "It is profitless to imagine a hypothetical world in which men no longer organize themselves in groups for purposes of conflict" (Carr 1946, 231). Therefore, statesmanship must be driven by the need to control this side of human nature.

Conflict and insecurity, however, are also seen to be rooted in the anarchic structure of international relations. As Butterfield puts it, "the difference between civilization and barbarism is a revelation of what is essentially the same human nature when it works under different conditions" (1950, 31; compare Schuman 1941, 9; Schwarzenberger 1951, 14; Spykman 1942, 141). Within states, human nature usually is tamed by a hierarchical political structure of authority and rule. In international relations, anarchy prevails. Therefore, the evil, egoistic side of human nature is more easily, and much more regularly, expressed.

It is important that we be clear about the technical sense of anarchy used by students of international relations. Anarchy does *not* imply chaos or the complete absence of order. Rather, anarchy is the absence of political rule, of a "hierarchical" political order based on formal subordination and authority (Waltz 1979). Hedley Bull (1977) thus speaks of international relations as taking place in an "anarchical society," an ordered society of states, but one without international government. There is considerable order in our current anarchic international political system. That order, however, is not the hierarchical order characteristic of domestic politics.

States in international anarchy face a profound "security dilemma" (Herz 1951; Jervis 1978). Because of the absence of international government, each state must provide for its own protection through "self-help"; that is, by marshaling its own power or drawing on the power of friends and allies. But such power, even if it is intended entirely for defensive purposes, will appear as threatening to other states. They too must defend themselves, through self-help means. The power they are forced to acquire, however, will appear threatening to other states, who will respond . . .

The result is constant fear and an incessant need to acquire, maintain, demonstrate, and exercise power. The realist emphasis on the anarchic structure of international relations thus focusses our attention on the constraints of power and security faced by all states, whatever their internal composition, immediate goals, or ultimate desires. In such a world, power politics must ordinarily dominate other interests and objectives.

Although egoism and anarchy both point to the centrality of power and security in international relations, the character of any particular realist theory may be significantly influenced by the relative emphasis given to anarchy or human nature. In fact, many so-called structural realists go out of their way to distinguish their work from realist theories that emphasize human nature.[2] For example, John Herz

[2] Keohane (1986a) uses the vocabulary of "structural" and "classical" realism to mark this contrast. Although this terminology has rapidly become standard in the field it is misleading, for there are significant "structural" elements in "classical" realists such

stresses that his realism, which emphasizes the structure of inter-national anarchy,

> is distinguished from that of Hans Morgenthau, who sees the chief cause of power politics in innate human aggressiveness, or of Reinhold Niebuhr, who finds its deepest ground in human pride and sinfulness. Such factors, to be sure, may constitute additional grounds for conflicts and war, but the security dilemma remains an inescapable basic condition, even in the absence of aggressivity or similar factors. (Herz 1976, 10; compare Waltz 1979, 62–63)

Neo-realism, which in the last dozen years has come to dominate the study of international relations in the United States, is essentially a structural realism (see Keohane 1986b).

It is important not to overstate this distinction, which is largely a matter of emphasis. Realists who emphasize structure must make motivational assumptions about states and individuals. For example, Christian saints, Homeric heroes, and Hobbesian egoists would be likely to behave very differently in the identical anarchic environment. Conversely, those who emphasize human nature usually recognize at least quantitative differences in behavior in anarchic and hierarchic structures. For example, Morgenthau gives considerable attention to the structure-induced patterns of behavior of the balance of power (e.g., 1954, Chs. 11–14, 21). In addition, in recent years there has been a growing awareness of the importance of the interaction of structural and non-structural factors in the behavior of states and their leaders.

Nonetheless, the difference in emphasis does distinguish structural realism, especially in its contemporary neo-realist forms.[3] Further-more, because anarchy is more susceptible to amelioration than human nature, an emphasis on structure may permit greater theoreti-cal allowance for change, diversity, and the expression of nonrealist elements in human nature and international politics. "The essential nature of man may not be altered, but human behavior in general is sometimes improved, by the establishment of an order of things which

as Thucydides and Morgenthau. Whatever the labels, however, commentators today typically distinguish between realists who emphasize human nature and those who emphasize international anarchy.

[3] A more "scientific" approach, including an emphasis on explanation rather than prescription, also gives most neo-realist writings a very different "feel." Even when considering the same topics there are important differences in their typical approach as, for example, Waltz insists in his discussion of balance of power (1979, 118–22). Furthermore, neo-realists often present hierarchic domestic politics and anarchic international politics as qualitatively different realms that must be studied within logically incompatible theoretical frameworks (Waltz 1979, Chs. 5, 6). In sharp constrast, many earlier realists – notably Morgenthau and Niebuhr, as well as the realists discussed in the preceding chapter – wrote about both domestic and inter-national politics, applying a single set of concepts and categories.

has the effect of reducing temptation," and in some instances "a healthy disposition of forces can be attained for long periods which, so to speak, makes human nature better than it really is" (Butterfield 1960, 25; 1950, 33).

Power and politics

Realists tend to equate politics, and especially international politics, with the pursuit and use of power. As Morgenthau puts it, emphasizing human nature, "the aspiration for power over man . . . is the essence of politics" (1946, 45; compare 1948, 13). From a more structural perspective, John Herz argues that realism rests on "a recognition of the inevitabilities of power politics in an age of sovereign states" (1976, 79; compare Schuman 1941, 261, 282). Human nature and international anarchy are the underlying forces that lead to the realist emphasis on power and security.

There are, however, strong and weak versions of the realist commitment to power politics. Consider, for example, the following passages from Nicholas Spykman:

> International society is . . . a society without central authority to preserve law and order, and without an official agency to protect its members in the enjoyment of their rights. The result is that individual states must make the preservation and improvement of their power position a primary objective of their foreign policy. (1942, 7)

> In international society all forms of coercion are permissible, including wars of destruction. This means that the struggle for power is identical with the struggle for survival, and the improvement of their relative power position becomes the primary objective of the internal and the external policy of states. All else is secondary. (1942, 18)

The first of these passages is modest and beyond dispute: the pursuit of power must be *a* primary objective of any state. The second, however, advances an extremely radical claim: power and security must be *the* primary objectives of *both* the internal and external policy of *any* state. As we shall see in greater detail as we proceed, this tension between strong and weak claims for the political priority of power – and, more generally, between a "pure" and radical realism and a realism open to a variety of (sometimes extensive) qualifications or "hedges" – is common, even characteristic, within the realist tradition.

Most realists, for all their emphasis on power, also insist on the importance of struggling against the ultimately insuperable tendency toward power politics. Even if power politics cannot be eliminated, some of its most destructive consequences can be mitigated. For example, Georg Schwarzenberger argues that "a presentation of the motivations of power politics in terms of self-interest, suspicion, fear and lust for power would be open to justified criticism if the necessary qualifications of this analysis were not made with equal emphasis" (1951, 158). Herz likewise insists that his work is "not meant as a defense of, or resignation to, the extremism of political realism often meant in practice." He even argues that "the mitigation, channeling, balancing, or control of power has prevailed perhaps more often than the inevitability of power politics would lead one to believe" (1976, 11, 97).

These hedges make realism more "realistic," in the ordinary sense of that term. An account of international politics that ignored everything other than egoism, anarchy, power, and interest would be at best a crude and often a misleading oversimplification. Furthermore, as we have already seen, realists typically recognize another side to human nature and politics, even if they insist on its subordination to power and security.

Such hedges involve deviations from or restrictions on fundamental realist premises, however. It would be irresponsible to caricature all realists as radical exponents of the most extreme versions of all four realist premises, or to insist that any deviation from the radical ideal is illegitimate, not truly realist. Nonetheless, too many qualifications may threaten the distinctiveness of the realist position. And, unless their range can be specified with some precision, hedges and exceptions may appear as ad hoc qualifications that seriously erode the explanatory and predictive power of realist theories. Furthermore, at a certain point the "hedges" may become as important as the realist "core" that they supposedly surround.

There is, however, a wide range of intermediate positions between an unqualified realism and the point at which nonrealist outweigh realist elements in a theory. This suggests that we should think of a continuum of realist perspectives across the range of agreement marked by the four defining premises. At one end are "radical" realists, such as the Athenian envoys to Melos in Thucydides' History, who adopt extreme versions of all the realist premises. At the other end lie what we can call "hedged" realists, who admit quite a substantial space for nonrealist elements in their theory. For example, Carr argues that "we cannot ultimately find a resting place in pure realism" (1946, 89; compare Niebuhr 1944, 126; Herz 1951, v; Keohane 1984). Placing individual theorists precisely on this continuum is not important, but it is essential that we recognize the great range of particular positions within the realist tradition.

If we combine this dimension of strength or purity with the differing emphases on human nature and international anarchy noted earlier, we can already see that "realism" encompasses a surprisingly diverse array of views. In fact, different realists may give such differing emphases and interpretations to realist premises, and combine them in such a great variety of ways, that one is tempted to speak of realist traditions in the plural. Nonetheless, all do share a concern with power and security, which is seen as the central problem of international relations, because of human egoism and international anarchy. (For another way of classifying realist views, see "Ethical judgment as judgment within a tradition," Chapter 1.)

The national interest

Power is, and is likely to continue to be, exercised principally by and in relation to nation-states. Most realists therefore advocate a statecraft of the national interest. "The main signpost that helps political realism to find its way through the landscape of international politics is the concept of interest defined in terms of power" (Morgenthau 1954, 5). Where a common good enters into realist analyses, it is the good of a national rather than a subnational, international, or global community. Furthermore, realists define that good in terms of interest rather than morality. A realist ethic of the national interest is therefore typically both statist and amoral. This section focusses on the special place accorded to the state and its interests. The following section will consider the place of morality in realist theories of foreign policy.

Although the idea of the national interest is central to most realist theories, individual realists give very different accounts of its precise meaning and significance. A few see the national interest as nothing more than the expression of collective selfishness and power. For example, Frederick Schuman argues that "economically dominant classes within each State ... tend to dictate the specific purposes in terms of which the national interests of the State are expressed" (1941, 264). In fact, if we start from strong realist assumptions about human egoism, it is hard to see how or why politicians would adopt the perspective of the nation, rather than seek their own personal interests (or the interests of their families, friends, associates, neighbors, or class).

If we begin from international anarchy, however, the special place accorded to the nation and its interests may appear in a very different light. Whatever its internal character, and however its interests are defined, the state is a standard, almost necessary, instrument for the realization of most political values in the contemporary world. Achieving most political ends, whether domestic or international, requires the minimum domestic security that in our world typically can be provided only by the state, even if not all states do in fact provide it all the time. "The state, though not the source of value, indeed remains the indispensable condition of value" (Osgood and Tucker 1967, 323). Pursuit of the national interest thus appears as a fact of international political life imposed by the existence of an anarchical society of states and has an instrumental value of considerable significance.

Probably the most characteristic realist account of the national interest, however, is provided by Morgenthau, who argues that there is a real and in some sense objective national interest and that good statesmanship involves neither more nor less than its pursuit. The national interest thus provides both a descriptive account of the rules of international politics and prescriptive rules for international political success. States "act as they must, in view of their interests as they see them" (1962a, 278; compare 1970, 382). "The objectives of foreign policy must be defined in terms of the national interest" (1948, 440).

A policy of pursuing the national interest, however, implies a control of reason over passion that is incompatible with Morgenthau's account of human nature. "Reason, far from following its own inherent impulses, is driven toward its goals by the irrational forces the ends of which it serves" (Morgenthau 1946, 154). But if reason is the servant of egoistic passion and the will to power, it cannot play the guiding role Morgenthau requires of it. And if "reality is dominated by forces which are indifferent, if not actively hostile, to the commands of reason," if there are indeed "unresolvable discord, contradictions, and conflicts which are inherent in the nature of things and which human reason is powerless to solve" (Morgenthau 1946, 172, 206), then a politics of the national interest becomes a dubious enterprise. At best it involves a never-ending, and always ultimately unsuccessful, struggle against precisely those elements of human nature and political reality that lie at the heart of the realist analysis of politics.

Niebuhr reveals a similar tension. He argues that "a prudent self-interest" – which is what the rational national interest amounts to – is "an achievement almost as rare as unselfishness" (1932, 45). "Reason may as easily enlarge the realm of dominion of an imperial self, as mitigate expansive desires in the interest of the harmony of the whole" (1944, 50; cf. 1934, 16). In fact, Niebuhr argues that in most nations "the force of reason operates only to give the hysterias of war and the imbecilities of national politics more plausible excuses than the average man is capable of inventing" (1932, 97). Yet he also holds that reason may mitigate egoistic desire, that "reason is something more than a weapon of self-interest" (1944, 54).

Niebuhr is also acutely aware of the problematic character of the collective perspective embodied in the idea of the national interest. Because it rests on an expanded, collective idea of interest that may require the subordination, even the sacrifice, of personal interests, the national interest may seem like a moral advance. The national interest, however, is likely to be pursued in an essentially egoistic way with respect to other states. And this higher egoism is often pursued in extremely brutal and destructive ways in international relations. Niebuhr thus speaks of the "ethical paradox" of patriotism, which "transmutes individual unselfishness into national egoism" (1932, 91).

For Morgenthau and Niebuhr, such ambivalence reflects the realist vision of a bifurcated human nature. Human nature is fundamentally corrupt, but it also contains what Niebuhr calls rational, moral, and religious "resources" (1932, Chs. 2, 3) that can help us evade some of its worst consequences. A rational politics of the national interest attempts to mobilize the "better" side of human nature to check the "worse" side that provides realism with its political starting point.

Realists who stress international anarchy reach a remarkably similar conclusion. In a world of international anarchy, the state is one of the few relatively stable means by which social interests and values can be secured. Therefore, its interests have a special instrumental value.

If there is an escape from the political problems posed by human nature and international anarchy, realists locate it in a rational politics of moderation and restraint in pursuit of the national interest. This pursuit can never be entirely successful. In addition, whatever success is obtained may come only at great material or moral cost. But realists present a politics of power in the pursuit of the national interest as the only plausible alternative to an even more violent world, and an even more narrowly selfish and destructive pursuit of interest.

Politics and morality

The realist emphasis on power, security, and the national interest typically leads to a theory of statesmanship that counsels excluding morality from foreign policy. As George Kennan puts it, "the process of government . . . is a practical exercise and not a moral one" (1954, 48). For the purposes of this volume, this is probably the most interesting aspect of realism.

"The problem of international morality can be stated simply. Are

93

groups in international society subject to the same, or comparable, moral principles which govern relations between individuals?" (Schwarzenberger 1951, 218). Realists answer this question with a more or less forceful "No," largely as a corollary of the principle of an international politics of power and interest. Morgenthau refers to this as the "autonomy of the political sphere" (1954, 10). Politics is governed by the demands and restrictions imposed by the national interest rather than by morality.

Most realists do allow an instrumental political role for morality. "Justice, fairness, and tolerance ... can be used instrumentally as moral justification for the power quest, but they must be discarded the moment their application brings weakness. The search for power is not made for the achievement of moral values; moral values are used to facilitate the attainment of power" (Spykman 1942, 18; cf. Schwarzenberger 1951, 225, 227). Thus Henry Kissinger, while US secretary of state, characteristically praised the historical role of American values in US foreign policy because they "contributed to our unity, gave focus to our priorities, and sustained our confidence in ourselves," and he defended an ongoing commitment to these values because otherwise "this nation ... will lose its bearings in the world" and its interest will thereby be harmed (1977, 200, 204). Typically, however, realists insist on excluding *intrinsic* considerations of morality from foreign policy, although their arguments for this conclusion vary greatly.

Some realists hold that moral values are relative and thus cannot be legitimately applied to other countries or cultures. For example, Carr claims that "supposedly absolute and universal principles ... [are merely] the unconscious reflections of national policy based on a particular interpretation of national interest at a particular time" (1946, 87). Somewhat more agnostically, Kennan argues that "our own national interest is all that we are really capable of knowing and understanding" (1954, 103). "Let us not assume that our moral values ... necessarily have validity for people everywhere" (1954, 47).

Many realists, however, reject value relativism. For example, Morgenthau argues that "there is one moral code ... [which] is something objective that is to be discovered" (1979, 10; cf. 1960, 222–23, 252; 1962c, 237). He even rejects the idea of a separate, less stringent ethical code for politics (1946, 178–80, 195–96). Nonetheless, Morgenthau too insists that moral standards, though universal, are not appropriately applied to the judgment of political acts.

Morgenthau rests his argument largely on human nature. "Man cannot achieve [justice] for reasons that are inherent in his nature. The

94

reasons are three: man is too ignorant, man is too selfish, and man is too poor" (Morgenthau 1970, 63). To demand moral behavior in foreign policy would thus be foolishly unrealistic. In fact, because others cannot be counted on to act morally, it risks exposing one's state to unnecessary danger.

Structural realists typically take a different route to a similar conclusion. "The cleavage between individual morality and international morality corresponds to the difference between social relations in a community and those in a society bordering on anarchy" (Schwarzenberger 1951, 231). "The nature of international society . . . makes a disparity between principle and practice inevitable" (Tucker 1968, 61). Whether because of human nature or international anarchy – or, most typically, because of the reinforcing interactions of the two – realists hold that the "facts" of international politics, and the political necessities to which they give rise, ordinarily require that morality give way in foreign policy.

Another standard realist argument, however, appeals instead to the nature of political office:

> When the individual's behavior passes through the machinery of political organization and merges with that of millions of other individuals to find its expression in the actions of a government, then it undergoes a general transmutation, and the same moral concepts are no longer relevant to it. (Kennan 1954, 48)

The task assigned to political leaders is to pursue the interests of the community that they represent. As a result, there is a "difference in the moral principles that apply to the private citizen in his relations with other private citizens and to the public figure in dealing with other public figures" (Morgenthau 1979, 13).

Such arguments take at least two forms. Some realists suggest that politics is an essentially amoral realm.

> Government is an agent, not a principal. Its primary obligation is to the *interests* of the national society it represents . . . its military security, the integrity of its political life and the well-being of its people. These needs have no moral quality. They are the unavoidable necessities of national existence and therefore are subject to classification neither as "good" or "bad." (Kennan 1985/86, 206)

Others, however, give at least a conditional moral force to the demands of the office of the statesman. For example, Robert Tucker argues that "the statesman has as his highest moral imperative the preservation of the state entrusted to his care" (Osgood and Tucker 1967, 304 n. 71).

This moral imperative to an amoral foreign policy – a paradox to which we will return below – points to a characteristic realist discomfort. Few if any realists are happy with the need to exclude morality from foreign policy. Morgenthau goes so far as to argue that "it is the tragedy of man that he is incapable, by dint of his nature, to do what Christian ethics demands of him" (Morgenthau 1962c, 15; cf. 1946, 221; Kennan 1954, 49). The subordination of morality to political necessity is not a matter of preference but rather a regrettable choice forced upon political leaders by the unsavory realities of human nature and international anarchy.

It is therefore not surprising that most realists hedge the amoral statesmanship that they describe or advocate. At minimum they allow moral considerations a place in international affairs if they do not conflict with considerations of power and interest (e.g., Schwarzenberger 1951, 22, 224). Some even admit that moral principles are "operative but not controlling" in international relations (Thompson 1985, 52). In fact, the separation of morality and politics often turns out to be less sharp than some of the general theoretical arguments quoted above might suggest. For example, Kennan commends "morality in governmental method, as a matter of conscience and preference on the part of our own people" (1954, 49).

Even Morgenthau, perhaps the most vociferous advocate of the autonomy of politics, argues that "nations recognize a moral obligation to refrain from the infliction of death and suffering under certain conditions despite the possibility of justifying such conduct in the light of a higher purpose, such as the national interest" (1948, 177). "Morality is not just another branch of human activity ... it is superimposed upon [it], limiting the choice of ends and means and delineating the legitimate sphere of a particular action altogether. This later function is particularly vital for the political sphere" (1962a, 326). I can see no way in which such claims can be reconciled with Morgenthau's general theory of politics and statecraft, for they place at least some moral considerations above the national interest and deny the autonomy of politics. But even if they can be reconciled, it is informative to see the extent to which Morgenthau feels compelled to hedge his principles.

Many other realists adopt a position that is at least as heavily qualified. For example, Carr contends that "political action must be based on a co-ordination of morality and power" (1946, 97). In fact, once all the hedges have been added, many, perhaps even most, realists typically argue that *both* must be taken into account, even if morality usually must be set aside. As Niebuhr puts it, "nations are ...

subject, as are individuals, to an internal tension between the claims of the self and the larger claims of love" (1960, 160). One might even argue that the explication of this tension is as important to many realists as their advocacy of an amoral foreign policy.

Such hedges certainly increase the practicality and plausibility of realism in particular cases. They do so, however, by diluting its distinctive character and at the risk of inconsistency. Furthermore, realists typically apply these hedges in an apparently ad hoc or, at best, intuitive way that has led critics to contend that in the end the theory provides little practical guidance or social scientific insight. There is nothing inherently problematic with hedges, but without an account of when the rule applies and when the exceptions do – something that most realists do not even attempt – the power and value of the theory are radically reduced.

Prudence and raison d'état

There are at least two partial exceptions to the general realist tendency to exclude morality from international relations. A few realists argue that statecraft must involve "prudence" in a moral sense of the term that can be traced back to Aquinas and Aristotle (see "Twentieth-century arguments: Christian realism," Chapter 13). Herbert Butterfield is a prominent representative of this strand.

> When we speak as though there were a separate ethic for the statesman, a peculiar substance called political morality, we are already moving into a world of trick mirrors and optical illusions ... We must not allow that there can be a difference in the quality of the decision in these cases or a difference in the ethical principles involved. (1960, 23)

Butterfield concludes that "political action may be assessed according to the brilliance of its conception or the degree of its success, but it also has to be measured against the principles of morality" (1960, 23). In a similar vein, Kenneth Thompson argues that "somewhere between moralism and cynicism, an ethical dimension exists" (1966, 75).

It is important to note that "prudence" here is not simply instrumental reason, the selection of means to achieve some given end. Rather, means are matched to ends within a context in which the choice of means and ends alike is constrained by ethical principles. The reason in operation here is much more like Thomistic or Kantian practical wisdom, which has a substantive moral dimension, than purely instrumental or technical reason. (For discussion of the

97

natural-law conception of practical wisdom, *prudentia*, see "Practical reasoning and moral dilemmas," Chapter 6).

One might ask whether the resulting position still deserves to be called realist. For example, the "hedges" may seem to have completely obscured the realist "core" when Thompson argues that "international society is not bereft of certain broader principles of justice, freedom, and order . . . States in formulating their foreign policies seek points of correspondence between what they do and the broader principle" (1966, 77). But Butterfield and Thompson, although they represent a minority view, both call themselves realists, are considered realists by most other commentators, and are strongly committed to the other three realist premises. We see here one more example of the diversity of the realist tradition, but also another instance in which hedges and diversity, if pushed too far, may weaken the overall coherence of the perspective.

The second exception to the realist exclusion of morality from foreign policy is represented by the *raison d'état* (reason of state) tradition, which is typically traced back at least to Machiavelli (Meinecke 1957; d'Entreves 1967, Ch. 5). Although also a minority view, especially in this century, it is much more clearly a part of the realist tradition.

States are seen as "individualities . . . spiritual substances"; "there is a living, unique, inherent principle in each of our great states, by which all its foreign affairs and internal developments are shaped" (Ranke 1973, 119, 123; cf. Meinecke 1957, 1). And the state is viewed as a *source* of value, not merely an instrument necessary for the achievement of other ends. "The State is in itself an ethical force and a high moral good" (Treitschke 1916, 106). In its extreme forms, the state may even be presented as the highest of goods and the source and necessary condition for the realization of all other values.

Raison d'état accepts a sharp separation between politics and the principles of morality that govern individual relations. "Moralists . . . must recognize that the State is not to be judged by the standards which apply to individuals, but by those which are set for it by its own nature and ultimate aims" (Treitschke 1916, 99). But these standards (and the arguments of reason of state that they ground) are held to be *ethical*, however different they may be from those of ordinary morality, which apply to relations between individuals.

The practical political excesses with which this position was rightly or wrongly associated during the Second World War have effectively destroyed its contemporary political plausibility. Nonetheless, there are strong parallels to such arguments in the tendency of many realists to give at least a provisional moral status to the state. Consider, for example, Kissinger's argument that "a nation's survival is its first and ultimate responsibility; it cannot be compromised or put to risk" (1977, 204), or Thompson's observation that "the nation state is both the problem-child of international relations and the highest *effective* expression of genuine moral consensus" (1985, 54).

In fact, when we look more closely we find that realist appeals to the national interest often involve an implicit appeal to some such moral standing for the state. For example, Morgenthau contends that "the state has no right to let its moral disapprobation of the infringement of liberty get in the way of successful political action, itself inspired by the moral principle of national survival" (Morgenthau 1954, 9). This paradox of a moral ground for an amoral foreign policy is usually obscured by realists. It is, however, remarkably common and, in some ways, necessary.

Paradoxical as it may be, realism without an appeal to higher values seems implausible, unrealistic, especially as a prescriptive theory of statecraft. As Robert Osgood notes,

> it is certainly utopian to expect any great number of people to have the wit to perceive or the will to follow the dictates of enlightened self-interest on the basis of sheer reason alone. Rational self-interest divorced from ideal principles is as weak and erratic a guide for foreign policy as idealism undisciplined by reason. No great mass of people is Machiavellian. (1953, 446).

Without an (at least implicit) appeal to the value of the nation and its interests, realism is likely to have little if any practical attraction or impact.

Whether realism can provide a sound basis for such an appeal, however, is not clear. *Raison d'état's* rejection of universal values for national values is unattractive to most contemporary realists. Value relativist realists can accept the rejection of universal values but, in acting internationally on their own values, they would seem to have no reason to expect others to give them any special weight or consideration. And, as we have seen, most realists do in fact explicitly deny the direct relevance of moral values to international politics, in sharp contrast to the *raison d'état* tradition.

This would seem to leave open only a secondary, indirect or instrumental place for morality in foreign policy. It is not at all clear, however, that this would provide sufficient grounds for the assumption of some moral standing for one's state. The problem of the moral standing of the state requires much more careful attention than has been common in the realist literature.

Realism and international issues

We have now considered each of the major premises of realism. To illustrate and further develop this overview, this section will briefly outline representative realist approaches to four international issues with substantial moral dimensions: war, intervention, economic relations, and human rights. I draw my examples principally from the work of Robert W. Tucker, who has written important books on two of these four issues, and Hans Morgenthau, perhaps the best known and most cited twentieth-century realist.

War

Realists typically present war as a standard, if destructive, instrument of statecraft, a continuation of politics by other means. "The threat of physical violence . . . is an intrinsic element of politics" (Morgenthau 1954, 27) and, in international relations, war is the ultimate backing for that threat. In its extreme form, this leads to the claim that "war is nothing more than a powerful embodiment of politics" (Treitschke 1914, 140). More moderate realists argue only that given the nature of the contemporary international system "no determinate limits may be drawn to the evil that may be threatened, or done, if necessary for the preservation and continuity of the state" (Osgood and Tucker 1967, 289, 323).

War – both the initial resort to war, and conduct in war – requires justification. For the typical realist, however, that justification is a matter of interest, not justice. In fact, Tucker argues that the very idea of the just war is incoherent. "In principle, there has never been a way by which the state's necessities can be acknowledged yet the measures by which these necessities may be preserved always limited" (Osgood and Tucker 1967, 320). If one adopts the perspective of the statesman, which "presupposes as an ultimate end the preservation and continuity of the state" (Osgood and Tucker 1967, 304), there is no escaping the force of the demands of the national interest (Tucker 1966, 50). Furthermore, even granting the theoretical coherence of the idea of the just war, realism's emphasis on egoism and the corrupting power of passion leads to skepticism over its practical application. "Modern just war doctrines share the fate of their predecessors in being scarcely distinguishable from mere ideologies the purpose of which is to provide a spurious justification for almost any use of force" (Tucker 1960, 43; cf. Schwarzenberger 1951, 33; Osgood and Tucker 1967, 313).

War thus is likely to present a genuine moral dilemma. The statesman faces "the necessity to choose, and yet the inability to justify a choice, between moral claims which, although regarded as equally compelling, have become irreconcilable" (Tucker 1960, 166). Considerations of justice are real and important – but so are the demands of statecraft. This dilemma is recognized by a variety of other moral and political perspectives. What is distinctive about realism is its solution. When the exigencies of statecraft and the demands of justice cannot be reconciled, realists argue that political leaders must choose injustice, even if it means war.

Intervention

Intervention is also treated by realists as an ancient and honorable instrument of statecraft. "From the time of the ancient Greeks to this day, some states have found it advantageous to intervene in the affairs of other states on behalf of their own interests and against the latter's will. Other states, in view of their interests, have opposed such interventions and have intervened on behalf of theirs" (Morgenthau 1967, 424). Therefore, "it is futile to search for an abstract principle which would allow us to distinguish in a concrete case between legitimate and illegitimate intervention" (Morgenthau 1967, 430).

Once more, the standard realist justification appeals to interest and avoids moral considerations. "The traditional doctrine justifies intervention as a measure necessary to preserve the vital security interests of the state" (Tucker 1985, 4). Legal standards have indeed been elaborated, and the legal rule of nonintervention can be given strong moral support (e.g., Walzer 1977, Chs. 4, 6). In practice, however, "intervention cannot be limited by abstract principles" (Morgenthau 1967, 430). In fact, moral and legal standards usually are used simply "to discredit the intervention of the other side and to justify one's own" (Morgenthau 1967, 425), as illustrated by the contortions of legal offices in the foreign ministries of intervening states. "All nations will continue to be guided in their decisions to invervene and their choice of means of intervention by what they regard as their respective national interests" (Morgenthau 1967, 430).

This does not mean that realists typically advocate intervention. The most prominent American realists have often opposed major US interventions, which they have considered to be based on ideology or some other factor extraneous to the national interest. For example, Morgenthau was an early and vocal critic of US involvement in

Vietnam (e.g., 1962b, 2, and Ch. 27; 1970, 33) and Tucker criticized the Reagan Doctrine of supporting anti-communist insurgencies in the third world (1985). In fact, in the United States, where moral and ideological concerns have often served to justify intervention, a consistent application of realist principles would almost certainly lead to far less intervention. What is distinctive about the realist approach, however, is that rather than start from a principled position on intervention or nonintervention, each particular case is judged on instrumental grounds of interest.

Economic relations

The same patterns of argument can be seen if we turn from the "high politics" of war and intervention to economic issues and "new" issues such as human rights. Particularly striking is Tucker's powerful realist attack on the demands for a new international economic order in *The Inequality of Nations*.

The demands of third world states for massive transfers of wealth, Tucker argues, "merely reflect the ubiquitous operation of reason of state" (1977, 61). Weak third world states are simply seeking to further their own national interests, to increase their wealth at the cost of richer and more powerful Western states. To the realist there is nothing surprising about this. But it provides no reason for the governments of developed countries to give special consideration to the interests of third world states – unless it is also in their national interest.

Redistribution has also been called for in the name of "a humanitarian conception of equality" (Tucker 1977, 130). This cosmopolitan, rather than state-centric, perspective seeks "a justice for individuals that can be guaranteed only by the atrophy of the sovereign powers states continue to claim" (1977, 137). Not surprisingly, Tucker argues that such fundamental structural change in the international system shows "few signs of materializing" (1977, 157). "What evidence we have points to the conclusion that the great majority persists in drawing a sharp distinction between the welfare of those who share their particular collective and the welfare of humanity, and to assume that the collective is quite entitled to what its members have created" (1977, 139–40). The nation-state and the state system are historically contingent forms of international political organization. Nonetheless, most realists see it as possessing continuing strength and vitality, despite repeated claims of their obsolescence or imminent demise.

Furthermore, Tucker argues that a new international economic order, whether statist or cosmopolitan, would threaten to create a situation in which order no longer rested on power, leading to "a decline in both power and order" (1977, 93). The current international order, based on power and self-help, is hardly ideal. It does, however, ease some of the more extreme consequences of anarchy. Unless authoritative international institutions replace this order – a prospect that hardly seems realistic in either sense of the term – the result will be an international society that "promises to be a more disorderly one than the international society we have generally experienced in the past" (1977, 170; compare Bull 1977). This defense of an admittedly imperfect but functioning order as the least unacceptable of several morally unattractive alternatives is characteristic of the general approach of realists.

Human rights

Realist accounts of human rights in international relations also typically emphasize the intractability of moral problems and the persistence of traditional patterns of politics.

> It is difficult to see any promise in an American policy which sets out to correct and improve the political habits of large parts of the world's population. Misgovernment . . . has been the common condition of most of mankind for centuries and millennia in the past. It is going to remain that condition for long into the future, no matter how valiantly Americans insist on tilting against the windmills. (Kennan 1977, 45).

Human rights violations rest on ineradicable flaws in human nature. Furthermore, international anarchy and the associated principle of sovereignty limit international action to ameliorate the problem.

Realists also characteristically argue that the pursuit of human rights mistakes the nature of foreign policy. "American policy-makers would do better to concentrate on those areas of international relations where the dangers and challenges are greatest" (Kennan 1977, 45), that is, on the national interest defined in terms of power. Such an argument is often reinforced by relativist moral arguments. For example, Kennan argues that "there are no internationally accepted standards of morality to which the US government could appeal if it wished to act in the name of moral principles" and, in drawing the contrast between morality and the national interest, he speaks of "our interest rather than just our sensibilities" (1985/86, 207, 209). In much the same vein, Morgenthau talks of "the issue of what is now called human rights. That is to say, to what extent is a nation entitled and

103

obligated to impose its moral principles upon other nations?" (1979, 4).

Other realists are skeptical of the substance of alleged human rights policies. For example, Schwarzenberger (1951) treats human rights under the heading "Power Politics in Disguise." Likewise, Kissinger argues that the aim of the Carter human rights policy was "to give the American people, after the traumas of Vietnam and Watergate, a renewed sense of the basic decency of this country, so that they may continue to have the pride and self-confidence to remain actively involved in the world" (1978, 160). It is almost as if Kissinger can conceive of no purpose for human rights other than as an instrument in the pursuit of other "real" national interests. This is in many ways the perfect summary of the realist approach to moral issues in international relations.

Realism: a theory of international politics?

To this point I have stressed description and analysis over evaluation. In this final section I want to take a more critical look at the realist tradition, with special attention to the typical realist arguments against morality in foreign policy. I will argue that although realism provides important insights into certain perennial problems of international politics, it is essentially a tradition of negative argument.

Many realists readily admit a primarily negative purpose to their work. For example, Carr writes that "*The Twenty Years' Crisis* was written with the deliberate aim of counteracting the glaring and dangerous defect of nearly all thinking, both academic and popular, about international politics in English-speaking countries from 1919 to 1939 – the almost total neglect of the factor of power" (1946, vii). Likewise, Niebuhr, in the preface to the 1960 reprinting of *Moral Man and Immoral Society*, notes that his "central thesis was, and is, that the Liberal Movement both religious and secular seemed to be unconscious of the basic difference between the morality of individuals and the morality of collectives," a difference that "refutes many still prevalent moralistic approaches to the political order" (compare Schwarzenberger 1951, xv; Tucker 1977, ix; Kennan 1984, vii).

As a result, most of the more powerful and effective arguments of the realists are essentially negative. For example, Carr is at his best in his brilliant critique of the liberal doctrine of the harmony of interests (1946, Ch. 4), and Niebuhr's realism is most penetrating in his attacks on the sentimental and moralistic illusions of his fellow liberals and radicals (e.g., 1932, Ch. 2) and in unmasking the pretensions of those in power (e.g., 1932, Chs. 5, 7, 8). But, for more positive purposes, many realists abandon realism as one-sided.

Both Carr and Niebuhr explicitly reject realism as a positive theory of politics. "Consistent realism excludes four things which appear to be essential ingredients of all effective political thinking: a finite goal, an emotional appeal, a right of moral judgment and a ground for action" (Carr 1946, 89). "Mature thought combines purpose with observation and analysis. Utopia and reality are thus two facets of political science. Sound political thought and sound political life will be found only where both have their place" (Carr 1946, 10). "The moral cynicism and defeatism which easily result from a clear-eyed view of the realities of international politics are even more harmful" than unchecked moralism (Niebuhr 1944, 126; cf. Herz 1951, v).

Those who do try to pursue a consistent positive realist theory ultimately fail in their effort to exclude morality categorically from international relations. Realists certainly are correct to remind us that sometimes, even regularly, the demands of morality conflict with the national interest defined in terms of power. But this is only a caution against idealism, not an effective argument for an amoral foreign policy. *All* objectives of foreign policy may at one time or another compete with the national interest thus defined. For example, arms races may in some instances lead to war and alliances may prove dangerously entangling. Realists rightly refuse to conclude from this that we should eschew arms or allies. They should also abandon their categorical attacks on morality in foreign policy.

Even the appeal to the special office of the statesman, perhaps the strongest of the realist arguments against morality in foreign policy, proves to be essentially negative. Butterfield presents the dilemma in a particularly striking form: "If an individual consents to make self-sacrifice – even to face martyrdom before a foreign invader – it is not clear that he has a socially recognizable right to offer the same sacrifice on behalf of all his fellow-citizens or to impose such self-abnegation on the rest of his society" (1953, 11). We can allow that political leaders may be guilty of grievous political misconduct if, in the pursuit of some moral goal, they were to sacrifice the sovereignty or independence of the country, let alone the lives of its citizens. But the same is true of the pursuit of alliances or economic objectives. Realists, however, would (again rightly) never think of excluding alliances or material gain from foreign policy because they may be pursued with excessive zeal. Once more a valuable caution against moralistic excesses is inflated into an unsound general rule of statecraft.

Most moral objectives can be pursued at a cost far less than national survival, sometimes even at little or no cost to the national interest defined in terms of power. And there is no reason why a country cannot, if it wishes, include certain moral elements in its definition of the national interest. Even if security, independence, and prosperity are unavoidable necessities of national political life, there is no reason why a government must limit itself to the pursuit of these necessities. The fact that the *primary* obligation of a government is to the national interest, no matter how narrowly defined, does not mean that this is its *sole*, or even ultimate, obligation. Realism establishes only the need for caution in the pursuit of moral objectives, an essentially negative – if often very useful – lesson.

An appeal to structure will not rescue realist amoralism. Art and Waltz claim that "states in anarchy cannot afford to be moral. The possibility of moral behavior rests upon the existence of an effective government that can deter and punish illegal actions" (1983, 6). But this is obviously false, even if we set aside their confusion of morality and law. Just as individuals may behave morally in the absence of government enforcement of moral rules, so moral behavior is possible in international relations. The costs of such behavior do tend to be greater in an anarchic system of self-help enforcement, but states often can act morally in international relations with safety, sometimes even with considerable success. There may be good policy reasons in particular cases to pursue an amoral, or even immoral, policy, but there are no general theoretical reasons why such a policy must or ought to be required, or even be the norm.

There is an undeniably valuable positive core to the realist emphasis on self-interest as the source of social conflict. There is also a valuable positive core to the realist emphasis on the constraints imposed on foreign policy by the existence of international anarchy. But the principal use of realism is to counter idealism and moralism, both in general and in particular policy debates, to clear away one recurrent set of impediments to effective international political theory and action. Once the attack on idealism has been concluded, the principal positive contribution of realism is to remind us of the limits of rational and moral reform. This is extremely valuable, especially in countries such as the United States that have well-established traditions of idealist international thought and practice. It is, however, only a starting point for theory or for action.

If this account of the nature and contribution of realism is correct, we would expect a cyclical resurgence of realism in response, to revivals of idealist thought and practice. This is precisely what we have seen over the last sixty or seventy years in the American study of international relations. Realism initially arose in the interwar period in response to extreme versions of legalist liberal internationalism (see "Liberal internationalism: liberals as promoters of international organization," Chapter 10). By the publication of the second edition of Morgenthau's *Politics Among Nations* in 1954, idealism had been largely discredited. But positive developments in the study of international relations were leaving realism behind; in fact, they often took the imprecision, inconsistency, and other theoretical inadequacies of realism as a starting point. By the early 1970s, with the increasing prominence of topics such as transnational politics, international interdependence, and political economy, along with the rise of world system theory, peace studies, and world order studies, nonrealist perspectives had carved out a substantial space for themselves. Not surprisingly, this led to a realist reaction, in the form of structural neo-realism (see Keohane 1986b).

Perhaps the most interesting feature of contemporary neo-realism, for our purposes, is its striking lack of attention to moral issues. Whereas earlier generations of realists often seemed preoccupied, even obsessed, with attacking moralism in foreign policy, most neo-realists do not even bother with morality. For example, Kenneth Waltz's *Theory of International Politics*, the most important work in the neo-realist revival, contains no index entry for ethics, justice, or morality, and his account of the classical theory of *Realpolitik* fails to mention its hostility to morality in foreign policy (1979, 117).

This may be seen as a desirable theoretical advance. Rather than devote energy and resources to essentially negative harping on the dangers of moralism, neo-realists are focussing their attention of the development of positive explanatory theory. But when it leads to an undefended advocacy of an amoral foreign policy – as in Art and Waltz's virtually offhand, and entirely unsupported, remark that anarchy makes the pursuit of moral goals in foreign policy impossible – neo-realism represents a dangerous and discouraging regression.

Although there is no reason why neo-realism must move in this direction, its structuralism does suggest that it is theoretically inclined to ignore moral considerations, which operate primarily at the individual or state level (rather than at the level of the international system). Whatever we may think of the arguments of earlier realists, they gave a prominence to moral issues that helped to keep ethical debate alive, even as they strove to keep moral concerns out of foreign policy. Were neo-realist structuralism to forestall such debate, it would be a sad development.

We can imagine a more optimistic future, however, in light of the relatively limited scope and aspirations of most neo-realist theorists. If neo-realist structuralism is seen as a matter of division of labor, or as a very rough first approximation rather than a comprehensive theory of international relations, it leaves space within the field for the discussion of moral issues. We cannot expect realists of any stripe to give central place to moral concerns. Nonetheless, we may be able to hope for neo-realism to allow moral concerns a place in the study and practice of international relations that earlier generations of realists denied. There may even be a new opening for at least a constructive interchange between realists and those more actively concerned with moral issues in international relations.

Suggested reading

E. H. Carr, Reinhold Niebuhr, and Hans Morgenthau are the three founding figures of twentieth-century realism. Carr's principal work in international relations is *The Twenty Years' Crisis* (1946). Chapters 1–6 still make interesting reading, although the discussion of morality in international politics (Chapter 9) is highly idiosyncratic.

Morgenthau's textbook *Politics among Nations*, first published in 1948, had an immense impact on the American study of international relations. It is still in print in an edition revised by his former student, Kenneth Thompson. Chapter 1 in all editions after the first provides a succinct general overview of Morgenthau's realism. A much better indication of the character and range of Morgenthau's thought is provided by his essays, most of which are collected in *Politics in the Twentieth Century* (1962) and *Truth and Power* (1970).

The best place to begin reading Niebuhr is probably his *Moral Man and Immoral Society* (1932). Although not as philosophically or theologically refined as *The Nature and Destiny of Man* (New York: Charles Scribner's Sons, 1941), it is the most powerful and most often cited of Niebuhr's political works. Pages xi–xxv, 1–32, 40–50, 83–98, 106–12, 137–41, and 168–80 provide a good feel of the general argument. *The Children of Light and the Children of Darkness* (1944) offers a good introduction to Niebuhr's later work, which moves away from his earlier leanings towards Marxist class analysis.

Two essays by eminent US practitioner-theorists should be noted. George F. Kennan's "Morality and Foreign Policy" (1985/86) is perhaps the best short statement of the realist position on the proper role of morality in foreign policy. Henry Kissinger's "Morality and Foreign Policy" in his book *American Foreign Policy* (3rd edn., New York: W. W. Norton, 1977), provides a clear statement of an instrumental political approach to morality in American foreign policy.

The most important figure in the recent revival of realism in the study of international relations is Kenneth Waltz. Waltz's work is the focus of Robert Keohane's edited volume *Neo-Realism and Its Critics* (1986). Keohane's own article, "Theory of World Politics: Structural Realism and Beyond," offers an excellent summary and mildly critical evaluation. The volume's excerpts from Waltz's *Theory of International Politics* (1979) provide the essence of this authoritative statement of the neo-realist perspective. The articles by Ruggie and Cox are among the best critiques of neo-realism available. Another important critique is Alexander Wendt, "The Agent-Structure Problem in International Relations Theory" (*International Organization* 41 (Summer 1987): 335–70).

Special note should also be made of Michael Joseph Smith's *Realist Thought from Weber to Kissinger* (1986). This is the best book-length study of the twentieth-century realists available, undertaken from a sympathetic but critical perspective. It can also be used as a guide to further reading.

References

Art, Robert J. and Kenneth N. Waltz. 1983. "Technology, Strategy, and the Uses of Force." In *The Use of Force*, 2nd edn., ed. Robert J. Art and Kenneth N. Waltz. Lanham, MD.: University Press of America.

Bull, Hedley. 1977. *The Anarchical Society: A Study of Order in World Politics*. New York: Columbia University Press.

Butterfield, Herbert. 1950. *Christianity and History*. New York: Charles Scribner's Sons.

1953. *Christianity, Diplomacy and War*. London: The Epworth Press.

1960. *International Conflict in the Twentieth Century: A Christian View*. New York: Harper & Brothers Publishers.

1979. *Writings on Christianity and History*. Ed. C. T. McIntire. New York: Oxford University Press.

Carr, Edward Hallett. 1946. *The Twenty Years' Crisis, 1919–1939: An Introduction to the Study of International Relations*. New York: Harper and Row.

d'Entreves, Alexander Passerin. 1967. *The Notion of the State: An Introduction to Political Theory*. Oxford: Clarendon Press.

Gilpin, Robert. 1986. "The Richness of the Tradition of Political Realism." In Keohane 1986b.

Herz, John H. 1951. *Political Realism and Political Idealism: A Study in Theories and Realities*. Chicago: University of Chicago Press.

1976. *The Nation-State and the Crisis of World Politics*. New York: David McKay.

Jervis, Robert. 1978. "Cooperation under the Security Dilemma." *World Politics* 30: 167–214.

Kennan, George F. 1954. *Realities of American Foreign Policy*. Princeton: Princeton University Press.

1977. *The Cloud of Danger: Current Realities of American Foreign Policy*. Boston: Little, Brown & Co.

1984. *American Diplomacy*, expanded edn. Chicago: University of Chicago Press.

1985/86. "Morality and Foreign Policy." *Foreign Affairs* 64: 205–18.

Keohane, Robert O. 1984. *After Hegemony: Cooperation and Discord in the World Political Economy*. Princeton: Princeton University Press.

1986a. "Theory of World Politics: Structural Realism and Beyond." In Keohane 1986b.

Keohane, Robert O., ed., 1986b. *Neo-Realism and Its Critics*. New York: Columbia University Press.

Kissinger, Henry A. 1977. *American Foreign Policy*, 3rd edn. New York: W. W. Norton.

1978. "Continuity and Change in American Foreign Policy." In *Human Rights and World Order*, ed. Abdul Aziz Said. New York: Praeger Publishers.

Meinecke, Friedrich. 1957. *Machiavellism: The Doctrine of Raison D'Etat and Its Place in Modern History*. New Haven: Yale University Press.

Morgenthau, Hans J. 1946. *Scientific Man Versus Power Politics*. Chicago: University of Chicago Press.

1948. *Politics among Nations: The Struggle for Power and Peace*. New York: Alfred A. Knopf.

1954. *Politics Among Nations: The Struggle for Power and Peace*, 2nd edn. New York: Alfred A. Knopf.

1960. *The Purpose of American Politics*. New York: Alfred A. Knopf.

1962a. *Politics in the Twentieth Century*, vol. 1. *The Decline of Democratic Politics*. Chicago: University of Chicago Press.

1962b. *Politics in the Twentieth Century*, vol. 2. *The Impasse of American Foreign Policy*. Chicago: University of Chicago Press.

1962c. *Politics in the Twentieth Century*, vol. 3. *The Restoration of American Politics*. Chicago: University of Chicago Press.

1967. "To Intervene or Not to Intervene." *Foreign Affairs* 45: 425–36.

1970. *Truth and Power: Essays of a Decade, 1960–70*. New York: Praeger.

1979. *Human Rights and Foreign Policy*. New York: Council on Religion and International Affairs.

Neibuhr, Reinhold. 1932. *Moral Man and Immoral Society: A Study in Ethics and Politics*. New York: Charles Scribner's Sons.

1934. *Reflections on the End of An Era*. New York: Charles Scribner's Sons.

1944. *The Children of Light and the Children of Darkness*. New York: Charles Scribner's Sons.

1960. *Reinhold Niebuhr on Politics: His Political Philosophy and Its Application to Our Age as Expressed in His Writings*. Ed. Harry R. Davis and Robert C. Good. New York: Charles Scribner's Sons.

Olson, William and Nicholas Onuf. 1985. "The Growth of a Discipline: Reviewed." In *International Relations: British and American Perspectives*, ed. Steve Smith. Oxford: Basil Blackwell.

Osgood, Robert E. 1953. *Ideals and Self-Interest in America's Foreign Relations*. Chicago: University of Chicago Press.

Osgood, Robert E. and Robert W. Tucker. 1967. *Force, Order and Justice*. Baltimore: The Johns Hopkins Press.

Ranke, Leopold von. 1973. *The Theory and Practice of History*. Ed. Georg G. Iggers and Konrad von Moltke. Indianapolis: Bobbs-Merrill.

Schuman, Frederick L. 1941. *International Politics: The Western System in Transition*, 3rd edn. New York: McGraw-Hill.

Schwarzenberger, Georg. 1951. *Power Politics: A Study of International Society*. New York: Frederick A. Praeger.

Smith, Michael Joseph. 1986. *Realist Thought from Weber to Kissinger*. Baton Rouge: Louisiana State University Press.

Spykman, Nicholas John. 1942. *America's Strategy in World Politics: The United States and the Balance of Power*. New York: Harcourt, Brace.

Thompson, Kenneth W. 1966. *The Moral Issue in Statecraft: Twentieth-Century Approaches and Problems*. Baton Rouge: Louisiana State University Press.

1985. *Moralism and Morality in Politics and Diplomacy*. Lanham, MD: University Press of America,.

Treitschke, Heinrich von. 1914. *Treitschke: His Doctrine of German Destiny and of International Relations*. New York: G. P. Putnam's Sons.

1916. *Politics*. New York: Macmillan.

Tucker, Robert W. 1960. *The Just War: A Study in Contemporary American Doctrine*. Baltimore: Johns Hopkins University Press.

1966. *Just War and Vatican Council II: A Critique*. New York: Council on Religion and International Affairs.

1968. *Nation or Empire? The Debate over American Foreign Policy*. Baltimore: Johns Hopkins University Press.

1977. *The Inequality of Nations*. New York: Basic Books.

1985. *Intervention and the Reagan Doctrine*. New York: Council on Religion and International Affairs.

Vasquez, John A. 1983. *The Power of Power Politics: A Critique*. New Brunswick, NJ: Rutgers University Press.

Waltz, Kenneth N. 1979. *Theory of International Politics*. New York: Random House.

Walzer, Michael. 1977. *Just and Unjust Wars*. New York: Basic Books.

Wight, Martin. 1978. *Power Politics*, rev. ed. New York: Holmes and Meier.

6 NATURAL LAW AND INTERNATIONAL ETHICS

JOSEPH BOYLE

A tradition of "natural-law" ethics identified

The expression "natural law" is perhaps most commonly used to name a family of views concerning the nature of law, namely, those jurisprudential views united by their common rejection of the position, called legal positivism, according to which law can be identified and understood without reference to moral considerations (Fuller 1964, 95–106; 1968, 112–19; see also "The evolution of international law," Chapter 2, and "Law, morality, and international affairs," Chapter 3). Used in this way, "natural law" names a theoretical position or proposition which is accepted by many who have little else in common, and whose various efforts of inquiry do not emerge from or add up to anything like a unified tradition. Agreement on one or more propositions, however important or basic, neither presupposes a common tradition of inquiry nor brings scholars into a unified tradition.

Among those who hold the natural-law position in jurisprudence, however, there is an identifiable group whose work does have features of inquiry within a shared intellectual tradition. Members of this group reject legal positivism because of a common commitment to a set of moral and political views and to a set of analytical strategies that can reasonably be described as belonging to the "natural-law tradition." This natural-law tradition of inquiry is comprised of the ethical investigations of scholastic moral philosophers and theologians, particularly within Catholicism since the time of Aquinas. These investigations have common roots in the Hebrew-Christian Scriptures, make use of many categories and arguments of the Greek philosophers, especially Aristotle and the Stoics, and have precedents in the writings of St. Augustine and other fathers of the church.

The ethical and political writings of Aquinas provide an especially important and authoritative source for natural-law inquiry. His conception of natural law, which implies (but is not identical with) the rejection of legal positivism, provides the reference for the expression "natural law" within the tradition. For Aquinas this expression refers to the most basic prescriptions of morality and practical reason; they are *laws* because of their prescriptive character, and *natural* because they are naturally known by human beings and are founded on those desirable activities which perfect and fulfill human beings. These activities, which are often referred to simply as "goods," include such things as knowing reality, relating to others in a decent way, and staying alive and healthy. So, what is natural in this sense is contrasted with what is derivative, established by human convention or decision, or knowable only through special divine revelation. Furthermore, on Aquinas's conception, natural law is the foundation not only of morality in the narrow sense, but of all normative discussions of law, human community, and politics. For all these are within the domain of morality as he conceives it: the domain in which practical reason, deliberation, and the exercise of human choice are operative (*S.t.*, 1–2, Prologue).[1]

Aquinas's theory of natural law, which emerged within the tradition of Christian medieval theorizing, became the foundation of a distinctive, Thomist tradition of moral inquiry during the sixteenth century, via a sustained effort of commentary on Aquinas's ethical and political writings. Even theologians who were concerned with the polemics of the Counter-Reformation period or interested in problems that Aquinas did not address frequently presented their analyses as commentaries on his work.

The writings of Spanish Jesuits and Dominicans during this period, most notably of Francisco Suarez and Francisco de Vitoria, constitute a particularly important development of the natural-law tradition, especially in relation to political and international issues. These writers faced a cultural and international situation very different from Aquinas's: the exploration of the new world and the conflicts between the emerging nation states provided a new context with new problems (Hamilton 1963; Midgley 1976, 62–94). In response, they amplified and formalized just-war theory, began reflecting on the mutual rights and duties of primitive peoples and explorers, and enriched the concept of

---

[1] Text references will follow a standard method of referring to Aquinas's work. The reference here is to the Prologue of the second part of the *Summa Theologiae*. This part of the *Summa* is further divided into two parts: the first part of the second part (which deals with ethical theory) and the second part of the second part (which deals with applications). Since the Prologue is contained within the first part of the second part, it is cited as "1–2." The argumentation of this work is divided into questions, which are further divided into articles. Citations indicate questions by "q." followed by the indication of articles within the question by "a." Where the reference is to a response to an objection within an article, "ad" follows the indication of the article.

the *jus gentium* – the common customs of humankind that, according to natural-law theory, have normative force in the absence of formally promulgated law.

The influence of Aquinas and his commentators on Catholic moral theology has continued throughout the modern period (see Jonsen and Toulmin 1988), and the twentieth century has seen a significant development of the natural-law tradition. This development began about one hundred years ago when the scholarly study of Aquinas was revived within Catholicism. Although the focus of this revival was not primarily on Aquinas's ethical and political writings, the application of modern scholarly techniques to these writings produced a far clearer picture of Aquinas's moral and political views than had previously existed. In particular, the work of French Dominicans in the interwar period sufficiently clarified many of Aquinas's key moral concepts and arguments to allow their introduction into modern discussions.[2]

Natural-law theorizing has also entered the broader, secular discussion of political and international issues, and not simply in Catholic countries or parts of the world. The political writings of Jacques Maritain are perhaps the best known of such efforts within the English-speaking world (1951, 1966). Contemporary work in this spirit can be found in the writings of John Finnis, his associates, and their neoscholastic critics (Finnis 1980; Fortin 1982; Hittinger 1987).

In short, the natural-law tradition is a fairly robust tradition of moral and political inquiry. It is not primarily a tradition of international ethics, but the key concerns of the tradition have application in this arena, as the natural-law contribution to the doctrine of the just war indicates.

Natural law and the dialogue of international ethics

Scholarly development of the natural-law tradition in this century has been closely related to the development of what is often called "Catholic social teaching." During the last hundred years, popes, bishops, and groups of bishops have issued a series of analyses of various social and political issues, including war and peace, poverty, and international cooperation (Freemantle 1963; Gremillion 1976). This material draws heavily – if not always explicitly – from the

---

[2] Little of this literature is available in English. Perhaps the most useful and accessible source is in the notes and commentaries to the relevant volumes in the multivolume translation of the *Summa Theologiae*: *Somme Theologique* (Desclee: Paris Tournai, Rome, 1930 and continuing).

natural-law tradition, and has spurred the development and refinement of the tradition (Calvez and Perrin 1961).

The close connection between Catholic moral and social teaching and the natural-law tradition is one reason that tradition might interest those concerned with the normative study of international relations. The natural-law tradition of moral inquiry provides the theoretical elaboration and underpinning for the political and social judgments of a large, international community whose members are sure to participate in discussions of international ethics.

The connection between Catholic teaching and natural-law inquiry can lead one mistakenly to expect substantial agreement among moralists in the tradition. In fact, natural-law theorists agree significantly less than might be expected of thinkers who share both an intellectual approach and a religious community. Neither common respect for Aquinas's writings, nor the shared use of his concepts and language has led natural-law thinkers to widespread agreement, either with Aquinas or with one another, about specific normative issues or about the precise justification of their judgments.

Given the extension of the natural-law tradition over time and diverse cultures, these differences of emphasis are not surprising. The differing social, intellectual, and political contexts within which natural-law theorists have worked have shaped their concerns and inspired them to develop the tradition creatively. Aquinas, for example, has virtually nothing to say about rights, yet rights are a central concern of twentieth-century natural-law theorists like Maritain and Finnis.

Even when natural-law theorists have addressed the same or very similar problems, they have frequently disagreed. For the application of moral principles to difficult cases, the moral reasoning usually known as casuistry, is complex and difficult, and even more so in political and international affairs. Mistakes are easy to make and conclusions are controversial. These conclusions depend not only on moral principles and conceptual analysis but also on empirical judgments and interpretations that are not simply a function of one's basic normative outlook. For example, disagreements about the precise character of the acts and intentions that together comprise the West's nuclear deterrent have led natural-law theorists to different moral evaluations of the deterrent; and differing judgments about the impact of various economic arrangements have led natural-law theorists to disagreements and indeterminacies in evaluating various economic schemes and property arrangements.

Aquinas would have found this phenomenon unremarkable. He

115

notes that, as moral analysis must take into account more and more of the specific details of actions, sound moral judgment becomes more difficult (S.t., 1–2, q. 94, a. 2; q. 100, a. 3).

Disagreements within the natural-law tradition have not, however, been limited to questions of casuistical detail. Some ambiguities and disagreements concern very fundamental matters, and affect judgments about political and international issues. The theoretical disagreements that affect the normative judgments of natural-law theorists tend to be those which arise from long-standing ambiguities and imprecisions of the tradition's basic analytical categories. For example, the pivotal notion of the "common good," which will be discussed further below, is notoriously opaque and a source of controversy within the tradition. Similarly, those working within the tradition are not always clear about the role within practical thinking of the virtuous person's practical wisdom (what Aquinas called *prudentia*, often misleadingly translated as "prudence") in assessing the concrete details of difficult decisions.

However, despite differences, ambiguities, and disagreements within the natural-law tradition, it provides a common, theoretical language that has been developed through centuries of analytical use by scholars within different cultural contexts. It also provides a set of approaches that raise distinctive questions and highlight as morally important aspects of international relations that other moral approaches tend to downplay or overlook.

For example, contemporary discussions of warfare and deterrence include a significant concern about the moral relevance of the intentions of various agents and polities involved (Finnis et al. 1987, 77–103, 180–81). The natural-law tradition has much to say on this issue. For, since Aquinas's famous discussion of the intentions involved in self-defense (S.t., 2–2, q. 64, a. 7) – which is widely regarded as the first statement of the doctrine of the double effect – the tradition has highlighted the role of intention within moral evaluation, and so provides a rich source for anyone concerned about the moral character of deterrent intentions.

Natural law, common morality, and consequentialism

The general normative outlook of thinkers within the natural-law tradition has clearly been shaped by the moral convictions of post-Reformation Catholicism. For the most part, these moral convictions are not specific to post-Reformation Catholicism, but have been the common property of Eastern and Western Christians, Protestants, and Catholics from the beginning of the Christian era. Indeed, given the roots of Christianity in the Hebrew Scriptures and the mutual interactions of Rabbinic Judaism and early Christianity, we may refer to this set of moral convictions as "Judeo-Christian morality." Alan Donagan has usefully named the nonreligious component of this ethical outlook "common morality." On this account there are two nonreligious components of this morality: it includes obligations that apply to actions which are not specifically religious, and it holds that these obligations can be known by rational investigation, independent of any religious revelation (Donagan 1977, 6–8, 26–31).

"Common morality," used in Donagan's sense, clearly does not refer to a robust and easily identifiable tradition of inquiry, in the way that "natural law" does. Nor does this expression pick out the values of a distinct and homogeneous group who live a shared way of life (see Chapter 13 on the discontinuities among communities rooted in the Hebrew or Christian scriptures). But there are commonalities among the values lived by members of communities who profess loyalty to the Hebrew or Christian scriptures, and Jewish and Christian theologians have to some extent consciously developed a common body of moral doctrine. In short, "common morality," does refer to a set of historically identifiable efforts of inquiry and communities of shared values.

On Donagan's account, natural-law theorizing is related to common morality as one of several possible elaborations or interpretations of the latter. Donagan prefers the elaboration developed in Kant's ethical writings, and he plainly supposes that the Rabbinic tradition provides another. Different elaborations of common morality lead to significant differences in detail, particularly concerning the evaluation of concrete actions whose moral character is opaque or ambiguous. But there is a common core of doctrine about the content and application of moral principles and precepts. Not surprisingly, this common core of moral doctrine defines the basic normative outlook of the natural-law tradition and allows us to locate it within the spectrum of views about foreign relations. In particular, four features of common morality determine what is central to the normative outlook shared by natural-law theorists. Three are discussed immediately below; the fourth is treated in the next section.

First, common morality takes the precepts of the Mosaic decalogue as established beyond question, even though these precepts are most often regarded as the implications of more fundamental moral principles such as the love commandments or the Golden Rule (or, in the Kantian interpretation, as the implications of the categorical imperative or, in the Thomist, as those of right reason).

117

Second, common morality understands some of the precepts of the decalogue as embodying absolute prohibitions of some kinds of actions. The prohibitions against adultery and murder, for example, are understood by virtually all who accept common morality as exceptionless (although there is a complex and controversial casuistry around the fuzzy edges of the ideas of murder and adultery). The exceptionless character of such precepts is taken to hold even in the face of grave necessity, and even when there is a strong positive obligation to promote an overriding good or avoid an exigent disaster. This idea is expressed in the maxim "the end does not justify the means," which is perhaps best understood as a restatement of St. Paul's dictum that one must not do evil that good may come of it (Romans 3:7–8; Donagan 1977, 149–57).

Natural-law theorists give this dictum a specific interpretation by applying the tradition's view of intention. In effect, the tradition holds that when St. Paul's dictum is applied to actions that harm human beings, their absolute prohibition refers only to actions in which these harms are intended; the same harms brought about as side effects of otherwise good actions might make those actions wrong but do not do so necessarily and in all cases. This idea underlies the well-known doctrine of the double effect (Mangan 1949; Boyle 1980; Anscombe 1982; for the utilitarian view of double effect, see "Implications for world affairs," Chapter 8). This interpretation of St. Paul's dictum presupposes that there are some kinds of harms, such as killing an innocent person, which are never permissible. Plainly, not all adherents of common morality accept absolute prohibitions of *this* kind (Donagan 1977, 163). Still, most do hold that once an action is classed as prohibited by one of the precepts of the decalogue, no further consideration can overturn it.

Third, according to common morality moral norms are systematically "agent relative": they direct the actions of agents, not the production of outcomes. Thus, the norm proscribing murder is addressed to every person and directs each not to murder. It is not, fundamentally, a rule directing that there be no murders or that the number of murders be minimized. This aspect of common morality is much more an assumption than a claim for which proponents of common morality have explicitly argued. Still, it is hardly a dispensable assumption. It is closely related to ideas that are fundamental to common morality: for example, that one's choices and intentions are within one's power (and thus are one's responsibility) far more fully than the outcomes of these volitional acts, and that the moral law is a participation in God's providential governance of the universe to

118

enable human beings to carry out their real but *limited* creative responsibility.

These three characteristics of common morality show that the natural-law interpretation of common morality falls within the spectrum of deontological ethical theories such as Kant's and various forms of intuitionism, and is deeply resistant to consequentialist interpretation (Donagan 1977, Ch. 6; see also "Kantian ethics: Kant's general theory," Chapter 7). There is considerable disagreement, even among those who regard themselves as consequentialists, about how to characterize consequentialism.[3] Anthony Ellis's characterization (on the first page of Chapter 8, this volume) is useful: consequentialism is based on the idea "that the only relevant factor in deciding whether any action or practice is morally right or wrong is its overall consequences viewed impersonally. The agent is morally obliged to perform any action, no matter what, if and only if it has the best consequences or, as it is also put, if and only if it maximizes the good." Its impersonal concern for maximizing the good means that consequentialism is, at its deepest level, agent neutral, and implies that all specific moral norms have exceptions: it would be irrational to be blocked by an absolute rule from doing what, all things considered, would be best.

Thus, in spite of important similarities in doctrine and language, the natural-law tradition and consequentialism are opposed at a very deep level. The basic similarities arise because both include a general test for the rightness of actions, and so are ethical theories in the full sense of the expression, and because both regard the category of the good as fundamental to practical reason and moral evaluation.[4] But these similarities are far less significant than the deep divergences concerning the agent neutrality of the moral point of view, and concerning the closely related question of whether *maximizing* is a correct way of articulating concern for the good.

The respects in which common morality is non-consequentialist have important practical implications for the conduct of moral inquiry

[3] The term was introduced by Anscombe [1958] 1981a, 33–36: she used the expression to name any moral theory according to which hopes for good results are sufficient to override traditional prohibitions. For useful contemporary discussions see Raz (1986, 268–71) and Sumner (1987, 165–75).

[4] Of course, some moralists with roots in the Christian tradition have accepted consequentialism. See Schneewind (1976) for an account of the development of utilitarianism by William Paley in an explicitly Christian context. One of the major schools of thought within contemporary Catholic moral theology, often dubbed "proportionalism," appears to accept a limited form of consequentialism; its proponents regularly maintain that proportionalism is rooted in the tradition and constitutes a legitimate development (see Curran and McCormick 1979). I believe that none of these approaches takes sufficiently seriously the deep opposition between the agent neutrality of consequentialism and the agent relativity of common morality.

– both generally and in international relations. The most obvious is that some possibilities for action that are appropriate on consequentialist grounds, and that could be morally right if they maximize the good, are simply out of the question according to common morality. One example is the interpretation of the just-war doctrine's requirement of noncombatant immunity. According to common morality, this requirement applies the prohibition against murder to the context of warfare (Anscombe 1981b; Finnis et al. 1987, 86–90, 298–300). Consequentialism, however, evaluates this requirement much more contextually: such killing might be justified if necessary to shorten a brutal war or to defeat a particularly vicious enemy (see "Implications for world affairs," Chapter 8).

This difference in approach exemplifies a more general difference in the conduct of moral inquiry, a difference that holds even when the issues do not concern the application of norms regarded as absolute within common morality. Generally, theorists within common morality approach concrete moral questions by using a form of casuistry, not consequentialist calculation. This latter involves projecting, comparing, and evaluating consequences in the light of their overall impact on the good. Common morality's casuistry proceeds very differently: possible actions are considered in relation to already established principles and norms (even when, as in the natural-law tradition, the ground of these principles and norms is the good), and the investigation is designed to clarify which of the norms applies. The key problem in this inquiry is to determine the character of a given act in terms which relate it to moral principles. Thus, although the consequences of actions are often relevant to how they are characterized and so can lead to fuller descriptions of actions which sometimes change their moral evaluation, the procedure does not involve a calculation and comparison of likely outcomes.[5]

The difference in how consequentialists and theorists working within common morality debate the morality of nuclear deterrence exhibits in a striking way this general difference of approach. The consequentialist debate centers on the likely outcomes of maintaining or dismantling the deterrent. Those who favor the deterrent argue that maintaining the deterrent will likely prevent great evils, such as

[5] Anscombe (1981a, 36) draws attention to the difference between consequentialist calculation and casuistry. See Donagan (1977, 66–71) for a useful account of the structure for deriving precepts from basic principles. My characterization of casuistry differs from that of Jonsen and Toulmin (1988, 1–20). They downplay the role of general moral principles and consequently seem to regard casuistry as a more piecemeal effort to articulate and apply moral intuitions. Still, on their account or mine, casuistry is a different sort of moral reasoning than what consequentialists suggest we should do.

nuclear war or domination of the world by an aggressor, and that the likelihood of the bad outcomes of the deterrent, particularly nuclear holocaust, occurring is sufficiently small as to be negligible. Consequentialists who reject the deterrent reverse these evaluations of the outcomes (Finnis et al. 1987, 177–237; "Implications for world affairs," Chapter 8). The debate among adherents of common morality has a different focus. The likelihood of the good and bad outcomes of maintaining or abandoning the deterrent are considered, but the focus of the discussion is on the question of whether the deterrent embodies an intent forbidden by the prohibition against murder. This leads to such non-consequentialist questions as whether the deterrent threatens innocents, whether it is a bluff, and whether conditional intentions are real intentions in the morally relevant sense (Finnis et al. 1987, 104–74; Walzer 1977, 269–83).

The universalism of common morality and natural law

The agent relativity of common morality does not make it identical with what some contemporary philosophers call the "morality of common sense." Common-sense morality gives primacy to the obligations associated with a person's specific relations with definite people, such as family members and fellow citizens. These obligations are also real and important according to common morality, for they provide much of the normative shape of a person's day-to-day moral existence. The promises, commitments, and capacity for mutual aid that bind people into a community create special obligations for both members and leaders of the community. But these obligations are not foundational nor immune from criticism in light of the precepts of the decalogue or of moral principles like the Golden Rule. According to all the theoretical interpretations of common morality, such obligations are justified "from the outside" by more general moral considerations and, like all other responsibilities, are governed by St. Paul's dictum. Communal obligations and values may not be pursued at the cost of doing moral evil as defined by general moral standards.

This difference between common morality and common-sense morality is one aspect of the former's fourth important characteristic: its universalism. Both the principles and the most basic norms of common morality provide directions for the treatment of all human beings. This idea runs very deep within common morality. All humans are made in God's image; all share a common human nature; the Golden Rule guides relations with any human being who may be

121

affected by our actions; and anyone can, in the relevant circumstances, be one's neighbor.

Consequently, common morality, like consequentialism, natural-rights theories, and other universalist approaches to ethics, rejects those forms of relativism that locate basic moral standards in the lived values of specific communities. Thus, protecting the values which find concrete shape in the life and institutions of a people cannot justify actions which disregard the basic human rights of outsiders. Therefore, although credible and immediate threats to a community's very existence may *excuse* the terrible things nations sometimes do to enemies and other outsiders in situations of extreme emergency, they do not *justify* such actions.[6]

This aspect of common morality's universalism does not imply that humankind is a kind of community, although some adherents of common morality have apparently thought this. But common morality's universalism does have implications relevant for understanding the moral relationships between peoples and nations. For common morality implies that all humans have something in common – their humanity – and that this humanity grounds moral obligations. Thus, prior to any kind of social contract or agreement among different peoples, and so prior to any actual community among them, there are some moral bonds between all humans. Thus, common morality rejects the extreme picture of international life (held by some political realists and contractarians) that depicts relations among nations as taking place in a pre-moral or amoral context because of the lack of community and recognized common authority that must obtain in a world of sovereign nations (see "The structure of contractarian arguments," Chapter 9).

All people are thus held to have certain rights that other people – including their own political authorities and the members and authorities of other communities – must respect. The accounts of natural rights provided by adherents of common morality vary considerably, but none take rights as an irreducible category of moral and political analysis. Instead they see rights as implied by the fundamental principles of common morality that have been formulated in terms of each person's obligations to others (Finnis 1980,

---

[6] Walzer (1977, 251–83) argues that the condition of supreme emergency allows a nation thus threatened to set aside such parts of the war convention as the requirement of noncombatant immunity. His argument can be understood in several ways, but insofar as Walzer means to justify otherwise immoral actions because of their necessity for turning aside a threat to the life and values of a given community, he departs radically from the traditional moral views that underlie much of his analysis of war.

198–230; for some reservations, see Fortin 1982; see also Chapter 7 of this volume).

Moral concern for those outside one's community is not limited on this conception to a set of rules requiring noninterference and refraining from harmful actions. The principles of common morality plainly imply a more positive concern for the welfare of people outside one's own community. For the general positive obligations to others included within common morality are not limited to people with whom we are bound in community by contract, political ties, or common locale. We are obliged to help whoever we can (when this is compatible with fulfilling other duties) and to be ready to form and promote decent relations with them. Thus, for example, consequentialists and adherents of common morality agree that when many in the third world face imminent starvation relatively wealthy people in richer parts of the world have a serious moral obligation to come to their aid ("The Kantian-deontological approach to international affairs," Chapter 7).

This general duty to help others is the most basic ground within common morality for interference in the internal affairs of one nation by outsiders, including other nations and international bodies. The specific implications of the general duty to provide help depend on a number of highly contingent factors, including respect for a nation's sovereignty and awareness of the limits of outside aid. But the normative ground is there, and it is not merely permissive; in extreme circumstances it can justify the use of force.

Another aspect of the universalism of common morality is a broadly epistemological claim about who can know, and so be directed by, the principles and norms of morality. This epistemological claim proposes that since the principles and basic precepts of common morality are accessible to human reason, they can be known by anyone capable of thought and action. This idea is emphasized by the natural-law tradition, but it is also part of common morality. Its roots go back at least to St. Paul's letter to the Romans in which he maintains that there is, written on the human heart, a moral law that serves much the same purpose for gentiles as the Mosaic law serves for Jews (Romans 2:15; Donagan 1977, 1–9).

Many who reject the foundationalist epistemological views of traditional philosophy are likely to find this claim incredible. In short, this is an area in which adherents of common morality, including those within the natural-law tradition, need to confront epistemological objections more fully. These objections arise from contemporary concerns about the relativity and possible incommensurability of

123

conceptual schemes and from historicist and coherentist objections to foundationalism.[7]

These epistemological difficulties should not, however, obscure the moral significance of this aspect of common morality's universalism. For its universalism is connected to its belief in the dignity of the human person. All mature humans are held to have the capacity for moral self-criticism and improvement; no one is simply stuck with a set of values that cannot be criticized by appeal to a higher standard. Thus, moral dialogue with others has a chance to succeed because, at the most basic level, neither one's own contribution to the dialogue nor that of others is simply a function of values and concerns to which the other party cannot have access (see Murray 1960, 5–139, 275–336 for an application of this idea to a pluralistic society). This has obvious implications for one enduring strand in the political realist argument: the view (which goes back at least to the arguments of the Athenian generals at Melos) that moral discourse between nations can have nothing more than emotive force because of the lack of shared values (see Walzer 1977, 5–20; "Thucydides," Chapter 4).

There are, of course, authoritarian abuses within common morality, such as the traditional just-war rule that citizens should not fight for their country if they *know* the war is unjust, but that otherwise they should give their political leaders the benefit of the doubt (Walzer 1977, 39). But even these abuses do not imply that individuals should abandon their own personal evaluation of what they are being asked to do. Indeed, it seems to me that the universalism of common morality provides a basis for criticizing such authoritarian abuses.

Practical reasoning and moral dilemmas

The two preceding sections have emphasized how much of the normative outlook of the natural-law tradition is shared with other interpretations of common morality. However, some of the features that distinguish natural-law theorizing from other interpretations of common morality are also important for understanding its contributions to the ethical discussion of international relationships. Two normatively important areas in which common morality remains indeterminate, while the natural-law tradition provides distinctive analyses, are: (1) the conception of how moral dilemmas are to be

---

[7] See Donagan (1977, 17–26) for an effort to distinguish the kind of foundationalism to which common morality seems committed from the Cartesian epistemology of pre-Sidgwickian intuitionism; for a natural-law account that seeks to separate claims about self-evident principles from intuitionism, see Grisez et al. (1987, 106–114).

resolved, and (2) the conception of political life and authority. The first of these areas will be considered in the remainder of this section; the second in the next section.

The two best known ways in which the natural-law tradition has dealt with apparent conflicts of obligations have already been noted: the use of the doctrine of the double effect to make precise the application of the Pauline principle to an important class of hard cases, and the use of the category of practical wisdom or *prudentia* to account for the highly contextualized and contingent character of human decisions. The application of this idea to the decision-making of political leaders requires some further comment.

The place of *prudentia* within the natural-law account of practical reasoning and decision-making is neither altogether clear in Aquinas's writings (*S.t.* 1–2, q. 58) nor uncontroversial within the tradition. Still, the main lines of Aquinas's account are clear enough to reveal its importance for dealing with difficult decisions. This account depends upon Aquinas's view that all practical decision-making is governed by the principles of natural law, but that many decisions and policies do not follow from these principles by a rigorous process of deduction and analytical thought.

According to natural-law theorists the fundamental principles of all practical thinking, and so of morality, are natural in several ways. Although natural-law theorists disagree on the details of how these principles are natural, all agree with Aquinas in holding that the most fundamental grounds of moral judgments are natural in the sense that they are readily known by mature human beings, and in the sense that they are somehow closely related to human nature (see *S.t.* 1–2, q. 94, a. 2). But only these basic principles are held to be natural; all other practical judgments are derivative. And there are several forms of derivation.

The writings of natural-law theorists, beginning with Aquinas, are filled with examples of the rational, analytic derivation of specific moral norms from general principles. The structure of this reasoning is deductive, although the truth of the premises that relate kinds of actions to moral principles is not established deductively but largely by informal conceptual analysis. According to Aquinas, this sort of analytical reasoning in its most simple form justifies the precepts of the decalogue and in its most complex and fallible forms justifies the results of well-conducted casuistry (*S.t.* 1–2, q. 100, a. 2). But it is clear that in his view this kind of reasoning is not sufficient for decision-making to be fully responsive to basic moral principles.

Prudentia is necessary to resolve such indeterminacies as remain

125

after rational analysis has done its best. *Prudentia* is not primarily skill in analytical thinking; it presupposes a feel for the concrete emotional appeal of the particulars of action that requires possession of the moral virtues (*S.t.* 1–2, q. 58, a. 5), and includes a responsiveness to the possibilities for doing good that is irreducible to reasoning (*S.t.* 2–2, q. 49).

Practical wisdom is necessary for the moral perfection of every person, but it has a special application in the decision-making of leaders of communities. For within a community common decisions are necessary, and these common decisions frequently concern matters that moral analysis leaves indeterminate. Since common action and the reasonable coordination of interactions will be difficult if not impossible unless community members regard these decisions as morally binding (even if only defeasibly so), they have moral authority (Simon 1951, 19–71; Finnis 1980, 231–59).

Thus, according to the natural-law tradition, law and political decision-making, insofar as they are human activities subject to rational control, are essentially related to moral principles and norms. Their purpose is to implement and make concrete in the life of a community those components of a rich and full communal existence that morality demands we respect and political society exists to promote and protect. Thus, the goals of political decisions, including the law, are essentially moral; they include setting up the conditions for the peaceful and just pursuit not only of the necessities of life but also of life's full flourishing and perfection in activities such as science, religion, play, and excellent achievement. But most laws and policies are not simple implications of the moral norms which demand respect and concern for worthwhile human activities. Invention and decision are necessary to implement these moral purposes and make moral objectives concrete (*S.t.* 1–2, q. 95, a. 2; Finnis 1980, 281–90). Consequently, political leaders need the virtue of practical wisdom to properly fulfill their social role. There is, of course, no guarantee that they will have it but, insofar as their decisions are compatible with rationally derived moral principles, their authority remains.

This view of practical wisdom, I believe, is among the deepest reasons why the natural-law tradition does not accept as a matter of moral principle anything like Kant's "global rationalism" (see "Kantian ethics: Kant's general theory" and "Kantian internationalism," Chapter 7). The general moral norms governing the relations between all the peoples of the world do not settle what particular sort of society world leaders should at any particular time seek to fashion. That will depend on a variety of contingent factors, including the technological and political possibilities for mutual aid and cooperation. The casuistry needed for specific practical judgment must take these factors into account, and what cannot be done for all times and places. Moreover, the complete development of this casuistry at any given time is not generally sufficient to provide fully determinate guidance for decisions. Instead, casuistry terminates with a set of positive obligations which need to be ordered and given concrete form in specific actions and policies. For that, reasonable human decision is needed, and this in turn requires the practical wisdom of leaders.

This acknowledgment of contingency shows that the natural-law tradition has the resources to counter the objection, often made by politicians and political realists, that moralistic approaches to political and international decisions do not accord to political leaders the discretion they need to do their job. Like political realists, natural-law theorists believe that political leaders must make prudent decisions that take into account the possibilities for effective action and the interests of the polity for which they bear responsibility. But the possibilities they consider and the interests they prudently pursue must be evaluated by moral standards. Likewise, natural-law theorists recognize the necessities faced by politicians, but resist regarding them as justifying actions contrary to the moral law. A political authority may feel compelled by these necessities, but necessities cannot justify immoral actions. For these necessities do not ordinarily make the consideration of morally acceptable alternatives impossible and, if deliberation and choice are possible, it is possible, even though very difficult, to choose to follow the moral law. When necessities do make deliberation and choice impossible, then there are grounds for excuse but not justification.

Thus, the natural-law tradition resolves conflicts between morality and political necessity in favor of morality. There is, however, another version of the problem of "dirty hands" that is best seen as a conflict within morality itself – the conflict between common moral standards and the special responsibilities of political leaders. According to this view, political leaders are often tragic figures who face strict moral dilemmas: they must face hard choices in which there is no alternative but to do something immoral. Aquinas directly addresses this question of "moral perplexity." He maintains that there are no moral dilemmas in the strict sense. The underlying reason seems to be that morality is a matter of thoroughgoing practical reasonableness and practical reason is consistent and sufficient for the conduct of human affairs.

But Aquinas admits that, even though practical reason itself is not at

127

fault, a person can face moral dilemmas because of prior immorality. Consequently, unless the prior immorality is rejected, people can face options all of which are immoral. Thus, for example, established hatreds and injustices between peoples can be taken by their leaders as unalterable, and so lead them to face a set of options all of which are seriously wrong. The natural-law prescription is to change the set of options by removing the standing immoralities. Unwilling to do that, political leaders should not pretend that the evil they choose is morally justified even if it is the lesser of the evils they could choose (Donagan 1977, 143–49, 180–89).

The common good and the complete society

In considering the distinctive natural-law approach to political and social life, the notion of the common good emerges as pivotal. The centrality and international relevance of this idea is suggested by its analytical function within natural-law theory: the common good is the basis for the authority of political society and its leaders, and so for its limitation and criticism.

In spite of its importance, the notion of the common good within the natural-law tradition has remained somewhat unclear and indeterminate. It has been a source of sometimes acrimonious debate within the tradition and is regarded by many outside the tradition as either hopelessly vague or pernicious. These difficulties go back (at least) to Aquinas. He frequently speaks of the common good of political society as more noble and more divine than any advantage, benefit, or interest of its members could be, and sometimes refers to the relation between the common good of a society and the private or individual goods of its members as that of whole to part (see DeConinck 1945 for a complete listing of the relevant texts). This suggests a subordination of the interests of individual persons to the interests of political society that most people and most natural-law theorists now reject. It also appears to invest political leaders with authority out of all proportion to the kind of justification available in the tradition.

In spite of these difficulties, some features of the natural-law tradition's conception of the common good are clear and uncontroversial, and some recent developments of the idea point towards needed clarifications.

It is clear that, according to the tradition, every community has a common good. The pursuit of benefits common in some way to a group is a necessary condition for that group's being a community (Finnis 1980, 157). For if each member of a group pursues only interests that are private and defined independently of the interests he or she has as a participant in a cooperative enterprise, there simply is no basis for common action and cooperation. Thus, even a purely contractual relationship has a common good: the fair consummation of the exchange specified in the contract.

It is also clear enough why the tradition holds for a connection between the common good of a community and the authority within it: as already noted, the need for authority, and so its justification, arises because of the requirements for common and coordinated action within a community. Such common and coordinated action is the pursuit of the community's common good. Thus, the common good is not simply a category of political analysis, but a general category for the normative analysis of communities and social relationships.

Consequently, to the extent that the peoples and nations of the world are able to unite in cooperative action to address common concerns, the object of the common action and the resolution of the common concerns becomes a common good of humankind, and a basis for genuine authority in the international arena. The existence of such community, at least incipiently, is suggested by the *jus gentium*, the common customs of humankind, which natural-law theory has always regarded as authoritative (Finnis 1980, 238–45). The fuller development of the international community is reflected in the body of international law and in various international organizations such as the United Nations. Such laws and bodies can have moral authority even if they lack mechanisms of enforcement.

Since people form communities in different ways for different purposes, very different sorts of benefits and interests can be common goods. Thus, the more or less definite goals of various organizations can be common goods, as can the much more open-ended and long-term values and concerns of friends, families, and polities. What the tradition calls "external goods," such things as property and other instrumentalities, can plainly be held commonly within a community. Except when the use of external goods is the precise purpose of the human association, they are not the common good which defines a community, but are related to it instrumentally.

The common goods of communities can be related to the individual benefits of their members in a variety of ways. Generally, the common goods of communities include at least some benefits of their members, including some that are fundamental. Thus, for example, in families the common good of the group includes many fundamental benefits which the adult members seek for themselves as family members and for other members of the group, for example, survival, friendship, and

129

the development of virtue. Similarly, the values of international cooperation, solidarity, and security are not only parts of the common good of humankind but of every individual nation.

It follows that the common good of any community is not simply the sum of the individual interests and benefits of its members, but includes whichever of the interests and benefits of its members the community aims to realize via cooperative actions. Consequently, natural-law's notion of the common good is not simply an additive conception, like most utilitarian conceptions (see "The origins of utilitarianism," Chapter 8). Nor is it a purely instrumental conception, like most contractarian conceptions (see "The structure of contractarian arguments," Chapter 9). Furthermore, natural law's general conception of the common good does not, in contrast to many more modern teleological approaches to practical issues, exclude morally defined components: justice and other virtues can be among the benefits people seek in cooperative action, and so can be part of the common good. Thus, not surprisingly, the tradition holds that justice is an essential element of the common good of political society.

The full nature of this common good emerges only in the explanation of two distinctive and closely related aspects: (1) the fact that political society is not a voluntary association, and (2) the fact that political authority appears to have altogether special prerogatives, especially the legitimate use of force.

Just as a family is not a voluntary association for those born into it, neither is a political society. While it is usually possible to leave decent political societies by emigrating or renouncing citizenship, the obligations of citizenship are not recognized as purely consensual. Neither political authorities nor upright citizens regard the obligations which political society imposes as requiring the consent or agreement of all on whom they are imposed. It follows that the common good of political society, whatever that precisely is, must be unlike the common goods of most human communities whose essential contours and content depend upon the decisions of their members. Thus, according to natural-law theory, social contracts cannot create political obligation. Actual agreements can (but plainly often do not) implement the requirements of a polity's common good, and contractarian strategies, such as Rawls's device of the original position, can reveal some of the implications of the common good, especially fairness (see "Modern contractarianism," Chapter 9). But, while natural law admits that people can freely create a polity, it does not admit that people are justified in giving it any shape they choose.

There are important human values, realized only in political society, which constrain any such choices.

The special prerogatives of political authority also demand that the common good of political society (which, on natural-law grounds, alone can justify them) be distinctive. Unlike the legitimate decisions of other authorities, the decisions of political leaders involve more than an appeal to the conscience of those obliged to obey them. The use of sanctions and force is uniquely justified in the proper exercise of political authority. Furthermore, in dealing with other polities and foreign entities, political authority is justified in regarding its own enactments as final and decisive; it is held to be justified in claiming sovereignty, in recognizing no other authority as superior to its own.

This does not mean, of course, that the claims of political authorities to special prerogatives are beyond moral criticism. "An unjust law is no law at all," a tag that is often used to characterize natural-law theorizing, makes plain that political authorities are subject to criticism in the light of the common good and other moral considerations. These same moral considerations sometimes require that people go along with unreasonable political decisions. Thus, it is common doctrine within the natural-law tradition that, while laws and political decisions not justified by the common good have no inherent authority, upright citizens must go along with them if disregarding them will lead to great harm to the common good (see Finnis 1980, 351–60 for a standard treatment).

Natural-law theorists attribute the two specific characteristics of the common good of political society to the fact that political society is a "complete" or "perfect" society. It is because political society is a complete community that its common good is neither optional nor dependent upon the decisions of its members, and that this common good justifies the final, sovereign authority of its leaders.

The notion of a complete society is originally Aristotelian (see Finnis 1980, 160), and continuing disputes about the precise way in which Aristotle understood "complete" indicate important areas of indeterminacy in this notion within the natural-law tradition (see Gerson 1988). Thus, Maritain and Finnis understand "complete community" in a way that does not preclude the possibility that, given certain levels of communication and interdependence, the entire world might be a complete society (Maritain 1951, 187–216; Finnis 1980, 150), whereas others within the tradition see this as beyond the naturally given limits within which political society can effectively function (Messner 1965, 517).

Although the matter requires far more study than it has so far

131

received, it seems to me that Finnis and Maritain are correct in thinking that the more contextual and less "naturally" defined conception of "complete" societies is more compatible with the deep logic of the natural-law tradition than interpretations which regard the size of a polity as somehow naturally settled. For their understanding of complete community fits well with the tradition's conviction that the actual arrangements of political institutions are based upon reasonable convention and decision, and are not settled once and for all by naturally given factors.

More importantly, this more contextual understanding of complete community is sufficient for the main purpose the idea serves: to explain the nonvoluntary character of political society and the special authority of political leaders. A community can rightly demand the moral allegiance of its members independently of their wishes and commitments, and if necessary carry out its authoritative decisions by the use of force only if the community meets two conditions. The first is that it be an all-round community in which all the benefits which human beings have reason to seek are somehow in view. Communities defined by a common commitment to only some human benefits cannot reasonably claim complete jurisdiction over human affairs, and cannot reasonably exclude people coercively from deciding which benefits they will choose to pursue, or how they will structure their pursuit of them. The second condition is that the coordination of action in pursuit of the whole set of human interests and benefits can reasonably be undertaken only by the authority of a community actually capable of coordinating all the actions which people might undertake in respect to all these interests. Thus, although the family is an all-round community, authority within any family is not as such capable of coordinating interactions between families and between families and other institutions.

These essential conditions of a complete society reveal the core content of the common good of political society: this good must include all the interests human beings might have insofar as the pursuit of the interests has a communal dimension which requires the decisive regulation and coordination provided by public authority. Since decent human interactions are governed by the requirements of justice, and all people have or should have an interest in the fair distribution of the benefits and burdens of social cooperation, the justice which public authority can realize is the central, invariant component of political society's common good, which Aquinas describes as the "common good of justice and peace" (*S.t.* 1–2, q. 96, a. 3).

Which communities meet the conditions of a complete society, and so are capable of pursuing the common good of political society, is a contingent matter. Thus, it may be that a single worldwide community is now, or will be in the future, the most plausible "complete society." Contrary claims about the sovereignty of nations would not be decisive if the authoritative coordination of the human interactions bearing on the whole set of human interests were shown to be best achieved by international arrangements that significantly qualify the sovereignty of nation-states.

In short, the natural-law tradition's conception of the common good of political society needs considerable development to make its precise implications for international relations clearer and more determinate. But it is clear enough that this notion does not justify the leaders of a nation in ignoring the interests of people and communities outside their own jurisdiction. The exercise of such sovereignty as any polity can rightly claim is limited by moral principle. Moreover, the common good of political society provides a basis for evaluating the claims of the leaders and the authority structure of any particular polity to be those uniquely capable of regulating and coordinating the whole range of human interactions within that group of people. The kind of sovereignty associated with the modern nation-state is not a naturally fixed moral reality, but needs a justification which in the present world it may lack.

Suggested reading

Aquinas's most important works are translated into most modern languages, and are readily available in English in several editions. His famous discussion of law, including natural law, occurs in questions 90 to 100 of the first part of the second part of the *Summa Theologiae*; his discussions of war and peace, justice, and the ethics of killing are in the second part of the second part. A useful collection of these and other important texts is: St. Thomas Aquinas, *On Law, Morality and Politics*, ed. W. Baumgarth and R. Regan (Indianapolis: Hackett Publishing Co., 1980). The most useful recent translation of the *Summa* is the sixty-volume Blackfriars edition. The most valuable volume is St. Thomas Aquinas, *Summa Theologiae: Latin text and English translation, Introductions, Notes, Appendices and Glossaries*, volume 28, *Law and Political Theory (1a2ae. 90–97)*, ed. Thomas Gilby (London and New York: Blackfriars, Eyre & Spottiswoode, McGraw-Hill Book Company, 1966).

Although his interpretation of Aquinas's ethical theory remains controversial, John Finnis (1980) provides the most thorough and useful recent synthesis of Thomistic legal and political thinking. Hittinger (1987) and Fortin (1982) develop the controversial issues; Grisez, Boyle and Finnis (1987) develop a response to some of the analytical issues raised. Maritain (1951, 1966) and Simon (1951) are also competent and influential examples of natural-law thinking based on a careful reading of Aquinas. The first chapter of Simon's book is a classic exposition of natural-law political philosophy. Messner (1965), though not as useful for understanding Aquinas, provides a mass of detail and reference to the considerable European literature.

Many of the works of later natural-law theorists are not available in modern English translation. Bernice Hamilton (1963) provides an accessible introduction to the sixteenth-century writers and literature.

Finnis, Boyle, and Grisez (1987) use natural-law categories and strategies to argue that nuclear deterrence is immoral. Michael Walzer (1977) shows the influence of natural-law thinking on the development of just-war doctrine. Alan Donagan (1977) develops the idea of common morality, shows the deep similarities between Kantian ethics and the natural-law tradition, and provides a number of illuminating discussions related to natural-law thinking and the ethical issues of international affairs. Taken together, these three books show the analytical relevance of natural-law thinking to international moral questions.

References

Anscombe, G. E. M. 1981a. "Modern Moral Philosophy." In *Ethics, Religion, and Politics: Collected Philosophical Papers*, vol. 3, 26–42. Minneapolis: University of Minnesota Press.

    1981b. "War and Murder." In *Ethics, Religion and Politics: Collected Philosophical Papers*, vol. 3, 51–61. Minneapolis: University of Minnesota Press.

    1982. "Action, Intention and 'Double Effect.'" *The Proceedings of the American Catholic Philosophical Association* 54: 12–25.

Aquinas, Thomas. 1942. *Summa Theologiae*, 5 volumes. Ottawa: Institute of Medieval Studies.

Boyle, Joseph. 1980. "Towards Understanding the Principle of Double Effect." *Ethics* 90: 527–38.

Calvez, Jean-Yves and Jacques Perrin. 1961. *The Church and Social Justice: The Social Teaching of the Popes from Leo XIII to Pius XII*. Chicago: Henry Regnery Company.

Curran, Charles and Richard McCormick, eds. 1979. *Readings in Moral Theology*, No. 1, *Moral Norms and Catholic Tradition*. New York: Paulist Press.

DeKoninck, Charles. 1945. "In Defense of St. Thomas: A Reply to Father Eschmann's Attack on the Primacy of the Common Good." *Laval Theologique et Philosophique* 1–2: 9–109.

Donagan, Alan. 1977. *The Theory of Morality*. Chicago: University of Chicago Press.

Finnis, John. 1980. *Natural Law and Natural Rights*. Oxford: Oxford University Press.

Finnis, John, Joseph Boyle, and Germain Grisez. 1987. *Nuclear Deterrence, Morality and Realism*. Oxford: Oxford University Press.

Fortin, Ernest. 1982. "The New Rights Theory and Natural Law." *The Review of Politics* 44: 590–612.

Freemantle, Anne, ed. 1963. *The Social Teachings of the Church*. New York: New American Library.

Fuller, Lon. 1964. *The Morality of Law*. New Haven, CT: Yale University Press.
1968. *Anatomy of the Law*. New York: Frederick Praeger Publishers.

Gerson, Lloyd. 1988. "Aristotle's Polis: A Community of the Virtuous." In *Proceedings of the Boston Area Colloquium in Ancient Philosophy*, vol. 3, ed. John Cleary, 203–25. Lanham, MD: The University Press of America.

Gremillion, Joseph. 1976. *The Gospel of Peace and Justice: Catholic Social Teaching Since Pope John*. Maryknoll, NY: Orbis Books.

Grisez, Germain, Joseph Boyle, and John Finnis. 1987. "Ultimate Principles, Moral Truth, and Ultimate Ends." *The American Journal of Jurisprudence* 22: 99–151.

Hamilton, Bernice. 1963. *Political Thought in Sixteenth-Century Spain: A Study of the Political Ideas of Vitoria, DeSoto, Suarez and Molina*. Oxford: Oxford University Press.

Hittinger, Russell. 1987. *A Critique of the New Natural-Law Theory*. Notre Dame: University of Notre Dame Press.

Jonsen, Albert and Stephen Toulmin. 1988. *The Abuse of Casuistry: A History of Moral Reasoning*. Berkeley: University of California Press.

Mangan, Joseph. 1949. "An Historical Analysis of the Principle of Double Effect." *Theological Studies* 10: 41–61.

Maritain, Jacques. 1951. *Man and the State*. Chicago: University of Chicago Press.
1966. *The Person and the Common Good*. Notre Dame: University of Notre Dame Press.

Messner, Johannes. 1965. *Social Ethics: Natural Law in the Western World*, revised edition. St. Louis MO: B. Herder Book Co.

Midgley, E. B. F. 1976. *The Natural-Law Tradition and the Theory of International Relations*. New York: Harper and Row.

Murray, John Courtney. 1960. *We Hold These Truths: Catholic Reflections on the American Proposition*. New York: Sheed and Ward.

Raz, Joseph. 1986. *The Morality of Freedom*. Oxford: Oxford University Press.

Schneewind, J. B. 1976. *Sidgwick's Ethics and Victorian Moral Philosophy*. Oxford: Oxford University Press.

Simon, Yves. 1951. *Philosophy of Democratic Government*. Chicago: University of Chicago Press.

Sumner, L. W. 1987. *The Moral Foundation of Rights*. Oxford: Oxford University Press.

Walzer, Michael. 1977. *Just and Unjust Wars*. New York: Basic Books.

7 KANT'S GLOBAL RATIONALISM

THOMAS DONALDSON

The impact of Immanuel Kant (1724–1804) on moral theory is ubiquitous. Kantian interpretations of ethical issues in medicine, economics, sociology, and politics flourish. Of special importance is the rapidly emerging influence of Kant on the literature of international affairs; as I hope to show, the Kantian tradition in application to international affairs offers a comprehensive, sophisticated methodology of interpretation. This methodology is agent-centered, places emphasis on moral motives, and allows principles to trump consideration of consequences. From the Kantian perspective, realism turns out to be sadly misguided; ideals prove to be a surer guide than empirical certainty; and cosmopolitanism becomes mandatory.

Kantian ethics

Kant's general theory

By Kant's own admission, his theory of morals provides the foundation for his political philosophy, including its international dimension. Best known for the *Critique of Pure Reason* (Kant 1929), in which he undertook a "Copernician"-style revolution in metaphysics that made experience beholden to the experiencing mind, Kant in his later moral writings utilizes much of the terminology and analysis presented in his earlier theoretical reflections. If our understanding of reality is conditioned by pure concepts known prior to experience (called by Kant *a priori* in order to distinguish them from concepts known after experience, called *a posteriori*), as he had argued in the first Critique, then similarly our action is subject to rational conditions established by pure, *a priori* concepts. He argues for this view especially in the *Groundwork of the Metaphysics of Morals* (Kant 1964a), and in the *Critique of Practical Reason* (Kant 1949) (the second Critique). According to Kant, all rational, purposive behavior must accord with conditions known independently from experience. The most important of these he calls the "categorical imperative," which bids us to treat others as having value in themselves, and to act in accordance with principles that are valid for all other actors.

Kant's general moral theory is thoroughly "deontological" in character. Indeed, most common definitions of "deontology" apply directly to his views. For example, it is common to define deontological theory as "agent-centered," i.e., as placing emphasis on an agent's moral motives, and as allowing principles and precepts to override consideration of consequences.[1] Both are hallmarks of Kantian analysis. Indeed, so pervasive is Kant's influence that moral and political theorists often find it difficult to define "deontology" apart from Kant's philosophy. Frequently enough, to say that something is "Kantian" is tantamount to saying it is deontological, and vice versa.

The word "deontology" is derived from a Greek word meaning duty, and signifies moral reasoning that is agent-centered and that construes right action as action of a certain form or kind. On a deontological view, an action's form frequently includes reference to a guiding principle held valid for relevantly similar acts under relevantly similar circumstances. Hence, Kant's emphasis on universalizable principles fits neatly into this framework. Deontology's agent-centeredness, which insists that motive is a key to evaluating an act, follows Kant's well-known distinction between an action merely done *in accordance* with obligation and one done *for the sake of* obligation. (Kant argues that the latter but not the former has moral worth.) Kant's deontological concepts emphasize the characteristics of an agent's actions in contrast to the actions' consequences, especially those characteristics which relate to motivating principles. In this sense, Kant's view is at sharp odds with the moral theory known as consequentialism, which holds that the only relevant factor in deciding whether any action or practice is morally right is its overall consequences (for a discussion of consequentialism as one aspect of utilitarianism, see the opening section of Chapter 8).

According to Kant, reason is the faculty that discovers moral principles, and it is reason, not inclination or interests (including state interests), which certifies right action. When reason guides action, the behavior is said to be motivated by "duty."

---

[1] The term, "agent centered," is often used in a loose and confusing manner. At a minimum the term implies that one's motives, i.e., what one aims at, and not merely the actual consequences of one's act, are relevant to the evaluation of the act. But it has also been interpreted to mean that deontological reasons are often not explainable in terms of "neutral" moral values, i.e., values with relevance to all moral agents, since the particular relation of the agent to the outcome is essential. "Deontological reasons," as Thomas Nagel puts is, "have their full force against your doing

Hence, acting from duty is not to be interpreted as acting in obedience to local, state, or even international law, since such law may be unreasonable. Instead, every moral obligation is linked to the idea of moral rationality, a link independent of an actor's position, place, or status. By tying rationality to the heart of moral deliberation, Kant thus makes a crucial move against the Aristotelian natural-law tradition, dissolving the hierarchy subordinating practical to theoretical reason. (Interestingly enough, the Aristotelian tradition also assigns a critical role to reason; see "Practical reasoning and moral dilemmas," Chapter 6). For Kant the same underlying rationality functions both in theoretical and practical endeavors. Reason is the faculty that seeks the unconditioned, which is to say that it seeks that which has no further cause or explanation. But reason *finds* the unconditioned, the categorical imperative, in practical activity while it cannot find it in theoretical activity. This occurs because in theoretical activity reason is doomed always to seek a further cause or explanation. Hence, for Kant practical reason is in one important sense prior to theoretical reason: its task is to guide theoretical reason.

The essence of acting morally for Kant does not lie in achieving self-interest or national interest, even when those pursuits are "enlightened" ones. Nor does it lie, as Aristotle believed, in actualizing human potential. Rather, it lies in responding to a demand of reason. This demand, the categorical imperative, implies that we all possess equal and unqualified value, a moral fact that entails, in turn, that we must act for the sake of that equal value.

The split envisaged by Aristotle and the modern scientific mind between the soft, changing realm of practice and the unchanging objects of natural science is absent in Kant. Reason apprehends the moral imperative just as it apprehends the axioms of geometry or of theoretical physics. This allows Kant to say: "Two things are unceasing sources of awe for man: The starry heavens above us, and the moral law within us" (Kant 1949, 113).

The categorical imperative, as the highest of moral principles, is the universal of universals, the principle that serves as a guide to the discovery of all subordinate moral principles. It is not simply a rule of conduct but also a criterion or test of the moral validity of particular rules. Kant formulates his famous imperative in a variety of ways, but the most important concepts it manifests are (1) maxim-universalizability, and (2) the notion of rational beings as having value as ends in themselves.

something – not just against its happening" (1986, 177). See Nagel's discussion of agent-centered deontological theory, and of agent-relative reasons (1986, 164–85).

138

By the former Kant means that one ought only to act such that the principle (or "maxim") of one's act could become a universal law of human action. As H. J. Paton puts it, we ought not act on maxims that fail to facilitate a "harmony of purposes among rational beings" (Paton 1947). By the latter notion Kant means that one must treat other rational beings as having value in themselves; in particular, the imperative bids us never to treat rational agents as mere means to our, or anyone else's, ends.

Problems with the general theory

More than most philosophers, Kant is subject to misinterpretation. He has been accused of making moral decisions in a causal vacuum, with no consideration of consequences; and, indeed, Kant refused to make consequences the moral litmus test of action. But this does not mean that the consideration of consequences is morally irrelevant. In clarifying Kant's theory, we note first that *hypothetical* consequences play an obvious role in the process of universalizing principles, since in imagining a world following a hypothetical maxim we imagine the empirical consequences of rule adoption. Empirical facts, Kant asserts repeatedly, are to be the "empirical spring" of moral reflection. However, Lewis White Beck illustrates the sense in which Kant *did* believe consequences to be irrelevant with the following example: Suppose two soldiers volunteer for a dangerous mission. Of course the consequences they pursue are an integral part of what makes their proposed act worth doing. That is to say, our evaluation of their action is influenced by our moral evaluation of the hoped-for consequences of the mission itself. But in what sense, then, does Kant mean that consequences do *not* matter? Suppose both try as hard as they can but, through fortune, one fails and is killed; then how are we to evaluate the two acts morally? For Kant, each deserves the same moral praise or blame despite the fact that the outcomes of the two acts were quite different (Beck 1960).

Another persistent confusion involves the level of specificity in framing maxims when attempting to universalize them. Should maxims be framed in general terms, such as "Never make a lying promise," or, in specific terms, such as "Canadians should never misspell their names on their income tax forms"? Kant knew well that excessively specific principles were inappropriate candidates. The proper level of generality must be struck – an activity which itself must be informed by moral rationality. For example, in his famous discussion of the lying promise, Kant knew well that a maxim considered by

John Doe reading "If one is named John Doe, has a birthmark below his left ear, and lives in Konigsberg, then he may borrow fifty dollars without intending to repay it," is too specific. On the other hand the principle "repay any debt," is too general since it would require that a starving man repay the only money he possesses to buy a loaf of bread. To solve the problem of striking the proper degree of generality, many modern theorists interpret Kant's test to read: "Could I will that everyone in the world would follow this principle under *relevantly similar conditions?*"

Hence a sufficient level of generality is essential for Kant when framing principles, and making conditions too specific leads to confusion. It leads Steven Luper-Foy, for example, to accuse Kant of inconsistency at the international level. "Note," he writes, that Kant's theory neglects the fact that "people in relatively poor nations would favor bringing about a global order in which everyone acts from the maxim that goods should be fairly equally distributed" while, in contrast, the rich would "endorse a maxim of inequity, according to which wide disparities are tolerated." Or, he argues, "People in France (say) could refuse to provide aid to those in other nations because the French could become and remain happy and rational were they part of a global order in which everyone acted from the maxim that all and only French people are to receive aid" (Luper-Foy 1988, 11–12). But the earlier analysis shows why Luper-Foy's interpretation is a confusion. For Kant, a morally relevant condition of similarity when prescribing principles of action for foreign aid or international economic transfers would *not* be being French, or rich, or poor. The subject of the categorical imperative is never more specific than that of a "rational being," and it is morally irrelevant that one is a French rational being, or a rich rational being, or a poor rational being. Indeed, this helps explain the affinity between Kant and the twentieth-century US philosopher, John Rawls. Rawls explicitly acknowledges that his theory of justice, with its veil of ignorance, owes much to Kant (Rawls 1971).

Kantian epistemology

Kant's insistence on the gulf between reason and nature, and between theoretical and practical reason, is apparent in the division of subject matter between his first and second Critiques. The first Critique investigates theoretical reason; it begins with experience of the world and moves to a discovery of *a priori* concepts and principles. The second Critique investigates practical reason; it begins with *a priori* principles and concepts (in particular, the categorical imperative), and then moves to human action. While such epistemological distinctions appear arcane, and while Kant's own awkward style of exposition aggravates this appearance, they are important in understanding the application of his moral philosophy to international affairs.

Consider, for example, Kant's refusal to let empirical fact ground morality. While Hobbes thought it possible to argue from the essentially self-interested nature of man to a theory of morals, Kant believes such a task wholly impossible. Even if he thought people were thoroughly self-interested (and he did not) Kant would have denied fundamental moral import to any mere fact about human nature. This is because he believed the way the world *is* cannot be used to derive the way it *ought* to be.

A few simple epistemological distinctions underlie Kant's separation of what he sometimes called the "realm of nature" and the "realm of freedom" (i.e., of morality). As mentioned earlier, knowledge has two sources for Kant, the *a priori* and the *a posteriori*. The former is connected to rational reflection, the latter to experience. *A priori* knowledge is marked by two characteristics, necessity and universality. Thus, for example, the *a priori* propositions "every event has a cause," or "all rational beings ought to treat other rational beings as ends in themselves and not merely as means," are said to be both necessary and universal while not depending upon experience for their warranty. The sense of necessity we sometimes feel in ethics, i.e., that something "must" be done or "must" not be done, is from Kant's perspective, a clue to the judgment's *a priori* character. Consider our likely reaction to the possibility of someone's discriminating against a nation simply because its inhabitants happen to be black. If our reaction is that one *must* not discriminate in this manner, Kant will ask where our sense of "must" is derived. It cannot come, he will reply, from the empirical situation itself, for this can never ground rational necessity (things can always be imagined otherwise), but rather from what we rationally impose on the situation, i.e., from what *we* demand. It comes, in other words, from a demand of reason in application to action.

Hence the categorical imperative, which is the essence of rational morality, is said by Kant to be *a priori*, and to contain no *a posteriori* or empirical elements. But as soon as the categorical imperative is applied to a practical context, he grants that empirical considerations intrude. This happens because the purposes and desires of the particular kind of rational being we are, i.e., a human being, are particular and *a posteriori*. Experience must be consulted to know, for example, that

141

humans must eat to survive, that blacks are victims of systematic discrimination, and that the world food supply is adequate but maldistributed. It is no surprise, then, to find Kant writing in the preface to the *Groundwork of the Metaphysics of Morals* (Kant 1964a) that moral philosophy has both an empirical and a non-empirical part. Ethics has an empirical part relating to anthropology, and it has a rational, non-empirical part which is *a priori*.

Kantian internationalism

Most international theorists correctly interpret Kantian morals as entailing implicit universalism. R. J. Vincent, for example, compares Kant's theory to the Christian doctrine expressed in St. Paul's epistle to the Galatians: "There is neither Jew nor Greek, there is neither bond nor free, there is neither male nor female; for ye are all one in Christ Jesus" (Vincent 1986, 35). Kantian morals also demand a full-blown freedom for the moral agent, and this freedom becomes Kant's preoccupation in the political realm. "Since every restriction of freedom through the arbitrary will of another party is termed coercion," Kant writes, "it follows that a civil constitution is a relationship among free men who are subject to coercive laws, while they retain their freedom within the general union with their fellows. Such is the requirement of pure reason, which legislates *a priori*, regardless of all empirical ends" (Kant 1971a, 73).

Kant's international theorizing contrasts to the "cooperative" emphasis of Hobbesian and Rawlsian theories. Both Hobbes and Rawls emphasize the fruits of cooperation in their interpretation of justice. For Hobbes the incentives of cooperation, and for Rawls the mere fact of cooperation, are essential to positing the obligations of justice. Hence, on both conceptions, justice in the international realm becomes suspect where cooperative schemes appear scarce and fragile. For Kant, in contrast, existing or potential cooperation, considered merely as an empirical matter, is largely irrelevant when framing the responsibility of global actors. Charles Beitz is surely wrong, then, when he asserts that for Kant "international economic cooperation creates a new basis for international morality" (Beitz 1979, 144). The basis for international morality must remain for Kant what it is for domestic morality: the moral demand of reason. Morality justifies cooperation; not the reverse. While international cooperation may, as an empirical matter, make it more possible to create a league of nations, the reasons why we want a league or, for that matter, any form of international cooperation, derive from our *a priori* concepts of morality (the idea of cooperation or "reciprocity" in the thought of Hobbes, Kant, Rawls, and Beitz is discussed in Chapter 9).

Kantian cosmopolitanism affirms the existence of cross-cultural moral truth, at least to the point of affirming a cross-cultural basis for moral truth, and stands opposed to cultural relativism or extreme realism, which denies that moral concepts have any international purchase. It stands opposed, then, to what Steven Forde has called the "thoroughgoing" realist position in Chapter 4 of this volume. For the cultural relativist, either there is no ethical truth or else such truth is merely the consensus of an individual culture. Cultural relativism thus appears to defend tolerance and condemn imperialism while condemning attempts to elevate local morality to the status of universal morality. From the perspective of such relativism, as Vincent notes, Kantian "universality" appears to be little more than a well-disguised attempt to make the values of a particular culture general, and documents such as the Universal Declaration of Human Rights, passed by the United Nations in 1948, become "futile proclamations, derived from the moral principles valid in one culture and thrown out into the moral void between cultures" (Vincent 1986, 38).

Called by some the "anthropologist's heresy," cultural relativism has not fared well as a philosophical doctrine. Philosophers are quick to note that cultural relativism, contrary to appearances, bears little resemblance to tolerance. If a culture disapproves of the Shiite Moslem practice of having women wear veils, yet owing to its tolerance believes nonetheless that it should refrain from forcing its views on Shiite Moslems, then tolerance counts as a *moral*, not a relativistic, value. Many also observe that virtually no person can live with cultural relativism's severe consequences because consistent cultural relativism demands jettisoning more than naive relativists imagine. Granted, when toying with the prospect of relativism, most are willing to allow that prejudice and custom infect many cultural norms. It is only custom that makes British rules of etiquette that require, for example, the fork to be used in the left hand, "better" than American rules of etiquette. But for most people the moral buck stops somewhere. First-century Romans followed a law under which, if a slave owner was killed by one of his slaves, *all* of his slaves were executed, even ones entirely innocent of the murder, and the law was applied strictly to households of three hundred and more slaves. We may predict that many people considering such extreme examples will leaven their cultural relativism.

Hence, Kant's categorical imperative stands as a clear alternative to relativism and extreme realism. It is, in a word, a "cosmopolitan" doctrine that treats all humans, by virtue of their shared rationality, as citizens of a single moral order.

It is important to remember, however, that for Kant the demand of practical rationality, not an actual consensus, underlies cosmopolitanism. No matter how striking or intriguing attempts to establish international morality on the basis of cooperative possibilities or cultural evolution may be, these empirical considerations carry, for Kant, no fundamental moral weight.

Kant's point applies even to R. J. Vincent's recent, fascinating attempt to suggest that the existence of universal human rights may be predicated on the recognition of the existence, or future emergence of, a "single cosmopolitan culture." Vincent speaks of this single cosmopolitan culture, "which is spread across all indigenous cultures, and which carries to each of them what are, in some at least geographical sense, global human rights." "All over the world," he notes, "individuals have been pulled away by its [the common culture of modernity's] operation from their traditional attachment to the local community." In this way, he argues, we are returned in an important sense to the "single moral universe of the natural rights theorists" (Vincent 1986, 56).

Vincent realizes that there is a Kantian objection to this proposal, and that the existence of a common, emerging global culture cannot in itself define and justify international rights. The attempt to ground the legitimacy of rights on the emerging global culture, he writes, "may be a grandiose version of the naturalistic fallacy – deriving statements about how people ought to behave from statements about how in fact they do behave" (Vincent 1986, 53). From Kant's perspective this is correct. No matter how awe-inspiring the international convergence of diverse cultures upon a single set of values may be, the convergence is from Kant's vantage point merely an empirical fact. And, as in law, an empirical convergence of value may be either right or wrong.

For Kant, international morality must be based not on any empirical fact or probability, but simply on the authority of the categorical imperative, the demand of practical reason that informs the activity of all rational agents. Whether or not globalism, moral consensus, or global cooperation actually emerges, Kant would defend the existence of global obligations, and their corollaries, global human rights. Even if the world were, and appeared destined to be, a barbarous Hobbesian free-for-all, with each nation insisting upon its own peculiar morality, Kant would argue that practical reason forbids indiscriminate killing, intentional lying, and other acts violating our hypothetical postulated citizenship. This is because even if there were no possibility of realizing the outcomes prescribed by the categorical imperative, practical reason demands that we must act *as if* there were.

Kant's own application of moral philosophy to the international realm occurs primarily in two works, the "Metaphysical Elements of Justice" (one of the two sections of the *Metaphysics of Morals* [Kant 1964b and 1965]), and *Perpetual Peace* (Kant 1971b). Three guiding concepts that appear in these works unlock his entire approach: (1) the view of the state as a moral person, (2) the original, communal ownership of the earth and its resources by all persons, (3) the demand to strive for perpetual peace.

The first is a metaethical rather than normative concept. It asserts that the state is a moral person, living in a condition of natural freedom and subject to a social contract with other states. This is a statement about the structure of moral rationality, not about how someone ought to behave. Kant's remarkably strong doctrine of the moral personhood of the state, which envisages the nation state as subject to most if not all of the obligations to which individuals are subject, marks the Kantian perspective as theoretically spare yet metaphysically ambitious. It is spare because the ordinary problem of reducing collective acts of organizations to those of individual persons (what philosophers sometimes refer to as the issue of "methodological individualism") disappears for Kant. It is ambitious because the metaphysical baggage it carries is suspicious to the modern mind. The view of the collective as a "big person" has unsettling implications for temperaments honed by science and analytic rigor. Nonetheless, Kant remembers to identify other actors as morally significant in international affairs. In the section entitled "Definition of the Law of Nations" in *The Metaphysical Elements of Justice* (Kant 1965) he writes that the principal difference between the state of nature that exists among individuals or among families and that which exists among nations is only that the Law of Nations is concerned both with the relationship of "one state to another," and with "relationships of individuals in one state to individuals in another and of an individual to another whole state" (Kant 1965, 115).

According to Kant, each state has an "original right" to defend itself from harm, but the state of nature, sometimes referred to as the state of "war," is regarded by him as "unjust in the highest degree" (Kant 1965, 116). It follows that a confederation of states in accordance with the concept of a social contract is mandatory to afford mutual protection against aggression. Like Bentham and other eighteenth- and nineteenth-century reformers, Kant hoped to modify existing practice to allow a somewhat more centralized order, and thus reduce the

145

uncertainty of international rules while preserving the basic sovereignty of individual states (Nardin 1983, 21–22). Kant's confederation or "alliance" involves no sovereign authority and can be renounced by individual states at any time. In turn, it requires constant renewal. Kant believed that a world government patterned after national governments would be impossible to govern, owing to the vastness of the territories involved. For any individual state in the confederation of states, self-defense turns out, for Kant, to be the only justification for going to war, but the notion of self-defense is interpreted with sufficient liberality to include preemptive attacks under special circumstances.

The remaining two concepts are normative or prescriptive. Kant asserts that all nations originally held the earth's land in community, a view he believes follows from the earth's possession of a limited boundary. Charles Beitz has even suggested a comparison between Kant's position and Rawls's notion of original possession, with the attendant Rawlsian insistence on the moral arbitrariness of original holdings. Whether this interpretation can be sustained is not entirely clear. Although never specific about the rights and duties that flow from this original possession, Kant does clearly believe that communal possession carries weight even after the social contract is in place; for he notes that the rights and duties flowing from original communal possession justify attempts at open trade and inform the establishment of certain universal laws regarding the intercourse of nations (Kant 1965, 352–53). And, in contrast to neo-Hobbesian thinkers such as David Gauthier, he condemns, on the grounds of original communal possession, attempts to colonize primitive peoples such as the American Indian when there is no voluntary contractual agreement from all sides (Gauthier 1986).

The third and final concept posits lasting or perpetual peace as a necessary ideal and condemns all acts, by individuals or nations, that would prevent such a peace. Combining the categorical imperative with his general doctrine of peace, Kant defines an "unjust enemy" as one who adopts a maxim that if universalized would make lasting peace impossible. In *Perpetual Peace* (Kant 1971b), Kant argues that we must act in accordance with the idea of perpetual peace even if it appears unlikely to be realized.

On this point – which demonstrates the vast gulf between the function of the theoretical and moral realms in Kant's philosophy – even Charles Beitz, who grasps much of its subtlety, underestimates Kant's theoretical radicalism. Beitz correctly notes that many objections to Kant misrepresent the relation between ideal theory and the real world, and that "the ideal cannot be undermined simply by pointing out that it cannot be achieved at present." In order to understand Kant's point, he argues, one must distinguish between impediments to change that are modifiable over time and those that are unalterable (Beitz 1979, 156). Presumably while the latter may sometimes count as sufficient reasons for not demanding compliance with obligations of peace, the former cannot. But Kant's doctrine is more radical even than this. In *The Metaphysics of Morals* he writes that "what duty requires is that we act in accordance with the Idea of such an end (i.e., of perpetual peace), even if *there is not the slightest theoretical probability that it is feasible*" (Kant 1964b, emphasis added). Kant's only nod to practicality is that the "impossibility of the end cannot be demonstrated." His rationale for apparently denying the well-known philosophical dictum that "ought implies can" is that individual acts consistent with perpetual peace may be possible even if pessimism about the cooperation of others and inherent psychological dispositions of humanity make perpetual peace seem implausible.

Kant's own verdict, by the way, is positive. In "Idea of a Universal History from a Cosmopolitan Point of View" (Kant 1963a), he argues in typical *a priori* fashion for the possibility that our actions occur in the context of a providential scheme. The implications of our nature are not visible through examination of single members of the species, but appear only in the context of society at large and succeeding generations, and for Kant this is a clue to the prospect of a long-term plan. Even the development of an individual's creativity requires a social context and multigenerational learning; and, because nature's implanting of creative possibilities in humanity presumes that such possibilities could be developed, we may hope that a form of civil society will emerge which fosters such development. Do we not have reason to hope, Kant asks, that republican constitutions and, in turn, the league of nations requisite for maintaining international society in a state of peace, will emerge? While Kant's use of abstract reason to deduce conclusions about future events has drawn sharp criticism, such arguments make clear his own optimism about the possibility of international peace.

Even lacking the prospect of peace, all of us are obliged to push for republican forms of government (which Kant regarded as more likely to keep the peace), to honor treaties with other states, and to refrain from acts that impede peace. We must also work to preserve peace through international institutional arrangements, especially through the "confederation" of states mentioned above. For Kant, the absence of hostilities is not equivalent to the peace demanded by our moral ideal, for unless the absence of hostilities is supported by formal institutions, the constant threat of war remains (Kant 1971b, 98). Peace, according to Kant, is a juridical rather than a natural condition (Nardin 1983, 283).

Kant's seeming optimism, for which he is roundly criticized, is nonetheless limited. His international moralism is tempered by his recognition of the great difficulty that any international confederation that lacks the power of sanction will have protecting a system of moral practices. Kant cynically questions the efficacy of international law so long as nations themselves are free from external sanction. And he dismisses defenders of international law such as Vattel, Pufendorf, and Grotius, as "sorry comforters" whose codes "do not and cannot have the slightest *legal* force, since states as such are not subject to a common external constraint" (Kant 1971b, 103).

Because his doctrine of peace proscribes all acts inconsistent with the end of peace, Kant's view here may be called the moral "doctrine of possible peace." It has an important corollary, often overlooked by interpreters, which I shall call the "doctrine of possible personhood." In *The Metaphysics of Morals* (Kant 1964b and 1965) Kant advances this doctrine by insisting that even if war is under way, measures may not be undertaken that have the effect of making "a subject of that state unfit to be a citizen." He continues by saying that if such measures were employed by the state, they would thereby make the state unfit to be considered a person in relation to other states in the eyes of the Law of Nations, and this, in turn, would destroy the mutual faith necessary to generate an enduring peace in the future (Kant 1965, 120). This doctrine of possible state personhood rules out a vast assortment of acts, according to Kant, including the use of spies, borrowing by the public treasury to finance war, conquest, plundering, employing poisoners or assassins, spreading false rumors, and even using guerrillas who "wait for individuals in ambush."

The picture that emerges of Kant's international doctrines is one of specific norms tied to an underlying moral theory. To simplify: the moral law, i.e., the categorical imperative, is the source of the idea of perpetual peace and this idea, in turn, informs national and individual obligations to foreigners and foreign nations. The notion of "possible state personhood" is analogous to the respect for persons mandated by the categorical imperative's prescription that we treat other rational agents as having worth in themselves, and never as mere means to ends.

Kant's moral doctrine clearly has application to international affairs beyond the rather narrow concerns of war and peace which Kant tended to emphasize. For example, as Onora O'Neill and others have argued, Kant's notion of "possible state personhood" in his theory of law could plausibly oblige a rich nation to save the lives of starving persons in a poor nation, especially when that notion is conjoined with the imperfect obligation of benevolence he describes in the *Groundwork* and elsewhere. And Kant's full-blown concept of state personhood implies, as Kant's own discussions tend to confirm, that states share virtually every general universalizable obligation possessed by rational individuals. Hence such personal obligations as keeping promises, refraining from lying, and furthering the happiness of individuals have direct application to states. The extension of individual morality to large organizations, which might be called the "moral person" view of organizational agency (Donaldson 1982, Ch. 2), has been articulated in the twentieth century by philosopher Marshall Cohen, who defends against Hobbesian detractors the view that states are subject to the same general moral obligations as individuals (Cohen 1984, 299–346).

None of this implies that Kant was unaware of the significant moral differences separating individuals and states. Nardin is correct to include Kant in the influential group of eighteenth-century European thinkers such as Montesquieu, Voltaire, Burke, and Martens who recognized the society of states as a distinct, historical institution not to be confused with the broader, global society of individual persons. And he is probably also correct to assert that, in contrast to Hobbes and his followers, Kant views international society as depending not on a simple coincidence of state interests, but on a shared conception of an authoritative body of practices and rules (Nardin 1983, 309). Yet, in embracing this latter conception, Kant did not distinguish fundamentally between the moral agency of individuals and states. The association of states necessary to preserve peace entails special obligations much as a unique set of relations among a group of persons entails special obligations. States, like persons in unique relationships, must recognize specific moral problems and moral precepts; the universalizable imperatives that rationality imposes remain the same for states and individuals. For example, in *Perpetual Peace* Kant affirms a nonintervention principle as a "preliminary article" based on respect for the internal procedures of individual state governance of individual states and in the interests of preventing hostilities. But, in citing this specific, state-oriented obligation, Kant not only relies on his general theory of individual morality to identify the goal of perpetual peace; he also invokes a notion of "respect" for state autonomy reminiscent of the

149

"respect" for individual autonomy that pervades his general moral writings.

The Kantian-deontological approach to international affairs

The broad outlines of the contemporary deontological tradition, which includes representatives as disparate as Rawlsian social-contract theory and Gewirthian rationalism, are Kantian in form. Kant's historical impact on this contemporary form of philosophizing is difficult to exaggerate, and the form itself probably constitutes the dominant contemporary tradition of moral reasoning among philosophers. Even those rare contemporary deontologists who do not pay respects to Kant espouse theories with many resemblances to his.

It is worth noting in this vein that most contemporary rights-based theories are also deontological theories with Kantian affinities. Rights are principles that assign claims or entitlements to someone against someone (Feinberg 1966; 1970), and are usually interpreted as "trumping" or taking precedence over consequential claims made in the name of collective welfare (Dworkin 1977). Hence, both in their similarity of form (as a principle universally applicable to relevantly similar situations), and in their similarity of function (as taking precedence over collective, consequential considerations), they satisfy two key deontological/Kantian criteria. While it is possible to defend rights from a consequential perspective, that is, in terms of their ability to generate the maximal good, the validity of rights on this view is always beholden to their consequential power. For these and other reasons, most philosophers who view rights as fundamental moral notions consider themselves deontologists rather than consequentialists (for a more detailed discussion of the nature of rights, see "Rights in a cross-section of world society," Chapter 12).

Neo-Kantians such as Alan Donagan have claimed to discover Kantian precepts in the broad context of what in the first chapter we called "common morality," especially formulations of traditional Western morality such as those of Judaism and Christianity. Kant would have agreed with this view, for he repeatedly reminds his readers that in presenting his own theory of morality he is not pretending to discover *new* normative concepts, but only to articulate more precisely what is embedded in the insight of ordinary morality. And he explicitly compares the "respect" demanded by the categorical imperative to "love" in the Christian tradition. One way Donagan defends his view that Kantianism squares with common morality is by focusing upon the second rather than the first formulation of Kant's categorical imperative (i.e., the imperative of treating others as ends in themselves rather than as mere means). Donagan argues that this principle is fundamental to the Hebrew-Christian tradition. One notable implication is that two streams of moral reflection ordinarily thought to be disparate – the truths of reflective rationality and religious tradition – intersect on critical issues, as the natural-law tradition has maintained since the thirteenth century.[2]

As interest in international affairs has grown, so too has the application of deontological and Kantian perspectives to international problems. Deontological theorists such as Alan Gewirth, Henry Shue, Alan Donagan, Terry Nardin, Onora O'Neill, and Marshall Cohen have explicitly affirmed the use of deontological concepts in international affairs. Their interpretation contrasts sharply with that of consequentialists such as Peter Singer, Shelly Kagan, and Russell Hardin, who are inclined to factor even international principles through consequential considerations.

Deontologists war among themselves, sometimes in the international arena, as Onora O'Neill's critique of rights-based approaches to international affairs and her subsequent recommendation of a duty-based approach reveals. The issue she discusses is whether international problems can be handled exclusively through a doctrine of rights, as appears to be the tendency of many contemporary theorists, or whether they submit more easily to a morality purged of rights talk, one that substitutes duties for rights. In the same context, many argue, we should add the concept of Kantian imperfect duties to our international conceptual tool box.

Others have joined O'Neill in asserting that the present preoccupation with rights in the international realm is misplaced (O'Neill 1988). Duties, not rights, they say, should be our deontological focus, not only because rights are a relatively new historical invention, but because duties ground rights: rights entail duties of forbearance or action by those who are bound to respect them. They argue, then, that one has nothing to lose, and everything to gain, by moving from talk of rights to duties. One advantage of speaking of duties stems from the notion of the so-called "imperfect" duty formulated by Kant. Whereas all rights and all perfect duties require specific actions or omissions by moral agents on behalf of either all others or at least specified others, imperfect duties require omissions or actions for unspecified others, but not for all others. The advantage, claims O'Neill and others, of approaching international problems such as hunger and poverty by

2 See Donagan (1977).

way of a theory of obligations is that we are not restricted to considering those perfect obligations that correspond to human rights. The construction of duty can be used to identify principles of imperfect obligation and, in turn, human needs. O'Neill writes:

> Wherever there is endemic hunger, and the poor health and raised death rates that hunger brings, we know that the material conditions necessary for human agency to grow and survive are fragile and failing ... Because human beings are vulnerable and needy, a commitment to act on principles that can be shared by all has to include a commitment to develop capacities to act ... Neither developing human potential nor offering needed help can be a matter of justice. Nor could either be a matter of perfect obligation for the standard reason that neither is the sort of policy that we can enact completely. We cannot develop all the potential of all human beings. (O'Neill 1988, 81–82)

O'Neill, nonetheless, seems vulnerable to an interpretation of rights that allows something other than perfect duties as rights-correlatives. As long as all the duties correlative to rights are perfect duties, her argument appears to preclude a doctrine of rights as a comprehensive international moral perspective, insofar as such a doctrine misses the imperfect duties of, for example, charity. But what if one allows different classes of duties as correlative to rights, one class of which is the imperfect duty to aid the deprived? Short of an argument exhibiting that rights can have no such correlatives, which O'Neill herself fails to provide, rights doctrines appear to regain comprehensive scope and impact.[3] If the defense of rights is successful, it suggests once again that the language of rights and the language of duty are not as different as many imagine (for further discussion of the relationship between rights and duties, see the beginning of Chapter 12).

While the various contemporary theories of ethics, including most versions of consequentialism and deontology, exhibit normative convergence to a surprising degree and speak with univocal force in condemning, say, governmental torture of political dissidents or non-defensive war, they often clash on more complex issues. Deontologists have historically viewed the plight of the noncombatant with alarm in an era of nuclear deterrence, citing the proscription against the killing of the innocent, while consequentialists denounce principled sticklers and point to the lessened probability of nuclear war through deterrence.

The "functional specialization" argument exemplifies how different

---

[3] Another criticism of Onora O'Neill's argument which reaches the same conclusion by a slightly different route is Aiken (1988).

background theories may suggest different conclusions. This argument about international institutions takes the form of a stipulative definition. Frequently, the *function* of a given international organization, such as the International Monetary Fund (IMF), is to promote a certain good. The IMF's function is to promote exchange stability and to provide short-term assistance in balance of payments problems. The "functional specialization" argument claims that the IMF is not obliged to promote development, distributive justice, or human rights, since that is not what the organization was designed to do. For the purpose of promoting development, for example, we already have institutions such as the World Bank. To take other examples, it is often argued that the *function* of the multinational corporation is to maximize return on investment for its shareholders, not to serve as a moral exemplar; and that the *function* of the nation-state is to secure the welfare of its citizens, not those of other nations.

These specialization arguments are frequently devices for limiting the moral responsibility of international agents, and are consequential in character. Typically those asserting them presume that overall good is enhanced by specialization. That is to say, good is maximized by having institutions that focus upon balance of payments problems or upon serving the welfare of a specific citizenry. Those who want to refute such claims commonly employ deontological arguments, and assert that universalizable principles, such as human rights, must be respected by all persons and organizations regardless of a given organization's function or design. Hence, insofar as the IMF or multinational corporations fail to exercise the correlative duties attached to human rights, deontologists will say that they have failed morally, even though they may have succeeded in achieving their mission. (In fairness, it should be noted that consequentialists, too, may criticize the specialization arguments, but only to deny the empirical connection between the instance of specialization at issue and maximal overall welfare; also see Chapter 12 for a discussion of the rights of multinationals and groups besides the state.)

Still another area of controversy in which deontological arguments are common is the interpretation of global responsibility generally. For example, in *Law, Morality, and the Relations of States*, Nardin considers whether the efficient accommodation of aggregate interests among nations can itself give rise to moral duties. This issue has a clear answer from the Kantian-deontological perspective. No matter how efficient a coordination strategy is from the perspective of game theory, and no matter how efficiently the observance of international moral precepts secures the maximal satisfaction of the aggregate interests of nation-states, such considerations cannot be morally decisive from a Kantian perspective. Rather, what is decisive is whether the precepts embody the moral rationality governing all human behavior – precepts that deserve respect regardless of consequences.

The apparent imperfections of the Kantian-deontological tradition are topics of intense philosophical debate. It is often said, I believe correctly, that Kant's international doctrine suffers from incompleteness. For example, we should like to know how Kant's sketch of nations understood through the social contract fits with his broader moral theory of the categorical imperative. And we should like to know how his extreme view of the moral agency of states jibes with his attachment of morality to the rationality of the individual. While individual persons clearly have a single ego and manifest autonomous rationality, something Kant refers to as the "noumenal" self, it is difficult to imagine the noumenal counterpart of, say, the Soviet Union or Monaco.

Another frequently voiced criticism of the Kantian-deontological tradition concerns the formulation of moral principles. So few principles appear to be truly universalizable that the further specification of principles, in turn, seems necessary, and critics assert that this process cannot proceed without fundamental reference to consequential considerations. Like the principle, "never lie," the principles "never harm innocents" and "never intervene in the affairs of sovereign nations" seem susceptible to specifiable, if rare, counterexamples. Article 2(4) of the United Nations Charter instructs all states to "refrain in their international relations from the threat or use of force against the territorial integrity or political independence of any state or in any other manner inconsistent with the Purposes of the United Nations." But even here, in one of the strongest proscriptions on intervention, two exceptions are identified: namely, self-defense and force authorized by the UN Security Council. But what, critics will ask, is to guide the UN Security Council in its deliberations about intervention if not consequential considerations? And, if the exceptions defining application of deontological principles are hostage to consequential considerations, then are the principles themselves not also hostage? (For a discussion of some of these tensions in modern international law, see "Contradictions and comparisons," Chapter 3).

Whatever the outcome of such disputes, the thrust of the Kantian-deontological moral tradition in application to international events is clear: the tradition warns us of the pitfalls of allowing the end to justify the means, and of reducing the good for all humankind to the prejudices of a single community, collective, or nation. Whatever the flaws of the Kantian-deontological tradition, indeed, no matter what verdict we finally reach on the correctness of deontological moral logic, this insistence on principle over calculation stands as its practical raison d'être.

Suggested reading

Kant's moral theory is articulated primarily in six writings: *Groundwork of the Metaphysics of Morals* (1964a), *Critique of Practical Reason* (1949), *The Metaphysics of Morals* (which contains "The Metaphysical Principles of Virtue" (1964a) and "The Metaphysical Elements of Justice" (1965)), *Lectures on Ethics* (1963b), "On the Common Saying: 'This May be True in Theory, but it does Not Apply in Practice'" (1971a), and *Perpetual Peace* (1971b).

Kant discusses general moral philosophy far more than international affairs, and asserts that his moral interpretation of international affairs is meant to follow directly from his general moral philosophy. For that reason one cannot hope to understand the former without the latter. It is wise to begin with the *Groundwork* (1964a), and proceed next to the *Critique of Practical Reason* (1949). The *Groundwork* (1964a) assumes the perspective of ordinary moral experience and then delineates moral principles. The work is brief and accessible. The second Critique (1949), however, is a more formidable undertaking. It adopts the reverse order of exposition from that taken in the *Groundwork*, beginning with principles and moving to an explanation of ordinary moral experience. And because the discussion frequently makes use of technical terminology used in Kant's epistemology, readers should have some acquaintance with Kant's project in the *Critique of Pure Reason* (1929). The understanding of both the *Groundwork* and the *Critique of Practical Reason* works is enhanced by reading H. J. Paton's *The Categorical Imperative* (Paton 1947) or Lewis White Beck's *A Commentary on Kant's Critique of Practical Reason* (1960). Paton's book remains, in my opinion, the best overall treatment of Kant's moral philosophy.

Kant frequently wrote for a popular audience, and two such writings are helpful in rounding out his moral theory: *Lectures on Ethics* (1963b), which contains his university lectures on topics of ethics, and "On the Common Saying: 'This May be True in Theory, but it does Not Apply in Practice'" (1971a), which offers a defense of the role of theory in practical affairs.

For a detailed analysis of the many formulations of Kant's categorical imperative, see Aune (1979) and Doore (1985).

To find Kant's specific discussions of international obligations, especially the obligations of nation-states, one should read especially *The Metaphysics of Morals* (1964a and 1965) and *Perpetual Peace* (1971b). Also helpful are the many passages scattered throughout the Kantian writings that describe his broad, morally constituted view of history. These have been collected in a single volume: *Kant on History* (1963a).

For an historical analysis of Kant's philosophy which reveals Kant's position in the evolution of European thought, see Lewis White Beck, *Early German Philosophy* (Cambridge, MA: Harvard University Press, 1969).

References

Aiken, William. 1988. "World Hunger, Benevolence, and Justice." In *Problems of International Justice*, ed. Steven Luper-Foy, 67–83. New York: Westview Press.

Aune, Bruce. 1979. *Kant's Theory of Morals*. Princeton, NJ: Princeton University Press.

Beck, Lewis White. 1960. *A Commentary on Kant's Critique of Practical Reason*. Chicago: University of Chicago Press.

Beitz, Charles R. 1979. *Political Theory and International Relations*. Princeton, NJ: Princeton University Press.

Cohen, Marshall. 1984. "Moral Skepticism and International Relations." *Philosophy and Public Affairs* 13: 299–346.

Donagan, Alan. 1977. *The Theory of Morality*. Chicago: University of Chicago Press.

Donaldson, Thomas. 1982. *Corporations and Morality*. Englewood Cliffs, NJ: Prentice-Hall.

Doore, Gary. 1985. "Contradiction in the Will." *Kantstudien* 76: 138–51.

Dworkin, Ronald. 1977. *Taking Rights Seriously*. Cambridge, MA: Harvard University Press.

Feinberg, Joel. 1966. "Duties, Rights and Claims." *American Philosophical Quarterly*, 3: 137–44.

  1970. "The Nature and Value of Rights." *Journal of Value Inquiry* 4: 243–57.

Gauthier, David. 1986. *Morals By Agreement*. Oxford: Oxford University Press.

Kant, Immanuel, 1929. *Critique of Pure Reason*. Trans. Norman Kemp Smith. London: St. Martin's Press.

  1949. *Critique of Practical Reason and Other Writings in Moral Philosophy*. Trans. L. W. Beck. Chicago: University of Chicago Press.

  1963a. *Kant on History*. Trans. L. W. Beck, R. E. Anchor, and E. L. Fachenheim. Indianapolis: Bobbs-Merrill.

  1963b. *Lectures on Ethics*. Trans. Louis Infeld. New York: Harper & Row.

  1964a. *Groundwork of the Metaphysics of Morals*. Trans. H. J. Paton. New York: Liberal Arts Press.

  1964b. "The Metaphysical Principles of Virtue." Trans. James Ellington. Part II of *The Metaphysics of Morals*. New York: Bobbs-Merrill.

  1965. "The Metaphysical Elements of Justice" [1797], Part I of *The Metaphysics of Morals*. Trans. John Ladd. Indianapolis: Bobbs-Merrill.

  1971a. "On the Common Saying: 'This May be True in Theory, but it does Not Apply in Practice'" [1793] in *Kant's Political Writings*. Trans. H. B. Nisbet and ed. Hans Reiss. Cambridge: Cambridge University Press.

  1971b. "Perpetual Peace" [1795] in *Kant's Political Writings*. Trans. H. B. Nisbet, ed. Hans Reiss. Cambridge: Cambridge University Press.

Luper-Foy, Steven, ed. 1988. *Problems of International Justice*. Boulder, CO: Westview Press.

Moore, G. E. 1903. *Principia Ethica*. Cambridge: Cambridge University Press.

Nagel, Thomas. 1986. *The View from Nowhere*. New York: Oxford University Press.

Nardin, Terry. 1983. *Law, Morality, and the Relations of States*. Princeton, NJ: Princeton University Press.

O'Neill, Onora. 1986. *Faces of Hunger: An Essay on Poverty, Development and Justice*. London: George Allen and Unwin.

1988. "Hunger, Needs and Rights." In *Problems of International Justice*, ed. Steven Luper-Foy. Boulder, CO: Westview Press.

Paton, H. J. 1947. *The Categorical Imperative: A Study in Kant's Moral Philosophy*. Philadelphia: University of Pennsylvania Press.

Rawls, John. 1971. *A Theory of Justice*. Boston, MA: Harvard University Press.

Vincent, R. J. 1986. *Human Rights and International Relations*. Cambridge: Cambridge University Press.

8 UTILITARIANISM AND INTERNATIONAL ETHICS

ANTHONY ELLIS

Utilitarianism, in its modern form, is the detailed articulation of two basic premises. The first is that the only thing that is intrinsically good, or good in itself, is well-being. Other things may be good, of course, but only because they are conducive to well-being (or utility, as it is sometimes expressed). Over the question of what constitutes well-being utilitarians have differed. The most famous have identified it simply with happiness, but recent utilitarians, as we shall see, tend to reject this view. The second premise, whose modern theoretical articulation is known as consequentialism, is that that the only relevant factor in deciding whether any action or practice is morally right or wrong is its overall consequences, viewed impersonally. The agent is morally obliged to perform any action, no matter what, if and only if it has the best consequences or, as it is also put, if and only if it maximizes the good. These two thoughts yield the idea that all of our moral duties can be reduced to one: that we should try to maximize well-being or utility. The history of utilitarianism has been the attempt to articulate these thoughts in detail.

The origins of utilitarianism

Although utilitarianism is popularly thought of as a nine-teenth-century British tradition, utilitarian thinking can be found as early as the late seventeenth century in the work of Richard Cumberland (1672). In the eighteenth century it influenced the philosophy of the British empiricists Berkeley (1712), Hutcheson (1725, 1755) and Hume (1740, 1751), as well as theological writers such as John Gay (1731), John Brown (1751), Abraham Tucker (1768–78), and William Paley (1785). Of those thinkers, the greatest by far was David Hume.

Hume is not really a utilitarian in the modern sense, however. In its modern form, utilitarianism is a *normative* doctrine, laying down a standard of right action. Hume's intent, on the other hand, was to *describe* the phenomena of morality and, more specifically, to explain

158

how our actual moral reactions have arisen. His central claim was that moral judgments do not result from the exercise of reason but are rather the expressions of feeling. The feeling of moral approval, Hume argued, is mainly aroused by the disposition in people to promote the public good. But he went a step further, and asked why it is that we approve of this disposition. His answer was that such a disposition is useful or, as he put it, has utility. It is not that it is simply admirable in itself; rather, we approve of it because we see that the exercise of this disposition is likely to promote the public good.

It is with the work of Hume that we find the first serious attempt to apply to questions of politics a mode of ethical thinking which, if not strictly utilitarianism, has affinities with it. Arguing against the contractarian tradition, he held that the consent of the governed is not the basis of governmental authority, which is based rather on the *utility* of government. (Hume's argument against the social contract is still discussed today; see "Contemporary issues in contractarianism," Chapter 9.) Unlike the nineteenth-century utilitarians, however, Hume was skeptical of the capacity of humans to organize large-scale political and social change; this, along with his utilitarianism, produced a decidedly conservative approach to politics. The public interest would be served best by working within the broad moral and political structures that we have inherited.

Hume also argued that the institution of *property* (which he thought of as being the major part of justice) is also based on utility. The obvious opponent here is the natural-law tradition, which held that people have a natural right to acquire property. Hume held that there was no such right; his view was simply that the institution of property is conducive to the public good, and that this is the sole basis of its legitimacy.

Hume was not, however, strictly speaking a utilitarian. For one thing, as we have seen, his intentions were not normative. And when he speaks of utility, he does not mean well-being, or anything of that sort; nor is there in Hume's writings the idea that utility is to be *maximized* in the utilitarian's sense. His claim was merely that we have come to approve of moral constraints and conventions because they have utility – they are useful because they serve the public good. What he means by utility and the public good is little more than the man in the street would mean by those phrases.

There can, however, be no doubt about the claim of Jeremy Bentham to be an authentic utilitarian. He and his writings were at the center of the immensely important nineteenth-century school of utilitarian writers and politicians, and the tradition can almost be defined by reference to his writings. And here we find for the first time in the tradition a clear conception of the connection between moral judgment and political action. Bentham's interest in moral philosophy was practical, and he thought that one should simply work out the correct ethical principles and then apply them directly in political action. About this he was very optimistic.

Bentham's abiding interest was the law, and at the center of his intellectual temperament lay an obsessive desire for clarity, order, and system. One way in which this expressed itself was in a contempt for moral and legal systems that had grown up piecemeal and whose mode of expression was in terms that were emotive and obfuscating. Bentham set himself to provide a rational, systematic theory of law that could cut through the jumble he thought English law was at the time and replace it with something clear, rational, and comprehensible. At the heart of his philosophy of law was the claim that the function of the law, and of government, is the promotion of the general happiness, and he stated more clearly, and starkly, than anyone before him what the promotion of the general happiness, for utilitarianism, amounts to.

He went back to first principles, and these were very simple. Like many of his predecessors, he believed that all motivation was self-interested and that, more specifically, one could act only to promote one's own happiness. And happiness, in Bentham, is scarcely distinguished from pleasure, happiness consisting simply in pleasurable states of mind and unhappiness in painful ones. He also believed that our only moral duty was to promote the general happiness – indeed, that to talk of duty in any other way was simply to talk gibberish. There would seem to be a tension here between our *motive* (which can only ever be self-interest) and our *duty* (which is to promote the general good); it seems, then, that it must be impossible to do our duty. But the tension can be resolved: there are factors that make it in our own interest to pursue the general happiness. The most interesting to Bentham were those that are provided by the government through the law: the various sorts of punishment and penalty (various sorts of pain) that the law exacts for actions that damage the general happiness.

Or *should* exact for this reason. In Bentham, more clearly than in any of his predecessors, utilitarianism is a *normative* doctrine, and Bentham was a reformer. He expressed an indebtedness to Hume; but where Hume was a Tory, Bentham was a Radical. He did not believe that the major political and legal institutions of his time were calculated to promote the general happiness, as he understood that phrase. He also thought, unlike Hume, that once we had a clear view of what these institutions ought to be like it would be a compassable task to rectify them.

Bentham faced head on the question of the measurement of happiness. "Pleasures then, and the avoidance of pains, are the *ends* which the legislator has in view: it behoves him therefore to understand their *value*. Pleasures and pains are the *instruments* he has to work with: it behoves him therefore to understand their force, which is again, in another point of view, their value" (Bentham 1789, 38). And, possibly, it was his obsession with order that led him to enunciate his infamous "felicific calculus," which proposes seven dimensions along which pleasure and pain are to be measured. (The most important of these are intensity, duration, and extent, or the number of people affected.)

Some have thought that Bentham did not intend the felicific calculus to be taken too seriously but, be that as it may, it does respond to what is a serious question for utilitarianism. According to utilitarianism in its Benthamite form (which was the orthodox form until the middle of this century) we are to maximize pleasure. That is to say: we are to produce the best balance of pleasure over pain that we can. Clearly, this requires that pleasures and pains be measurable in some way; and, equally clearly, if this is to be done then there are various dimensions along which they must be measured. In fact, we do seem to measure pleasure and pain in some way, and along various dimensions. We say, for instance, that one performance of a piece of music gives us *more* pleasure than another. Nor do we find absurd the idea of trading off a mild but enduring pain for a short but intense one (though it must not be *too* intense). And we very naturally say that one person lived a *happier* life than another. And so on. We seem to make such judgments; explaining *how* we make them is no easy matter. *Duration* is the least problematic dimension. How we compare the *intensity* of two experiences of pleasure, however, is hard to say. The problem is compounded when we try to compare the pleasures and pains of different people, when we try to make *interpersonal comparisons*. Often, we do not know enough about other people's experiences, but the problem goes deeper, and many consider the idea of interpersonal comparisons to be simply incoherent. This issue is still unresolved.[1]

Benthamite politics and foreign policy

We can see from the foregoing sketch why the utilitarian tradition had the identity it had throughout the nineteenth century. It bore the stamp of Bentham quite generally, and identified itself, not

[1] The most useful modern treatment is in Griffin (1986).

only with the General Happiness Principle, but with a commitment to clarity, rationality, system, calculation (all thought of as composing a "scientific" approach), individualism, social reform built upon these, and laissez-faire economics. Hence it came to be thought of as the doctrine of cold, hard calculation, devoid of any sense of the importance of human feeling. Dickens, for instance, attacked utilitarianism in this way in *Hard Times*; and it is true that the utilitarians' commitment to hard rationality and to laissez-faire economics led them to such policies as support for the New Poor Law. But, taken as a critique of utilitarianism as a doctrine, the novel is inept. For one thing, the critique is itself couched in broadly utilitarian terms (as Bentham had said attacks on utilitarianism would generally be – see Bentham 1789, 14) since the characters who represent the utilitarian tradition are faulted because their behavior leads to great unhappiness. It would be a very stupid utilitarian who ignored the importance of human feelings to human happiness. And though utilitarianism is committed, at some level, to the view that calculations of human happiness enter into morality, the theory can be divorced from the broadly "scientistic" motivations that led Bentham and some of his followers to this view. There are other ways of arriving at utilitarianism.

Utilitarianism can also be divorced from the radical approach to politics that was part of its nineteenth-century identity. Indeed, the political program utilitarianism required in any given circumstance will usually be a matter of contention, since it is seldom clear which program will best promote the general happiness. Bentham's own thought illustrates this. In his earlier days he believed in firm rule by the rational legislator. He later came to believe, as did most of the utilitarians, in democracy. The argument was stated classically by James Mill.[2] According to utilitarianism, government, or the state, can only be an instrument of the community, an instrument whose purpose is to secure the general happiness. Mill argued that the only people with a natural and settled interest in the general happiness are the people in general, not those in political power. Democracy, however, gives rulers a self-interested motive for pursuing the general happiness, namely their desire to continue to govern. Macaulay objected[3] to this argument on the ground that it was excessively abstract, insensitive to the diversity and complexity of the human condition. Clearly, the soundness of the argument does depend upon

[2] James Mill's most significant contribution to the utilitarian tradition was as a popularizer through a number of articles in the *Encyclopaedia Britannica*. His argument for democracy is in one of them, the *Essay on Government* (1820), reprinted in *Utilitarian Logic and Politics*, edited by Lively and Rees (1978).
[3] In Macaulay (1829).

very complicated and contentious empirical premises about the behavior of rulers and voters. Any argument that tries to support a system of government, or a political program, on the basis of the General Happiness Principle will require such premises, premises that cannot be derived from the General Happiness Principle itself. The utilitarians, however, did not see this as a disadvantage; quite the reverse. Their view was that if we could agree on the relatively simple ethical idea that our duty is to secure the general happiness, then the rest of morality, political as well as individual, would reduce to a matter of empirical calculation. Morality and politics would thus approximate to a science, and this was thought to be a major source of the intellectual authority of the doctrine.

Such calculations may be very complex, of course, and this may partly explain another interesting fact about the nineteenth-century utilitarian tradition. Utilitarianism may seem at first sight to provide one with a powerful political rhetoric, with its appeal to the general happiness, or the public good. Such an appeal was often made, both in Parliament and elsewhere. But those radical political thinkers influenced by utilitarianism (known as the Philosophical Radicals) also made constant appeal to other notions such as justice, fairness, liberty, and humanity (on this, see Marsh 1979, 53f). The empirical question of whether flogging seamen would contribute to the general happiness may have seemed a complicated one; the claim that it was inhumane made a more direct appeal

But if that is part of the explanation, it is indeed only a part. Two other points must be made. The first should already be clear. The identity of the nineteenth-century utilitarian movement has as much to do with Radicalism as with the General Happiness Principle; and the former does not always sit in obvious consistency with the latter. The second point is a philosophical one, and more complicated. It may be argued that an adherent of utilitarianism is not precluded from appealing to such notions as justice since, properly understood, these notions are not competitors with the General Happiness Principle. Rather, they are to be derived from it. Of course justice is important, but only because it contributes to the general happiness. This, in a way, had been argued by Hume and was to be argued again by J. S. Mill. Whether the argument is correct, and to what extent it was in the minds of the Philosophical Radicals, are, however, matters for dispute.

We have seen something of the involvement of utilitarianism in the domestic politics of the nineteenth century. What did it have to say of international affairs? Only a small portion of Bentham's enormous corpus of writing is given over to this issue, and this was not published until after his death. However, his views were by then well known through the work of James Mill, who expounded them in an article in the *Encyclopaedia Britannica* (1824–5).

The utilitarians were fundamentally cosmopolitan; the citizen of a nation is also a citizen of the world (Bentham 1843, 537) whose basic duty is to the good of mankind in general. Of course, we have duties to particular sections of mankind that we do not have to other sections – our families, friends, countrymen, and so on – but this is so only because and insofar as utility is maximized by recognizing such duties. Similarly, utility is maximized by accepting the natural disposition that a government has to foster the interests of its own citizens (Bentham 1843, 544), but a government's fundamental duty is again to mankind in general. So Bentham can write that it should be a crime for a nation "to do more evil to foreign nations taken together . . . than it should do good to itself," or even "to refuse to render positive services to a foreign nation, when the rendering of them would produce more good to the last mentioned nation, than it would produce evil to itself" (1843, 538).

When Bentham speaks of a crime here he means a crime in *international law* – a phrase which, it seems, he himself coined – and the purpose of international law could be only one thing: "The most extended welfare of all the nations on the earth" (1843, 538). Now it is sometimes thought that Bentham and James Mill should be unsympathetic to the whole notion of international law, since they adhered to what has become known as the "command theory" of law. This theory, which held that a law is nothing but the command of a sovereign, backed by a threat, was popularized by another of Bentham's disciples, the influential jurisprudent John Austin (1832). In the case of international law there may seem to be no sovereign, and hence no command and no threat; in that case, there could be no law. This was indeed the position that Austin held; "international law," though bearing some analogies to law, was not law properly so-called. Even if one could in some way identify the sovereign with the very states that are subject to international law – Austin held that, in a democracy, the sovereign is to be identified with the electorate – there still seems to be no effective system of sanctions. Bentham, however, took a more flexible view. He did not require that the sovereign be a body separately identifiable from the subjects; and, further, though he thought that there could be no *obligation* without a sanction, he did not think that there could be no *law* without a sanction. (On Bentham's conception of law, see Hart 1982, Chs. 5 and 6.) No doubt international law is very different from domestic law, but it is law nonetheless and is not without effect.

International law was not without defect either, in Bentham's view and, in order better to achieve its end, it required above all two things: codification and a tribunal to settle differences between nations. Such a tribunal would probably need no coercive powers other than public opinion. However, Bentham also mentions that refractory states may be put under the "ban of Europe" (1843, 554) – referring presumably to the various legal disabilities that James Mill countenances (1824–5, 33) – and even, "as a last resource," may be forced to comply with the tribunal's judgment by an armed contingent furnished by the several states (Bentham 1843).

The major benefit to be achieved by this was that states would go to war less frequently: "Establish a common tribunal, the necessity for war no longer follows from difference of opinion" (Bentham 1843, 552). Bentham also thought that England and France should withdraw from their colonies, and, indeed, from foreign entanglements generally, since these were prone to cause the sort of complicated conflict that led to war.

Bentham thought that, in any case, colonialism never worked for the general good. For the colonial power, colonies were never a source of true profit; in addition, they corrupted domestic government. Nor was colonial rule good for the colonies, which, in general, would be better able to look after their own interests. So, though utilitarianism must be unsympathetic to such ideas as that of the *intrinsic* right of peoples to self-government, Bentham was nonetheless staunchly anti-colonialist. (J. S. Mill was perhaps not so staunch: see 1863, 9.)

J. S. Mill and his successors

The paradigm of nineteenth-century utilitarianism is often taken to be John Stuart Mill but there is little to be said for this estimate. His main contribution to the tradition (*Utilitarianism*, 1863) was to state the doctrine more articulately than Bentham had done, and to try to defend it against some of the objections that were current (many of which will not strike the modern reader as serious). Whether in doing this he was true to the essence of utilitarianism is still a matter of dispute.

As to government, he argued (1859, 1861) that, although different conditions require different types of rule, the type that would, in civilized conditions, promote the general happiness of its citizens was a democratic one (democracy, in Mill's conception, involving an

165

extended, though not universal, suffrage and voting by means of the "single transferable vote" system). And, like Bentham, he thought that national self-determination was in general likely to promote the general good, if only because a nation is more likely to know its own good than is another nation. On the other hand – like most Victorians – he thought it permissible, despite the difficulties, to impose European rule upon "barbarous" nations as long as this was for their improvement.

Most of these points, including his ambivalent attitude to the doctrine he set himself to defend, can be seen in his short essay, "A Few Words on Non-Intervention" (1862). His view was that armed intervention in the affairs of another state is rarely justified. This is, of course, a view common to many traditions, for reasons both fairly obvious and available to the utilitarian. For one thing, the success of an intervention, even at the most immediate level, is not always assured. Concerted action by many nations is unlikely; and even a relatively isolated nation can generally find support somewhere – however self-interested – which may produce unexpected alliances, altering the balance of world power dangerously. Even if some immediate success is achieved, intervening nations often find it difficult to extricate themselves and may thus produce international friction. Armed interventions have also usually been more expensive, both in lives and money, than expected. So the track record has not been good and this must, for anyone, create a major – but defeasible – presumption against such interventions. (For a discussion of this issue, see also McMahan 1986.)

One exception to the general rule Mill recognized was the case in which a "civilized nation" intervenes in the affairs of an "uncivilized" people. Here the presumption can be overridden, for two reasons: an intervention is more likely to be in the interests of an uncivilized people than a civilized one; and "barbarians" cannot enter into the reciprocity that is, according to Mill, the basis of international morality. (Mill says there are many reasons, though he gives only these two; no doubt one of the others would be the superior chance of success that a "civilized" people often has against an "uncivilized" one.) Unsurprisingly, J. S. Mill, like his father, always opposed self-rule for India.

It should already be clear that the considerations Mill appeals to are not ones that sit naturally with utilitarianism. The question for a utilitarian is not whether an intervention serves the interests of the people whose affairs one is intervening in, nor whether one is dealing with a people with whom one can have reciprocal relations, but whether the intervention would be in the *general interest*. It might be replied that the good of a people, if identified with its general happiness, is itself conducive to the general good, so that in pursuing the good of one nation one is thereby pursuing the general good. Similarly, it might be held that it is for the general good that international relations be based upon reciprocity, so that the appeal to reciprocity is not an appeal to something other than the general good. These are complicated matters about which different views are possible, and work on the place of rules and institutions in utilitarian theory (to be discussed below) has clarified, though not simplified, the issue. It is hard to believe that Mill was clear about it.

I have remarked upon the uncertain chance of success that armed intervention usually carries, but this was not the consideration that Mill emphasized in this essay. In the case of relations between equally developed states, Mill thought, the only difficult question about intervention is whether it is justified to intervene on the side of a people in arms for liberty against its own government. It is worth seeing why he thought the answer was generally no. Such intervention would not generally be for the good of the people themselves because, to put it more starkly than does Mill himself, if a people has not sufficient love of freedom to ensure that they can achieve it by themselves in these circumstances then they are not "fit" for it. (If the government is receiving external help then, Mill thought, the case is otherwise.) Why did Mill hold this view? He presumably thought that a people will be hard to oppress for long, once they have set their minds on freedom; if, on the other hand, they, or sufficient of them, have not set their minds on it then they will not have the will to keep it once they have been given it, and it will be only a matter of time before they are enslaved again. So the costs of the intervention will not have been justified. Such a line of reasoning is perfectly consistent with utilitarianism. Its plausibility, however, is another question, and it may be, as Michael Walzer has suggested (1977), that the underlying thought that drove Mill here is not really a utilitarian one, but rather the thought that freedom achieved except by one's own efforts is – simply in itself – not worth having. If Walzer is correct, this argument is one of Mill's many attempts, not always successful, to align utilitarianism with a less rigid moral code.

The next significant contribution to the tradition was that of Henry Sidgwick[4] – to whose profundity we cannot do justice here. He clung to the view that the only good is pleasure, but rejected what the

[4] Sidgwick ([1874] 1907). I rely throughout on the seventh edition of *The Methods of Ethics*.

utilitarians had accepted almost unanimously for two hundred years, namely that an agent is able to pursue only his own happiness. It is now generally agreed that this is false (see Rachels 1986, Ch. 5), and, insofar as utilitarianism is a normative doctrine, it need have no commitment to it.

He also broke with the utilitarian tradition over another matter that is not essential to it. Since the eighteenth century utilitarianism had been squarely empiricist, accepting that the only knowledge we can have is gained by the five senses. This leaves moral knowledge hard to account for, and Hume had concluded that there was in fact no such thing: moral judgments were merely expressions of emotion. Sidgwick argued that moral principles were the deliverances of reason: we should pursue the general happiness simply because that is the rational thing to do. This he called the Principle of Rational Benevolence, and it has seemed to many to be the source of utilitarianism's authority.

Unfortunately, Sidgwick thought, the principle that it is rational to pursue one's *own* good seemed as compelling as the Principle of Rational Benevolence. This is unfortunate because, unless there is a God, these two principles will sometimes diverge, and it is unclear what the rational solution to this will be. Sidgwick regarded this as "the profoundest problem of Ethics" (Sidgwick 1874, 386, n. 4), but never solved it to his own satisfaction (Sidgwick 1907, Bk. III, Ch. ii and concluding chapter).

He also saw another question that has been extensively discussed recently: should we aim to maximize *total* utility or *average* utility (Sidgwick 1907, 415f)? The difference is easy to see in what is, for the utilitarian, a genuine issue. Imagine two different sizes of world population. The first is relatively small, and the level of happiness, for most people, is relatively high. The second is very large, and the level of happiness for most people very low. Further the *average* amount of happiness is higher in the first than in the second, but the *total* amount of happiness is higher in the second than in the first. Which should a utilitarian aim for? (Clearly, the answer to this question will have relevance to our world population policy.) Sidgwick thought that we should aim for total happiness, but he did not seem to be aware of its paradoxical consequences (discussed extensively in Parfit 1984).

Sidgwick touches on another issue that has been much discussed recently, namely the problem of distribution. Utilitarianism requires us to maximize utility, but if we could do this *either* by concentrating intense utility in a few people *or* by spreading it thinly through a larger number, which should we do? It is sometimes said that J. S. Mill argued that it was an implicit part of utilitarianism that we should opt for the latter (though a careful reading of the relevant passage suggests that he is not really addressing this point: see Mill 1863, 335f). Sidgwick is clear that utilitarianism in itself can find no way of discriminating in value between the two alternatives, and must be supplemented by a further principle; he opts for a principle of equality (Sidgwick 1874, 416f; this issue is also discussed in Parfit 1984).

The nineteenth-century tradition ended with G. E. Moore. Although he is sometimes referred to as a utilitarian, he did not think of himself in this way. Certainly, he was a consequentialist, believing that our sole duty was to produce the most good that we could. But he rejected a utilitarian conception of the good, holding, for instance, that beauty was intrinsically good, independently of anyone's appreciation of it (Moore 1903, 83f). And, recognizing a multiplicity of goods, he rejected the characteristically utilitarian desire for order and unity in ethical theory (1903, 222f). He did, however, think that the *highest* goods were "personal affections and aesthetic enjoyments" (1903, 189).

The major effect of Moore's work was to lay the utilitarian tradition almost entirely to rest for fifty years. This was partly a result of his ferocious attack on hedonism, commonly thought to be a definitive part of it. But, more generally, his claim that deriving ethical conclusions from non-ethical premises commits what he called "the Naturalistic Fallacy" was enormously influential; his view was that one must simply "intuit" what was good and bad. And this, rightly or wrongly, left the impression that there was little scope for normative ethics. Moore's intuitionism fell out of favor in the 1930s and 1940s, largely in the aftermath of logical positivism, but the ensuing climate was no more sympathetic to normative ethics. It was dominated, first, by emotivism, which held that moral judgments were simply expressions of emotion, and then by prescriptivism, which held that moral judgments were a form of personal commitment.[5] It was not until the 1960s that utilitarianism flowered again.

Act and rule utilitarianism

In 1961 J. J. C. Smart published *An Outline of a System of Utilitarian Ethics* (Smart and Williams 1973), and this is still the best short account of the doctrine. In particular, it is a good popular introduction to some of the technical aspects of utilitarianism. Unlike Sidgwick, Smart accepted that moral judments were fundamentally a

[5] For an account of these schools, see Hudson (1970).

matter of feeling, and this meant that utilitarianism could not be *proved*. He saw it as simply the working out of a widely shared feeling, namely generalized benevolence, and believed that its basically empirical approach to ethical matters would appeal to the scientific temperament. He acknowledged that some people would never accept utilitarianism, but thought it likely that no ethical system would appeal to everyone.

Smart wrote at a time when a particular issue dominated discussions of utilitarian theory, and much of his monograph is given over to it. This is the question of the place of rules, or social institutions more generally, in utilitarian theory. This issue has given rise to two versions of utilitarianism, known as act utilitarianism and rule utilitarianism.

Act utilitarianism holds that the utilitarian criterion is to be applied directly to particular acts; the right act is always that which maximizes utility. Rule utilitarianism holds that the utilitarian criterion is to be applied not to particular acts but to general rules or principles. The correct rules are those the general observance of which maximizes utility, and the correct action is always that which is in accord with such a rule even if, in a particular circumstance, it fails to maximize utility.

A very schematic example will make the difference clear. Should nations observe their treaties? An act utilitarian will say that this depends entirely upon the circumstances: when observing treaties maximizes utility then they should do so; when violating them maximizes utility then they should not do so. A rule utilitarian response will be more complicated. First, we must decide whether the general observance of the rule that treaties should be observed would maximize utility. The answer is probably that it would. Second, we must decide whether in any particular circumstance a nation should observe a treaty. The answer will be that it should, since doing so accords with a rule the general observance of which maximizes utility.

The advantages of rule utilitarianism were basically two. First, act utilitarianism seemed unable to account for the duties that most people are convinced that they have, such as, for instance, the duty to fulfill commitments even where doing so fails to maximize utility. Rule utilitarianism thus brings utilitarianism more nearly into line with our ordinary moral thought. Second, it seems that a society whose members actually tried to practice act utilitarianism would inevitably *fail* to maximize utility. The most interesting cases where this might happen concern what are known as "coordination problems." In a drought, for instance, when the government has imposed restrictions on the use of water, an act utilitarian will reason that his secretly using a small amount of water over the permitted amount will maximize utility, and he will therefore do so. For either others will adhere to the restriction or they will not. If they do not, then the restriction will be ineffective and his own adherence would have been futile. If, on the other hand, they do, then *his* non-adherence would make no significant difference to the amount of water saved; it would, however, vastly augment his own utility and thereby the general utility. So, whatever others do he should not adhere to the restriction. However, in a society of act utilitarians all will follow this correct reasoning and there will be no water. Utility will thus not be maximized. (The relevance of this problem to the international regulation of scarce resources is obvious.) Rule utilitarianism avoids at least some of these problems by requiring utilitarian agents not to apply utilitarian reasoning to actions that are already covered by an acceptable rule.

The difference between the two theories, however, may be less sharp in practice than this account makes it appear. An act utilitarian can use rules (such as that one ought to fulfill one's commitments) even if only as rules of thumb, guides for maximizing utility in a particular case. Even when he *thinks* that it would maximize utility to deviate from the rule he may be justified in placing greater trust in the rule and following it. He is not, after all, infallible. And a rule utilitarian may mitigate the rigor of his position, holding that, though the mere fact that, say, breaking a promise would clearly maximize utility does not make it permissible, one does not have to keep a promise at *all* costs; at some level, it becomes right to deviate from the rule.

Smart was an act utilitarian. Of course, he thought, it was useful to have conventional moral rules, since they helped to maximize utility. But, if that was their point, it seemed like "rule-worship" to follow them when they clearly did not do this.

This seemingly plausible point did not, however, end the issue, and in 1979 R. B. Brandt argued that the question for moral theory is what moral code a fully rational person would choose for a society he had to live in (Brandt 1979). His answer was that he would choose a code that would maximize utility. Such a code would not be act utilitarianism, however, since the attempt to follow this would not achieve that aim, for reasons that are now familiar. It would be a "plural code" of the sort that we have now (though not necessarily with the particular rules that we have). This, then, is a full-blown version of rule utilitarianism (Brandt 1979).

In 1963, R. M. Hare, who had been the father of prescriptivism, began to work towards a utilitarianism that is now much discussed

(Hare 1963; and more thoroughly worked out in Hare 1981). Like most modern utilitarians, he thinks of the individual good as consisting in one's desires being fulfilled, rather than in happiness, and this conception is known as "preference utilitarianism." The notion of happiness had eventually come to seem too problematic: in particular, it seemed difficult to believe that it could be measured in the way required by the theory. Desires, it was thought, could be ordered according to their strength and this, with the aid of decision theory, would give us a systematic way of measuring the good. He then argued that a sympathetic identification with the desires of others would make us come to identify with those desires as we identify with our own. We should thus come to want the satisfaction of desires generally, ranked according to their strength and with no concern for *whose* desires they were. And, Hare argued, this would lead us to desire the maximum satisfaction of desires generally.

In his later writings (Hare 1981; and, for a simpler account, see Hare 1972) he worked towards a theory that combined the advantages of both act utilitarianism and rule utilitarianism. Though in principle the right act is always that which maximizes utility, Hare argued, in making moral decisions we should not usually consider the consequences of each individual act. Doing so would not in fact maximize the good, since we should often go wrong. Rather, we should generally follow those rules that have been tried and tested – for example, rules against lying, cheating, stealing, and so forth. Indeed, we should try to mold our sentiments, and those of our children, to make it psychologically difficult for us to act against them save in exceptional circumstances. So Hare does not suggest that utilitarian thinking should replace an adherence to many of our moral principles. Indeed, the fact that a general adherence to these principles maximizes utility explains, in his view, why they have grown up.

Implications for world affairs

Having traced the content and history of utilitarianism, we may now ask more explicitly what some of its implications for world affairs are, and we should start by making explicit the understanding of international society that emerges from utilitarian thought. According to the utilitarian tradition, the ultimate locus of value is the individual, and the reason for this is simply that it is individuals, not communities, that can be happy or unhappy, have desires satisfied or unsatisfied, and so on. We may speak of a community as wanting something, but this, utilitarians believe, can always be translated into some set of statements about the individuals that compose the community.

This individualism need not, of course, deny that communities are important. On the contrary, human beings are communal animals, and one's good is bound up in all sorts of ways with one's place in the various communities of which one is a member. But the value of any community is no more than the value of the individuals that make it up.

The value of states is, then, merely instrumental, though what they are instrumental toward needs to be stated carefully. Their immediate function is the protection of the individual and his or her community. But their pursuing this parochial end is justifiable only because it is their most efficient way of maximizing the *general* good – the good of all sentient beings everywhere. In principle, there might be other ways. There have always been those, for instance, who have favored world government as an ultimate ideal, and if the establishment of world government would indeed maximize utility then that would settle the matter. Hare, for instance, has argued that it would not (1989, 71f), and probably most utilitarians have taken this view; for a utilitarian, this is perhaps a complicated empirical matter, but that is all that it is.

It should now be clear what is the status of international society. States are a fact of international life, in much the way that clubs, firms, sports teams, and so on, are a fact of domestic life. (They do not have such a clear legal identity, perhaps; that reflects a difference between international law and domestic law.) It is equally a fact of life that states will have conflicting aims; and this would be inevitable even if they were all consciously committed to the same utilitarian ideal, for they would differ about how to realize it. However, as far as utilitarianism is concerned, states should be committed ultimately to the positive pursuit of a common end, namely the general good, and their joint actions and legal conventions should reflect this.

This puts states in an uncomfortable position since they are pulled in two directions. On the one hand, they have a derivative duty to their own citizens; on the other hand, their fundamental duty is to the world at large. And, as the problem of world hunger may show, there may be circumstances in which promoting the good of their own citizens is not compatible with pursuing the more general goal.

We shall end by asking what a utilitarian approach to the morality of war would look like. Utilitarians have usually recognized that war is sometimes justified, and it will be useful to compare utilitarian thought about war with the just-war tradition. The latter starts from the duty of a government to protect its citizens. We have seen that, for utilitarianism, the duty of a government is to promote welfare generally. However, as we have also seen, a utilitarian may also hold that it is for the general good that "every state regards itself as bound to afford to its own subjects protection, so far as it is in its power, against all injuries they may sustain either from the subjects or the government of another state" (Bentham 1843, 544). "The utility of the disposition" is, he says, "evident." If this reasoning is accepted, the two traditions need not conflict here: they will agree that a government has a duty to protect its citizens. Any disagreement will be about what it is permissible to do in pursuit of this duty.

The just-war theory divides the morality of war into two questions: When is it permissible to go to war (*jus ad bellum*)? And what actions are permissible in the pursuit of a just war (*jus in bello*)? About the first question utilitarianism and the just-war theory need not, broadly, be in dispute. The just-war theory recognizes the peculiar awfulness of war and seeks to limit the occasions when it is lawful to partake in it. Anyone wishing to limit the ravages of war is likely to be sympathetic to the sort of rules it lays down (for a brief account, see McKenna 1960). This will include most utilitarians, who have generally agreed with Bentham that war rarely does more good than harm and thus is rarely justified. Of course, about the *precise* content of the rules there may be disagreement.

On the second question there will be a divergence. The just-war theory's rules governing military action in war contain a marked and irreducible deontological element (for the notion of deontology, see "Natural Law, common morality, and consequentialism," Chapter 6; and "Kantian ethics: Kant's general theory," Chapter 7), and a comparison here is instructive. A central element in the just-war theory is the idea that noncombatants may not be attacked. The rationale for this is that one may attack only those who are posing a threat, and noncombatants do not pose a threat. Deliberately killing a noncombatant is murder, and that is an action of a sort that is standardly prohibited in deontological systems. On the other hand, injury, and even death, may be inflicted on them so long as (1) this is militarily necessary; (2) the injury is proportional to the gain; and – crucially – (3) the injury, though foreseen, is not intended. It is over this last condition, which appeals to the doctrine of the double effect, that the just-war theory conflicts with utilitarianism.

According to the doctrine of the double effect, it is permissible, when militarily necessary, to bomb a munitions factory, knowing that civilians will be unavoidably killed, so long as one does not actually *intend* the deaths of those civilians. On the other hand, it is impermissible, however militarily necessary, to bomb civilians in order to break their morale since, in this case, one must be *intending* civilian deaths. Now we may question whether there is any real distinction between intended consequences and foreseen though unintended ones. But even if there can be shown to be such a distinction, we may question whether it can have any moral significance. As far as utilitarianism is concerned, it cannot. This is a consequence of the central doctrine of utilitarianism. All that matters is that welfare be maximized and, if that is true, it cannot matter *how* this occurs, or fails to occur. There is no focus on the *nature* of any action we may perform beyond the question: did it causally contribute to maximizing welfare?

This approach has the effect of breaking down many of the moral distinctions that we customarily cling to. For instance, there will be no ultimate moral significance in the distinction between killing someone and simply allowing them to die. In both cases, the outcome is the same and that, for utilitarianism, is all that matters. Thus, if people die of starvation in the third world when aid from me would have saved them, then I am morally responsible for those deaths. It follows that I am morally obliged to do what I can to save these people.[6] Similarly, there can be no moral distinction between civilian deaths that are intended and those that are merely foreseen but unintended. All that matters from the utilitarian perspective is the outcome, and the outcome may be the same in both cases: the death of a number of civilians and some progress towards winning the war. If the outcome is really the same, it cannot matter how that outcome is brought about. As we have already seen, this is a very general principle to which utilitarianism is committed. (For another discussion of the distinction embodied in the doctrine of the double effect, see "Natural law, common morality, and consequentialism," Chapter 6.)

A real example will bring out the contrast. It is hard to see how a proponent of the just-war theory could support the British area bombing of German cities in the Second World War; the clear intention was to kill civilians, and that is enough, from the just-war perspective, to make it impermissible. From the utilitarian perspective the only question would be whether such action promoted the general welfare; in the particular case this comes down to such questions as whether it hastened the end of the war, whether it made a postwar settlement easier, whether it set a harmful precedent, and so on. On such counts, it is now generally agreed, the net effect of the strategy was bad. It would thus not be legitimate from the utilitarian perspective; but that

---

[6] For an influential discussion of this topic, from a broadly utilitarian perspective, see Singer (1972).

illegitimacy has nothing directly to do with the fact that the death and injury involved were inflicted upon civilians. A utilitarian may argue, of course, that attacking civilians would rarely promote utility. This seems to be the position of James Mill (Mill 1824–5).

This enables us to see, in a general way, how utilitarians would view the issue of nuclear deterrence. Is it permissible for a state to use this strategy? From most deontological perspectives, the question is doubly complicated. Determining whether the strategy actually *works* is itself extremely complicated. There is, however, the further question of whether it is *permissible* even if it does work. Many people think, for instance, that since it would be impermissible actually to use nuclear weapons it is impermissible to intend to use them in the way required by the strategy (for example, see the discussion of nuclear deterrence under "Natural law, common morality, and consequentialism," Chapter 6). But this second issue is also complicated (see, for instance, Lackey 1984). From the utilitarian perspective, however, the question does not arise. It is permissible, indeed obligatory, to do whatever promotes welfare. There are few circumstances in which the actual use of large-scale nuclear weapons could be calculated to do that; but if *threatening* to use them does so, then there is no further moral question. We are left only with the first question: does it work?

As I have said, however, the question of whether deterrence works is extremely complicated. It requires that we weigh the known and estimated costs against the known and estimated benefits. To this debate the utilitarian tradition has nothing distinctive to offer, and utilitarians differ in their conclusions.

The account so far may seem to leave no room for the rules of war that are taught to soldiers, rules that absolutely prohibit the ill treatment of prisoners of war, the pillage of towns, and so on. Would utilitarianism not permit such actions if they maximize utility? The simplest form of act utilitarianism clearly would. But a slightly more sophisticated position would ask what rules of war it would maximize utility to instill in soldiers. In the world as we know it, it seems likely that utility would be maximized by instilling into them fairly specific rules from which they are prohibited from deviating (see Brandt 1972 and Hare 1972).

Utilitarianism, and consequentialism more generally, are thriving amongst academic philosophers. (For some of the most significant recent work see Parfit 1984, Griffin 1986, and Hardin 1988.) We may end by asking briefly what popular support it may have. Public discussion of ethical issues reveals over and over again an adherence to a basic idea – the idea with which we started – that the right action is the one that produces the most welfare. It is an easily revealed assumption of most participants in the debates about government secrecy, nuclear deterrence, air piracy, foreign intervention, and so on. But it is also an assumption that rubs shoulders uneasily with other, contradictory, assumptions, often in the mind of the same person; and it is only to that extent that F. R. Leavis's diagnosis of our age as a "technologico-Benthamite" one is accurate. Some think that an acceptance of this pluralism is the major cause of our inability to think seriously about ethical issues. Others, however, think that an acceptance of it is what seriousness here demands.

Suggested reading

The most comprehensive account of the history of utilitarianism is still Ernest Albee's *A History of English Utilitarianism* (New York: Collier, 1962; 1st edn. 1902). It does not, however, deal with the more recent developments. More up to date, though much briefer, is Anthony Quinton's *Utilitarian Ethics* (London: Macmillan, 1973). The works of Jeremy Bentham and J. S. Mill are classical sources for the nineteenth century. The most important are Bentham's *Introduction to the Principles of Morals and Legislation* ([1789] 1970) and J. S. Mill's *Utilitarianism* ([1863] 1987). Relevant extracts from both can be found in *Utilitarianism and Other Essays: J. S. Mill and Jeremy Bentham*, edited by Alan Ryan (Harmondsworth: Penguin Books, 1987). More sophisticated, and recently very influential, is Henry Sidgwick's *Methods of Ethics* (the seventh edition of 1907 is the standard edition).

Utilitarianism has been extremely influential in the second half of the twentieth century. The most impressive contribution to the tradition has probably been Derek Parfit's *Reasons and Persons* (1984); but it is long and complex. Slightly easier to read, though by no means easy, is James Griffin's intelligent and cultivated *Well-Being: Its Meaning, Measurement and Moral Importance* (1986). R. M. Hare's *Moral Thinking: Its Levels, Method and Point* (1981) is probably the easiest to read of the recent significant contributions to the tradition. Amongst recent critics of utilitarianism none has been more influential than Bernard Williams, and an invaluable introduction to his critique can be found in his contribution to Smart and Williams, *Utilitarianism: For and Against* (1973). The other essay in this book, by J. J. C. Smart, is a defense of utilitarianism, and remains one of the best introductions to its central doctrines.

There have been many attempts to apply utilitarianism to practical issues. R. M. Hare has been a pioneer in this respect, and some of his writing is collected in *Essays on Political Morality* (1989). One of these essays, "Rules of War and Moral Reasoning," appeared originally in *Philosophy and Public Affairs*, 1972, vol. 1, as part of a symposium with R. B. Brandt, another important contributor to the tradition. Since its inception, *Philosophy and Public Affairs* has published a steady stream of articles concerned with international ethics, many of them broadly in the utilitarian tradition. Probably, none has been more influential than Peter Singer's "Famine, Affluence, and Morality" (*Philosophy and Public Affairs*, 1972, vol. 1), an article which – if its argument is correct – demonstrates just how uncomfortable, for most readers of this book, an acceptance of utilitarianism would be. For a later version of the argument, see Singer's *Practical Ethics* (1980), Ch. 8.

References

Austin, John. [1832] 1954. *The Province of Jurisprudence Determined*, ed. H. L. A. Hart. London: Weidenfeld and Nicolson.

Bentham, Jeremy. [1789] 1970. *Introduction to the Principles of Morals and Legislation*, ed. J. H. Burns and H. L. A. Hart. London: Methuen.

   1843. *Principles of International Law*. In *The Collected Works of Jeremy Bentham* vol. 2, ed. John Bowring. Edinburgh: William Tait.

Berkeley, George. 1712. *Passive obedience*. London: H. Clements. Reprinted in *Berkeley's Collected Works*. vol. 4, ed. A. C. Fraser. Oxford: Clarendon Press, 1901.

Brandt, R. B. 1972. "Utilitarianism and the Rules of War." *Philosophy and Public Affairs*, vol. 1.

   1979. *A Theory of the Good and the Right*. Oxford: Clarendon Press.

Brown, John. 1751. *Essays on the Characteristics*. London.

Cumberland, Richard. 1672. *De Legibus Naturae*. Selections reprinted in *Eighteenth-Century British Moralists*, ed. D. D. Raphael. Oxford: Clarendon Press, 1969.

Gay, John, 1731. *A Dissertation Concerning the Fundamental Principle of Virtue or Morality*. London. Prefixed to Archbishop King's *Essay on the Origin of Evil*; reprinted in *British Moralists*, ed. L. A. Selby-Bigge. New York: Dover, 1965.

Griffin, James. 1986. *Well-Being. Its Meaning, Measurement and Moral Importance*. Oxford: Clarendon Press.

Hardin, Russell. 1988. *Morality within the Limits of Reason*. Chicago: University of Chicago Press.

Hare, R. M. 1963. *Freeedom and Reason*. Oxford: Clarendon Press.

   1972. "Rules of War and Moral Reasoning." *Philosophy and Public Affairs*, vol. 1. Reprinted in Hare 1989.

   1981. *Moral Thinking: Its Levels, Method, and Point*. Oxford: Clarendon Press.

   1989. *Essays on Political Morality*. Oxford: Clarendon Press.

Hart, H. L. A. 1982. *Essays on Bentham: Studies in Jurisprudence and Political Theory*. Oxford: Clarendon Press.

Hudson, W. D. 1970. *Modern Moral Philosophy*. London: Macmillan.

Hume, David. 1740. *A Treatise of Human Nature*, book III. London.

   1751. *An Enquiry Concerning the Principles of Morals*. London.

Hutcheson, Francis. 1725. *An Inquiry Concerning the Original of our Ideas of Virtue or Moral Good*. London.

   1755. *A System of Moral Philosophy*. Glasgow: R. and A. Foulis.

Lackey, D. 1984. *Moral Principles and Nuclear Weapons*. Totowa: Rowman and Allanheld.

Lively, Jack and John Rees eds. 1978. *Utilitarian Logic and Politics.* Oxford: Clarendon Press.

Macaulay, Thomas. 1829. "Mill's Essay on Government: Utilitarian Logic and Politics." *Edinburgh Review.* Reprinted in Lively and Rees 1978.

McKenna, Joseph C. 1960. "Ethics and War: A Catholic View." *American Political Science Review,* vol. 54.

McMahan, Jeff. 1986. "The Ethics of International Intervention." In *Ethics and International Affairs,* ed. Anthony Ellis. Manchester: Manchester University Press.

Marsh, Peter, ed. 1979. *The Conscience of the Victorian State.* Syracuse: Syracuse University Press.

Mill, James. 1820. *Essay on Government.* Reprinted in Lively and Rees 1978.

    1824–5. *Law of Nations.* In "Articles Reprinted from the Supplement to the *Encyclopaedia Britannica.*" London: J. Innes, probably 1824–25.

Mill, John Stuart. 1859. *On Liberty.* Reprinted in *On Liberty and Considerations on Representative Government,* ed. R. B. McCallum. Oxford: Clarendon Press, 1946.

    1861. *Considerations on Representative Government.* Reprinted in *On Liberty and Considerations on Representative Government,* ed. R. B. McCallum. Oxford: Clarendon Press, 1946.

    1862. "A Few Words on Non-Intervention." *Fraser's Magazine,* February. Reprinted in *Dissertations and Discussions,* 3 vols. London: Longmans, Green, Reader and Dyer, 1867.

    [1863] 1987. *Utilitarianism.* London. Reprinted in *Utilitarianism and Other Essays: J. S. Mill and Jeremy Bentham,* ed. Alan Ryan. Harmondsworth: Penguin Books.

Moore, G. E. 1903. *Principia Ethica.* Cambridge: Cambridge University Press.

Paley, William. 1785. *The Principles of Moral and Political Philosophy.* London.

Parfit, Derek. 1984. *Reasons and Persons.* Oxford: Clarendon Press.

Rachels, James. 1986. *The Elements of Moral Philosophy.* New York: Random House.

Sidgwick, Henry. [1874] 1907. *Methods of Ethics.* London: Macmillan.

Singer, Peter. 1972. "Famine, Affluence, and Morality." *Philosophy and Public Affairs,* vol. 1.

    1980. *Practical Ethics.* Cambridge: Cambridge University Press.

Smart, J. J. C. and B. Williams. 1973. *Utilitarianism: For and Against.* Cambridge: Cambridge University Press.

Tucker, Abraham. 1768–78. *The Light of Nature Pursued.* London, published under the pseudonym "Edward Search."

Walzer, Michael. 1977. *Just and Unjust Wars: A Moral Argument with Historical Illustrations.* New York: Basic Books.

9 THE CONTRACTARIAN TRADITION AND INTERNATIONAL ETHICS

DAVID R. MAPEL

Although the contractarian tradition is relatively new compared to other traditions of ethical and political thought such as natural law, the idea of the social contract has frequently dominated modern political philosophy. In the seventeenth and eighteenth centuries, the tradition was developed and criticized by such influential thinkers as Hobbes, Locke, Rousseau, and Kant. In the nineteenth and early twentieth centuries, its influence declined in contrast with more recent traditions such as utilitarianism and Marxism. Yet contractarianism has shown great staying power, and today it is again one of the most influential traditions in political theory, largely due to the work of contemporary American philosopher John Rawls.

All contractarian arguments have a common structure, and it is this common structure that unifies the tradition. At the same time, the tradition is broad enough to permit a wide range of disagreements. The first section of this chapter presents a logical analysis that maps the common structure of contractarian arguments. With this map in hand, we will be better able to understand why the contractarian tradition has often yielded radically different conclusions across a variety of issues in international ethics.

The second and third sections of this chapter illustrate the historical range and diversity of the tradition by discussing some of the most influential classical and contemporary contractarian theorists who have written on international ethics. As we shall see, classical contractarians have been pessimistic about the possibility of international justice, whereas contemporary contractarians emphasize the possibility of international reciprocity and social cooperation. In contrast with classical authors, contemporary contractarians also focus more directly on specific issues within international ethics, such as military intervention and global distributive justice.

The final section discusses some recent issues in the contractarian tradition. As I try to show in the case of US foreign policy, the contractarian tradition continues to exercise an indirect but significant influence on practical politics. At a philosophical level, the tradition also continues to inspire lively debate. In particular, contemporary contractarians disagree about "reciprocity": that is, about the idea of "a return in due measure" by each member of a cooperative scheme. Traditionally, contractarians have viewed reliable expectations of reciprocity or cooperation as a necessary condition of social and political justice. Since classical contractarians saw little or no reliable reciprocity in international society, they concluded that duties of justice between states were relatively weak or nonexistent. More recently, some contemporary contractarians have argued that there is more reciprocity and therefore greater scope for principles of justice in international society than has frequently been thought. This contrast reflects the debate within the tradition about the degree and kind of cooperation required to bring claims of social and political justice into play. Nevertheless, all contractarians recognize that reciprocity is generally weaker and less reliable in international than in domestic society. Because reciprocity is of special significance in international society, the attention paid to this idea by the contractarian tradition has made it an important source of ethical reflection about international relations.

The structure of contractarian arguments

Contractarian arguments use a procedure of collective choice, the social contract, to show how legitimate political institutions might arise. More recently, the social contract has also been used to justify principles of social justice. The basic idea behind the device of the social contract is that the acceptability or fairness of the initial contractual situation transfers to the institutions or principles that are chosen in that situation. For example, in Locke's version of the social contract, individuals in a "state of nature" agree to transfer some of their natural rights to the political community, thereby establishing a government. That government is legitimate only insofar as it rests on and is limited by an original contract between individuals who are initially free and equal.

Obviously, in making any contract individuals must take into account their general circumstances, various moral considerations, and their own wishes and desires. Contractarian arguments merely reformulate these conditions at a higher level of abstraction. Thus, the structure of all contractarian arguments can be broken down into three elements: a description of the "circumstances of justice," a description of the moral constraints built into the initial contractual situation, and a theory of rational choice. The first two elements set up a framework for deliberation and choice. An account of rational choice then tells us which principles or institutions individuals would choose within that framework. Since any contract must reflect the circumstances that inspired it, describing the initial choice situation is the most important part of any contractarian argument and the principal source of diversity within the tradition. As we shall presently see, it is also the point at which contractarianism most clearly draws on other traditions of political thought.

The first step in all contractarian arguments is to define "circumstances of justice." In its most demanding sense, this means determining the circumstances that must obtain for justice to have any meaning, raising basic questions about the scope of justice. As coined by David Hume and reinterpreted by recent contractarians such as Rawls, however, the phrase more often refers to the less demanding idea of "the normal conditions under which human cooperation is both possible and necessary" and, even more specifically, to the conditions that are necessary for "the emergence of just institutions" (Rawls 1973, 126). Thus Rawls, following Hume, lists interdependence, vulnerability, moderate scarcity of goods, limited generosity, and roughly equal capacities and aptitudes as the main circumstances of justice (see Hume 1740, bk. III, pt. II, sec. ii, and Hume 1751, sec. III, pt. I; also see Donaldson 1991).

Contractarian descriptions of the circumstances of justice vary in their assumptions. One description of circumstances might assume that individuals (or states) are altruistic and law-abiding; another might assume that they are highly competitive and inclined to break the law in the absence of sanctions. Obviously, such motivational assumptions set limits on the sort of social and political arrangements to which parties to the social contract can reasonably agree. The presumed material circumstances of cooperation also vary. Contractarians make different assumptions about the level of material scarcity and economic interdependence in a society, and also about a society's stage of social and political development.

Some of the circumstances of justice that are characteristic of domestic society, such as limited generosity, also clearly obtain in international society. The extent to which other circumstances obtain, such as roughly equal capacities, remains a matter of debate. With respect to circumstances of justice, then, the contractarian tradition exhibits a range of more or less "optimistic" assumptions about the possibility and ease of social cooperation. For example, whether contractarians are "realists" or "cosmopolitans" in international ethics depends partly on how favorable they think circumstances of justice are to international cooperation.

The second element in all contractarian arguments is a description of the ethical constraints that are built into the initial choice situation. As critics outside the tradition have often pointed out, contractarians must rely on extra-contractarian assumptions in order to explain the moral force of the contract. For example, Locke's social contract presupposes that individuals already possess certain natural rights. Those rights are not justified in contractarian terms; rather, they explain the moral force and scope of the contract itself. Until recently, contractarians have generally assumed that parties to the social contract possess a fairly full and detailed knowledge of their situation. Since Rawls's hypothetical contract theory, however, many contractarians have limited the information available to individuals in the initial choice situation, to keep agreement from being influenced by "morally arbitrary" factors such as knowledge of one's class position or natural talents. As we shall see, followers of Rawls have extended his argument to international society by imagining that states meet to agree on principles of global justice under similar conditions of ignorance about their own stage of economic development and level of natural resources.

Given this reliance on extra-contractarian moral assumptions, there are few, if any, "pure" contractarians. Few political thinkers simply presuppose a contractual situation without further justification. Rather, the contractarian tradition permits a range of more or less "moralized" descriptions of the initial contractual situation. Hobbes's "state of nature" illustrates one extreme version, in which extra-contractarian moral constraints have minimal importance. Rawls's theory illustrates the other extreme, in which the agreement of the contractors is all but dictated by the normative constraints built into Rawls's initial situation or "original position."

In one sense, there is nothing unusual about the contractarian reliance on extra-contractarian assumptions; political theorists outside the contractarian tradition also ordinarily draw on several other traditions of political thought at once. Machiavelli, for example, can be read as a *"quattrocento"* humanist concerned with the virtue of princes; a "civic" humanist concerned with the vigor of republican government; or a "realist" concerned with the economy of power (for humanist and civic republican readings, see Skinner 1978, 123–39, 180–6; for a realist reading, see "Machiavelli," Chapter 4). In another sense, however, the extent to which the vocabulary and concepts of contractarianism mesh with other traditions is unusual. In principle, the method of the contract is available to theorists working in almost every other major ethical tradition. There are even a few contemporary theorists, such as John Harsanyi, who argue that parties to the social contract would choose to organize their society according to utilitarian principles (Harsanyi 1975, 594–606).

Historically, however, contractarians have almost always rejected utilitarianism. Instead, they have generally claimed that the moral constraints embedded in the initial choice situation express distinctive, non-utilitarian principles of justice. Hobbes, Locke, and Rousseau all argue that the domestic social contract rests on individual rights; Kant's account of a federation of states is motivated by a non-utilitarian conception of moral duty; and Rawls argues that his theory expresses a distinctive, non-utilitarian notion of justice as fairness. While not hesitant about explaining the contractual situation in terms of extra-contractarian principles of right or justice, contractarians are generally hesitant about explaining it in terms of good consequences. In contractarianism, what can be done in the name of good consequences is generally limited in two ways: by the normative constraints represented in the contractual situation and by the institutions or principles chosen by the contractors. These limitations on the importance of consequences might seem to make contractarianism somewhat irrelevant to international society, where the importance of consequences in guiding state action appears to loom large. But, again, the applicability of contractarian principles to international society depends on whether there is enough reciprocity in international society to make the social contract a rational undertaking.

Although limited in importance, a concern with consequences does enter all contractarian arguments in essentially the same way. Once the circumstances of justice and the moral constraints of the initial-choice situation have been described, all contractarian arguments also need a third element: a theory of rational choice to explain why parties to the social contract agree to certain institutions or principles. Contractarian theories of rational choice are generally instrumental in character: individuals (or states) are left to form their own preferences, which are not subject to criticism as long as they are not mutually contradictory or otherwise irrational in some weak, formal sense. At this point, however, some classical and contemporary contractarians differ significantly. Classical contractarians such as Hobbes understand instrumental rationality primarily as directed at minimizing important kinds of harm; contemporary contractarians more frequently understand instrumental rationality as maximizing preferences or goods within the framework of the social contract. In Rawls's work these two ideas are combined in the idea of "maximizing the minimum" share of goods individuals in domestic (or international) society might receive. All of these theories of rational choice are skeptical about the possibility of reaching agreement about final ends.

Contractarians are reluctant to prescribe final ends for individuals (or states) for two reasons. First, as we have already seen, the contractarian tradition tends to regard parties to the contract primarily as holders of rights or duties and only secondarily as "maximizers" of goods. Second, contractarians are somewhat skeptical about our ability to reach theoretical agreement about final ends, and even more skeptical about our ability to arrive at practical agreement about such ends. As a practical matter, contractarians generally think that the best we can hope for is agreement on a more or less extensive set of instrumental goods, the chief of which is some form of political society. If such practical agreement about final ends is difficult to reach in domestic society, it is even more difficult to reach in international society, where an even greater range of views about the best way of life prevails. In these circumstances, most contractarians have regarded agreement on the common procedural value of the rule of law as the best that states can achieve.

At this point, there are obvious connections between contractarianism and the liberal tradition. Liberals who begin from a qualified skepticism about the possibility of political agreement tend to favor contractarian arguments because the contractarian tradition does not require individuals (or states) to agree to more than a "thin" or instrumental theory of goods. Liberals who begin from strong deontological views about rights or duties also often tend to favor contractarian arguments because the initial contractual situation can be easily set up to reflect those kinds of ethical constraints. Typically, liberals hold both views, being skeptical about final ends and inclined towards strong views of the "right" or justice. Hence, the prevalence of contractarian arguments in the liberal tradition.

In contractarianism the common good receives a rather bare and instrumental definition. Among contractarians, the idea of the common good may amount to no more than the absence of social war, the creation of a common authority, the protection of basic rights, the equitable distribution of certain instrumental goods, or perhaps the possibility of "social union" or harmony between smaller associations. There is nothing in the contractarian tradition that corresponds to the more robust notions of the common good found in other traditions such as natural law. It is true that in Rousseau, Kant, and Rawls, the social contract also appears as a condition of another ideal of individual welfare or excellence, namely individual autonomy. Nevertheless, autonomy is a much less exacting ideal than the natural-law idea of virtue. Similarly, the idea of a domestic political community appears as a mediating link between individual and government in the contractarian theories of Locke and Rousseau, while the idea of a moral or cosmopolitan international community appears in Kant and the work of Rawlsians such as Charles Beitz. With the partial exception of Rousseau, however, all of these notions of community and the common good are explicable primarily in terms of respect for the principles of the contract itself.

Contractarianism is an individualistic political tradition, then, not in the sense that it necessarily posits "atomistic" individuals who have no social ties, but in the sense that it rejects any ideal of a natural or organic relationship between individuals and the community. Instead, the artificial device of the social contract is used to establish critical standards for evaluating basic social and political relationships and institutions, as well as all de facto distributions of political power. By the same token, authority in the contractarian tradition is based on actual or hypothetical agreement, not on the wisdom of rulers who discern the common good. This conception of authority has its roots in the contractarian emphasis on the free, equal, and separate status of each individual, and in its philosophical and practical skepticism about agreement concerning final goods, whether individual or communal.

To summarize: the contractarian tradition is distinguished by the device of the social contract, which brings together a description of the circumstances of justice, various extra-contractarian moral assumptions, and an instrumental theory of rational choice. It is further distinguished by its rejection of utilitarianism at a foundational level, by skepticism about the possibility of agreement about final ends, and by an emphasis on the free, equal, and separate status of individuals who consent to social and political institutions. Individual contractarians explain and emphasize these ideas somewhat differently. Nevertheless, the tradition can be identified by a common vocabulary and approach. This vocabulary also has considerable rhetorical power, which is another reason why the tradition has proven so influential.

Classical contractarianism

Hobbes, Locke, Rousseau, and (in international ethics) Kant are the classical figures in the contractarian tradition. Unfortunately, their writings about international relations are for the most part scattered or incomplete. Yet, despite the fragmentary character of this work and their deep disagreement about the nature of the social contract in domestic society, these writers share a common, skeptical view of the scope of ethics in international relations. In particular, they share a deep pessimism about international circumstances of justice. For all of them, international relations is a "state of war," not in the sense of actual fighting, but in Hobbes's sense of a "known disposition thereto." With the partial exception of Locke, all of them regard individuals outside of civil society as primarily motivated by scarcity, fear, or a desire to dominate. In this situation, promise-breaking and anticipatory violence are often mere counsels of survival. Thus, while all of these writers recognize the possibility of international law, all have doubts about its efficacy. More importantly, none of them think that international government is as possible or as desirable as domestic government, albeit for somewhat different reasons. In these general respects, classical contractarianism has deep affinities with classical realism (see "Early modern realism," Chapter 4).

According to Hobbes, before the social contract individuals live in a state of nature which is also a "war of all against all." This war is generated by the natural motives mentioned above, together with equality of power and the absence of any central authority with effective power. Under these conditions, anticipatory violence is often the most rational strategy for survival and is morally permissible, given the natural "right" of each individual to judge and to do whatever is necessary to his or her self-preservation. In other words, there is little or no reliable reciprocity in the individual state of nature and no authoritative interpretation of the requirements of justice. As a consequence, Hobbes says that in the state of nature nothing can be considered just or unjust.

Nevertheless, Hobbes also says that there is a "law" of nature that directs individuals to seek peace insofar as they can without risking their own survival. Unfortunately, there is so much insecurity in the individual state of nature that it is usually impossible to act on this duty. Conditions in the state of nature are so intolerable that individuals are either driven to create a government by means of the social contract or (more frequently) willing to submit to conquest, which Hobbes regards as an equally legitimate way of founding the state. The state that is created by contract or conquest is the "Leviathan," a "mortal god" who possesses an almost absolute authority. Since the sovereign of this state defines justice, his actions cannot be either just or unjust. There is no right of rebellion against the sovereign, nor any other recourse against his laws save by the sovereign's own permission.

Once the domestic state has been created, however, matters outside become more ambiguous. On the one hand, the state now cushions individuals from the worst consequences of the individual state of nature. In addition, the state is much more capable of surviving in the international arena than are individuals before the domestic social contract. Hence, at the international level both individuals and the state are more able to seek peace. By the same token, however, there is now much less urgency to do so, since individuals are protected by the state, while the same natural motivations of scarcity, fear, and glory still tend to guide foreign policy. In other words, a central government is no longer a *necessity*, as it was in the domestic context. Given these more moderate circumstances of justice in international society, the observation of common rules of conduct is sometimes reasonable (although such rules lack an essential feature of law for Hobbes, namely, a central authority that can interpret and enforce them). Yet the sovereign's primary duty is still to protect himself and his subjects, even if this requires breaking treaties and violating agreements. As a result, the standing of international law is always precarious. Hobbes's experience of the English Civil War and his sense of logical consistency also rule out the possibility of states agreeing to a world federation, since Hobbes thought that the sort of division or limitation of authority characteristic of federations was both dangerous and nonsensical. Ironically, states remain in a war of all against all at the international level because the state has successfully eliminated that war at the domestic level.

As many commentators have noted, Hobbes's description of international circumstances of justice resembles Locke's description of domestic circumstances of justice, since Hobbes recognizes the possibility of a somewhat greater degree of reciprocity in the international state of nature. Of course, Locke also clearly postulates various natural moral duties and rights in the state of nature, while it remains a matter of scholarly controversy whether Hobbes's laws of nature are essentially prudential or moral in character (for two different views of this issue see Oakeshott 1962, 248–301; and Kavka 1986, 338–85). But if we leave this complex issue aside, Locke differs from Hobbes primarily in arguing for a right of punishment in the state of nature, more limited rights of government, a right of domestic rebellion, and rights against conquest. In contrast with Hobbes, Locke's notion of a natural right of punishment brings him closer in international ethics to that part of the natural-law, just-war tradition that rules out conquest yet regards some punitive wars as morally legitimate. For Hobbes, such punitive wars are clearly a matter of prudence rather than justice, whereas wars of conquest may be justified in terms of the natural right of self-preservation, which overrules the natural law to seek peace. Yet while Hobbes is more permissive than Locke, their views of international ethics are essentially similar: both recognize only limited possibilities for international law and reciprocity, and both place the preservation of the state first.

In many respects, Rousseau is even more pessimistic. The creation of the state in civil society eliminates violence at the domestic level, only to exacerbate it at the international level. War is an artificial relation between states, not a natural relation among men, and should be fought according to civilized conventions. But the advent of the state system increases the source of all evil for Rousseau, namely, a form of social interdependence that breeds and magnifies inequality, dependency, and resentment. Rather than cushioning the individual from deadly conflict, the state system makes an unprecedented level of organized violence possible and draws the individual into it. For Rousseau, observation of international law, the balance of power, and even international federations are not expressions of a true common interest, but merely temporary tactics of international competition. At the domestic level, things are even worse: threats from abroad are used to justify inequality and tyranny at home, while the individual's conscience is hopelessly divided between the demands of good citizenship and the dreadful exigencies of the international state of nature. Finally, Rousseau argues that political authority is legitimate only if it expresses a democratic "general will," which is in turn only possible in a small society. This problem of scale makes Rousseau quite suspicious of the virtue of large states. It also makes it impossible for something as large and heterogeneous as a world community to have a general will (for discussion of the practical impossibility of the law of nature functioning as a universal general will, see Forde's treatment of Rousseau under "Early modern realism," Chapter 4). A world government clearly would be illegitimate. The only permanent solution to international conflict is therefore a world of small, virtuous, autarkic republics, each based on Rousseau's understanding of the domestic social contract. In international society as we know it, neither a world government nor a world federation is possible; in an international society of small republics, neither would be required (Hoffmann 1965).

Like Rousseau, Kant thought that individuals have a right to republican government and that a world of republics is a necessary condition of perpetual peace. From this point on, however, Kant and Rousseau diverge. First, Rousseau located the origin of the conflict between passion and reason in society, while Kant located it in a human nature that is always able to choose between the two. Secondly, although Kant was pessimistic about human beings freely choosing to act on their duty to pursue peace, he speculated that providence working through history might drive them to it through the demands of international commerce and the growing costs of war. War would eventually become too unprofitable for human beings to pursue any longer. Unlike Rousseau, the sort of republics on which Kant pinned his hopes were commercial and juridical in character, not autarkic and highly political. Kant's speculative history leads away from contractarianism and towards Hegelianism and Marxism in the nineteenth century. Nevertheless, as we shall see below, there is still an echo of Kant's view of history in some contemporary versions of contractarianism.

Although Kant thought that a world of republics was a necessary condition of perpetual peace, he did not think it a sufficient condition without further legal guarantees. At this point, however, Kant apparently wavered between the ideal of a world state, which he thought would be the only means of making such guarantees effective, and the ideal of a world federation or "league of peace," which would preserve state sovereignty and independence, but at the price of effectiveness. Kant's providential theory of history explains his hope for a moral transformation of the human race that might make the second solution workable. But this idea of a world federation remains a distant aspiration, and in the meantime moral individuals must resist the very war-making capacity that provides the hidden mechanism for realizing their moral aspirations (Pangle 1976, 361). In the end, we arrive at a dualism very characteristic of Kant: actual states exist in a Hobbesian state of nature, where wars are neither just nor unjust because there is no guarantee of reciprocity and no common judge: yet, despite the prospect that we shall continue in this condition, individuals must hope and act as if an international social contract is not impossible.

Modern contractarianism

Turning from classical to more recent contractarianism, we find several striking differences. First, classical contractarians doubt the wisdom of relying too extensively on international law and question the possibility of employing a social contract to create a world federation or government. The classical contractarians tend to be "realists" in practice, even if they also sometimes entertain distant cosmopolitan aspirations, like Kant. In contrast, contemporary contractarian theorists of international ethics often begin with a critique of realism. Part of this shift results from a recent perception of increased international interdependence and reciprocity, while part reflects a more explicit "Kantian" division between normative and empirical theory. Second, in contrast with the classical writers, contemporary contractarians focus more directly on specific issues in international ethics such as intervention, nuclear deterrence, and global distributive justice. We can fill out our understanding of contractarianism by attending to some of these differences.

One of the clearest examples of the difference between classical and contemporary contractarianism is found in Charles Beitz's recent attempt to extend John Rawls's theory of justice to international relations (Beitz 1979). Beitz begins with a critique of both the descriptive and normative aspects of "Hobbesian" realism. According to Beitz, Hobbes's equation of the individual and international states of nature depends on four analogies. Like the individual state of nature, the international state of nature is supposedly characterized by: (1) actors of a single kind; (2) with relatively equal power; (3) who are independent of each other; and (4) with no reliable expectations of reciprocal compliance in the absence of a common superior. Beitz argues that empirically none of these analogies holds for modern international circumstances of justice. Instead, there are significant non-state actors, such as the IMF and the UN; state power is very unequal; there is a significant degree of interdependence; and there is also a fair degree of international reciprocity in the absence of any effective central authority. International circumstances of justice are more favorable to cooperation than Hobbesian realists admit, and attempts to pursue international peace and justice often do not entail irrational risks (Beitz 1979, 35–50).

Of course, each of these contentions has been challenged. For example, it has been argued that nuclear weapons once again equalize state vulnerability (Gauthier 1969, 207–8); that international interdependence is more productive of conflict than cooperation; and that international reciprocity is no more than a short-term tactic (for the last two criticisms echoing Rousseau, see Tucker 1977, 132–40). We cannot discuss these issues here. The point is simply that disagreement about the circumstances of justice among contemporary contractarians explains much of their disagreement about international ethics. Important as this is, however, it is not as crucial as controversy about the normative constraints that should be built into descriptions of the initial contractual situation.

As we have just seen, Beitz rejects the analogy between individuals and states that underlies the Hobbesian empirical description of the international state of nature. But Beitz also rejects any normative analogy between persons and states. The state is not a moral "person," and it does not have a moral interest in sovereignty that corresponds to individuals' moral interest in autonomy. Instead, Beitz follows the logic of Hobbes's own account in noting that the state is merely a *condition* of individual welfare, while departing from Hobbes in arguing that it is not always an indispensable condition. Beitz recognizes no distinctive "morality of states"; whatever moral standing the state has derives from a morality for individuals (Beitz 1979, 71–76). Obviously, this rejection of the person-state analogy goes far beyond the rejection of one version of contractarianism. That analogy is also part of the traditional normative justification of international law (for further discussion of the state as a *magna persona*, see "Origins of the tradition," Chapter 2).

In addition, Beitz disagrees with recent theorists like Michael Walzer who argue that the traditional rule of nonintervention rests on a right to communal autonomy. Walzer's contractarianism is of a *very* extended sort, however. According to Walzer the "community rests most deeply on a contract, Burkeian in character, among 'the living, the dead, and those who are yet to be born'" (Walzer 1985, 219). Walzer explains that, in his work, "Contract . . . is a metaphor" for the idea of a shared historical development of a political culture (Walzer 1985, 219). Underlying this metaphor is the individual right to be governed only by consent. Beitz is skeptical that individuals in the modern world consent to their governments in any meaningful sense, and he argues that actual consent by itself doesn't legitimize anything unless it is in accordance with principles of social justice (Beitz 1979, 77–83). In the absence of actual consent (since all states are inherently compulsory), individual and state principles of conduct must derive from a Rawlsian *hypothetical* contract.

The basic idea of Rawls's contract is that in imagining a collective decision about principles of social justice, we should allow individuals only enough information to reach a rational choice, but not enough information to take advantage of knowledge of their own special circumstances. In applying this approach to the problem of international justice, we are to imagine individuals choosing principles of international cooperation without knowledge of their particular identities, interests, or generation and place in society. We must also

192

imagine that these individuals are ignorant of their society's history, level of development and culture, level of natural resources, and role in the international economy. As noted above, Rawls argues that in such situations it is rational to choose principles of justice that maximize one's minimum share should one turn out to be the least-advantaged member of society. As applied by Beitz, this argument leads to sweeping principles of global justice: each *person* in international society is to have an equal right to the most extensive total system of equal basic liberties compatible with a similar system of liberty for all; and all basic international social and economic inequalities are to be arranged so that they are to the greatest advantage of the least well-off, consistent with a just savings principle and fair equality of opportunity (Beitz 1979, 143–53).

Rawls's own brief discussion of international justice leads to more conservative results, largely because he assumes that questions of justice do not arise in a world of relatively self-sufficient nations where there is little economic cooperation or reciprocity (Rawls 1973, 377–79). As we have seen, this assumption is part of the classical contractarian view: in contrast with other traditions such as utilitarianism, contractarianism generally holds first, that circumstances of distributive or social justice principally arise between members of a cooperative scheme, and second, that the state is the largest of such schemes. While contractarians also generally believe in a few "natural" or extra-contractarian duties of justice, their focus is on the sort of justice that comes into play *within* a scheme of social cooperation. For this reason, contractarians have traditionally viewed redistribution among nations as a matter of charity, not obligation.

Beitz, however, departs from Rawls and the classical contractarians primarily in arguing that requirements of justice are relevant whenever "social activity produces relative or absolute benefits [beyond a certain threshold] that would not exist if the social activity did not take place" (Beitz 1979, 131). Given this very broad interpretation of the circumstances of justice, the world economy must be viewed as a "cooperative scheme" even in the absence of deliberate cooperation. Together with Rawls's hypothetical contract, this view of the circumstances of justice makes international redistribution not a matter of charity, but a moral duty. Other traditional principles of international society are also transformed. For example, the principle of nonintervention now applies in principle only to states that are socially just. To prohibit intervention against unjust states would be to place an unjustifiable obstacle in the way of reform. Of course, there may be other prudential and moral considerations for thinking that intervention is normally impermissible, and even for setting up an absolute prohibition on intervention as a matter of positive international law. But in principle, intervention cannot be ruled out on the grounds of state autonomy alone.

Obviously, these views illustrate one sort of continuity within the contractarian tradition, running between Kant and modern theorists such as Rawls and Beitz. Like Kant, Beitz (and perhaps Rawls) is hopeful that economic interdependence will make it possible to move away from the current state system toward a more cooperative set of arrangements. Like Kant, Rawls and Beitz also draw a sharp distinction between the contractarian ideal and politics in the non-ideal world (for some of the differences between Kant, Rawls, and Beitz on the topics of economic interdependence and the relationship between ideal theory and non-ideal politics, see "Kantian internationalism," Chapter 7). For example, Rawls's theory provides little guidance in explaining how we resolve conflicts between the need to reform institutions and the need to honor expectations formed under present institutions. In such cases, we must fall back on an intuitive balancing of various principles, and in radically unjust situations we may have to fall back on consequentialism. As Beitz remarks, "if this is true, then political change in conditions of great injustice marks one kind of limit of the contract doctrine" (Beitz 1979, 171). Nevertheless, the Rawlsian contract does have important practical implications, perhaps the most fundamental of which is that we cannot subscribe to the "statist" view that foreign aid is a matter of charity rather than duty. Finally, like Kant, Beitz exhibits some ambivalence about the state as a mechanism for change. Although for Beitz global principles of justice ultimately apply to persons, not states, and although states often constitute an obstacle to reaching persons directly, it may be that the state system is the only practicable (and perhaps even the morally best) means of applying principles of global justice. Whether this is so depends on further empirical assumptions about how the state system can be expected to develop.

Contemporary issues in contractarianism

Contemporary moral and political theorists disagree sharply about whether Rawls's contract *does* yield the principles of justice discussed above. More fundamentally, theorists argue about whether Rawls's extra-contractarian description of the initial-choice situation *should* be set up to yield such principles. Many theorists believe that the Rawlsian contract excludes too much information without good justification (for an introduction to this controversy, see Daniels 1975).

The area of disagreement among contemporary moral and political philosophers that is most relevant to contractarianism in international ethics, however, concerns the connection between morality and rational choice. Crudely stated, "Kantians" argue that morality can often fundamentally conflict with prudential self-interest. They therefore tend to set up the contract to reflect this strong view of moral requirements. On the other hand, modern so-called "Hobbesians" believe that it is a condition of the rationality and motivational efficacy of morality that it not fundamentally conflict with self-interest (Kavka 1986; Gauthier 1986). They therefore tend to set up the contract to reflect rational self-interest more directly. Hobbesian contractarians emphasize reciprocity as the main rational motive for acting morally in international affairs, and this emphasis once again leads to a more "realist" view of state relations.

Of course, it can be argued that the long-run prudential interests of strong nations require decent treatment of weak ones. But at best this sort of argument leads to the conclusion that (where there is not already a cooperative scheme) the rich need only "buy off" the poor to the extent necessary to forestall international instability. On this approach, international principles of beneficence are greatly limited. Similarly, the idea of common rational self-interest can lead to arguments for arms limitation or even disarmament. But the morality of nuclear deterrence itself becomes less problematic if international relations reflect a Hobbesian state of nature, where nothing can be considered just or unjust. In this situation, the issue of nuclear deterrence is largely a matter of prudence, not morality – assuming there is a strong distinction between the two (for example, see Morris 1985, 479–97).

These disagreements in international ethics reflect a theoretical disagreement more fundamental than any we have discussed. Contractarians disagree about more than how the circumstances of justice should be described or what sort of moral constraints should be built into the contractual situation. At a more fundamental level, they disagree about how much reciprocity is necessary before principles of justice become relevant at all. To resolve this matter, a more general theory of practical reason is required to explain the relationship between morality and prudential self-interest.

Such philosophical debates have only an indirect influence on practical politics. Nevertheless, the indirect influence of philosophers can be profound and lasting. As an illustration, we might observe that the most significant contractarian figure in the background of recent

US foreign policy is neither Rawls, Kant, nor even Hobbes, but probably Locke. Consider the intellectual defense that some writers have offered for the "Reagan Doctrine" in US foreign policy. That doctrine holds that it is permissible to provide military aid to insurgents who rebel against repressive non-democratic regimes but impermissible to provide aid to those who rebel against democratic ones. The Reagan Doctrine does not exhibit Hobbesian skepticism about rights of rebellion, Rousseauian skepticism about the virtue of large states, or Rawlsian skepticism about actual consent. Instead, an essentially Lockean view of the social contract in domestic society is used to decide which states are legitimate. In defense of the Reagan Doctrine, Lloyd N. Cutler, counsel to the US president from 1979 to 1980, invokes Locke directly: "Our Declaration of Independence, influenced by Vattel, Locke and other apostles of the eighteenth-century Enlightenment, proclaimed the rights of any people to rebel by force against a tyrannical regime . . . Is there a parallel right to rebel by force against a democratic regime that gives all its people the opportunity to vote in free elections open to any candidate? John Locke thought not" (Cutler 1985, 102–3). Cutler's defense of the Reagan Doctrine is unusual, however, in that he wishes to square that doctrine with existing international law, particularly Article 2(4) of the UN Charter, which appears to rule out resorts to force even when war is not declared. Other advocates for the Reagan Doctrine, such as Charles Krauthammer, dismiss such legal justifications and argue instead that international law can be ignored whenever reciprocity is lacking. As Krauthammer remarks, "unlike the domestic social contract, international law lacks an enforcer . . . If one country breaks the rules at will . . . [what] can possibly oblige other countries to honor that claim? The idea that international law must be a reciprocal arrangement or none at all is not new" (Krauthammer 1985, 24). Despite their disagreement over the international legal justification of the Reagan Doctrine, however, Cutler and Krauthammer agree with Locke that actual consent is the correct test of both national and international political legitimacy and that third parties have a moral right to help enforce the rights of others in the absence of an effective central authority.

Of course, we may question the application of this rationale for intervention. Are the insurgents or "freedom fighters" in question really committed to establishing a democratic government? More basically, we may question the connection between this "Lockean rationale" and Locke's own teachings: did Locke's social contract justify "democracy," or only the more limited ideas of the rule of law and the protection of a few basic rights? The vocabulary of a tradition can be misappropriated, and debates within a tradition are often precisely about such questions of appropriation and misappropriation. It seems clear, however, that despite a great deal of criticism at the philosophical level, eighteenth-century Lockean notions of legitimacy continue to have a strong influence on the way the US government approaches international affairs.

Finally, this Lockean emphasis on natural rights once again illustrates the extent to which contractarians depend on extra-contractarian assumptions and arguments. The most important external criticism of the tradition has always been that this reliance on extra-contractarian assumptions makes the contract itself an unnecessary shuffle: why not appeal directly to the moral considerations that justify the contract? (For the most famous example of this criticism, see Hume 1748.) Contractarians have responded to this sort of criticism in a number of ways.

First, even if the contract *is* only an organizational device, it is a powerful one. It allows us to draw together many empirical and ethical considerations in a systematic, compact, and elegant way. Rhetorically, the idea of the contract has great appeal. Philosophically, it serves as a useful bridge between moral and political theory. Second, in those cases where the social contract is arguably a reality, the contract gives individuals an important opportunity to exercise control over their own fate. The importance of such control is indicated by the original purpose of the contract for theorists such as Locke. For Locke, the social contract was important because it protected individuals from being bound even by *just* regimes unless they had first consented. On this Lockean view, freedom is an important value apart from its contribution to social justice (Simmons 1979, 61–71). Finally, some modern contractarians have offered sophisticated philosophical replies to this sort of external criticism. Rawls has argued that his contract really does introduce a distinct set of considerations that cannot be restated in extra-contractarian terms (for a detailed discussion, see Daniels 1979, 256–82). Recent theorists like David Gauthier have tried to derive the conditions of the contract almost entirely *from* a theory of rational choice rather than from moral assumptions brought *to* a situation of rational choice (Gauthier 1986).

Whether these kinds of arguments ultimately succeed, the main value of the contractarian tradition is surely that it directs our attention to one of the central issues in international ethics, namely the role of reciprocity. Of course, it might be said that the classical contractarians were *not* contractarians in international ethics, precisely because they thought that sufficient reciprocity did not exist in international affairs.

But even this view reflects a distinctive, important, and controversial view of justice. It raises basic issues that remain unresolved: To what extent are principles of justice independent of social cooperation? What exactly do we mean by reciprocity or a "return in due measure"? How much reciprocity must exist before principles of justice apply? More fundamentally, how should we understand the relation between morality and prudential self-interest? Other traditions focus less on the notion of reciprocity in explaining the idea of justice, and more on other considerations, like the common good (for example, compare the discussion of natural law under "The common good and the complete society," Chapter 6). But it can be argued that in international relations the idea of reciprocity is especially significant and problematic, given the absence of an effective central authority. For this reason, the contractarian tradition is likely to have a strong and continuing influence on ethical reflections about international affairs.

Suggested reading

For the major writings of the classical contractarians, see the suggested reading for Chapter 4 (Hobbes and Rousseau) and Chapter 7 (Kant). Locke's major presentation of the social contract is in the second treatise of *Two Treatises on Government*. Within this treatise Chapter 3, "Of The State of Nature," and Chapter 16, "Of Conquest," are especially relevant.

Aside from these primary sources, the beginning reader should look at Kenneth Waltz's *Man, The State, and War* (New York: Columbia University Press, 1954) and Stanley Hoffmann's critique of Waltz (Hoffmann 1965). Along with Thomas Pangle's essay (1976), Hoffmann's critique offers the best short comparison of the early contractarians on international ethics. Richard Cox's *Locke on War and Peace* (Oxford: The Clarendon Press, 1960) also presents an interesting, albeit more controversial, comparison of Hobbes and Locke. Since Hobbes has exercised more influence on international ethics than any other contractarian thinker, the reader may also wish to look at Murray Forsyth's "Thomas Hobbes and the External Relations of States," *British Journal of International Studies* 5 (1969), as well as a more recent collection of essays edited by Timo Airaksinen and Martin A. Bertman, *Hobbes: War Among Nations* (Aldershot: Gower 1990).

The secondary literature on Rawls's work is so extensive that readers should consult *John Rawls and His Critics: An Annotated Bibliography*, edited by J. H. Wellbank, Denis Snook, and David Mason (New York: Garland Publishing 1982) for detailed guidance, although Daniels (1975) is also a good starting point. Rawls's own discussion of justice between states is presented primarily in Chapter 6, section 58 of *A Theory of Justice* (1973). The last third of Thomas Pogge's *Realizing Rawls* enthusiastically explores the general implications of Rawls's theory for international society (Ithaca, NY: Cornell University Press,

1989). For a discussion of how Rawls's theory applies to a specific issue in international ethics, see Mark Wicclair, "Rawls and the Principle of Nonintervention," in *John Rawls's Theory of Social Justice: An Introduction*, eds. Gene Blocker and Elizabeth Smith (Athens: Ohio University Press, 1980), 289–308. For another (non-Rawlsian) attempt to apply contractarian reasoning to a specific issue, see Christopher W. Morris, "A Contractarian Defense of Nuclear Deterrence," *Ethics* 95 (1985): 479–97.

The idea of reciprocity as a precondition of social and political justice is perhaps the most distinctive feature of contractarianism. Charles Taylor offers a good point of entry into the contemporary debate about the scope of contractual justice and its relation to duties of justice that apply prior to social cooperation in "The Nature and Scope of Distributive Justice," in *Philosophy and the Human Sciences: Philosophical Papers*, vol. 2 (Cambridge: Cambridge University Press, 1985), 289–303.

References

Beitz, Charles. 1979. *Political Theory and International Relations*. Princeton: Princeton University Press.

Cutler, Lloyd N. 1985. "The Right to Intervene." *Foreign Affairs* 64: 96–112.

Daniels, Norman, ed. 1975. *Reading Rawls: Critical Studies of 'A Theory of Justice'*. New York: Basic Books.

1979. "Wide Reflective Equilibrium and Theory Acceptance in Ethics." *Journal of Philosophy* 76: 256–82.

Donaldson, Thomas. 1991. "Circumstances of Justice." In *The Encyclopedia of Ethics*, ed. Larry C. Becker. New York: Garland Press.

Gauthier, David. 1969. "Hobbes on International Relations." In *The Logic of Leviathan*. Oxford: The Clarendon Press.

1986. *Morals By Agreement*. Oxford: The Clarendon Press.

Harsanyi, John. 1975. "Can the Maximin Principle Serve as a Basis for Morality? A Critique of John Rawls's Theory." *American Political Science Review* 69: 594–606.

Hoffmann, Stanley. 1965. "Rousseau on War and Peace." In *The State of War: Essays on the Theory and Practice of International Politics*, 54–88. London: Praeger.

Hume, David. 1740. *A Treatise of Human Nature*, bk. III, pt. II, sec. ii., ed. L. A. Selby Bigge. 2nd edn. revised P. Nidditch. Oxford: The Clarendon Press, 1978.

1748. "Of the Original Contract." In *Essays: Moral, Political and Literary*, ed. Eugene Miller. Indianapolis: The Liberty Press, 1985.

1751. *Enquiries Concerning Human Understanding and Concerning the Principles of Morals*, sec. III, pt. I, ed. L. A. Selby Bigge. 3rd edn. revised P. Nidditch. Oxford: The Clarendon Press, 1975.

Kavka, Gregory. 1986. *Hobbesian Moral and Political Theory*. Princeton: Princeton University Press.

Morris, Christopher W. 1985. "A Contractarian Defense of Nuclear Deterrence." *Ethics* 95: 479–97.

Oakeshott, Michael. 1962. "The Moral Life in the Writings of Thomas Hobbes." In *Rationalism and Politics*. New Jersey: Rowman and Littlefield.

Pangle, Thomas L. 1976. "The Moral Basis of National Security: Four Historical Perspectives." In *National Security Problems*, ed. Klaus Knorr. Lawrence, KS: University Press of Kansas.

Rawls, John. 1973. *A Theory of Justice*. Cambridge, MA: Harvard University Press.

Simmons, A. J. 1979. *Moral Principles and Political Obligation*. Princeton: Princeton University Press.

Skinner, Quentin. 1978. *The Foundations of Modern Political Thought*, vol. 1. Cambridge: Cambridge University Press.

Taylor, Charles. 1989. *Sources of the Self*. Cambridge, MA: Harvard University Press.

Tucker, Robert W. 1977. *The Inequality of Nations*. New York: Basic Books.

Walzer, Michael. 1985. "The Moral Standing of States: A Response to Four Critics." In *International Ethics*, eds. Marshall Cohen et al. Princeton: Princeton University Press.

10 LIBERALISM AND INTERNATIONAL REFORM

MICHAEL JOSEPH SMITH

Central to liberalism, whether conceived as a tradition, an ideology, or as ethical doctrine, is concern for individual liberty. Liberals worry about how individuals can claim and preserve "a certain minimum area of personal freedom which on no account must be violated" (Berlin 1969, 124). The task of the state is to protect that minimum area from arbitrary violations by other people, governments, and institutions. Of course, on the difficult questions of how to define that protected area, which kinds of states and institutions are best suited to do so, and which means are permitted to guarantee and even to extend individual freedom, liberals disagree; indeed, their disagreement on such key issues has helped to keep the tradition vital. Liberals argue about the role of equality, about the nature and importance of democratic self-government, and about the proper relationship between state and society, between liberal tolerance and the shared values of community. Debates on these issues, both within the liberal tradition and between it and competing perspectives, place liberalism at the center of the contemporary discourse of political thought.

Liberalism's contribution to questions of international ethics is more problematic: as one sympathetic interpreter has put it, "international affairs have been the nemesis of liberalism" (Hoffmann 1987, 400). Whereas liberals can claim impressive victories in the realm of domestic politics, the relations among states have proven to be remarkably resistant to liberal reform. The world has yet to emerge from the "lawless state of savagery" Kant deplored in 1784. Liberals ranging from Richard Cobden to Norman Cousins have denounced political leaders for pursuing parochially defined national interest, for playing the traditional game of nations. A stubborn adherence to a "pathology of power," they argue, stands in the way of our achieving a "global humanist community." Yet liberal theorists and politicians have not lost hope. Whether from a sense of duty or from a deeply held belief in the eventual triumph of reason, they continue to urge, and seek to apply, ideas of limiting arbitrary power and protecting individual freedom to a milieu in which such freedom is regularly violated with impunity. Indeed this attempt to reform the international milieu is a defining characteristic of the liberal tradition in international ethics. Exponents of this tradition have asserted that if we can tame the struggle for power domestically, we can also do so in the realm of international relations (Kant [1784] 1970, 47; Cousins 1987; Johansen 1980).

Liberal theorists judge the obstacles to such reform very differently. Some, like Bentham, seem to regard international reform as an inevitable result of the spread of commerce and the application of rational principles. Others hold a more tragic optimisim: Kant, for example, believed that nations would recognize the need for an international federation to tame their "barbarous freedom" only "after many devastations, upheavals and even complete inner exhaustion of their powers." More recent writers proceed from a kind of apocalyptic premise that makes our very survival in an age of "self-annihilating weapons" dependent upon a fundamental change in the character of inter-state relations. Some of these differences in emphasis will come out below in the discussion of liberal notions of authority, conceptions of the common good, and attitudes toward existing institutions. Liberals are also divided on intervention in other states for the purposes of reform. These tensions cannot be overlooked. But, with some notable exceptions, most liberals in this tradition are convinced that the status quo will not do, that international politics as usual is a recipe for moral and political disaster. More than anything else, this conviction about the necessity for international reform is the identifying feature of the liberal tradition (Kant [1784] 1970, 47; Cousins 1987, 203).

Liberal premises

Reason and human nature

The authority of the liberal tradition taken as a whole derives from its faith in reason and in the application of rationally derived principles to human institutions. Liberals believe that disputes can and should be resolved by recourse to rational argument. Reason itself can be the ultimate arbiter. Kant rejected what he saw as the false dichotomy between theory and practice, claiming that "whatever reason shows to be valid in theory, is also valid in practice." Jeremy Bentham, concurred, asserting that if plans "have been bad in practice, it is because they have been bad in theory." Listening to those "practical men" who are "no friend to theories," Bentham wrote, "one would almost think that in the process of thinking there was something wicked, or at least unwise." Belief in the human capacity for reason is a hallmark of the liberal tradition (Kant [1784] 1970, 92; Bentham 1971, 200, 196).

One distinct group of liberals derives this faith from the view that human nature is essentially benign. Locke and Bentham, in their different ways, reject the notion that human beings are inevitably sinful and incapable of genuinely moral behavior. Bentham and the utilitarians also show great faith in the human capacity for rational understanding. On this view, the principle of utility, not a purportedly universal *animus dominandi*, will inevitably govern the relations between states as well as within states. Human nature, far from being an obstacle to the eventual triumph of rational arrangements, will eventually express its true interests in peace and a thoroughly reformed international system.

Liberals writing after the world wars are notably more defensive about human nature, but they nevertheless resist the dark conclusions of the realists. War, asserted G. Lowes Dickinson, "is not a fatal product of human nature; it is an effect of that nature when put under certain conditions." Writing in the midst of the First World War, Dickinson argued that "nothing will save us but the harnessing of human reason to human charity." And Alfred E. Zimmern, a favorite target of realist critics, could lament our "limited intelligence" and "muddled thinking" but remain convinced that human nature itself was pacific (see Smith 1987, 56–57). More recently, Richard Falk has written that "by being true to ourselves we will also help forge the still uncreated conscience of the human race" (Johansen 1980, xxvii). Liberal faith in our essential goodness – and in the potential efficacy of appeals based on reason – was shaken, but it survived.

Kant's view of human nature is less sanguine, his optimism more painful. He refers to the "unsocial sociability of men," that is, an innate conflict between our desire to avoid all restraints on our freedom and our "inclination to live in society" and therefore to accept the minimum restraints that make society possible. It is through this inner conflict that we take "the first true steps from barbarism to culture." Without our "asocial qualities" we would live an "Arcadian, pastoral existence" worthy of sheep, and our higher faculties would remain undeveloped. Thus Kant echoes the unflattering portrayal of human nature one finds, say, in Hobbes: he notes our "enviously competitive vanity and insatiable desires for possession or even power." But, unlike Hobbes or the realists, Kant finds in these

203

characteristics a providential design to force human beings to develop their natural capacity for reason and culture. "The sources of the very unsociableness and continual resistance which cause so many evils at the same time encourage man towards new exertions of his powers and thus towards further development of his natural capacities." This same providential design, of course, leads human beings to found a civil society; and eventually, after many years of wars, upheavals, and devastation, men will "take the step that reason could have suggested to them even without so many sad experiences – that of abandoning the lawless state of savagery and entering a federation of peoples" (Kant [1784] 1970, 44–45, 47).

Thus Kant shares the liberal tradition's faith in reason, but cautions that its triumph over power may not come soon and will by no means be painless. For Bentham and his school, in contrast, that triumph was virtually at hand. This vital difference can partly be explained by the key importance of welfare for the utilitarians as opposed to duty for Kant and his followers.

According to the British liberals, a rational appreciation of our individual interests and of the requirements of our own welfare would lead to the attenuation of national conflicts and the spread of trade and commerce across the globe. In his *Plan for a Universal and Perpetual Peace*, Bentham argues that "between the interests of nations there is nowhere any real conflict; if they appear repugnant anywhere it is only in proportion as they are misunderstood" (1927, 43). In the same plan, written with four other pamphlets on international law between 1786 and 1789 (but not published until 1843), Bentham presents two major propositions "dedicated to the common welfare of all civilised nations." First, he urged Britain (and all nations) to join in "the reduction and fixation of the [military] force of the several nations that compose the European system," that is, to pursue a general agreement for disarmament. Secondly, Bentham argues for the "emancipation of all distant dependencies" held by colonial powers ([1838] 1927, 43, 11). Underlying these propositions was an unshakable conviction that neither war, nor armaments, nor colonies served "the real interests" of any state. All were obstacles to the development of international trade and commerce: "Mark well the contrast. All trade is in its essence advantageous – even to that party to whom it is least so. All war is in essence ruinous; and yet the great employments of government are to treasure up occasions of war and to put fetters on trade" (Bentham [1838] 1927, 25).

By the time J. S. Mill wrote his *Principles of Political Economy* in 1848, the anti-mercantilist ideas of Adam Smith had virtually become commonplace. Mill not only praises the economic advantages of international commerce, but also points to its intellectual and moral benefits. Commerce would replace war as the principal means by which people would "come into contact with persons dissimilar to themselves." This contact was bound to improve the welfare and culture of all "civilized nations" by increasing the "communication [that] has always been, and is peculiarly in the present age, one of the primary sources of progress." Commerce, Mill concludes, "is rapidly rendering war obsolete, by strengthening and multiplying the personal interests which are in natural opposition to it. And it may be said without exaggeration that the great extent and rapid increase of international trade, in being the principal guarantee of the peace of the world, is the great permanent security for the uninterrupted progress of the ideas, the institutions, and the character of the human race" (1909, 581–82; see also Howard 1978).

Nineteenth-century British liberals identified a strong connection between international commerce, domestic welfare, and the foreign-policy stance of their country. For them, high military expenditures, balance-of-power machinations, and the pursuit of colonies all combined to divert attention from the business of promoting economic prosperity at home. States and diplomats could be expected to pursue such aggressive foreign policies – their own interests were at stake – but with the aid of a properly enlightened and led public opinion, rationality could triumph and state power could be limited. For this reason, figures like Richard Cobden were indefatigable in the promotion of their ideas; they sought nothing less than to educate and mobilize public opinion for the pursuit of peace.

Cobden, described by A. J. P. Taylor as "the most powerful reasoner who has ever applied himself to practical politics," is a fascinating exemplar of the liberal tradition because of his combination of unshakable conviction, tireless advocacy, and rhetorical power. Best known as a crusader for free trade (an 1842 title is emblematic: *Free Trade as the Best Human Means for Securing Universal and Permanent Peace*), Cobden successfully led the movement to repeal the protectionist Corn Laws and, throughout his long public career, consistently opposed an interventionist foreign policy. His ridicule of the balance of power as a reason for such interventionism is justly famous. After a survey of competing and self-contradictory definitions he concluded that "the theory of the balance of power is a mere chimera – a creation of the politician's brain – a phantasm, without definite form or tangible existence – a mere conjunction of syllables, forming words which convey sound without meaning." And yet wars are fought, armaments amassed, trade interrrupted, passions aroused for the sake of this "phantasm" (Taylor 1957, 46; Cobden 1903, 202).

Cobden, like Norman Angell after him, sought above all to refute the notion that wars could actually promote commerce and prosperity. The very idea seemed to him scandalous:

> How shall a profession which withdraws from productive industry the ablest of the human race, and teaches them systematically the best modes of destroying mankind, which awards honors only in proportion to the number of victims offered at its sanguinary altar, which overturns cities, ravages farms and vineyards, uproots forests, burns the ripened harvest, which, in a word, exists but in the absence of law, order, and security – how can such a profession be favorable to commerce, which increases only with the increase of human life, whose parent is agriculture, and which perishes or flies at the approach of lawless rapine? (Cobden 1903, 245–46)

The passage conveys a sense of the moral conviction that infused Cobden's program and is characteristic of the liberal tradition down to our own day. The basic liberal stance was concisely put by Cobden in an 1850 parliamentary debate: "The progress of freedom depends more upon the maintenance of peace, the spread of commerce, and the diffusion of education than upon the labours of cabinets and foreign offices." Or, in the words of the maxim with which he concluded his attack on the balance of power – a maxim he regarded as proven by the growth of American wealth and prosperity up to 1860 – "As little intercourse betwixt the *Governments*, as much connection as possible between the *nations* of the world" (Taylor 1957, 49; Cobden 1903, 216).

It is not my purpose here to survey dissenting arguments about British foreign policy through the course of the nineteenth century. But it is worth noting that arguments like Cobden's continued to be made by liberals writing much later. L. T. Hobhouse noted in 1911 that "it is of the essence of Liberalism to oppose the use of force, the basis of all tyranny" and thus liberals stand firmly against the "tyranny of armaments" and the "military spirit" which "eats into free institutions and absorbs public resources which might go to the advancement of civilization." Bertrand Russell, in *Why Men Fight* (1916) makes a similar argument: "The excessive power of the State, partly through internal oppression, but principally through war and the fear of war, is one of the chief causes of misery in the modern world, and one of the main reasons for the discouragement which prevents men from growing to their full mental stature" (Hobhouse 1911, 45; Russell 1916, 65–66).

All these liberals assume that there is no fundamental conflict of interests that necessarily divides states or human communities. Universal laws, if applied rationally and not subjected to wrongheaded interference, can ultimately lead to harmony among all peoples. For the British liberals, the engine that will pull all of humanity to the happy day when peoples trade peacefully without the bellicose intervention of tyrannizing states is an appreciation of the benefits to be derived from banishing war and the spirit of militarism. Increasing enlightenment, aided by the spread of commerce, will lead people to limit state power both domestically and internationally. For Kant and later nationalistic liberals (like Mazzini) on the continent, the path to universal peace is less smooth, littered with the sad experiences of wars, insurrections, and the increasingly costly military preparation for both. The first group argues that one should seek peace because it would increase the welfare and freedom of all mankind – seek peace and prosper. The second group sees international reform as an ethical duty, with the benefits being as much moral as material. The practical conclusion is identical – reform the anarchic state of international relations – but the reason and motivation of each is somewhat distinct.

Principles and consequences

Including Bentham and Kant in the same ethical tradition may at first seem perverse. These two founding fathers, after all, symbolize the great divide between deontological and consequentialist approaches to moral philosophy. But considered in the international context, their differences recede in importance. Whether Benthamite or Kantian, liberals agree on the importance of basing and judging one's acts, and of founding political institutions, on rationally derived and rationally defensible principles. Thus both deontologists and consequentialists scrutinize the international milieu to find such principles – and both groups find this milieu severely wanting. Neither Bentham nor Kant accepted the notion that change in institutions could only be a slow and organic process. Both were quite willing to urge fundamental change in long-standing practices or institutions on the basis of rational principles. Moreover, unlike Marxism and political realism, both hold a fundamental belief in the independence and efficacy of ideas: one's principles cannot be reduced to his class interests or to purportedly objective national interests. Ideas, in short, matter; they have an integrity and life of their own, and they can move people and policy.

Similarly, the behavior of states can reflect a commitment to ideas.

207

Liberal reformers do not accept that the foreign-policy behavior of a state has to reflect, in some vaguely deterministic way, that state's position in an international power hierarchy. States could – and ought to – act on what they considered to be right in principle. As John Bright put it in a parliamentary debate on Gladstone's occupation of Egypt in 1882:

> For forty years at least I have endeavoured, from time to time, to teach my countrymen an opinion and doctrine which I hold – namely that the moral law is intended not only for individual life, but for the life and practice of States in their dealings with one another. I think that in the present case there has been a manifest violation of International Law and of the moral law. (Taylor 1957, 81)

As strong believers in a protected area of individual freedom, liberals are committed to the notion of an autonomous sphere of free inquiry. For liberals, the notion of a search for truth is real; it has no ironic, postmodernist, overtones. Because ultimately the interests of all people are harmonious, this search for truth need not be a source of conflict, except for those who fear what exposure to the light of universal laws will do to their sectional or vested interests. Those devoted to the maintenance of "pathological power" may well resist the ideas of the cosmopolitan community of mankind. Bentham, Mill, Cobden, Bright, Angell, and Lowes Dickinson, and in the United States, James T. Shotwell and Nicholas Murray Butler all experienced and decried what they saw as a benighted refusal on the part of traditional statesmen to recognize the need for international reform. Yet they retained and nurtured a faith in the political efficacy of principled argument. A modern critic of liberalism has identified three characteristic liberal "illusions": "the belief in rational harmony, the illusion of ultimate agreement, and ... the idea that will and desire can ultimately be sovereign in human affairs" (Minogue 1963, 200).

Liberals, of course, deny that these beliefs are illusions, but the description of the beliefs themselves seems fair. Perhaps more than any other tradition, liberalism asserts the eventual primacy of moral argument over political expediency. Kant puts this argument in classically liberal terms:

> A true system of politics cannot take a single step without first paying tribute to morality. Although politics is a difficult art in itself, no art is required to combine it with morality. For as soon as the two come into contact, morality can cut through the knot which politics cannot untie. The rights of man must be held sacred, however great a sacrifice the ruling power may have to make. (Kant [1792] 1970, 125)

Although liberal utilitarians obviously would not define morality in the way that Kant does, they would still agree with his assertion that principle should come before "politics" even if this means a substantial change in current social arrangements. Indeed, as Hedley Bull characterizes the "universalist" view of international morality, achieving potential community of mankind is a moral imperative requiring "the overthrow of the system of states and its replacement by a cosmopolitan society" (Bull 1977, 26). Liberal reformers of both deontological and consequentialist persuasion do not shrink from the far-reaching consequences of acting on their principles. In this sense, the relationship between principles and consequences in the whole liberal tradition has broad implications for existing institutions. To be sure, consequentialists stress the shortcomings of current arrangements and the benefits to be derived from change as a way to justify their preferred reforms, whereas Kantians emphasize the requirement to seek peace through international reform as an overriding moral duty. The effect is to give liberal reformers two different, but not uncomplementary, arguments with which to appeal for public support.

Liberal internationalism

The common good and the problem of nationalism

Liberal conceptions of the good and common good are the subject of considerable controversy. Critics from both right and left complain that the liberal emphasis on so-called "negative freedom" (protecting the individual from outside encroachments by state or society), by defining liberty itself as the absence of constraint, has resulted in an impoverished, atomistic doctrine based on disembodied individuals. The debate often surfaces in discussions of human rights, where liberal adherents of "negative freedom" often define such rights in strict civil and political terms, while those who favor some version of "positive freedom" regard the essential human rights as social and economic. An emphasis on individualistic civil rights is often said to ignore the communal character of human life. Liberals like Maurice Cranston reply that to focus on these aspects is to "push *all* talk of human rights out of the clear realm of the morally compelling to the twilight world of utopian aspiration" (Cranston 1973, 68). This issue is canvassed fully under "Rights in a cross-section of world society," Chapter 12; its relevance here concerns the question of how liberals define the common good.

Liberals argue that the greatest strength of their approach is that it respects the right and the capacity of the individual to define his own conception of "the good." Only in this way, when individuals in a given society have the liberty to set their own goals – and, when necessary, to bring them into harmonious co-existence with the goals of others – can a true conception of common good emerge. As Hobhouse puts it, "every constructive social doctrine rests on the conception of human progress. The heart of Liberalism is the understanding that progress is not a matter of mechanical contrivance, but of the liberation of living spiritual energy." Thus, to many liberals the society that best serves the "common good" is a society that allows as many different conceptions of the good by liberated individuals as can be peacefully accommodated in a given society (Hobhouse 1911, 187; also see the comparison with the contractarian view of the common good in "The structure of contractarian arguments," Chapter 9).

There are, as some liberals have recognized, three main difficulties with such a rough definition of the common good. Will individuals be sufficiently free and educated to allow them to form a conception of the good? What happens when their conceptions clash? What are the boundaries of a given society? Here the differences among liberals are striking. Bentham, James Mill, Cobden, and Bright propose that a natural harmony of interests will inevitably assert itself as enlightenment proceeds and governmental interference withers. Bentham, of course, straightforwardly defines the common good as the greatest happiness of the greatest number. For him, the object of international reform is to make the greatest happiness principle "apply to all nations taken together." The principle can and should be applied globally: in this way artificial national differences will inexorably recede. To the extent that nations imagine their interests to conflict, Bentham suggests, they need greater instruction – presumably from him and his fellow "philosophic radicals." Bentham concludes confidently that "the more we become enlightened, the more benevolent shall we become" (Wolfers and Martin 1956, 181–82). Cobden's maxim that governments should leave international relations to individuals rests on the same assumption of an underlying harmony of interests throughout the world.

Common to many pre-First World War liberals is a comfortable belief in the spread of respresentative democracy and an inevitable pacification of the world. The principle of nationality is seen as entirely compatible with liberal ideas about ending of arbitrary power. Even Mazzini, the romantic prophet of nationalism who regards a period of liberating warfare as essential, and deplores Cobden's doctrine of non-intervention as cowardly, believes that liberalism and the nation go hand in hand (Howard 1978, 50). Thus many liberals see no conflict between the apparently particularist doctrines of nationality and the universalist claims of liberalism itself. The notion of self-determination and the ultimate harmony of interests through commerce and education are thought to be entirely complementary.

Other nineteenth-century liberals were less sanguine. In France, Charles Renouvier warned against the illiberal tendencies of nationalism. In Britain, Lord Acton argued that

> nationality does not aim either at liberty or at prosperity, both of which it sacrifices to the imperative necessity of making the nation the mould and measure of the State. Its course will be marked with material as well as moral ruin, in order that a new invention may prevail over the works of God and the interest of mankind. There is no principle of change . . . more comprehensive, more subversive, or more arbitrary than this. (Acton 1907, 299)

Liberals writing after the world wars, with fresh evidence of the evils of nationalism, follow Acton's line. Nationalism is deplored as an atavism, a barrier to enlightenment, an illiberal doctrine which prevents those who mistakenly cling to it from recognizing their genuine interests. Even self-proclaimed realists deplore the "balkanization, demoralization, and barbarization on a world-wide scale" that are said to be the result of nationalism. Reading the following passage from Hans J. Morgenthau, one might even be forgiven for numbering him among the liberal internationalists:

> Nationalism has had its day. It was the political principle appropriate to the post-feudal and pre-atomic age. For the technology of the steam engine, it was indeed in good measure a force for progress. In the atomic age, it must make way for a political principle of larger dimensions, in tune with the world-wide configurations of interest and power of the age. (1962, vol. I, 195)

But for the ritual reference to power in the concluding phrase, the passage might well serve as a summary of the postwar liberal attitude toward nationalism.

There can be no doubt that the twentieth century has strained the liberal faith in the benevolent effects of national self-determination. But, in general, that faith, rephrased to omit the specifically national content of self-determination, remains. Contemporary reformist authors continue to believe that a global common good can be achieved if the institutional and attitudinal obstacles can be overcome. They deplore rather than celebrate nationalism, and present the choice between parochial interests and cosmopolitan interests starkly. Writing in 1947, Francis B. Sayre declares that the postwar era could mark "a far better world if it be built actually upon human welfare rather than narrow national self-interest. The rampant nationalism of the nineteenth century must give way to a twentieth-century broad humanitarianism – a genuine concern for the individual welfare of men and women all over the world – if we and our civilization are to survive. It is not a matter of choice. It is a plain matter of survival." Writing nearly thirty years later as director of the World Order Models Project, Saul Mendlovitz asserts that "a global community has emerged and global governance is not far behind." Robert Johansen is confident that "people are capable of extraordinary attitudinal change and social adjustment when they feel that all persons will share the necessary sacrifices equally, when they are convinced that change is imperative . . . and when the need for change is related directly to the pursuit of higher values" (Sayre in Woodward et al. 1947, 136; Mendlovitz in Galtung 1974, xxi; Johansen 1980, 404).

Thus liberals have moved from regarding nationalism as a liberating doctrine compatible with the goals of limiting state power and pacifying the international competition to a recognition that unbridled nationalism has proven in the modern era to be one of the strongest ideological weapons in the armory of independent sovereign states. The dominant strand of the tradition since the First World War, therefore, has been to condemn nationalism insofar as it stands in the way of an emerging global community. At the same time, liberals continue to applaud self-determination, especially in the guise of anti-colonialism. They seem to believe that the particularist doctrine of nationalism can be transcended by a universalist conception of the self-determination of peoples. But liberals have never solved the problem of how and whether one can have the good effects of the latter without the ill effects of the former. The tradition remains profoundly ambivalent about nationalism and the idea of the nation-state.

The problem of intervention

Liberals are also ambivalent about intervention. Members of the tradition disagree over whether a liberal state may intervene to promote the rights of citizens in an illiberal state. The predominant strand in the tradition appears to be noninterventionist. Consider this assertion: "Social and political orders in one country or another changed in the past and may change in the future. But this change is the exclusive affair of the people of that country and is their choice. Any interference in domestic affairs and any attempts to restrict the sovereignty of states – friends, allies, or any others – are inadmissible." The author of these remarks was not Richard Cobden but Soviet premier Mikhail Gorbachev in a speech to the Council of Europe on July 7, 1989. Remarkable chiefly because of its source, this statement well expresses the noninterventionist position within the liberal tradition. In the speech Mr. Gorbachev follows a traditional liberal line of argument, asserting that "differences among states are not removable. They are ... even favorable, provided, of course, that the competition between the different types of society is directed at creating better material and spiritual living conditions for all people" (*New York Times*, July 7, 1989, A6).

Allowing for a different rhetorical style, one could easily exchange these remarks for those made by Cobden or Bright in the course of parliamentary debates on British policy in Europe. Compare the peroration of an 1854 speech by Bright:

> The past events of our history have taught us that the intervention of this country in European wars is not only unnecessary, but calamitous ... We have left Europe at least as much in chains as before a single effort was made by us to rescue her from tyranny. I believe if this country, seventy years ago, had adopted the principle of non-intervention in every case where her interests were not directly and obviously assailed, she would have been saved from much of the pauperism and brutal crimes by which our Government and people alike have been disgraced. This country might have been a garden, every dwelling might have been of marble, and every person who treads its soil might have been sufficiently educated. (Taylor 1957, 82)

As the passage suggests, the issue for liberals is how best to protect rights and promote prosperity at home and abroad. For noninterventionists, the best – indeed the only – way to promote institutional reform and to advertise the virtues of freedom is by example. One cannot by military intervention free foreign peoples from the chains of native tyranny; one must simply tend to one's problems at home and, as Bright puts it, "set a high example of a Christian nation, free in its isolation, courteous and just in its conduct towards all foreign states, and resting its policy on the unchangeable foundations of Christian morality" (Joll 1950, 146).

John Stuart Mill provides an interesting example of a liberal who tried to develop a doctrine of nonintervention that was discriminating rather than absolute. His argument has recently been revived by Michael Walzer in *Just and Unjust Wars*. Mill suggests that the decision whether or not to intervene "will be different according as the yoke which the people are attempting to throw off is that of a purely native government, or of foreigners." If a people are struggling against a foreign oppressor, intervention to help them is permissible. In an essay on the 1848 revolution in France he asks rhetorically: "Is any motive to such interference of a more binding character than that of preventing the liberty of a nation, which cares sufficiently for liberty to have risen in arms for its assertion, from being crushed by tyrannical oppressors, and these not even of its own name and blood, but foreign conquerors?" But when the tyranny is home-grown, Mill argues that only through an "arduous struggle to become free by their own efforts" can a people establish lasting institutions of freedom. In that case an outside liberal state would be limited to offering "the moral support of its opinion" (Mill 1882, 251, 258, 260; see also "J. S. Mill and his successors," Chapter 8).

The noninterventionist position within the liberal tradition may be more pronounced, and certainly among contemporary internationalists more common, but such liberals as Giuseppe Mazzini, Thomas Paine, or Woodrow Wilson have also made strong arguments on behalf of benevolent intervention. Here the argument is that liberal states have a responsibility to come to the aid of people struggling for their freedom abroad. Mazzini's pleas for English intervention in the struggle for Italian unification are emblematic. He urges the British to consider "war in the noble intention of restoring Truth and Justice, and of arresting Tyranny in her inhuman career, of rendering the Nations free and happy, and causing God to smile upon them benignantly, of crowning religious and political liberty, and making England proud and powerful." Through such intervention the British would gain "the sympathy and gratitude of the nations that she has benefited." Mill himself points out that devotion to the principle of non-interference is selective and that if only liberal states observed it, tyranny could be perpetuated (Mazzini quoted in Waltz 1959, 109–10; Mill 1882, 255).

More recently, the prominent liberal Arthur M. Schlesinger, Jr. employed similar arguments about arresting the spread of tyranny to support American intervention in Vietnam – even as realists like George Kennan and Hans Morgenthau opposed it. American intervention began with a consensus among orthodox liberal internationalists in the foreign-policy establishment that it was a worthwhile and necessary effort to assist a people struggling to establish their freedom. In an era of communist insurgency, they argued, it was important for the United States to demonstrate its commitment to help

214

people seeking to establish or maintain liberal, democratic institutions. According to this view, even if those institutions are flawed, our assistance is required if there is to be any chance of development toward democracy. A similar argument is made by partisans of the Reagan Doctrine like Norman Podhoretz or Charles Krauthammer, who are liberals re-christened as neo-conservatives (Smith 1989; also see "Contemporary issues in contractarianism," Chapter 9). Only after the domestic and international costs of the Vietnam war became overwhelmingly clear did liberal opinion turn against it. One assumes a similar dynamic changed the minds of Soviet policymakers about Afghanistan. The contrast between the Brezhnev Doctrine, promulgated in the wake of the Soviet invasion of Czechoslovakia, and the view of Mikhail Gorbachev just quoted is striking.

Liberals as promoters of international organization

The issue of intervention in the liberal tradition is closely connected to ideas about the need to reform existing institutions and to create new ones at the international level. Liberal disagreement about intervention largely turns on differing judgments about the effectiveness of intervention as a means toward the necessary reforms. But whether or not they sanction military interventionism, liberals of all stripes call for a double reform of existing institutions. At the domestic level, states need to adopt liberal, democratic reforms that limit the power of the state and guarantee the freedom of individual men and women through political participation. In the nineteenth century, this meant an end to absolutist monarchy and the introduction of parliamentary reform. In the twentieth century, liberals have opposed the tyrannies of fascism, communism, and military dictatorship. At the international level, states themselves must agree to limit their sovereignty, adopt the restraints of a genuine international law, and join in federations or schemes of world government. At least two of these plans for international organization have been realized and, arguably, have affected the conduct of international politics quite profoundly. Both the League of Nations and the United Nations have their philosophical origins in liberalism (Claude 1971, 78).

F. H. Hinsley (1963) describes a long tradition of liberal plans for replacing or reforming the current anarchic state system. The liberal tradition is replete with schemes to bolster international law, to create new international organizations and global institutions, and to establish means for individuals to pursue the cosmopolitan human interest

215

rather than a narrow national interest. Liberals are often unclear, however, about the priority of domestic and international reforms. Some write as if all states must first become democracies before genuine global reforms and effective international organization are possible. Woodrow Wilson, for example, had no doubt of this point: "Only the free peoples of the world can join the League of Nations. No nation is admitted to the League of Nations that cannot show that it has the institutions which we call free. No autocratic government can come into its membership, no government which is not controlled by the will and vote of its people." On this view, the key to peace is a world of democracies: "only a nation whose government was its servant and not its master could be trusted to preserve the peace of the world" (quoted in Claude 1971, 51).

At the same time, liberals recognize the obstacles that international anarchy places before states that wish to be both liberal and pacific. Without explicitly addressing the issue, Kant appears to regard the reforms as a mutually reinforcing process. New institutions will develop, old ones be superseded, "till, finally, partly by an optimal internal arrangement, and partly by common external agreement and legislation, a state of affairs is created, which, like a civil common-wealth, can maintain itself automatically." Other liberals are often not even this clear, and the problem of which reforms have to come first is sometimes fudged by invoking the image of an ascending spiral (Kant [1784] 1970, 48; Galtung 1974, Ch. 1). Still other writers in the liberal tradition emphasize the liberty of independent sovereign states and simply urge greater compliance to existing norms of international law (Schiffer 1954; Holbraad 1970; Nardin 1983).

Regardless of their position on the priority of domestic and international reform, liberals have been steadfast in their support for international organization, however imperfect. In the interwar period figures like Alfred Zimmern, Lord Robert Cecil, or Lowes Dickinson in Britain, James T. Shotwell, Raymond B. Fosdick, and Hamilton Holt in the United States all championed the cause of the League of Nations indefatigably (Divine 1967; Smith 1987, Ch. 3). The British League of Nations Union in 1934 even organized a nationwide canvass of British households, which it called the "Peace Ballot," designed to demonstrate popular support for the League and the principles of collective security and disarmament. Of the 11½ million replies gathered – as Taylor (1965, 379) points out, a "substantial majority of all house-holders" – more than 10 million responded affirmatively to the five questions designed to elicit such support. On only one question – should an aggressor be stopped by war – was there a split. Nearly

7 million "voted" yes, over 2 million said no, and another 2 million did not respond. American supporters of the League wrote hortatory articles and addresses decrying the United States' non-membership and proclaiming to a devoted band of liberal internationalists the manifold virtues of the League.

Although the League of Nations patently failed to mark a new era of international relations, liberals did not lose faith in international organization. If anything, the failure deepened their convictions about the necessity for an effective world body, and they redoubled their efforts to persuade politicans and citizens alike to create an institution devoted to the liberal ideals of freedom and human welfare. In the words of the Mexican delegate to the San Francisco conference that founded the United Nations:

> The [United Nations] Charter is not only an instrument of security against the horrors of war. It is also, for the people who have been fighting to uphold the principles of human dignity, an instrument of well-being and happiness against the horrors of a peace without hope, in which men would be subjected to humiliating privations and injustices. "Blood, sweat, and tears" comprise the glorious but provisional rule of war. It must not become the rule of peace. (Claude 1971, 68)

As Claude argues, the liberalism at the foundation of the United Nations system combined a nineteenth-century view of the pacifying effects of unfettered commerce with a twentieth-century conception of the need for institutional planning and functional organization. The founders realized that the goal of human welfare, first expounded by Bentham, requires more than governmental noninterference. It also requires coordination, planning, and functionally specific institutions. Claude likens the specialized agencies of the UN to "a kind of international New Dealism, an adaptation of the welfare state philosophy to the realm of world affairs" (1971, 79). In this sense, modern liberal supporters of the United Nations move beyond their forebears. They suggest that endemic problems of public health, poverty, and environmental pollution must be addressed internationally, by vital and effective international agencies.

These international agencies need not be global in scope, however. Liberals support regional associations like the European Economic Community as well as global institutions like the UN: the key liberal notion of economic welfare can drive and justify all manner of cooperative schemes as long as they are founded on democratic principles. To be sure, there is some tension between liberals like P. T. Bauer, who emphasize free trade and governmental nonintervention,

217

and those, like Amartya Sen, who have pointed out the distortions and imperfections of the international economic market. But the larger point is that the debate on the goals and character of international institutions – be they economic or political – occurs in a basically liberal framework. On these issues realists have little to contribute because they tend to regard all international institutions as either irrelevant or simply reflective of underlying power realities. And Marxists of whatever persuasion have mainly confined themselves to criticizing international institutions as exploitative or ineffectual; they have offered no positive contribution beyond a general recommendation for wholesale economic revolution. The hard questions of global distributive justice, the nature of the international trading system, the scope and enforceability of international law, and the problematic place of national self-determination in an interdependent world are debated in terms basic to the liberal tradition. Thus, despite frequent accusations of naiveté from realists, or of hypocrisy from Marxists, liberals have continually sought to translate their ideas into concrete international institutions, and can justifiably claim some success.

Liberal appeals for public support

In their appeals for public support, liberals draw on the distinct ideas of welfare or duty. Those who, like Kant, see international reform as a moral imperative, urge both political leaders and individuals to seek peace as a matter of urgent moral duty.

> Moral-practical reason pronounces within us the following irresistible veto: *there shall be no war*, either between individual human beings in the state of nature, or between separate states, which, although internally law-governed, still live in a lawless condition in their external relationships with one another. For war is not the way in which anyone should pursue his rights. (Kant [1797] 1970, 174, emphasis in original)

Kant presents the transformation of the international state of nature to a "law-governed" federation of states as a moral imperative. To shirk or deny the duty to seek peace would not only contradict the "moral law within us," it would "give rise to the execrable wish to dispense with all reason and to regard ourselves, along with our principles, as subject to the same mechanism of nature as the other animal species" (Kant [1797] 1970, 174). To be true to our essence as reasoning humans, we seek international reform. Woodrow Wilson echoed Kant in his appeals for the world to adopt a "peace without victory" after the First World War, and to found a League of Nations based on the universality of democratic self-determination. Wilson challenged the United States to provide an example to the world of a country guided not by the balance of power, but by a conception of right and duty in a world of democratic states. In contrast, liberals like Cobden, Bright, Gladstone, and Norman Angell followed the welfare arguments of the Benthamite strand of the liberal tradition. Angell, in his enormously popular *The Great Illusion*, attempts to demonstrate that war does not "pay," and that "military power is socially and economically futile and can have no relation to the prosperity of the people exercising it" (Angell [1908] 1939, 116).

In contemporary discourse, wholesale reform of the state system is said to be necessary because of the unprecedented nuclear menace. The prominent liberal president of the University of Chicago put this argument in its classic form in 1947:

> Before the atomic bomb we could take world government or leave it. We could rely on the long process of evolution to bring world community and world government hand in hand. Any such program today means another war, and another war means the end of civilization. The slogan of our faith must be, world government is necessary, and therefore possible. (Hutchins in Woodward *et al.* 1947, 105)

Jonathan Schell echoes Hutchins in his stark description of the choice now before us: "On the one side stand human life and the terrestrial creation. On the other side stands a particular organization of human life, the system of sovereign, independent states" (1982, 218). For many contemporary liberals, the nation-state system has become nothing less than a threat to our collective survival. Thus the sense of apocalyptic urgency that pervades much of the current literature, particularly at times when tensions between the superpowers are high.

How are we to weigh the appeals of these liberal internationalists? Hedley Bull notes tartly that "there is no lack of self-appointed spokesmen of the common good of 'the spaceship earth' or 'this endangered planet.' But the views of these private individuals, whatever merit they may have, are not the outcome of any political process of the assertion and reconciliation of interests." He concludes that "to define the interests of mankind is to lay claim to the kind of authority that can only be conferred by a political process" (1977, 85–86). Bull insists that liberal spokesmen "authenticate" their ideas by some recognized form of political process. Some liberal reformers seem to be heeding his advice. A global environmental group recently carried petitions with millions of signatures from many countries to the

United Nations; peace groups have sought to place disarmament petitions on local ballots. But many liberals would simply reply that existing political institutions choke off the possibility of genuine "authentication." Others, of course, hold a more sanguine view of the durability and indeed the appropriateness of the current state system; for these noninterventionist liberals, wholesale schemes for reform are misguided and illusory.

Political leaders ranging from Jean Monnet to Jimmy Carter and Ronald Reagan have used doctrines of the liberal tradition to distinguish and legitimize their positions on foreign policy. Carter's adoption of human rights in the 1976 presidential campaign as the key feature of his foreign policy was a liberal move. By emphasizing human rights Carter sought to distance himself from policies of the Nixon–Ford–Kissinger regime that, he argued, put amoral *Realpolitik* considerations above the ideals of human dignity and freedom. Ronald Reagan dropped the emphasis on human rights, but he too reached for liberal arguments to justify the so-called Reagan Doctrine as a "crusade for freedom" and a "campaign for democratic development" (*New York Times*, June 9, 1982; see also Doyle 1986). Carter and Reagan not only illustrate how liberal doctrines can be used, even distorted, to justify particular foreign policies, but also how the liberal tension on state intervention remains unresolved. Carter sought "moral intervention" on behalf of victims of human-rights abuses; Reagan sought popular support for a military aid to non-Marxist insurgencies on the ground that these were most likely to spread democracy. Clearly both thought that using the rhetoric of liberal rights would help to persuade others of the wisdom of their policy.

In other contexts, heads of state often adopt liberal rhetoric when acting in ways (e.g., agreeing on common standards of pollution or communication) that require some diminution (or extension) of state sovereignty as a traditional realist might define it. European leaders like Monnet or Adenauer have used familiar liberal welfare arguments to support the foundation and extension of the European Economic Community. Mikhail Gorbachev now uses such arguments on behalf of his notion of a "Common European Home." And, of course, virtually all statesmen and leaders of would-be states now bow rhetorically at the shrine of self-determination, though the contradictions inherent in this difficult concept remain largely unresolved.

The liberal tradition has also served to ground dissent from a perceived statist bias among most international leaders. In these terms, the tradition remains alive and vital: indeed, the debate on nuclear deterrence has revived its internationalist agenda with the prima facie persuasive claim that no "national interest" can justify the incineration of the planet. Liberal internationalists claim to offer a way beyond the straitjacket of sovereign states without requiring a reinvention of politics – only a reassertion of reason and rationality. The liberal tradition also remains at the center of ethical thought about international relations. The utilitarian, Kantian, and contractarian traditions; the attempt to work out an effective system of international law; and the recent concentration on human rights as both a cosmopolitan and inter-state concern can all be regarded as more specific outgrowths of a broader liberal tradition.

Many liberals are willing to work within the current state system while seeking to tame the most brutal aspects of its competition. A more visionary strand to the tradition envisions the end of national sovereignty and its replacement with supranational institutions that move "beyond the nation-state." The former view, optimistic as it is about the capacity of existing institutions to reform in fundamental ways, seems more in tune with mainstream scholars of international relations, who mainly concern themselves with issues of national security. The latter strand of the tradition tries to articulate the concept of a relevant utopia.

The importance of this enterprise should not be underestimated. An observer who predicted in August 1939 that by 1992 the ten West European countries, led by France and Germany, would have established a common market and currency and moved toward "a common home" for all Europeans would have been ridiculed. And the extraordinary events of 1989, when the peoples of central and Eastern Europe flooded into the streets to demand democracy and self-government, caught virtually all "realistic" analysts by surprise. The Soviets, it was said, would never relinquish their hold on their empire; they would never accept a reunified Germany; and even Soviet restraint would not necessarily translate into wholesale changes in the Warsaw Pact states. Kant or Bentham would perhaps have been less dismissive, and certainly not as surprised. For liberals have always kept faith with the notion that ideas move people, that all human institutions are capable of reform, and that the application of goodwill and reason can create new arrangements better suited to the protection and promotion of human welfare and freedom.

Suggested reading

Kant's essays "Perpetual Peace" and "Idea for a Universal History with a Cosmopolitan Purpose," collected in Kant (1970), are among the most important of the classic texts of liberalism as it relates to international affairs.

Nineteenth-century texts include Bentham's *Plan for a Universal and Perpetual Peace* ([1838] 1927); essays by Lord Acton (1976) that discuss the tension between liberalism and nationalism; and the writings of Richard Cobden collected in Cobden (1903). Significant selections from the works of these writers may be found in Wolfers and Martin, *The Anglo-American Tradition in Foreign Affairs* (1956). Though published in 1911, Hobhouse's *Liberalism* reflects a nineteenth-century outlook in its attempt to distill the essence of liberalism for lay readers.

F. H. Hinsley's *Power and the Pursuit of Peace* (1963) combines a scholarly survey of peace plans with a liberal interpretation of the evolution of the modern state system. Michael Howard's *War and the Liberal Conscience* (1978) is an evocative survey of liberal attitudes toward war from an eminent English military historian. Another English historian, A. J. P. Taylor, provides a readable introduction to Cobden, Bright, and others in *The Trouble Makers* (1957).

Isaiah Berlin's *Four Essays on Liberty* (1969) remains an important starting point for understanding liberalism today. Kenneth Minogue's *The Liberal Mind* (1963) offers a critique of liberal political attitudes in general; more specifically related to international relations is Michael Doyle's "Liberal Institutions and International Ethics" (1986), a spirited defense of a Kantian approach.

Several works stand out in the contemporary international relations literature. Hedley Bull's *The Anarchical Society* (1977) is an indispensable introduction to the issues of international order and reform, while Inis L. Claude's *Swords into Ploughshares* (1971) remains the best overall treatment of the ideas underlying contemporary international organization. Stanley Hoffmann's *Janus and Minerva* (1987) is a fine collection of essays by a leading scholar with a distinctly liberal sensibility. More visionary are Robert C. Johansen, *The National Interest and the Human Interest* (1980), and Norman Cousins, *The Pathology of Power* (1987). Many of Hans Morgenthau's essays in *Politics in the Twentieth Century* (1962) bear re-reading in the context of the liberal-realist debate, and reveal a mind far more subtle than the Morgenthau of *Politics among Nations* and one that is quite genuinely liberal.

On the issue of intervention, the classic treatment is still J. S. Mill's "A Few Words on Non-intervention" (collected in Mill 1882), followed by Michael Walzer's discussion of the same topic in *Just and Unjust Wars* (New York: Basic Books, 1977). The best recent overview of liberal thinking on human rights is R. J. Vincent's *Human Rights and International Relations* (1986); a special issue of *Daedalus* published in Fall 1983 also contains some provocative essays on the subject.

References

Acton, Lord. [1907] 1967. *The History of Freedom and Other Essays*. Freeport, NY: Books for Libraries Press.

Angell, Norman. [1908] 1939. *The Great Illusion – Now*. London: Penguin Books.

Bentham, Jeremy. [1838] 1927. *Plan for a Universal and Perpetual Peace*. Introduction by C. John Colombos. London: Grotius Society Publications, Sweet and Maxwell Ltd.

1971. *Handbook of Political Fallacies*, ed. by Harold A. Larrabee. New York: Thomas Y. Crowell, Apollo Editions.

Berlin, Isaiah. 1969. *Four Essays on Liberty*, Oxford: Oxford University Press.

Bull, Hedley. 1977. *The Anarchical Society*. New York: Columbia University Press.

Claude, Inis, L. Jr. 1971. *Swords into Ploughshares*, 4th edn. New York: Random House.

Cobden, Richard. 1903. *Political Writings*, 2 vols. London: Fisher Unwin.

Cousins, Norman. 1987. *The Pathology of Power*. New York: W. W. Norton.

Cranston, Maurice. 1973. *What Are Human Rights?* New York: Taplinger.

Doyle, Michael. 1986. "Liberal Institutions and International Ethics." *American Political Science Review* 80: 1152–69.

Galtung, Johan. 1974. *The True Worlds*. New York: The Free Press.

Hinsley, F. H. 1963. *Power and the Pursuit of Peace*. Cambridge: Cambridge University Press.

Hobhouse, L. T. 1911. *Liberalism*. London: Thornton Butterworth.

Hoffmann, Stanley. 1987. *Janus and Minerva: Essays on the Theory and Practice of International Politics*. Boulder, CO: Westview Press.

Holbraad, Carsten. 1970. *The Concert of Europe: A Study of German and British International Theory, 1815–1914*. London: Longman.

Howard, Michael. 1978. *War and the Liberal Conscience*. New Brunswick, NJ: Rutgers University Press.

Johansen, Robert C. 1980. *The National Interest and the Human Interest*. Princeton: Princeton University Press.

Joll, James, ed. 1950. *Britain and Europe: Pitt to Churchill*. London: A. & C. Black.

Kant, Immanuel. [1784, 1795, 1797] 1970. *Kant's Political Writings*, ed. by Hans Reiss. Cambridge: Cambridge University Press.

Mill, John Stuart. 1882. *Dissertations and Discussions*, vol. 3. New York: Henry Holt.

1909. *The Principles of Political Economy*, 9th edn., ed. by W. J. Ashley. London: Longman.

Minogue, Kenneth. 1963. *The Liberal Mind*. New York: Vintage Books.

Morgenthau, Hans J. 1962. *Politics in the Twentieth Century*, 3 vols. Chicago: University of Chicago Press.

Nardin, Terry. 1983. *Law, Morality, and the Relations of States*. Princeton: Princeton University Press.

Russell, Bertrand. [1916] 1930. *Why Men Fight*. New York: Albert and Charles Boni.

Schell, Jonathan. 1982. *The Fate of the Earth*. New York: Alfred A. Knopf.

Schiffer, Walter. 1954. *The Legal Community of Mankind*. New York: Columbia University Press.

Smith, Michael Joseph. 1987. *Realist Thought from Weber to Kissinger*. Baton Rouge: Louisiana State University Press.

1989. "Ethics and Intervention." *Ethics and International Affairs* 3: 1–26.

Taylor, A. J. P. 1957. *The Trouble Makers: Dissent over Foreign Policy 1792–1939*. London: Panther Books.

1965. *English History, 1914–1945*. Oxford: Oxford University Press.

Vincent, R. J. 1986. *Human Rights and International Relations.* Cambridge: Cambridge University Press.

Waltz, Kenneth W. 1959. *Man, the State, and War.* New York: Columbia University Press.

Wolfers, Arnold and L. W. Martin, eds. 1956. *The Anglo-American Tradition in Foreign Affairs.* New Haven: Yale University Press.

Woodward, E. Llewellyn *et al.* 1947. *Foundations for World Order.* Denver: University of Denver Press.

11 MARXISM AND INTERNATIONAL ETHICS

CHRIS BROWN

The nature of Marxism poses many problems to the student of ethical traditions in international relations. Neither "ethics" nor "international relations" are notions that sit easily within a Marxist framework, while the notion of Marxism as a tradition is, itself, suspect. Marxist notions of ethics and international relations will be the main subject of this chapter but, before these issues can be addressed, we must define the primary term, Marxism. What this involves is not the hopeless task of trying to identify the essentials of Marxism, but the more modest ambition of setting out a checklist of contemporary "live" political doctrines that can claim with some plausibility to be Marxist, along with a sense of their origins.

What is Marxism?

Approaching this latter task first, we can identify three stages in the political and doctrinal evolution of Marxism, described by Kolakowski as the periods of the Founders, of the Golden Age, and of the Breakdown (Kolakowski 1978). The major doctrines associated with the names of Marx and Engels – the Founders – emerged in the middle decades of the nineteenth century, and are to be found in *The German Ideology*, *The Communist Manifesto*, and *Capital*, vol. I (McLellan 1977; Marx [1867] 1976). These doctrines were a major inspiration of the socialist movements that came together under the banner of the (Second) International in the quarter century prior to the First World War – the Golden Age. The collapse of this international movement in 1914, followed by the success of the Bolsheviks in 1917, led to the Breakdown – the end of even the pretense that Marxism was a unified tradition and the creation of the current situation where the term Marxism has no clear, distinctive meaning.

The most revealing comment on the founding period of Marxism was made by Marx's near-contemporary, English socialist, writer, and designer William Morris. "You ought to read Marx," he suggested to a friend and comrade, "he is the only completely scientific economist on our side" (Thompson 1977, 761). This is revealing in two respects: it reminds us that Marx and Engels were contributing to an existing political movement rather than creating something from nothing, and that the nature of their contribution was as specialists, people with valuable technical knowledge. For Morris, to be a Marxist meant to adhere to the main lines of Marxian political economy and to the notions of class struggle and revolution implied by this approach. The laws of motion of the capitalist mode of production, the notion of surplus value, Marx's demonstration of how exploitation can take place under conditions of apparently free exchange, and predictions of increasing immiseration, crisis, and collapse – these are the ideas that Marx and Engels contributed. Morris and his contemporaries did not see Marxism as an overarching philosophy, providing at the very least a method for approaching all issues, if not, in fact, an answer to all questions. Few of Marx's contemporaries understood him to be a philosopher or, in the broad sense, an anthropologist – if only because the writings that might have fostered this understanding were not published until fifty years after his death in 1883. No socialist looked to Marx for an "ethics"; even if Marx had seen himself as providing a set of values by which to live – and he did not – socialists of his era believed themselves to be well provided for in this department.

This position changed somewhat under the Second International. From 1889 to 1914 the various socialist and labor movements of Europe were in communion with one another in the International, partly because the role of Marxism in the most important of these movements – in Germany and Austria-Hungary – transcended the limits implied by Morris's statement. Although many of Marx's early writings were still unavailable, the notion of Marxism as an ideology, a philosophy, even a way of life, took hold in this period. Along with major writings on political economy and political strategy Marxists began producing major works on epistemology, religion, and morality (Kolakowski 1978, vol. II; McLellan 1979) and came to regard Marxism as a sort of general-purpose method that can be applied to virtually everything, including subjects such as international ethics left untouched by Marx. If it makes sense to think of Marxism as a "tradition," it is the Marxism of the Second International – sometimes called classical Marxism – that best merits this description.

The Golden Age came to an end in 1914 with the collapse of the presumption of proletarian unity. The task of reconstructing this unity after the war was made impossible by the Bolsheviks' ascension to power in Russia in 1917. They were a party faction that had been on the disreputable fringe of the movement before 1914. From 1917 onwards the crucial issue in the international movement was whether the Bolshevik revolution was to be welcomed as the first step to the worldwide overthrow of capitalism or condemned for its employment of methods that few Marxists before 1914 – even those on the left, such as Luxemburg – could accept (Luxemburg [1918] 1961). The inability to compromise on this issue led to the development of hostile international movements – the continuing Second International and the new Third or Communist International – and a world in which competing branches of Marxism were each other's bitterest enemies. The gradual movement of the Second International parties towards accepting a pluralist democracy and a reformist role within the capitalist system, prefigured by the work of Bernstein and the tactics of trade unionists before 1914, intensified the mutual hatred between the successors of the age of unity, while the development of Stalinism, and of Trotskyism in reaction, further intensified the schism. Whereas before 1914 the term Marxism had a reasonably clear meaning, after 1917 this ceased to be the case.

What does the term mean today? Three traditions have a reasonable claim to the title. First in importance for most of the century, but perhaps beginning to lack centrality as a result of developments in the 1980s, is Marxism-Leninism or Soviet Marxism (Kolakowski 1978, vol. III). By contrast, Western Marxism or classical Marxism is an oppositional tendency within the advanced capitalist states, present in the academy rather than the factory or the mass party, characterized by a focus on philosophy and cultural criticism along with the more traditional concern of political economy, and claiming descent from Marx and Engels via Luxemburg and Gramsci (Anderson 1976; *New Left Review* 1977). The third tradition, third-worldist neo-Marxism, has some official status in the "South," and much academic support in the West; its "dependency" and "world-systems" notions are regarded as inherently un-Marxist by many on account of their exchange-oriented view of capitalism, but its adherents lay claim to the tradition and, on the basis of the importance of self-description, this claim must be taken seriously (Frank 1971, 1984; Amin et al. 1982; Goldfrank 1979; Wallerstein 1983).

It should now be clear that there is no single Marxist ethical tradition with respect to international affairs. However, to examine each past and present tradition in turn would be tedious. The first part of the discussion, divided into two sections, will examine two problems common to all variants of Marxism – the nature of ethics and the role of the state – from the perspective of classical Marxism, drawing on

Soviet and neo-Marxist sources only occasionally. The second part will examine the ethical doctrines that have emerged out of Marxism-Leninism.

Marxism, ethics, and morality

The contribution of Marx and Engels to the evolution of socialist doctrine in the nineteenth century was characterized by an absolute determination to avoid the emphasis on ethics and morality that was so much a part of most other socialist thought. The burden of Marx's political economy is precisely that propositions about the exploitative nature of capitalism and its ultimate demise not only can but should be cast in scientific rather than moral terms. Marx was deeply contemptuous of socialists who resorted to moral arguments, and allegedly burst out laughing whenever anyone used the word "morality" (Skillen 1977, 129).

Why this apparent contempt? The answer lies at the heart of the project of historical materialism. The materialist conception of history dictates that what is real is the production and reproduction of material life; this, the economic structure of society, "conditions the social, political and intellectual life process in general" (McLellan 1977, 389). It is the foundation upon which is constructed a superstructure that includes morality:

> The phantoms formed in the human brain are also, necessarily, sublimates of their material life process . . . Morality, religion, metaphysics, all the rest of ideology and their corresponding forms of consciousness, thus no longer retain the semblance of independence. (McLellan 1977, 164)

Morality is ideology, and thus represents the interests of a class; there neither is nor can be a view from nowhere, some source of independent criteria for moral judgment. An ethics can only be the reflection of particular material interests. To suggest that the proletariat should be governed in its behavior by a morality is the equivalent either of saying that the proletariat should act in its own interests – which is redundant – or that it should act in the interests of the bourgeoisie – which is reactionary. What it cannot be is the equivalent of saying that the proletariat should act in accordance with some transcendent code, because no such code exists (M. Cohen et al. 1980; Wood 1984; Geras 1985).

An obvious response to this position would be to accept that some aspects of morality are time-bound and class related, while resisting

228

the notion that all aspects of all moral codes can be so described. Kamenka argues, quite plausibly, that Marx does indeed have an ethical conception of the nature of human beings as free, self-determining subjects – as the philosophical anthropology contained in such early unpublished writings as the *Paris Manuscripts* demonstrates – and this would seem to offer the possibility of an ethic that was not simply ideology (Kamenka 1969; McLellan 1971). From another angle, Marx's apparent amoralism can be seen as the product of an understandable anger generated by the hypocrisy of bourgeois society that promotes a code of conduct that its own laws of motion make impossible to adhere to – the role of "conscience" being to force us to correct the distortions that society itself introduces (Skillen 1977, Ch. 4; Norman 1983, 187).

Both of these arguments have force, but they do not succeed in undermining Marx's critique of morality. Even if it is plausible to suggest that Marx's contempt for morality stems from his contempt for the morality of bourgeois society, this does not explain how a morality that does not reflect the material interests of a particular class is to appear. The notion of a free, truly human, being emerging once the divisions of class society are overcome, when "the practical relations of everyday life between man and man and man and nature generally present themselves to him in a transparent and rational form" (Marx [1867] 1976, 173), is of little relevance as long as class divisions persist and ideology is inevitable – even supposing that the goal of complete transparency between human beings makes sense in the first place, which is doubtful.

On a materialist account of morality and ideology, then, what reasons for action make sense? One possible response to this sort of question might be to reject it out of hand. As Norman comments

> The assumption behind ethical thought is that human beings are capable of distinguishing between better and worse kinds of life, better and worse kinds of society, and are capable of acting to change their lives and their society. Marx and Engels seem to imply that this is impossible. (1983, 181)

If all choices are made for us by our relationship to the economic structure of society, then the notion of choice is meaningless. Although for some purposes in the analysis of capitalism Marxist thought does reduce individuals to bearers of particular roles whose behavior is determined by these roles, as a general proposition Marxists do not want to suggest that choice is a meaningless notion. Most Marxist writers are, after all, men and women who have made conscious decisions to become Marxists in spite of, rather than because of, their class origins. Equally, the actual conduct of working-class politics always involves making choices and decisions, adopting strategies and tactics that seem, under the circumstances, to be "right." What can this notion of rightness involve?

The nature of Marx's project seems to imply that the answers to these questions can be cast in scientific terms. Individuals become committed to the cause of the working class because they come to see that the logic of capitalism as a mode of production involves the exploitation and immiseration of the workers, and leads inexorably to crisis, collapse, and the eventual emergence of socialism and communism. This process of commitment is essentially non-ethical – moral feelings may be involved, but unless accompanied by correct understanding, will prove unreliable. Right action is a matter of theory, not morality. It is not a question of doing the right thing in response to codes of conduct and principles, but of correctly grasping what courses of action correspond to the needs of the moment. These needs are shaped by the paramount necessity to hasten the achievement of successful proletarian revolution. In the sense suggested by Anthony Ellis at the beginning of Chapter 8, Marxism can be seen as "consequentialist," since the only factor determining whether an action is right or wrong is its overall consequences, viewed impersonally.

The idea that right action is a matter of scientifically determining the needs of the moment is difficult to accept in all its implications. It does, however, indicate a frame of mind that is prevalent amongst many classical Marxists, and distinguishes them from other contemporary radicals. This point can be illustrated by a brief digression into a modern "moral" international issue – the question of poverty and oppression in the "third world" – and the role of capitalism in its creation and elimination. The key issue here is whether, as Marx himself and later classical Marxists would assert, capitalism is to be seen as an ultimately progressive force, irrespective of the short-term consequences it may have for non-Western societies, or whether, as many third-world radicals, including some neo-Marxists, would hold, such a judgment could only be made from a perspective which privileges a Western insensitivity to other peoples and other cultures.

Marx's own writings on, for example, India, are clear on this; the "undignified, stagnatory and vegetative life" characteristic of pre-capitalist Indian communities brutalized their population, and, however bad the motives of the British were – and Marx was without illusions on this score – British rule in India constituted a historically progressive move (Avineri 1969, 94; McLellan 1971, 336). The damage capitalism was inflicting on India was a necessary part of a progressive movement of benefit to all, including, of course, the Indians themselves. A similar view was taken by at least some of the participants in the various debates on imperialism and colonialism in the Second International – including George Bernard Shaw as a representative of the Fabian Society (Shaw 1900, cited from Porter 1984). Of particular interest in this context is the work of a recent classical Marxist, Warren, whose posthumously published study of imperialism defends what he takes to be the classical position against the woolly-minded, romantic critique of capitalism offered by neo-Marxist dependency theorists (Warren 1980). Warren's point is that the (correct) classical view of imperialism as a progressive force breaking down the barriers of precapitalist stagnation has been sacrificed to the political needs of nationalist and bourgeois politicians in the third world who, unable to face the implications of an accurate diagnosis of the needs of their respective countries, take refuge in the politically easier step of blaming foreigners and external capital for their plight.

This position reflects a tough-minded consequentialist view of the world. As Luxemburg put the matter in another context, Marxism, unlike other varieties of socialism, has "no pretentions to keeping patches in its pocket to mend all the holes made by historical development" (Davis 1976, 122); to think of third world peoples as facing a "cruel choice" – to quote the title of a study by a non-Marxist radical – is to misstate the issue (Goulet 1977). There is no choice. The consequence of the incursion of capitalism into non-capitalist societies is to place them on the route to eventual liberation; insofar as this raises any ethical issue at all it is to be welcomed, irrespective of any short-run costs. This attitude may seem callous, indifferent to the suffering of the wretched of the earth, ethnocentric in its underlying value judgments, but this concern simply reflects the power of bourgeois notions of morality, which concentrate on surface phenomena and inessentials.

Much the same attitude can be identified in Marx and Engels's writings on the problem of war. In their studies of the Eastern Question and the Crimean War, for example, the point at issue is always the impact of this conflict on the overall balance of forces in Europe and thus on the prospects for revolution (Aveling and Aveling 1897; Molnar 1975). The rights and wrongs of the war, its justice, are never discussed at any length: what counts is whether it makes revolution more or less likely.

There are two problems with this principled hard-headedness.

231

First, there is the problem of determining accurately the consequences of action. In principle, right action is a matter of theoretically informed practice. The working-class movement, from its lived experience, learns to reach the right decision by learning to tell which lines of action hasten the desired end and which do not. This learning on the job, plus its growing strength, makes the movement ever more capable of delivering the right result. The problem with this, of course, is that it all sounds rather more romantic than the anticapitalist rhetoric of Warren's opponents. It is not necessary to be a Leninist to acknowledge Lenin's critique of working-class consciousness without the guidance of a party led by the more sophisticated and theoretically aware. But the problem, of course, is that this argument can so easily justify dictatorship by the party, its leaders, and, potentially, of its one leader. The problem with the Marxist notion that action should follow, not moral rules, but political analysis is one of distinguishing the products of analysis from the products of prejudice. For some utilitarian versions of consequentialism, the nature of the desired outcome that shapes action can simply be treated as given by the existing preferences of individuals; this cannot be so of the Marxist variant, where the outcome must be revolution and liberation.

This is a serious point, but more telling is the second set of problems associated with Marxist consequentialism, which concern the desire of Marxists to translate the outcomes of historical processes into something that can be morally judged. What Lukes describes as the paradox of Marxism and morality is that while Marx and his followers characterize morality as ideology, expressions of moral outrage inescapably permeate their writings (Lukes 1985, 1). Even in the apparently hard-hearted case of Marx's writings on India, the spirit of compassion for the sufferings of the victims of imperialism is there, especially when the latter stood up for themselves in the "mutiny" of 1857. Luxemburg may not have kept patches to mend the holes left by historical development, but her account of the destruction of natural economy in *The Accumulation of Capital* is written with a passion that belies any claim of uninvolved analysis (Luxemburg [1913] 1963, part III). Again, and of particular interest to students of international relations, the pre-1914 writings against militarism and war of Luxemburg and Liebnecht are obviously informed by the judgment that war would be a disaster for socialism, but it is difficult to avoid the conclusion that for these writers the simple, human disasters of war are equally terrible (Liebknecht [1907] 1972). In short, the paradox lies in the apparent inability of Marxists to avoid sliding into moral judgment.

232

This slippage cannot be accounted for by the needs of the revolution as defined by theoretically informed action. Even if it can be established that a particular historical process is inevitable, this does not provide the individual with a reason for working to help it to come to pass. The suggestion made most explicitly by Kautsky, but implicit in much of the tradition, that the inevitability of victory in itself creates a reason for commitment cannot be taken seriously (Lukes 1985, 17). Supposed historical inevitability could just as well lead to a state of resigned indifference, or to a determination to conduct a doomed resistance. Attempts by Marxists to escape from this dilemma have done little more than illustrate just how deeply it is embedded in their thought.

As an example of both these problems, consider Trotsky's formulation in his double-barrelled attack on Stalinist and bourgeois morals of 1938, *Their Morals and Ours*:

> A means can be justified only by its end. But the end in its turn needs to be justified. From the Marxist point of view, which expresses the historical interests of the proletariat, the end is justified if it leads to increasing the power of humanity over nature and to the abolition of the power of one person over another. (Trotsky et al. 1973, 48)

This is interesting not only because it explicitly links an ethical conception of human beings as self-determining subjects with a consequentialist account of right action, but also because it embeds a number of unspoken premises that increasing the power of humanity over nature rather than putting the two in a right relationship is desirable, that it is possible to create a world where the power of one person over another is abolished and, most centrally for this discussion, that so general and abstract a goal can actually be related in a practical way to means. This last point is developed by Dewey in an immediate reply to Trotsky; not wishing to reject Trotsky's refusal to posit some externally imposed absolutist conception of ethics, Dewey still insists on the need to distinguish different kinds of ends – "the final justifying end and ends that are themselves means to this final end" (Trotsky et al. 1973, 68). Dewey's point is that, in practice, the "final justifying end" does not determine right conduct for Trotsky (or other Marxists); instead he (and they) introduce the class struggle and other laws of the development of society – to use Trotsky's phrase – as objective guides to action without demonstrating that these "ends that are themselves means" are actually necessary to the achievement of liberation. Trotsky wants to argue that the ends determine the means, but he also wants to resist the implication drawn by his opponents that Stalin could justify the Terror on the same logic. His argument comes down to the assertion that when he authorized terror in the past it was in accordance with the objective needs of the revolution and justified by this end, but that when Stalin uses similar tactics it is not. Trotsky is unable to find a way to cast this argument in *moral* terms; what it comes down to is that Trotsky is claiming to be a better analyst of a situation than Stalin. This may be true, but it is not a moral argument.

Trotsky is interesting because he would accept that the ultimate goal of liberation is an ethical goal. What he cannot do is find a way of linking this goal to actual conduct; somewhere along the route an ethical commitment to a particular possible future is transformed into a practical commitment to the truth of a particular way of analyzing historical development. However, even in the case of Trotsky, who in the years of the revolution in Russia was responsible for a number of acts that would cause most Marxists to pause for thought, it is noteworthy that his defense of his conduct is not simply cast in consequentialist terms; on the contrary he goes out of his way to minimize the scope of the terror in 1919, and to raise arguments of a *tu quoque* nature. Even while rejecting such tricks, he cannot resist a dig at the bourgeois Swiss who pay homage to the terrorist William Tell (Trotsky et al. 1973, 50). Although Marxist thinkers who address these problems generally adopt versions of the ends–means formulation, in practice it is difficult to find forthright assertions of the need to breach "bourgeois" or "common-sense" morality in specific as opposed to abstract terms. Theoretical commitment to class morality is more usually accompanied by demonstrations that what looks like a break with bourgeois morality has been misunderstood or misinterpreted.

Having said this, it should be noted that commitment to consequentialism seems to be quite important in drawing lines between Marxists and other varieties of socialist. One of the reasons "neo" Marxists earn their qualifier is that they seem to drift in the direction of nonscientific socialism, while those thinkers of the Second International who explicitly admitted the need to import a deontological dimension into Marxism – usually of a neo-Kantian variety – were generally considered to have gone beyond the bounds of Marxist controversy (see Kolakowski 1978, vol. III, Ch. 12). It does seem to be the case that even when the economic analysis of Marxism remains intact, thinkers (and parties) who abandon Marxist consequentialism are considered by others, and often by themselves, to have left the tradition behind. To take a modern example, the attempt by Cohen to defend a rights-based interpretation of Marxist morality has attracted criticism even though his account of historical materialism is highly orthodox (G. A. Cohen 1988; Nielsen 1988; see also the discussion of Marxism and rights under "Rights in a plan of world politics," Chapter 12).

Marxism, international relations, and international society

Marx's concept of historical materialism and his critique of ideology lie at the root of his rejection of morality and ethics as nonderivative foci for consideration. A similar position can be identified as a prime reason for the downgrading of international relations as a subject for discourse within the Marxist tradition. The celebrated – if controversial – metaphor of "base" and "superstructure," outlined most effectively in the preface to *A Critique of Political Economy*, posits the state as part of the superstructure and implies that international relations, defined here as inter-state relations, are even further away from the base – "the economic structure of society, the real foundation" (McLellan 1977, 389; G. A. Cohen 1979). This does not imply a lack of interest in international relations, much less the state, on the part of the founders or their immediate successors. On the contrary, both Marx and Engels were deeply involved in foreign affairs and wrote extensively about them, mainly as journalists (Aveling and Aveling 1897; Molnar 1975). The point is rather that the founders produced no "Marxist theory" of the state or international relations; moreover – as will be seen below – when their immediate successors did create such a theory it was one-sided and positivist, imbued with "economism," and directed away from the sort of ethical issues with which this chapter is concerned.

When examining Marxist approaches to the state and international relations, it is thus general attitudes and predispositions that are significant, rather than fully worked through theories or philosophies. A further parallel can be found in the contradictions that characterize these predispositions: whereas Marxist thinking on the state and on the relations of states is wholly cosmopolitan and universalist in its thrust, it is only by taking advantage of politically significant particularisms that Marxism has achieved political success.

Marx's rejection of the moral significance of the state as a community is an unambiguous and pervasive feature of his work. The crude but effective formulae of the *Communist Manifesto* are refined but not rejected in his later work. What is central is the class struggle, and the state cannot stand above this struggle. "The executive of the modern

235

state is but a committee for managing the common affairs of the whole bourgeoisie" (McLellan 1977, 223). In *The Eighteenth Brumaire of Louis Bonaparte* (McLellan 1977, 300–26) Marx refined this statement to allow for the possibility that a state bureaucracy could develop its own interests, but he continued to reject the view that the state could be a mechanism for realizing the common interest, whether this common interest was conceptualized in terms of the liberal utilitarianism excoriated throughout his work, or in the Hegelian terms more intrinsically congenial to him, but rejected as early as 1843 in his unpublished manuscript *The Critique of Hegel's "Philosophy of Right"* (McLellan 1971). Following from this position Marx and Engels gladly accepted in the *Manifesto* the charge of desiring to abolish countries and nationality. "The working men have no country. We cannot take from them what they have not got" (McLennan 1977, 235).

Although this is clear, it is interesting to consider the sentences that follow this dismissal:

> Since the proletariat must first of all acquire political supremacy, must rise to be the leading class of the nation, must constitute itself *the* nation, it is, so far, itself national, though not in the bourgeois sense of the word. (McLellan 1977, 235)

This is by no means as clear-cut a dismissal of the idea of the nation as one might expect; it acknowledges that national ideas are unavoidable given the specificity of actual class struggle. However, Marx wishes to argue that the notion of nationality derived from these specificities is different from the (unspecified) bourgeois variety and, in any event, as the following sentences make clear, that political particularism is not a continuing problem:

> National differences and antagonisms between people are daily more and more vanishing, owing to the development of the bourgeoisie ... [to free trade, the market,] ... to uniformity in the mode of production and in the conditions of life corresponding thereto.
>
> The supremacy of the proletariat will cause them to vanish still faster. United action, of the leading civilised countries at least, is one of the first conditions for the emancipation of the proletariat.
>
> In proportion as the exploitation of one individual by another is put an end to, the exploitation of one nation by another will also be put an end to. In proportion as the antagonism between classes within the nation vanishes, the hostility of one nation to another will come to an end. (McLellan 1977, 236)

In these sentences Marx and Engels identify the basic problem that the state and inter-state relations pose for Marxist practice, but then optimistically assume away the contradictions that characterize this problem. The proletariat must become the nation, but its emancipation relies upon united action that crosses national boundaries, at least among the "civilized" (advanced capitalist or European?) countries. While becoming the nation as opposed to simply the leading class in the nation, the working class must also hold fast with other nations. In so doing, it will drain from the idea of nationhood the sense of exclusiveness characteristically associated with it. This identification of the tasks and problems of proletarian national/internationalism is perceptive, but is accompanied by assumptions that effectively wish away the problem. Marx's version of economic interdependence is assigned the role of reconciling the national and international allegiances of the proletariat. Meanwhile, the assumption that all conflict, whether of individuals or of states, reflects class conflict ensures that with the abolition of classes, international conflict will necessarily disappear.

These rhetorical moves allow Marx and Engels to hunt with the hounds and run with the hare; they can simultaneously assert the moral irrelevance of the state today, its emergence as a community after the triumph of the proletariat, and its unproblematic situation *vis-à-vis* the world community, while ignoring the problems involved in reconciling these positions. Although in later writings the authors of the *Manifesto* certainly move a great distance from the simplicities of this early work toward a far less functionalist account of the state, even the later work fails to address what have turned out in this century to be the real problems of political community (Gallie 1978). In part, this rhetorical elimination of the problems of the community reflects the nature of politics in the mid-nineteenth century, when the Manchester view that trade and open intercourse between nations would undermine particularisms was considerably more plausible than it would become two or three generations later. It also reflects the fact that Marx and Engels were never faced with the task of guiding an actual mass movement through the labyrinths of the national question.

The writers and thinkers of the Second International were. In the decades before 1914 the ethical status of national communities and the state became an issue of compelling political importance. The Austro-Marxist Otto Bauer, the Polish-German left-winger Rosa Luxemburg, and the Russian Social Democrat V. I. Lenin realized that answering the national question correctly was a precondition for revolutionary success, and none of these writers expected the national question to disappear with increasing interdependence. They saw that the necessary correspondence of proletarian nationalism and internationalism was something that would have to be worked for; it could not be taken for granted (Kolakowski 1978, vol. II; Munck 1986; Nairn 1977; Davis 1976). How to reconcile the necessity for internationalism with the evident national identification expressed by actual working classes was a key issue of the period. The debates are too complex to summarize adequately, but it is noteworthy that those movements that had the greatest practical successes were those most willing to harness national sentiment, while thinkers such as Luxemburg who advocated an uncompromising rejection of nationalism in the name of proletarian internationalism won many of the arguments while losing the war.

The politics of the Second International suggest that political movements that seriously desire to attract the loyalty of a mass population have to cast their message in terms that at least seem to correspond to local needs rather than to a theoretical cosmopolitanism. This lesson has been learned and relearned over the course of the century. In some respects, the problem has become more acute. All the writers of the Second International assumed as a matter of fact that the real contradiction in world politics was between capital and labor and that the real interests of workers in different countries corresponded – with the possible exception of minorities such as the "labor aristocracies" of the imperial centers identified by Lenin. The real political issue was to what extent it was legitimate to acknowledge the fears of those who were unable to grasp this reality by assuring them that their national "rights" would be maintained – irrelevant though such assurances were when the *real* interests of the international working class formed a nonconflictual unity.

In the late twentieth century, with the emergence of an international division of labor based on extreme differences in living standards, it is more difficult to make this assumption. Shifts in employment patterns in the world economy have created a situation in which, for example, the real interests of coal-miners in Britain, South Africa, Poland, and Australia do indeed appear to conflict; the support for the Multi-Fiber Arrangement given by textile workers in the West is a tacit recognition that the real interests of different proletariats may be different (Aggarwal 1985). While most mainstream Marxist thought continues to oppose protectionism and to identify the contradiction between labor and capital as central, the third-worldist neo-Marxist school, with its emphasis on unequal exchange and its stress on the exploitation of one nation by another, does acknowledge that one working class might be exploited by another (Emmanuel 1972).

If this position can be defended, it adds strength to the notion that particular communities have a moral significance that is in at least

238

potential contradiction to that of the wider community of all workers. This would suggest in turn that some kind of community of interest could exist between workers and capitalists within "their" state; and this suggestion is indeed implied by the popular distinction between "national" and "comprador" bourgeoisies. "National" bourgeoisies are, at least temporarily, allied with the workers against the forces of international capitalism, symbolized locally by the "comprador" bourgeoisie. However, such thinking is difficult to fit into even a highly revisionist Marxism; even those writers who see most clearly the need to find a theoretical basis for the centrality of the national community do not find this an easy task. Marxist thinking about the state simply does not readily cohere with any sense of community less inclusive than the international working class.

If the notion of the state as a community is difficult to work with in the tradition, the idea of a society of states, an international community composed not of individuals but of states, poses even greater problems. If the state itself is superstructural, then international relations must be part of the superstructure of a superstructure, and thus even farther from the heart of events, even less likely to form the basis for an ethic, than the state itself. The extensive work of Marx and Engels on international affairs, and in particular on war, meets this expectation (Molnar 1975). Predictably, international events are assessed and evaluated in accordance with their likely impact on the prospects of the revolution – thus demonstrating the expected consequentialist attitude – yet the mode of analysis seems strangely divorced from expectations. Rather than demonstrating that the behavior of states corresponds to economic interests, Marx frequently shows that this is not the case. He does not, however, convey a distinctive alternative sense of what governs state behavior or produces the logic of the state system. The only theory of international relations that can be discerned is Clausewitzian – and Marx and Engels were keen readers of *On War*.

Subsequent attempts to produce a Marxist theory of international relations have corrected Marx's lack of interest in economic determination, but not his lack of interest in the ethical dimension of the subject. Marxist theories of "imperialism" – which in the hands of Luxemburg ([1913] 1963), Kautsky ([1914] 1970), Hilferding ([1910] 1981), Bukharin ([1916] 1972), and Lenin (1968) is synonymous with a system of international relations and not simply with alien rule – have realized the aim of explaining the operation of the international system via the logic of capitalist accumulation, but they have not managed to theorize the idea of a community of states, nor have they attempted to

239

do so. In some respects this is surprising; Marxist theories of the state may not have achieved a viable understanding of the state as a community, but this has at least been recognized and addressed as an important topic (Jessop 1982). By contrast, the morality of states and the normative dimension of international relations seems not to have attracted the attention of theorists.

This omission could be regarded as a weakness in the tradition. Any number of issues in the world today, ranging from the destructiveness of nuclear war to the dangers of irreparable environmental damage, could form the basis for some sense of common interests shared not simply by peoples and classes, but also by states and their governments. Marxist writers within the Western "peace movement" have had some difficulty in deciding whether to view the threat of nuclear destruction as the product of capitalism or as a phenomenon that transcends class analysis; in the work of E. P. Thompson the latter view predominates, though his rather unclear notion of "exterminism" seems designed to stress the exceptional features of nuclear politics, rather than to form the basis for a wider understanding of the moral dimensions of a world of states (Thompson 1982). The idea that the threat to the environment posed by international pollution is tied up with capitalism rather than industrial society in general seems inherently implausible; as the Green movements in Europe have stressed, the Promethean desire to control and dominate fuels industrial society, and Marxists are at least as heavily implicated in this version of original sin as their opponents (Bahro 1983; Hulsberg 1988).

Official Marxisms and international ethics

In the twentieth century many people understand Marxism to be the ideology of the Soviet state. Although this judgment is plainly false, it reflects an important reality, that the government of the Soviet Union has been in the hands of men claiming the title of Marxists for over seventy years. In the late twentieth century, the official ideology of the Soviet Union is seemingly subject to self-critique; however, it is instructive to examine just what is being criticized. What are the main lines of Soviet Marxism, with special reference to the ethical dimension of international affairs? (Kubalkova and Cruickshank 1980, 1985; Lynch 1987; Light 1988).

Two general features of Soviet ethics seem of interest. First is the matter of authority and the role of the party. As suggested above, the basic Marxist position is that knowledge generated by theoretically informed practice is self-validating. In principle, Marxism is based on the priesthood of all (theoretically informed) believers, but in practice Marxists have generally worked with political structures – parties – and with leaders who are assigned, or assign to themselves, special powers to determine right conduct. The Leninist principle of democratic centralism, with the stress on the latter term, has, in the USSR, carried this tendency to extremes. Lenin's belief that left to their own devices, the workers would never achieve revolutionary consciousness provided the ideological justification for a leader-dominated and disciplined party, and the success of this party in 1917 imbued Leninist principles with a degree of authority that was effectively unchallengeable (Lenin 1968).

This iron discipline is wholly compatible with the second feature of Leninist ethical thought – the extremism of its consequentialism. "We say that our morality is entirely subordinated to the interests of the proletariat's class struggle ... Morality is what serves to destroy the old exploiting society and to unite all the working people around the proletariat" (Lenin 1968, 607). As suggested above, most Marxists who have publicly adhered to this position have in practice backed away from its implications, but this unwillingness to go to extremes has been less characteristic of Soviet than of most other varieties of Marxism, especially in the Stalin years. In international affairs these features operated as background in the 1920s through to the 1950s for a *Realpolitik* as cynical as any in the twentieth century, with the possible exception of that of Hitler's Germany. Such policy moves as the branding of Social Democrats as Social Fascists, the calls for a Popular Front, and the Nazi-Soviet Pact of 1939 reflected a hard-line consequentialist disregard for principle in the interests of the Soviet state (or the Fatherland of the Workers) made possible by rigid party discipline, an effective political police and, outside of the USSR, a portion of the intelligentsia willing to abandon even the most basic commitment to truth. As a state in the international system that wished to claim the rights that go with statehood, the USSR in this period adopted a state-to-state diplomatic stance that was formal and "correct." The extensive program of subversion generated by the Soviet Union and the assassination campaigns directed at Trotskyites and other enemies overseas were, when acknowledged at all, attributed to the Communist International (Comintern), a notionally independent body based in Moscow and controlled by the Soviet Communist party (Borkenau 1962; Ulam 1974).

The abolition of the Comintern in 1943 is best seen as a propaganda move to reassure the Soviet Union's Western allies in the war against the Third Reich, but in the course of the 1950s and 1960s the Soviet

Union's attitude toward the institutions of international society became less negative. The notion of "peaceful coexistence" came largely to dominate the previous assumption that war between capitalist and socialist states was inevitable, although the meaning of this phrase of Lenin's is by no means clear – indeed it seems capable of including whatever level of conflict between social systems the leadership of the party deems to be necessary, short of total war. For the rest, the change in Soviet behavior in the postwar era has not been matched by a similar evolution of doctrine. Those innovations that have emerged center on a recognition that not all nonsocialist states are alike, and on the need to theorize relations between the countries of the socialist bloc.

The first of these points concerns Soviet recognition of the notion of the "South." During the high cold-war period, the Soviet view of third-world neutralism mirrored that associated in the West with Secretary of State Dulles – that between good and evil there can be no true neutrals. Gradually since the early 1960s the Soviet Union has come to see the advantages for Soviet foreign policy of the idea of a third world, given that the emerging Southern agenda has been directed more to the failings of the West than to those of the Eastern bloc (and, of course, the Soviet Union refuses to accept any responsibility for the past sins of Czarist imperialism). However, Soviet Marxism is, in some respects, a handicap in its dealings with the emerging South; the Southern claim for a global redistribution of income is regarded by the USSR as the international equivalent of social democratic revisionism, while the moral arguments that accompany this demand are disparaged by comparison with the ethics of self-reliance espoused by the Soviet Union. The view that the South should put its own house in order is held in Moscow as well as Washington (Light 1988; Papp 1985).

Clearly, the countries of the socialist bloc have relations that go beyond the formal correctness that is the best that capitalist-socialist relations can achieve, but what this international socialist fraternity might involve is more troublesome. The Brezhnev Doctrine proclaiming the special rights and duties of the socialist commonwealth toward one another can be seen either as a genuine attempt to answer this question, or as a cynical rationalization of Soviet intervention to prevent developments in the socialist countries unwelcome to Moscow (Kubalkova and Cruickshank 1980, 1985; Jones 1989).

What these last paragraphs suggest is that while Soviet diplomatic behavior seems to indicate a general readiness to abide by the norms of international society, this position has been, for the most part, untheorized. This may be changing now with the emergence of the New Political Thinking (NPT) of President Gorbachev (Gorbachev 1987; Sakwa 1988). The NPT explicitly recognizes the sort of inter-state problems that in Western theory have been identified with inter-dependence; recent writings and speeches have implied a basis for a morality of states in the problems faced by "our common European (or Asian, or World) home." Clearly, this new thinking is intended to point to cooperation far beyond that mandated by peaceful coex-istence, and is intended to place inter-*state* relations on a new footing. However, Soviet spokesmen have suggested that inter*national* rela-tions remain within the orbit of Marxist theory. What is, as yet, unclear is first, what these two categories contain, and second, how they are to be articulated. It is clearly not the intention of the present leadership to return to the dual set of institutions of the Comintern era, but what the actual shape of the emerging Soviet approach to the world will be is something that remains to be seen (Kaldor et al. 1989). The NPT has undeniably shown a striking willingness to acknowledge past mis-takes. The account given above of Soviet foreign policy under Stalin, Krushchev, and Brezhnev would no longer be dismissed as cold-war propaganda but would today be acceptable.

The impact of Marxism on official international thought outside of the USSR is too big a subject to cover in this chapter. In the People's Republic of China, a distinctive international theory with a strong ethical dimension did emerge in the 1960s and 1970s with the Maoist notion of conflict between the countryside of the world and the cities with, of course, China leading the countryside (Kubalkova and Cru-ickshank 1985, Ch. 5). This notion is about as far removed from classical Marxism as it is possible to be while still leaving portraits of Marx and Engels hanging in the Great Hall of the People – Marx's view of the countryside is nicely conveyed by his description of Indian village life as "rural idiocy" (Avineri 1969, 94) – and, in any event, seems no longer to be heeded within the PRC (Yahuda 1983).

Neo-Marxist thought about development and underdevelopment has helped form the attitudes of at least some Southern participants in the North–South dialogue (Hoogvelt 1982, Chs. 5 and 6). The gap between neo- and classical Marxism has been discussed above; it seems likely that it is those features of neo-Marxism that are furthest from the classical approach that have proved most attractive to Southern governments (Warren 1980). The willingness to think in terms of international as well as class exploitation undoubtedly appeals to Southern nationalist leaders, while the moralizing nature of some neo-Marxist writings has also been a necessary, if un-Marxist, condition of their acceptance. However, on balance it seems that neo-Marxism has been more important in shaping the rhetoric of the South in the North–South dialogue than in providing a usable intellectual framework; Southern elites have taken what is congenial to them from the dependency approach – largely the critique of the West – while ignoring less attractive aspects, such as the critique of Southern elites. In the long run, the impact of this thinking on the South may actually be most important for the emerging dialogue of cultures in world politics. For all their willingness to criticize aspects of industrialism that Marx himself greatly favored, neo-Marxists do represent a conception of Western modernity that may be of some importance in the face of non-Western critiques of this notion.

Full circle

The end of the twentieth century appears to be a time of crisis for Marxism both as a governing ideology and as a scholarly framework within the academy. In the Soviet Union, the New Political Thinking is clearly designed to remain within the Marxist tradition, but whether it can succeed is open to debate. The dramatic developments of the last two years have removed Marxist governments from power in most East European states. It seems that in states where Marxism has been long established, the tradition is losing its legitimacy. The role of morality in delegitimizing these regimes may be important (Lukes 1990).

The retreat from Marxism is equally apparent in the South. The mood of "new realism" that has overtaken Southern economic policy in the 1980s is under threat from radical populism, but hardly from Marxist movements. The areas where Marxism is still a "live" doctrine are largely those where external forces have given a degree of credibility to its teachings. Decades of US anticommunism in Central America seem to have linked Marxism with the opponents of corrupt local regimes, while apparent Western support for the regime in South Africa has preserved the credibility of communism in that region. Apart from these special cases, Marxism seems almost everywhere to be in retreat.

Marxism's position in the Western academy is rather more complex and paradoxical. On the one hand, Marx's status as a major theorist of modernity is now widely recognized, and scholars identifying themselves as Marxists play a more important role in philosophy and the social sciences than would have been conceivable a generation ago. On the other hand, with recognition has come a dilution of the distinctive quality of Marxism. The influential school of analytical Marxists, which attempts to combine the techniques of Anglo-American analytical philosophy with the study of traditional Marxist topics, would be regarded by the orthodox as straying far from the tradition (Cohen 1978; Elster 1985; Roemer 1982, 1986; Wright 1985, 1989). The "world systems" school, although undoubtedly influenced by Marx, develops an understanding of the dynamics of capitalism that is highly unorthodox (Warren 1980; Brenner 1977). Moreover, Marxism is no longer unambiguously at the cutting edge of contemporary radical social thought; the new schools of critical theorists, post-modernists, and post-structuralists either regard themselves as post-Marxists (building on the tradition but rejecting some of its core notions, as does, for example, Habermasian critical theory) or explicitly dismiss Marxism as simply one more theory of modernity that needs to be abandoned (Laclau and Mouffe 1985; Der Derian and Shapiro 1989; Hoffman 1987).

This may mean that Marxism has come full circle. The nineteenth-century attitude to Marx's work as providing but one voice in a wider radical conversation, with something distinctive to offer but no sovereignty over the rest of the discussion, seems an accurate account of today's situation. In terms of ethics, that "something" seems unlikely to be a central contribution to the debate. Marxism alone cannot provide a set of values by which to live. What, perhaps, Marxist thought can do is to provide a corrective to the vapid moralizing characteristic of much contemporary radical discourse. The hard-headed consequentialism that, taken as the whole story, is an unsatisfactory ethical position, can nevertheless play a positive role in checking the utopianism that is a necessary feature of radical thought but that left unrestrained can lead to disaster. International relations as an academic discipline is founded on the defeat of "utopianism" by "realism" in the 1930s and 1940s, a defeat that for much of the last four decades has left international relations as the new dismal science. If the discipline is now experiencing a revival of ethical thought, a key task is to ensure that any new utopianism is tempered by the tough-minded realism rightly insisted upon by the founding fathers of the discipline. This is an area in which Marxist thinking has much to offer.

Suggested reading

In David McLellan (1977) can be found some of the key texts that explain why Marx regards morality and ethics with such hostility. *The German Ideology* (159–92) contains the clearest statement of Marx's view that ideas are determined by material circumstances and not vice versa; the *Communist Manifesto* (221–48) exemplifies this position. For an illustration of Marx's hard-headed consequentialism on an international issue, see his writings on British rule in India (332–37). Lenin's views on morality were, if anything, rather more consequentialist than Marx's. The best brief account of Lenin's view that whatever serves the interests of the working class is morally right can be found in his address "The Tasks of the Youth League" given in 1920 and printed in V. I. Lenin (1968).

The secondary literature on Marxism and ethics is dominated by Steven Lukes's *Marxism and Morality* (1985). Lukes argues that Marx's consequentialist approach to ethics has had a disastrous effect on socialist practice; Marxists have been unable to offer moral resistance to abuses of power committed in their name. Chapters 1 and 6 contain the main arguments. Some other academic writers have contested the interpretation of Marx offered by Lukes (and in the present chapter). A collection of essays from the journal *Philosophy and Public Affairs* – Marshall Cohen, Thomas Nagel, and Thomas Scanlon, eds., *Marx, Justice, and History* (Princeton: Princeton University Press, 1980) – contains chapters by Allen Wood, G. A. Cohen, and Alan Gilbert giving a different and less consequentialist reading of Marx. The paper by Alan Gilbert is particularly interesting because it addresses the issue of war – see "Marx on Internationalism and War" (185–208).

For most Marxists, the most important international ethical issue is that of poverty and development in the third world and, in particular, the issue of whether the role of capitalism in the developing countries has been "progressive." Marx himself justified some instances of imperialism on the grounds that imperial rule would spread capitalism and thus, in the long run, enhance the prospects for socialism (see above for his writings on India). The modern "dependency" school opposes this view and sees capitalism as an oppressive force; a classic work here is Frank (1971); Chapter 1 gives the main argument. Immanuel Wallerstein's *Historical Capitalism* (London: Verso 1983) is a very brief account of his similar "world-system" approach; his attack on the idea of progress (97–110) is a key text for understanding the dependency position. Bill Warren's *Imperialism* (1980) is a stirring defense of the classical Marxist position; Warren sees capitalism as an historically progressive force (11–47) and regards the dependency theory of Frank and Wallerstein as part of a nationalist mythology, blaming foreigners for the faults of the new ruling classes of the third-world states (157–85).

The revolutions of 1989 in Eastern Europe were clearly based in part on a rejection of Marxist ideas on morality: see Václav Havel's "Politics and Conscience" in *Living in Truth* (London: Faber and Faber 1987). As yet there is little academic literature on this subject, but Steven Lukes's "Marxism and Morality: Reflections on the Revolutions of 1989" in *Ethics and International Affairs*, 4 (1990), extends the analysis of his earlier work cited above.

References

Aggarwal, Vinod. 1985. *Liberal Protectionism*. Berkeley: University of California Press.

Amin, Samir, Giovanni Arrighi, Andre Gunter Frank, and Immanuel Wallerstein. 1982. *Dynamics of Global Crisis*. London: Macmillan.

Anderson, Perry. 1976. *Considerations on Western Marxism*. London: New Left Books.

Aveling, Eleanor Marx and Edward Aveling, eds. [1897]. *Karl Marx: The Eastern Question*. Reprint. London: Cass Reprint of Economic Classics, 1969.

Avineri, S., ed. 1969. *Karl Marx on Colonialism and Modernization*. New York: Anchor.

Bahro, R. 1983. *From Red to Green*. London: Verso.

Borkenau, Franz. 1962. *World Communism*. Ann Arbor: University of Michigan Press.

Brenner, Robert. 1977. "The Origins of Capitalist Development." *New Left Review*, No. 104.

Bukharin, N. [1916] 1972. *Imperialism and World Economy*. London: Merlin.

Cohen, G. A. 1979. *Karl Marx's Theory of History: A Defence*. Oxford: Oxford University Press.

1988. *History, Labour and Freedom*. Oxford: Clarendon.

Cohen, Marshall, Thomas Nagel, and Thomas Scanlon, eds. 1980. *Marx, Justice and History*. Princeton, NJ: Princeton University Press.

Davis, H. B., ed. 1976. *The National Question: Selected Writings By Rosa Luxemburg*. New York: Monthly Review Press.

Der Derian, James and Michael Shapiro, eds. 1989. *International/Intertextual Relations*. Lexington, MA: Lexington Books.

Elster, Jon. 1985. *Making Sense of Marx*. Cambridge: Cambridge University Press.

Emmanuel, Arrighi. 1972. *Unequal Exchange: A Study in the Imperialism of Trade*. London: New Left Books.

Frank, Andre Gunter. 1971. *Capitalism and Underdevelopment in Latin America*. Harmondsworth: Penguin.

1984. *Critique and Anti-Critique: Essays of Dependence and Reformism*. London: Macmillan.

Gallie, W. B. 1978. *Philosophers of War and Peace*. Cambridge: Cambridge University Press.

Geras, Norma. 1985. "On Marx and Justice." *New Left Review*, No. 150.

Goldfrank, W. L., ed. 1979. *The World System of Capitalism: Past and Present*. Beverley Hills: Sage.

Gorbachev, M. S. 1987. *Perestroika: New Thinking for Our Country and the World*. London: Collins.

Goulet, Denis. 1977. *The Cruel Choice*. New York: Atheneum.

Hilferding, Rudolf. [1910] 1981. *Finance Capital*. London: Routledge and Kegan Paul.

Hoffman, Mark. 1987. "Critical Theory and the Inter-Paradigm Debate" *Millennium: Journal of International Studies* 16: 2.

Hoogvelt, A. M. M. 1982. *The Third World in Global Development*. London: Macmillan.

Hulsberg, W. 1988. *The German Greens*. London: Verso.

Jessop, Bob. 1982. *The Capitalist State*. Oxford: Martin Robertson.

Jones, Robert A. 1989. *The Soviet Concept of Limited 'Sovereignty' From Lenin to Gorbachev*. New York: St. Martins Press.

Kaldor, M., G. Holden, and R. Falk, eds. 1989. *The New Detente: Rethinking East West Relations*. London: Verso.

Kamenka, E. 1969. *Marxism and Ethics*. London: Macmillan.

Kautsky, Karl. [1914] 1970. "Ultra Imperialism." *New Left Review*, No. 59.

Kolakowski, Lezek. 1978. *Main Currents of Marxism*. 3 vols. Oxford: Clarendon Press.

Kubalkova, V. and A. A. Cruickshank. 1980. *Marxism-Leninism and the Theory of International Relations*. London: Routledge and Kegan Paul.

1985. *Marxism and International Relations*. Oxford: Clarendon.

Laclau, Ernesto and Chantal Mouffe. 1985. *Hegemony and Socialist Strategy*. London: Verso.

Lenin, V. I. 1968. *Selected Works*. Moscow: Progress Publishers.

Liebknecht, Karl. [1907] 1972. *Militarism and Anti-Militarism*. New York: Dover.

Light, Margot. 1988. *The Soviet Theory of International Relations*. Brighton: Wheatsheaf.

Lukes, Steven. 1985. *Marxism and Morality*. Oxford: Oxford University Press.

1990. "Marxism and Morality: Reflections on the Revolutions of 1989." *Ethics and International Affairs* 4: 19–33.

Luxemburg, Rosa. [1918] 1961. *The Russian Revolution*. Ann Arbor: University of Michigan Press.

[1913] 1963. *The Accumulation of Capital*. London: Routledge and Kegan Paul.

Lynch, Allen. 1987. *The Soviet Study of International Relations*. Cambridge: Cambridge University Press.

McLellan, David, ed. 1971. *Karl Marx: Early Texts*. Oxford: Basil Blackwell.

1977. *Karl Marx: Selected Writings*. Oxford: Oxford University Press.

1979. *Marxism after Marx*. London: Macmillan.

Marx, Karl. [1867] 1976. *Capital*, vol 1. Harmondsworth: Penguin.

Molnar, Miklos. 1975. *Marx, Engels et la Politique Internationale*. Paris: Gallimard.

Munck, Ronald. 1986. *The Difficult Dialogue: Marxism and Nationalism*. London: Zed Books.

Nairn, Tom. 1977. *The Break-up of Britain*. London: New Left Books.

New Left Review. 1977. *Western Marxism: A Critical Reader*. London: New Left Books.

Nielsen, K. 1988. "Arguing about Justice." *Philosophy and Public Affairs* 17: 3.

Norman, Richard. 1983. *The Moral Philosophers: An Introduction to Ethics*. Oxford: Clarendon.

Papp, D. S. 1985. *Soviet Perceptions of the Developing World in the 1980s*. Lexington, MA: Lexington Books.

Porter, Bernard. 1984. "Fabians, Imperialists and the International Order." In *Fabian Essays in Socialist Thought*, ed. Ben Pimlott. London: Heinemann.

Roemer, John. 1982. *A General Theory of Exploitation and Class*. Cambridge: Harvard University Press.

1986. *Analytical Marxism*. Cambridge: Cambridge University Press.

Sakwa, Richard. 1988. "Gorbachev and the New Soviet Foreign Policy" *Paradigms* 2: 1.

Shaw, G. B. 1900. *Fabianism and the Empire*. London: G. Richards.

Skillen, Anthony. 1977. *Ruling Illusions*. Hassocks: Wheatsheaf.

Thompson, E. P. 1977. *William Morris: Romantic to Revolutionary*. London: Merlin.

1982. *Exterminism and Cold War*. London: New Left Books.

Trotsky, Leon, John Dewey, and G. Novack. 1973. *Their Morals and Ours*. New York: Pathfinder.

Ulam, A. B. 1974. *Expansion and Coexistence: Soviet Foreign Policy 1917–1973*. New York: Praeger.

Wallerstein, Immanuel. 1983. *Historical Capitalism*. London: Verso.

Warren, Bill. 1980. *Imperialism: Pioneer of Capitalism*. London: Verso.

Wood, Alan. 1984. "Justice and Class Interests." *Philosophica* 33: 1.

Wright, Erik Olin. 1985. *Classes*. London: Verso.

1989. *The Debate on Classes*. London: Verso.

Yahuda, Michael. 1983. *Towards the End of Isolationism: China's Foreign Policy after Mao*. London: Macmillan.

12 THE IDEA OF RIGHTS IN INTERNATIONAL ETHICS

R. J. VINCENT

If, in our search for the most pervasive ethical tradition, we were to take currently popular usage as our guide, then rights would have a strong claim to the prize. Talk of rights is so widespread and, some would say, so shrill that it sometimes seems to be all, in the popular mind, that ethics is about. To the rights of man have been added the rights of women and of children, including unborn children. To the rights of states have been added the rights of nations and peoples, of races and classes. To the rights of human beings and the associations they form among them have been added the rights of animals, and of trees, and of stones. Rights talk, as it is now often called, is also a popular activity in international relations, where, as will be set out below, human rights have become part of the everyday language of diplomacy.

Whether this popularity justifies elevating rights to the status of one of the great categories of ethical discourse along with (in Nardin's formulation in Chapter 1) political realism, common morality, consequentialism, and international law is another question. It may be argued that rights, read as interests, are assimilable to realism. It may also be argued that rights are an aspect of common morality, one of the principles we have in mind when we think of ethics as fidelity to moral principle. It is also possible to give a consquentialist account of rights, and to accommodate them in the law of nations. It may therefore be that rights do not themselves constitute a paradigm of moral thought but have their place and content determined by the ethical system in which they are embedded.

We may illustrate this by reference to a number of the ethical traditions examined in this book. In the tradition of natural law (see Boyle, Chapter 6) rights have gained a more prominent role in the twentieth century, but the fundamental thrust of the tradition is to set out the principles of right reason which should apply to all human beings whatever their conception of their rights. In the contractarian tradition (see Mapel, Chapter 9), on the other hand, subjective conceptions of what one's rights are (in the state of nature) and ought to be (in the state) are a much more prominent determinant of the shape of an ethical system. But in Kant's "global rationalism," which Donaldson describes in Chapter 7, duties are preferred to rights, and the distinction between perfect and imperfect duties is thought to give a more comprehensive view of the ethical terrain than the discussion of human rights. In the tradition of international law, both classical and modern (see Chapters 2 and 3), rights are but part of a much broader moral schema. However, this part is sometimes very prominent, as in the doctrine of the fundamental rights of states associated with the work of Wolff and Vattel in the eighteenth century and, in contemporary international law, in such instruments as the Charter of Economic Rights and Duties of States. But rights do not themselves constitute a legal tradition; rather they correlate with duties in a system of law whose character is determined by other considerations: constitutions, conventions, the common-law tradition, and so on.

It is therefore doubtful whether the "rights tradition" is coherent enough to be called a paradigm or an ethical system. But there is a rights tradition in the more rudimentary sense of an idea that has a history, that has been transmitted from one generation to another and adapted in the process. We can trace the evolution of the concept of a right from its prehistory in the ancient world to its ubiquitous presence in contemporary world politics (Vincent 1986, Ch. 2; Dagger 1989; Shapiro 1986; Tuck 1979). This chapter is not about that evolution, but we may note the chief stations along the way. The ancient world contributed the idea of universality, the vision of natural law caught by Cicero's observation that "we cannot be freed from its obligations by Senate or People, and we need not look outside ourselves for an expounder or interpreter of it. And there will not be different laws at Rome and at Athens, or different laws now and in the future, but one eternal and unchangeable law will be valid for all nations and for all times" (Cicero 1928, 211). The Renaissance and the Reformation added the idea of the dignity of the individual together with the decisive significance of individual conscience. Together these produced the modern idea of a right as, in Francisco Suarez's formulation, "a certain moral power which every man has, either over his own property or with respect to that which is due to him" (Suarez 1944, 30). Rights became the foundation of political theory in the classical accounts of the social contract by Hobbes, Locke, and Rousseau, and this development worked itself out in political practice in the American and French Revolutions, which were undertaken to vindicate rights.

In terms of practical significance the eighteenth century recorded the high-water mark of the theory of rights, which provided both the reason for and the justification of the revolutions. The nineteenth century produced a good part of the classical criticism of rights in the work of Bentham, Hegel, and Marx but, despite these assaults, the idea of rights has, as we have seen, retained its place in the contemporary world. Nor is this just the failure of popular doctrine to keep up with scientific discourse. Rights remain a constructive component of political theory. In the contemporary discussion of natural law, rights (as human rights) have been taken to express "virtually all the requirements of practical reasonableness" (Finnis 1980), and are defended as egalitarian and non-consequentialist. Rights are also prominent in contemporary contributions to social contract theory (Nozick 1974; Rawls 1971). And, perhaps most surprisingly, contemporary utilitarian doctrine, traducing its nineteenth-century dismissal of rights and especially of natural rights, has sought to find room for an account of rights (Sumner 1987).

These observations return us to the importance of the paradigmatic context in which ideas of rights occur. But, before we move on, we should note a feature that all uses of the idea of rights have in common. The language of rights denotes a particular moral attitude. Someone claiming his or her rights is not begging or pleading, and the appropriate response if the claim is met is not gratitude. If the claim is *not* met, the appropriate response is indignation, not mere disappointment (Feinberg 1966). This is because rights have come to be understood as part of one's status as a person (Melden 1977) and, as such, they have forced their way into the most unlikely ethical theories.

The connection of the idea of rights with the idea of human dignity has given rights a greater role than that of simply correlates of duties in a conceptual scheme that connects rights-holders to duty-bearers. It is tempting but too neat to regard rights and duties as different ends of the same normative relation (Benn and Peters 1959). This terrain is philosophically complex (Feinberg 1966; Hart 1967; Lyons 1970), but rights do not always have to find a correlate in duties to be well-founded. From a political point of view, we may note the distinction between "I know my rights" and "I know my station and its duties."

We shall return to the distinctiveness of rights in the conclusion to this chapter. In the main body we focus on placing rights in international ethics in two different ways. First, we will take a cross-section through world society to identify the principal levels at which the idea of rights can be identified. Second, we will map out the place of rights in contemporary international ethics by looking down onto the political blocs that have until very recently shaped the international conversation about rights.

Rights in a cross-section of world society

Rights, according to Suarez, are moral or legal possessions. One persuasive account of the syntax governing their usage is as follows: rights-holders (subjects of rights) have a claim to some substance (the object of a right) that may be asserted, or demanded, or enjoyed, or implemented, or enforced (the exercise of a right) against some individual or group (the bearer of the correlative duty) on this or that ground (the justification of a right) (Gewirth 1982, 2; Vincent 1986, 8–9).

This syntax may help us discern the significance of rights at three different levels of world politics: (1) the level at which individuals are said to inhabit a great society or humankind; (2) the level at which states coexist in a society of states; and (3) the level at which groups other than states (such as multinational corporations and liberation organizations) jostle together in world society. The kinds of rights characteristic of each of these levels may be different: at the first level, the great society of humankind, we might expect to be dealing primarily with natural or human rights; at the second level, the society of states, we might expect to be dealing with the rights of states in international law; and, at the third level, the half-world between the first two, we might expect to encounter a mixture of claims based on both the idea of a common humanity and on rights recognized in the society of states.

The individual level

The association of human rights with individual human beings is, in the West, so strong as to make any other way of thinking about them seem to require a special justification. Who are the subjects of rights? Individuals. It is individuals (usually male individuals) who populate the imagined "state of nature" of liberal political theory, and individuals who make the social contract that facilitates their departure from this state of nature. And it is individual interests and purposes, prominently expressed in the form of rights, that continue to set limits to the encroachment of social arrangements.

What do these individuals have rights to? In the same classical liberal political theory, they have rights to life, liberty, and property (and, in twentieth-century liberalism, to welfare too). These are the moral possessions referred to at the beginning of this section as the shorthand definition of a right. The right to life entails, in most liberal formulations, the right to security against violence and, in many, but not all formulations, the right not to be deprived of the means to subsistence. The right to liberty means, in most liberal formulations, "freedom from" something (a government, the interference of other individuals), a private space within which an individual's own purposes may be worked out. Some formulations add "freedom to" participate in something, a public space within which some larger liberty is enjoyed through a general will. The right to property means a claim to stable possession of, for example, land, so that what is sown will also be reaped by the owner. A right to property involves, literally, possession. But the metaphorical idea of a right as an individual's possession is important in pinpointing the modern conception of a human right. It tells what political possessions (life, liberty, etc.) everyone ought to have, and it makes those values so much a part of an individual as if they belonged to him or her by nature.

Individuals claim rights differently according to the situation. Stating, insisting, protesting, justifying, or explaining are all modes of rights talk used in different circumstances. But two ideas distinguish rights from other forms or moral discourse. First, as was stressed at the outset, rights talk tends to denote a particular moral attitude associated closely with human dignity. Rights are thought of as part of an individual's status as a person, and the language in which they are expressed reflects this. Second, rights – especially natural rights, and expecially when abused – are invoked to explain the circumstances in which individuals find themselves. Thus, for instance, in the doctrine of the French revolutionaries, ignorance or neglect of or contempt for human rights is the cause of public misfortune. It is also a popular explanation of contemporary global miseries to say that this or that society, or world society as a whole, has paid insufficient attention to human rights.

Then there is the question of the duties that correlate with rights. It has been argued, in relation to the idea of universal human rights, that rights exist in a strong and in a weak sense (Raphael 1977). Everyone has both kinds. But rights in the strong sense are held against everybody else and rights in the weak sense are held against a particular section of humanity. Everyone has a right to life against everyone else: there is a general duty to respect it. But, if everyone has a right to, say, education, it is against a particular government: the duty is laid only upon a responsible authority. This formulation

254

reveals a certain liberal habit of thought according to which civil and political rights are regarded as negative rights, requiring as a correlate only an undemanding noninterference, whereas economic and social rights are positive rights, requiring substantial provision by the responsible agency. This habit of thought has recently been comprehensively scrutinized and its inadequacies revealed. A better formulation of the connection between rights and duties is that of Henry Shue who suggests that all basic human rights have three correlating duties: duties to *avoid* depriving, duties to *protect* from deprivation, and duties to *aid* the deprived (Shue 1980). According to the circumstances, the duty bearers may be different (individuals, states, multinational corporations), and the nature of the duty may change (to avoid depriving the participants in a subsistence economy, to protect refugees from assault, to aid in a natural disaster). Basic human rights require all three kinds of response.

The final issue at this level is justification, the reason this or that right should be taken seriously. In the natural-rights tradition there are three persistent aspects of justification, each of them associated with the idea that the claims we now call human rights are indeed universal. The first is the idea of nature (of Greek origin). The second is the idea that universality includes every human being and not merely every member of a particular category (discernible in Roman and Christian thought). The third is the idea that rights spring from the individual conscience, which is the ultimate foundation of politics (promoted by the Reformation and underpinning the liberal political theory that produced the American and the French Revolutions).

The idea of nature is important for the justification of values held to be the birthright of all individuals because it provides a standpoint from which circumstances – what happens to be – can be criticized. A notion of what human beings are like by nature leads naturally to a theory of how they ought to be treated, and this can be compared to how they are actually treated and provide a reason for change. This is the tradition of natural law and, although the content of that law changes over time, its continuity of concern with what ought to be rather than what is forms an important root of the idea of rights.

Quod semper but also *quod ubique*; what is always and what is everywhere. The idea that rights should be honored wherever human beings live is a second feature of the justification of natural or human rights. If human rights are indeed human then they should be species-specific, not culture-specific. If they are derived from a theory of right reason that is everyone's inheritance, then the exclusion of this or that individual can only be arbitrary. Theorists of change, or of the expansion of rights to cover new categories of things or new classes of people, have a script based on this principle. This is what is by nature due; it should thereby apply to everyone; insist on your rights. This justifies the extension of rights to Protestants, or slaves, or blacks, or women, or anyone or any category of people to whose humanity mundane arrangements give offense.

An offense against rights is registered in the individual conscience. Human rights are about everyone's due, and they stem from the original sovereignty of the individual to make such arrangements as he or she reasonably wills with society. The idea that the individual conscience is the ultimate forum of politics is central to rights-based political theory, and is repeatedly used to justify this or that political innovation (it will enhance the liberty of the individual) or protest against it (it will make indefensible inroads into individual liberty). So conventional has this kind of thinking become in the West that it seems natural. When, for example, a contemporary professor of jurisprudence describes individual rights as "political trumps held by individuals" to be used against the imposition of collective goals, we admire his metaphor and adopt it ourselves, but the thesis does not surprise us (Dworkin 1977).

The level of inter-state relations

The syntax we suggested to govern our discussion of rights has worked out relatively unproblematically in relation to individuals because it requires no effort of the imagination to understand individuals holding rights to something, claiming that something from others, and calling up this or that justification of the transaction. But it is not obvious, least of all to students of international relations, that states should be thought of as holding rights just as individuals do. States are seen as the locus of interests, but not, except in an artificial way that invites hypocrisy, of responsible moral action. However, for the purposes of this discussion, we will apply our syntax to states as rights-holders, even though the agents who act for states are individuals and collections of individuals (Carr 1966, 149).

Certainly, the idea of states as subjects of rights has become orthodox in what has been called "the morality of states" or "the legalist paradigm" or "liberal statism" (Beitz 1979; Walzer 1977; Falk 1981). The tradition of international law, especially at the apogee of positivist doctrine in the nineteenth century, not only takes states to be the principal subjects of its rules but also excludes the claims of any rival actors to the status of subjects. According to the positivist orthodoxy, states were the subjects of international law, individuals merely its objects. And the continuing vitality of this idea is revealed in the observation of a contemporary professor of international relations that "in some sense, there are really no people in the world, only states" (Miller 1981, 16).

This, however, reduces to absurdity an idea that begins not with the exclusiveness of states but with the universality of individual obligation. Princes, as individuals, were obligated to natural law as individuals whether acting in their private or their public capacities. Only later, with the consolidation of states and the emergence of the doctrine of reason of state, did the state itself take on the obligations of the prince, and the idea of a special morality of states begin to emerge. We need not retell this story here (Meinecke 1957; Vincent 1978) but we do need to notice that the doctrine that states are the (exclusive or not) subjects of international law derived from a doctrine of individual obligation.

What do states have a right to? In the language of the United Nations Charter the basic claims are to territorial integrity and political independence; the new states that have just won their political independence claim economic sovereignty too, to make the political independence mean something. We might see in these claims of states the international equivalent of those basic rights of individuals familiar in the domestic arena: the right to security (of the territory), the right to liberty (of the independent polity), and the right to subsistence (of the state as an economic unit).

How do states claim their rights? In the first place we may note how commonplace the use of the language of rights has become in international politics. The declarations and resolutions and agreements that Jones details in Chapter 3 as the output of states and of international organizations are replete with moral claims often expressed in terms of rights. These rights are not only the human rights and fundamental freedoms that constitute the common good, but also and more fundamentally the procedural rights that protect state autonomy or, perhaps, the plural good. This connects, secondly, with the moralism of states. States may or may not act morally, but they readily reach for a moral defense of action, and a policy arrived at from a calculation of interests is often presented to the world in the language of rights: it was the right to life of American citizens that triggered the United States' intervention in Panama; Britain went to war in the Falklands in defense of the principle of self-determination; the Soviet Union intervened in Czechoslovakia in defense of the rights if not the duties of the whole socialist commonwealth. The requirements of power politics were, in each case, politely ignored. This is not a peculiar hypocrisy of international relations. We are now accustomed to the cricketers' argument that a tour to South Africa is being undertaken in defense of an individual's right to choose. But the procedure is so prevalent in the world of states as to make that world the paradigmatic example of the homage paid by vice to virtue. Lest this should give the argument too zestful a realist thrust, we may note that it is also possible that states act on the grounds that they publicly give and not for some other unspoken purpose, and that the rights and duties set out in the books on international law provide a reason for action as well as an excuse for it. In any event, they form a canon in terms of which action can be judged.

If states have rights in international law, the bearers of the correlative duties are, in the standard formulation, other states. This reciprocal relationship is taken to provide the sanction in international law, as well as a description of the system. What secures fidelity to the law is the knowledge that failure to adhere to it will release others from their obligation to observe it. In general I observe your territorial integrity because in doing so I reinforce a system in which you are expected to observe mine. This state-to-state account of international rights and duties is not exhaustive, but it is the standard version.

The justification of the rights of states has two aspects corresponding to two questions: What is it that makes a state command moral respect? What is it about state behavior that allows us to drop our moral standards when judging it?

"Because it is there" is one standard, if uninteresting, response to the first question. The state has come to monopolize our political terrain and we have to make rules for it and not another institution. But the more reflective defense of the rights of states in the Western liberal tradition appeals to a more or less explicit social contract. A state commands respect if it is an association "of individuals with their own common interests and aspirations, expressed within a common tradition" (Benn and Peters 1959, 361) (the less explicit version). Or a state commands respect if it is an expression of the liberty of individuals such that they agree to join the community it protects (the more explicit version). Thus the justification for the existence of a state may be said to depend on a principle of individual self-determination judged as tacit consent in the former case and as open consent in the latter. Group self-determination derives from individual self-determination, and we are thus driven back to individuals to ground moral claims (Walzer 1977).

The second question, however, concerns a group not reducible to individuals. Because states are condemned to exist in a world of states, in which they can never be confident of their security, they make whatever security arrangements are necessary rather than act internationally according to some domestic conception of right. The tradition of *raison d'état* (or, more precisely, the part of that tradition that takes morality seriously) has supplied the moral defense for this. Justice presupposes order. Order is at least possible behind the protective wall of the state. Action to preserve the integrity of this wall is justifiable in the name of self-preservation even if it sets the precepts of ordinary morality aside. Thus the rights of states have been associated with the doctrine of necessity in a way that moralists claim severs them from true morality. Moralists of states, however, defend this as all that in reality is possible.

Neither individuals nor states

Individuals and states are not, as it is now commonplace to observe, the only actors in international politics. Multinational corporations, churches, terrorist groups, trades unions – the host of organizations that occupy the political space between individuals and states – are also in varying degrees subjects of rights in the international domain. Leaving aside international organizations that, as groupings among states, may be accommodated at the state and inter-state level, there are two kinds of nonstate groupings that are of interest here: groups that aspire to statehood (the PLO, the IRA), and groups that operate within the political structure formed by states without duplicating their functions (IBM, the Catholic Church).

What do such groups have rights to? Would-be states do not have rights merely in virtue of their aspirations, but international law does have a way of recognizing the successful presentation of their claims. Thus, for example, in the international law of internal war we can make rough distinctions between a rebellion that is to be treated as a domestic affair, an insurgency that gives its adherents some rights in international law, and a belligerency that makes of a warring faction the functional equivalent of a state (Falk 1968). In this way, it seems, international society has a way of recognizing the successful "presentation of a claim" and rewarding it with a grant of legitimacy. As to groups that are not states and do not aspire to statehood, the rights they seek are associated with access to sovereign territories: to buy and sell or to invest in the case of multinational corporations, to preach the word in the case of churches, to organize labor in the case of trades unions. Rights (and duties) such as these govern activity in the

259

transnational world that stretches across state frontiers without necessarily raising questions about the legitimacy of the state structure itself. This is the domain of what used to be called private international law.

How are such claims characteristically made? Groups engaged in shooting their way into international society are not normally mere gunslingers. They generally insist on the justice of their cause in language derived from the pronouncements about human rights whose legitimacy the club they wish to join has already endorsed. Thus the right of self-determination, which is Article 1 of both the International Covenants on Human Rights, is for them a principle of political action and not a mere cant phrase from the paper world of the United Nations. The appeal made by nonstate groups with nonstate objectives is different but connected. If the nationalist aspirant to club membership asks the club members to take the principles written into their constitution seriously, the nonstate accompaniment to the world of states asks them to consider what is necessary for a civilized life. Giving multinational corporations access makes possible, it is said, a reasonable standard of living. (Senator Moynihan, for example, described the multinational corporation as the most civilizing institution of twentieth-century world society.)

Who bears the correlative duties? For the most part states, for they are the gatekeepers both in admitting new full members and in determining who can be a privileged associate. But it is not only states that bear duties in respect of the rights asserted by nonstate groups. To show how this may be it is useful to return to Henry Shue's account of the duties that in general correlate with rights: duties to avoid depriving (which may fall on, say, exploitative corporations as well as states), duties to protect from deprivation (which may fall on nongovernmental organizations as well as states) and duties to aid the deprived (which may fall on individuals as well as states) (Shue 1980, 52–53). More concretely, a duty to avoid depriving may require a particular kind of provision from a mining company to a community habitually dependent on a subsistence agriculture that would be disrupted by development. (For another discussion of how human rights limit multinationals and other transnational agencies see "The Kantian-deontological approach to international affairs," Chapter 7.) Duties to protect from deprivation may fall on host communities responding to the plight of refugees. And duties to aid the deprived may fall on everyone confronted with the fact of poverty or starvation. But it is clear even from this formulation that states, as organizations for political action, are the most comprehensive duty-bearers.

The justifications of the claims of these nonstate actors are of two sorts. They may be expressed as (1) we are no different from you and we should therefore have the same rights as you; and (2) we are different from you but our presence is necessary if you are to live a decent existence. The first justification appeals to the rules of international society, claiming the same right of all (self-determining nations) to be different. The second justification appeals to the less well-established rules of a more inclusive world society, claiming the right to make different societies the same in respect of this or that value (the same market, the same revulsion against torture, the same recognition of personhood).

Qualified statism

We have now presented a cross-section of rights in international relations worked out at the levels of individuals, states, and nonstate groups. This organization is not meant to suggest a rough equality between the three modes of rights talk in the practice of world politics. For it is plain that the state bulks larger both as a repository of rights and as a location of obligation. Individuals do not exist as autonomous actors in world society at some Olympian level above the state, but receive their identity as members of a particular community corralled into the state. So evident is this that one of the chief offenses to human dignity in the twentieth-century world has been taken to be the plight of the refugee who abandons one state without the guarantee of a welcome by another. To be human is to be a citizen and, there being no global polis, this means affiliation with a section of humanity only. In the same way, groups other than states do not exist in some extraterrestrial void, but are barnacled to the states that make possible their relative security. International law, as the code of rights in world society, is the record, overwhelmingly, of the rights and obligations of states toward each other.

This does not strip our other levels of analysis of any meaning. The idea of the rights of individuals played a part, as we have seen, in producing the idea of the rights of states, and exists now as a vital component in the theory of what states are for, and as a central criterion for deciding what they can legitimately do. The idea of the rights of groups other than states demonstrates by its mere existence the incompleteness of the world of states, and constrains no less than the idea of individual rights what it is possible for states to do to their own citizens. The natural-law idea of a great society of humankind composed of all individuals in the world, and the transnational idea of

261

a kind of world society accommodating a host of different actors and institutions, have thus a practical effect as well as a mere theoretical existence.

Rights in a plan of world politics

The syntax that structured our discussion of a cross-section of rights in world society was presented from a Western point of view. But, in contemporary world politics, the discussion of rights, and especially of "human rights," takes place in a forum in which the West is joined by the East and the South. Accordingly, a satisfactory account of the imprint of the rights tradition on contemporary international ethics must include all of these standpoints. In the early 1990s, the great tectonic plates of world politics since 1945 seem to be breaking up, but it is too early to see the new shape of international relations. Accordingly, we should be aware of the ephemeral nature of the plan of world politics to be developed, even as we use it to establish the orthodoxy from which world politics are departing.

The West

Four central aspects of the Western position on human rights provide a framework for comparison with non-Western positions: individualism; the idea that human rights are held *against* the state; the primacy of civil and political rights; and universalism.

Human rights as the rights of individuals is a natural and habitual starting place in Western political thought and practice. Human rights are the rights of human beings, and human beings come in ones. The point of human rights is to preserve and nurture this individuality, so that theories of human rights as prerequisites to human agency have particular intuitive power in the West (Gewirth 1982).

The predator most likely to attack the rights of individuals is the state, and the story of rights in the West can be told, albeit rather Whiggishly, as the successive vindication of individuals' claims against the state. Every English schoolchild knows that the Magna Carta, the Petition of Rights, and the Glorious Revolution all enhanced individual liberty against the tyrannical prince, and equivalent landmarks are lodged in the American, the French, and every other Western political mind.

This same story as it is presented in contemporary world politics is predominantly a story of the rights that defend civil and political liberty. It is true that some modern liberal theories of human rights,

262

such as those of Henry Shue and Jack Donnelly, have shown the extent to which some minimal provision of economic and social rights is itself a prerequisite to human agency and therefore must be regarded as a basic right itself (Shue 1980; Donnelly 1989). But this is not generally the position defended by the leading Western governments when human rights are at issue in such institutions as the United Nations. Indeed, the very division of the two Covenants on Human Rights sponsored by the United Nations into one on civil and political rights and another on economic, social, and cultural rights indicates two factions in world politics, the former being the instrument of the Western party (Vincent 1989).

In the Western view this instrument should have a wider, even the widest application. For it is a central part of the orthodox Western account of human rights that they are the rights of everyone, of all individuals in the world, and not the privileges of those fortunate enough to belong to this or that section of humanity. Thus, at the Conference on Security and Cooperation in Europe at Helsinki and its several successors, the Western position has consistently been that the principle of nonintervention written into the Helsinki Final Act was no barrier to discussing or monitoring the human-rights records of any of the parties, because these were a matter of international concern and could not be protected by a claim of domestic jurisdiction. And, in North–South contexts, the West has frequently found itself in the position of defending the civil and political liberties of individuals against the argument that some communal imperative should set them aside (Ferguson 1986).

The East

In the Soviet Union and Eastern Europe (and we are speaking now of the recent past, not the present), Marxist-Leninist doctrine produced a quite different account of human rights from the orthodox Western view. It was not individuals but the group that dominated the moral scenery. Rights came from law, which came from government, which reflected the underlying economic relationships of any society. In capitalist society, the content of what are called human rights reflected the interests of the capitalist class. In socialist society, they reflected the interests of the proletarian class. And, because socialist society had transcended the individualist self-interest of bourgeois society, the social grouping that achieved this became itself the subject of rights.

As the converse to the Western formula, these (state) rights imposed

263

obligations on individuals. Socialist society had liberated the mass of the people from the serfdom of capitalism and provided a platform of economic emancipation from which they continued to benefit. Any rights that individuals claimed had then to recognize this achievement and not detract from it. Rights were enjoyed *through* the state not *against* it, and observing obligations to the state was the best way of protecting individual rights.

What makes this doctrine intelligible to an unsympathetic Western audience is the idea of the primacy of economic and social rights. The primary liberty in the socialist countries is economic: the freedom from exploitation that is delivered by having power in the hands of the working class. The absolute right to work is the sign of this freedom, different in kind from the freedom in the West to choose one's exploiter or to be unemployed (Hawkesworth 1980). And, because emancipation is fundamentally an economic process, economic and social rights found civil and political rights, which can never be asserted against the primary freedoms of socialist society.

The implication of this view is that, short of the revolution having taken place everywhere, human rights are not and cannot be universal. Socialist societies that have transcended individualist atomism open up the prospect of human emancipation, but the "freedom" trumpeted by Western societies is illusory. And when the West seeks to intervene in the name of universal human rights, this is seen as a stock pretense disguising the real exploitative motive within. In practice, socialist societies may have to acknowledge within their frontiers the Western tendency in regard to individual liberty, but according to traditional socialist doctrine, this reflects the configuration of forces in the world rather than a principled universalism.

The South

The group rights that are basic in the East reappear as central in the South. The group, not individuals within it, is the natural starting place for political thought and practice. Thus in traditional African thought it is social harmony and the preservation of the fabric of social life that is said to begin political enquiry, and this approach is more likely to produce obligations for individuals than rights. We can find similar patterns elsewhere in the third world – in Islam, for example, and in China (Vincent 1986, Ch. 3; Donnelly 1989, Ch. 3).

Starting with the group tends to produce a conception of individuality defined through it rather than against it, so that there is not a Southern doctrine of the "sacralized individual" (Legesse 1980) of the

West, but rather personhood understood as a set of incorporations into the group. In contemporary world politics this habit of thought made possible the idea, important in decolonization, that group freedom was a necessary preface to individual liberty, and that the latter was not possible in the absence of the former. External self-determination (as it came to be called) was prior to internal self-determination.

In the third world, also, the Eastern idea of the primacy of economic, social, and cultural rights has considerable force, and has sometimes been taken to be characteristic of Southern rather than Eastern doctrine in world politics (Donnelly 1981). It is not surprising, it may be said, that the part of the world that suffers the greatest economic and social deprivation should give priority to economic and social rights, and the idea of economic self-determination has been an important plank of the Southern platform at the United Nations, producing the demands for development in the third generation of human rights there. This idea is pressed as a collective right that, in the service of group emancipation, may impose uncomfortable obligations on the individual within third-world societies.

In regard to universality, two elements of Southern doctrine are of interest here. First, with regard to economic rights, the Southern view of the distribution of rights and duties in international politics is skewed in a way that tends to make the South the beneficiary of rights, and the North the bearer of duties. This is the result of either or both the arguments that the North as the colonial exploiter owes the South for past depredations, and that the principle of equal sovereignty requires a reallocation of economic as well as political resources. Second, with regard to social and cultural rights, there is an element of Southern doctrine that accepts the universality of the language of rights but uses it to protect plural conceptions of the good. Thus, the South might endorse a principle of self-determination that derives from the West, but then use it to legitimize non-Western and anticolonial conceptions of the "self." The effect of this might be to drive the First and Third Worlds apart rather than joining them together. It would therefore be a mistake to see the common language of a shared procedural principle as more significant than substantial political differences.

Rights as an issue in world politics

It was possible until very recently, without being too melodramatic, to present contemporary world politics as a great debate about human rights. The Western civil and political rights party confronted

265

an Eastern economic and social rights party, and both were in turn confronted (though the West more than the East) by a Southern party with a collectivist principle synthesizing the other two (Macpherson 1973). Whether they interpret their roles aggressively, as postures for others to assume too, or defensively, as tendencies to be maintained in their own parts of the world, some account of contemporary international politics could be given by reference to these parties and to their varying fortunes. But there was always an element of caricature about these positions. It may be, for example, that in certain parts of the West, notably the Scandinavian countries, economic and social rights were as well established as civil and political rights, so that the presentation of the argument between these groups of rights as an ideological battle between the blocs did violence to reality and was itself the prisoner of a cold-war perception of world politics. It may also be that within the Eastern bloc, the civil and political rights "party," while forced underground, never surrendered to the dominant orthodoxy of the priority of economic and social rights. It may in addition be true that the individualism mocked in the rhetoric of the South is honored in the practice and the beliefs of individuals and groups within Southern countries. For this reason, the cross-section is as important as the plan in placing rights in international ethics. This will be even more true as the established plan becomes a less reliable guide to the reality of world politics.

The new polarity that a revised plan would have to address may be that between democracies and non-democracies, instead of that between capitalism and communism, in which case the debate about rights in international politics might be absorbed into the question of how to democratize, and the issues may become the right to free elections, free trade, and openness. Or there may be a renewed emphasis on the North–South divide, in which case the debate about rights in international politics might refocus on the division between civil and political rights (the North) and economic and social rights (the South). In this regard, it is very interesting that a distinguished commentator has recently recast the dispute between West and East as a special case of that between North and South (Hassner 1990). In any event, we may continue to expect the question of rights to divide world society as much as to unite it.

The place of rights in international ethics

What conclusion then can we come to about the place of rights in international ethics? This is really two questions: one about the place of rights compared to other ways of thinking about ethics in international relations, the other about the part played by the idea of rights in the life of international society.

Taking the second question first, we may note the part played by rights in the conversation about ethics in international relations. As human rights, they have become a kind of *lingua franca* of ethics talk so that much of the discussion about ethics in international relations takes place making use of the vocabulary of rights (however slight the grammatical agreement). As the rights of states, they purport to govern the way actors in international society behave. And they provide a doctrinal lever for those who would enter international society or shape its development.

All this may be dismissed as merely language, but to some extent the conversation about human rights is setting out what is to be agreed upon as the content of civilized life within the states making up international society. Equally, there is a substantial sense in which international law collects together the rules of a functioning system of international cooperation. And nonstate actors show the importance of this in their anxiety to have the rules applied to them.

As to the first question about the place of rights as distinct from that of other traditions in international ethics, it would be a mistake to presume the existence of a single tradition of rights because of the frequency with which the language of rights is used. This is because of our earlier observation about the embeddedness of rights in other traditions. But what the language may be said to indicate is the utility of the discourse of rights for the protection of a plurality of interests, and out of these interests may come a continuing defense of rights.

Suggested reading

The place of rights in international ethics is most prominently the place of the rights of states. Richard Tuck said that in Hugo Grotius's work, the law of nature became "respect one another's rights" (1979, 67). And whether or not Grotius was the founder of international law, the rights of states was an important part of his treatment in *De Jure Belli ac Pacis* (1625) which is available in the Carnegie Classics on International Law translated in 1924 by F. W. Kelsey and reprinted by Oceana, New York in 1964. A recent treatment of the work of Grotius is Hedley Bull, Benedict Kingsbury, and Adam Roberts, eds., *Hugo Grotius and International Relations* (Oxford: Clarendon Press, 1990). The idea of the rights of states reached its apogee in Christian Wolff's doctrine of the fundamental rights of states as derived – like those of individuals – from nature (*Ius Gentium Methodo Scientifica Pertractatum*, 1764, trans. J. H. Drake, 1934, Carnegie Classics; New York: Oceana, 1964). The influence of this doctrine, mediated by the later positivist international lawyers' view of fundamental rights as presuppositions of the law of nations rather than as imprescriptible rights, can be felt down to the present day. See, for example, Robert F. Meagher, *An International Redistribution of Wealth and Power: A Study of the Charter of Economic Rights and Duties of States* (New York: Pergamon Press, 1979).

The idea of human rights, as distinct from those of states, has in the form of natural rights its mature statement in John Locke, *Two Treatises of Government*, ed. P. Laslett (New York: Mentor, 1965), and its brilliant polemical defense in Tom Paine's *The Rights of Man* (London: Dent, Everyman edition, 1969). The classical criticism of the idea is contained in Edmund Burke's *Reflections on the Revolution in France*, ed. C. C. O'Brien (Harmondsworth: Penguin, 1968); in Hegel's *Philosophy of Right*, trans. and with notes by T. M. Knox (Oxford: Clarendon, 1942); in Jeremy Bentham's *Works*, vol. 2, *Anarchical Fallacies* (Edinburgh: Wm. Tait, 1843); and in Karl Marx's *On the Jewish Question*, in *Karl Marx, Early Writings*, trans. and ed. T. B. Bottomore (London: Watts, 1963).

In contemporary international relations, an interesting development is the attempt to work out the relationship between the rights of individuals and those of states. Two works of theory are prominent: Charles R. Beitz, *Political Theory and International Relations* (1979), and Henry Shue, *Basic Rights* (1980). Jack Donnelly, *Universal Human Rights* (1989) and Michael Walzer, *Just and Unjust Wars* (1977) seek instructively to bring theory and practice together. And useful practical guides are David P. Forsythe, *Human Rights in World Politics* (Lincoln: University of Nebraska Press, 2nd edn., 1989) and Karel Vasek, *The International Dimensions of Human Rights*, 2 vols., rev. edn., ed. P. Alston (Westport, CT: Greenwood Press for UNESCO, 1982).

References

Beitz, Charles R. 1979. *Political Theory and International Relations*. Princeton: Princeton University Press.
Benn, S. I. and R. S. Peters. 1959. *Social Principles and the Democratic State*. London: Allen and Unwin.
Carr, E. H. 1966. *The Twenty Years' Crisis*. London: Macmillan.
Cicero. 1928. *De Republica*. Trans. C. W. Keyes. Cambridge and London: Harvard University Press and Heinemann.
Dagger, Richard. 1989. "Rights." In *Political Innovation and Conceptual Change*, eds. Terrence Ball, James Farr, and Russell L. Hanson. Cambridge: Cambridge University Press.
Donnelly, Jack. 1981. "Recent Trends in UN Human Rights Activity: Description and Polemic." *International Organization*, vol. 35, no. 4.
　1989. *Universal Human Rights in Theory and Practice*. Ithaca NY: Cornell University Press.
Dworkin, Ronald. 1977. *Taking Rights Seriously*. London: Duckworth.
Falk, Richard A. 1968. "The International Law of Internal War: Problems and Prospects." In *Legal Order in a Violent World*. Princeton: Princeton University Press.
　1981. *Human Rights and State Sovereignty*. New York: Holmes and Meier.
Feinberg, Joel. 1966. "Duties, Rights and Claims." *American Philosophical Quarterly*, vol. 3, no. 2.

Ferguson, J. A. 1986. "Human Rights and the Third World." In *Foreign Policy and Human Rights*, ed. R. J. Vincent. Cambridge: Cambridge University Press.

Finnis, John. 1980. *Natural Law and Natural Rights*. Oxford: Clarendon Press.

Gewirth, Alan. 1982. *Human Rights: Essays on Justification and Applications*. Chicago and London: University of Chicago Press.

Hart, H. L. A. 1967. "Are There any Natural Rights." In *Political Philosophy*, ed. A. Quinton. London: Oxford University Press.

Hassner, Pierre. 1990. "Europe Beyond Partition and Unity: Disintegration or Reconstitution?" *International Affairs*, vol. 66, no. 3.

Hawkesworth, Mary. 1980. "Ideological Immunity: The Soviet Response to Human Rights Criticism." *Universal Human Rights*, vol. 2, no. 1.

Legesse, Asmarom. 1980. "Human Rights in African Political Culture." In *The Moral Imperatives of Human Rights: a World Survey*, ed. Kenneth W. Thompson. Washington: University Press of America.

Lyons, David. 1970. "The Correlativity of Rights and Duties." *Nous*, vol. 4, no. 1.

Macpherson, C. B. 1972. *The Real World of Democracy*. New York: Oxford University Press.

Meinecke, Friedrich. 1957. *Machiavellism*. London: Routledge.

Melden, A. I. 1977. *Rights and Persons*. Oxford: Blackwell.

Miller, J. D. B. 1981. *The World of States*. London: Croom Helm.

Nozick, Robert. 1974. *Anarchy, State and Utopia*. Oxford: Blackwell.

Raphael, D. D., ed. 1977. *Political Theory and the Rights of Man*. London: Macmillan.

Rawls, John. 1971. *A Theory of Justice*. Cambridge: Harvard University Press.

Shapiro, Ian. 1986. *The Evolution of Rights in Liberal Theory*. Cambridge: Cambridge University Press.

Shue, Henry. 1980. *Basic Rights*. Princeton: Princeton University Press.

Suarez, Francisco. 1944. *Selections from Three Works*, vol. 2, *The Translation*, prepared by G. L. Williams. Oxford: Clarendon Press; and London: Humphrey Milford.

Sumner, L. W. 1987. *The Moral Foundation of Rights*. Oxford: Clarendon Press.

Tuck, Richard. 1979. *Natural Rights Theories: Their Origins and Development*. Cambridge: Cambridge University Press.

Vincent, R. J. 1978. "Realpolitik and World Community." *The Community of States*, ed. J. Mayall. London: Allen and Unwin.

1986. *Human Rights and International Relations*. Cambridge: Cambridge University Press.

1989. "Human Rights and Global Politics." Paper 24 in *Global Politics*. Milton Keynes: The Open University.

Walzer, Michael. 1977. *Just and Unjust Wars*. London: Allen Lane.

13 BIBLICAL ARGUMENT IN INTERNATIONAL ETHICS

MICHAEL G. CARTWRIGHT

Despite the popular tendency to appeal to the Judeo-Christian tradition as if it were a univocal source of moral teaching, the traditions that draw upon the scriptures of the Hebrew Bible, the Apocrypha, and the New Testament are irreducibly diverse. This is not to say that the Bible cannot be interpreted as a whole, and indeed the history of biblical interpretation is full of attempts to offer a pattern of relationship between the books of the Bible. But all such uses of Scripture are "imaginative construals" (Kelsey 1975, 103; Verhey 1984, 159, 232) of the text of the Bible in the service of some community (Birch and Rasmussen 1989, 141).

Within the diversity of traditions emanating from the Hebrew and Christian Scriptures, an ongoing argument about international issues has arisen among the living traditions that trace their origins to the writings of the Hebrew and Christian canons. Biblical argument also takes place within and among communities in which the Bible may not have religious and moral authority. For the latter, the Bible is a cultural document; for others it is "the Torah from Heaven" or the "Word of God" or "the Book of the Church." Among these diverse communities, no single tradition of biblical argument in international ethics has emerged. This chapter will discuss eight different uses of the Bible that correspond to different traditions of international ethics. In each case, I will describe how the Bible was used, and spell out the kind of authority that is presumed in biblical arguments. Thus, whether the appeal to the Bible supports arguments based on natural law or human rights, the kind of authority ascribed to the Bible is a critical issue in evaluating the appeal.

Since historically most interpreters using the Bible presume some notion of common morality, it is important to understand the kinds of appeals to the Bible that underwrite this conception of international ethics (on common morality, see "Common morality and international law," Chapter 1 and "Natural law, common morality, and consequentialism," Chapter 6). The first point to note about biblical arguments for common morality is that they draw upon diverse biblical texts even as they contrast markedly with one another about the relationship to ordinary morality. For this reason, the last part of this chapter explores the question of the rhetoric of biblical argument in international ethics.

The Bible and the traditions

In Western culture, there are three different canonical arrangements of the Bible: (1) the *Tanakh* or Hebrew Bible, (2) the Protestant canon of the Old and New Testaments, and (3) the wider or Catholic canon which includes the Apocrypha in addition to the Old and New Testaments. Even within a given canon, interpreting how a particular book (e.g. 1 Maccabees) is related to other books (Exodus or Matthew) in the Bible can be fraught with difficulty.

For example, in the Jewish tradition, the canon of Scripture is clearly marked into three sections: the Torah (the five books of Moses), the Nevi'im (the Prophets), and the Kethubim (the writings). The final books of the *Tanakh* (1984) are 1 and 2 Chronicles. In the Christian canon, the order is strikingly different: 1 and 2 Chronicles are buried in the middle of the "Old Testament" along with other historical narratives, while the book of Malachi, which mentions Elijah, the forerunner of the Messiah, is the last book of the Christian canon of the Old Testament.

Implicitly, the canonical arrangement of the Hebrew Bible and the Old Testament indicates the different patterns of interpretation in the two religious traditions. For Jewish interpreters, 1 and 2 Chronicles stand as a grave reminder of the failure of the kingship, and also support the centrality of temple worship in the post-exilic context of Judaism; for Christians, Malachi points forward to the New Covenant of Jesus, prophetically heralded by the Elijah-like figure of John the Baptist, and points backward to the covenant of Moses.

Non-religious approaches to the biblical canons yield other interpretations. Literary critics have identified thematic motifs in the Bible: creation, revolution, law, wisdom, prophecy, gospel, and apocalypse (Frye 1983), and literary classifications can shed light on some uses of Scripture in the moral discourse of international affairs. Formal thematic categories cannot, however, fully account for the myriad convergences and divergences in the use of the Bible in international relations literature. For example, the widespread use of "St. Paul's principle" by ethicists calls attention to nonreligious uses of Scripture. Yet lines of continuity can be traced, especially as the history of exegesis converges with scholarly assessment of the uses of Scripture in the historical religious communities of Judaism and Christianity.

One classical disagreement between Judaism and Christianity focuses on whether the cosmos is being redeemed, or if it awaits redemption (Goldberg 1991, 219). "To the Christian the Jew is a stubborn figure in an unredeemed world that is still waiting for the Messiah. And for the Jew the Christian is a heedless fellow who in an unredeemed world claims that redemption has somehow or another taken place."[1] As Reinhold Niebuhr once noted, much hinges on the meaning of "somehow or another" in the Christian claim that the world has been or is being redeemed. Contemporary heirs of Judaism continue to regard the world as unredeemed, and thus construe the canon of the Hebrew Bible differently from the way in which Christians use the "Old Testament."

Embedded in this dispute is a larger question: how is human history to be interpreted, given the differing visions of history embedded in Hebrew and Christian Scripture? From one Christian point of view, "If the gospel tells of agents rendered free before the reality of a redeemed universe, then the form which their agency assumes will correspond both to the intelligible order which they confront and to the freedom in which they act" (O'Donovan 1986, 186).

In other words, the ethical traditions of Christianity and Judaism are inextricably linked to particular interpretations of the biblical accounts of creation and redemption. Therefore, the way(s) in which the cosmos is depicted in a particular religious tradition in relation to the *telos* of history offers an important clue for understanding the role of biblical images in the tradition's ethical arguments about international relations. Whether one approaches the question of moral order from the narrative-based perspectives of a redeemed world, or unredeemed world, a "fallen" creation, a "new" creation, or from some "here and now, but not yet" vision of world peace is key to understanding biblical arguments in international relations.

Judaism

For the most part, Jewish visions of international order are discussed in terms of two covenants initiated by God: the Mosaic covenant and the covenant of God with "the children of Noah." Jewish biblical interpreters remind themselves as well as non-Jews or

---

[1] Reinhold Niebuhr quoting an unnamed Jewish philosopher in "The Wheat and the Tares," Sermon N–665 in the Union Theological Seminary Collection, Richmond, Virginia.

"Noachides" that Jews live in primary obedience to the Torah, the covenant with Moses (Exodus 19). But they also recognize that according to the Torah the Lord has a covenant with all of humanity, namely the Noachic covenant (Genesis 8:20–9:19). In fact, some Jewish theologians have argued that the highest *universal* authority in Judaism is not the Mosaic covenant, but the covenant with the children of Noah. However, the specifications of the Noachic covenant closely parallel several aspects of the Mosaic covenant. In fact, the ancient rabbis specified *seven* commandments that non-Jews or "Noachides" must keep, in contrast to the Torah commandments that Jewish faithful must perform (Borowitz 1980; 21).[2]

Jewish uses of the Noah's Ark narrative are notable for the absence of eschatological or future-oriented images. In part, this is because Jewish interpreters are reticent about what happens after the expected advent of the Messiah. In fact, there is no single view of what will happen to non-Jews when the Messiah comes at the culmination of history: "Views differ as to whether the ultimate stage of humanity will comprise both Judaism and Noachidism, or whether Noachidism is only the penultimate level before the universalization of all Torah" (*Encylcopedia Judaica* 1972, 1190).

Thus, within Jewish tradition, the covenant with Noah is understood as being the only covenant that applies universally to all people. The Mosaic covenant (also subject to divergent interpretations), constitutes a higher standard that only Jews are expected to obey. But, within the horizon of God's redemption (that is, within the narrative world of the Torah), "the nations" are expected to abide by the Noachic covenant.

This difference partly accounts for the distinction that is made by the prophets of ancient Israel when they denounce "the nations" that surround Israel. Thus the prophet Jonah appears to appeal "without saying so, to a *minimal code*, a kind of 'international law' when he condemns the excesses of Nineveh" (Walzer 1987, 89–90). Yet Amos, the eighth-century prophet from the Judean village of Tekoa, saves his most vociferous denunciations for the nation of Israel. When Amos does prophesy against the other nations the difference is striking: in these cases, Amos "limits himself to external behavior, violations of some sort of international law": do not violate treaties, do not kill innocent women and children, do not transport whole nations into involuntary exile (Walzer 1987, 91–92).

---

[2] According to the *Encyclopedia Judaica*, the Noachide laws include the prohibition of idolatry, blasphemy, bloodshed, sexual sins, theft, and eating from a living animal, as well as the injunction to establish a legal system.

Still later, in the context of the impending exile of the inhabitants of Jerusalem (587 BCE), Jeremiah urges the citizens of Jerusalem to "seek the peace" of the cities to which they will be sent in exile (Jeremiah 29: 5–9), and the prophet Ezekiel announces the word of the Lord: "This city of Jerusalem I have set among the nations, with other countries around her. And she has rebelled against my laws and my commandments more wickedly than those nations and countries; for her people have rejected my laws, and refused to conform to my statutes" (Ezekiel 5: 5–6). In these contexts, the particular vision of God found in the traditions of Torah is united with a sweeping vision of God's purposes in history. Ezekiel's harsh news is that it is the Lord God who is going to use the Babylonians to teach the Israelites a lesson. The chosen people are now to be punished, disciplined, and purified before the temple of Jerusalem is restored. Post-exilic prophets will once again call upon Israel to be a "light to the nations" but now the emphasis will be upon the temple, not the kingdom itself.

In the era after Auschwitz, Jewish interpreters have been less inclined to adopt Jeremiah's diaspora concept as the primary model for contemporary international ethics. Michael Walzer, for example, finds the stance of Amos more attractive, making use of two different appeals: (1) the minimal code of common morality by which the nations live; and (2) the particular rules that Israel is called to live by as God's chosen people. As long as we remember that the two sorts of rules are not the same, Walzer argues that both may be used in international social criticism: "The first rules tend toward universality, the second toward particularity" (1987, 93).

Some of Walzer's most important moral reflection has centered around the questions of "supreme emergency" (1977) and the validity of the national security interests of the modern nation of Israel in conjunction with the historic disputes with Israel's Palestinian neighbors. Some Jewish interpreters call upon the Bible, particularly the promise to Abraham and the story of the Exodus and the Promised Land of Canaan to support Israel's claim to sovereignty. Others, particularly the ultra-Orthodox Jews, reject the biblical arguments for the claims of the modern nation-state of Israel, arguing instead that Israel's sovereignty can only be reestablished when the Messiah comes. Thus, while biblical argument about international ethics in Jewish traditions has generally supported conceptions of common morality for "the nations," there are strikingly different expectations for "Jerusalem" as a *polis* among the nations of the earth.

The early church and medieval Catholicism

In contrast to the reticent Jewish interpretations of Noah's Ark and the Flood, early Christian uses of the narrative focused strikingly on present and future redemption of the world – even when these themes seemed to contradict one another. The Christian church itself has often been depicted metaphorically as Noah's Ark, as the image readily lends itself to St. Cyprian of Carthage's dictum – "outside the church there is no salvation." This image was particularly popular in medieval Catholicism after Christianity became the official religion of Catholic Europe, aligning church and empire against the barbarian nations.

Within medieval Catholicism, the authority of the Bible was defined in relation to church tradition. The Bible was understood to be the "Church's Book" and the ecclesiastical hierarchy determined what was correct interpretation of the Holy Scriptures. During this time, the "authoritative interpretation" (Grant and Tracy 1984) of the church took shape as a result of the practice of allegorical exegesis of the Bible. Following the model of St. Paul, who adopted this mode of interpretation in Galatians 4: 25–26, where he distinguishes between the earthly and the heavenly "Jerusalem" while explaining the difference between the Mosaic covenant and the "New Covenant" in Christ, medieval interpreters offered allegorical readings of Old Testament passages, interpreted through the New Covenant of Christ.

In the medieval period Christendom was often metonymically identified with the *polis* of Jerusalem: "These are the words of the Lord God: This city of Jerusalem I have set among the nations, with other countries around her" (Ezekiel 5: 5). The identification of the church with the city of Jerusalem led to the identification of Christendom itself with "the holy city," an association that had important implications for the way international relations was conceived in relation to the church.

Even as early as the fifth century, when St. Augustine wrote his famous reflections on the fall of the Roman Empire, he cast his neo-Platonic vision of history in terms of a vision of two cities, the "City of God" and the earthly city. Significantly, Augustine's history is written both as a defense of the City of God "against those [barbarians] who prefer their own gods to the Founder of this city" and as a chastening word to "the earthly city, which, though it be mistress of the nations, is itself ruled by its lust of rule." It is a history of the world written from the perspective of Christian faith. Thus, the City of God is traced back to the sons of Noah, as is the "city which is called Confusion [Babel]" (Genesis 11). According to Augustine, Noah's Ark prefigures the church, and the various kinds of animals prefigure the "various nations which were to be saved in the church" (1950, 3, 521, 530).

After Augustine, the church ordered its relations with the so-called "Holy Roman Empire" via the doctrine of the "two swords" – one religious and one secular. This marriage of ecclesiastical and civil authority in medieval Europe was based upon an allegorical reading of a single verse from Luke: "And they said, Lord, here are two swords. And he said to them, It is enough" (Luke 22:38). This theory not only justified the use of coercion by the church – including the persecution of dissenters and heretics – it also served as the implicit warrant for exerting papal power over recalcitrant rulers, and even launching crusades against the infidel nations (Johnson 1987, 144). As long as the medieval church was able to control the "authoritative interpretation" of Scripture, such allegorical arguments sufficed to legitimize the union of church and empire, but over time such justifications came to be seen as intellectually bankrupt and morally dangerous.

Subsequently, in the thirteenth century, St. Thomas Aquinas provided a more sophisticated argument for statecraft based on the conception of natural law. In defense of this notion, Aquinas appealed to Romans 1:20, where St. Paul argues that the righteousness of God has been revealed to both Jews and Gentiles: "Ever since the creation of the world God's invisible nature, namely, God's eternal power and deity, has been clearly perceived in the things that have been made. So they are without excuse." Aquinas, like biblical exegetes before him, followed the implications of St. Paul's claim that the Gentiles cannot simply plead ignorance of God, for God's power is displayed in "the things that have been made": there is a law in nature itself. This claim not only has implications for evangelization, but as a result it provides a basis for Christian nations to require that non-Christians live by certain minimum standards of morality.

The conception of natural law actually served two purposes within medieval Catholicism, both of which involved biblical argument. First, Aquinas found natural law useful as a heuristic device to explain why Christians were no longer bound to observe the "ceremonial laws" of Exodus and Leviticus but nevertheless were bound to observe the moral laws of the Old Covenant. In fact, in many of his arguments in the "Treatise on Law" (*Summa Theologiae*) Aquinas borrowed classifications and arguments from medieval Jewish exegetes such as "Rabbi Moses" (Maimonides) to work out the problem of the ceremonial law codes. Based on this use of natural law, Stanley Hauerwas has argued that natural law is not a principle that justifies a common morality, but is instead a "necessary exegetical principle" for reading the Old Testament as well as a reminder that "when confronted by God's law we are always sinners" (1990, 25).

But other scholars would argue that Aquinas's political writings demonstrate that his conception of natural law also served to clarify what is and is not permissible within the spheres of domestic and foreign relations and to determine where tension remains between human law and God's eternal law, of which the laws of nations, *jus gentium*, are one variety (see "A tradition of 'natural-law' ethics identified," Chapter 6, where the latter assessment of Aquinas's work is presumed). Within Aquinas's framework of law, civil government is understood to be *ordained* by God, as implied by Paul's letter to the Romans: "Let every person be subject to the governing authorities. For there is no authority except from God, and those that exist have been instituted by God. Therefore, he who resists the authorities resists what God has appointed, and those who resist will incur judgment. For rulers are not a terror to good conduct, but to bad" (Romans 13: 1–3). And yet, Aquinas would also argue that there is a time for overthrowing the tyrant, when he or she becomes like "the beast" of Babylon described in Revelation 13 (for discussion of the nature and limits of political authority in the natural-law tradition, see "The common good and the complete society," Chapter 6).

Also contributing to the complexity of biblical argument in medieval Catholicism is the distinction the Roman Catholic church made between the obligations of the clergy and the obligations of the laity with respect to Christian discipleship, creating a kind of "two-level ethic" (Lohfink 1984, 39). Within this framework, the priests and members of the monastic orders were held to a higher standard as specified in the teachings of Christ in the Sermon on the Mount (Matthew 5–7) – often called the "counsels of perfection" – while ordinary people were expected to follow the ordinary "precepts" as specified in Romans 13: 1–7 and the decalogue.

Given the overlap between church and empire within medieval Christendom, there was an implicit reliance upon common morality to preserve the order of society. And as early as Augustine, the foundations had been laid for the theory of a social order defined as a *corpus mixtum*, and symbolically imaged as a mixture of "wheat and tares" (Matthew 13: 24–30, 36–40), which are not to be prematurely sorted out. Within the world of Christendom, the social order was determined by the presence of the church into which a motley assembly of different peoples streamed as if to an ark, seeking a refuge from the

277

deluge that was held in check by the empire's power. The Crusades of the late Middle Ages remind us not only that the theory of just war applied primarily *within* Christendom – as an ordered means for Christians to kill Christians – but also of the very real limits of universality within the medieval *ecumene*.

Protestant arguments

The Protestant Reformation of the early sixteenth century broke the unity of medieval Catholicism by calling into question the validity of religious practices like the sale of indulgences. In place of the authority of Catholic tradition, reformers such as Martin Luther claimed that they would stand *sola scriptura*, "by the Bible alone." The leaders of the Reformation also accepted certain Catholic practices that were by no means explicit in the Bible. Nonetheless, Protestants believed that the basis for such practices was to be found in Christian Scripture.

The Protestant Reformation did not so much alter the *corpus mixtum* conception of medieval social order as it adapted the vision of coexisting "wheat and tares" (Matthew 13: 24–30, 36–44) within the emerging nations of Europe, under the principle of *cuius regio, eius religio* – each region or nation should have its own religion. Consequently, the Reformation helped to redefine the relations of countries formerly united by the vision of the Holy Roman Empire, creating a patchwork of Protestant and Catholic countries, with the so-called Anabaptists or "radical reformers" existing as minorities within the framework of the newly declared state churches. Both Luther and Calvin relied upon the governmental authorities in their regions to help implement the Reformation. Both would also appeal to Romans 13 as the basis for civil authority. Later, Thomas Erastus would provide the theoretical framework for what would come to be called the "state church," a rationale that Henry VIII of England would use to support the English Reformation from 1529 to 1559.

Thus, the Reformation contributed, though indirectly, to the eventual emergence of nation-states, making of early modern Europe a patchwork of countries, each of which had its own official religious affiliation – Catholic, Lutheran, Calvinist. In fact, in the religious wars of the early seventeenth century, Protestants fought Protestants as well as Catholics. When more irenic participants began trying to intervene in the religious and political strife of Europe, they turned again to the Bible to substantiate their arguments for international law.

It is against this backdrop that the work of the Dutch Protestant

Hugo Grotius (1583–1645) should be understood. Grotius wrote his famous treatise on the law of war and peace (*De Jure Belli ac Pacis*) in 1625, when relations among the incipient nation-states of Europe were tentative and ill-defined and Christian allegiances were disputed on the battlefield. Grotius's intention was to provide a basis for ordering relations between the warring factions of Europe, almost all of which were Christian.

Given this context Grotius naturally appeals to the Bible's authority. Ultimately, however, he is attempting to use the Bible to erect a secular authority, an authority that he would describe as "international law" (as Forsyth notes, Grotius's attempts in this respect were only partly successful; see "Origins of the tradition," Chapter 2). Thus, the argument adumbrated in the *Prolegomena to the Laws of War and Peace* is not based upon the Protestant tradition, nor is "Holy Writ" used as a primary warrant, despite his claims that he "frequently appeals to the authority" of the Bible.

In fact, Grotius's argument is based on the assumption that historical examples from secular history provide the requisite "illumination" (1957, 24, para. 38) for making ethical judgments in international relations. In particular, Grotius was intrigued by those "preferred ancient examples" of Greece and Rome. Grotius was so convinced of the merits of his insight that he claimed that history not only provided "illustrations" but that the "judgments" of history themselves "are not to be slighted, especially when they are in agreement with one another; for by such statements the existence of the law of nature, as we have said, is in a measure proved, and by no other means, in fact, is it possible to establish the law of nations" (1957, 30, para. 46). Judgments about history carry the primary weight in Grotius's argument, while judgments derived from Scripture are used only as a correlative or supporting means of justification.

As Grotius goes on to note, his appeals to the Old Testament assume that the Old Testament is never in conflict with the true law of nature. In fact Grotius believes the Old Testament can be used as a source of the law of nature as long as the distinction between the law of God – "which God sometimes executes through men" – and the law of men in their relations with one another is kept in mind (1957, 30–31). This distinction is a key proviso of Grotius's argument, yet the difficulty of maintaining the distinction is clearly evidenced at several points in the *Prolegomena to the Law of War and Peace*. In particular, Grotius recognizes that traditional uses of the New Testament run counter to this distinction. Grotius limits the use of the New Testament to explain "what is permissible to Christians" for "a greater

279

degree of moral perfection is enjoined upon us than the law of nature, alone and by itself would require" (1957, 31, para. 48).

What Grotius has done is to place himself and his fellow Protestants under a kind of double-bind with respect to the "law of nature": on the one hand, the law of nations can *only* be established with respect to the law of nature; on the other hand, in the New Testament "a greater degree of moral perfection is enjoined upon [Christians] than the law of nature." Here again we see a tension between the use of the Bible for a specifically religious ethic and the use of biblical arguments to nurture the notion of a common morality on which an emerging body of international law can be based. This tension would be reiterated in various ways within mainstream Protestant Christianity in succeeding centuries.

The Historic Peace Churches[3]

As the foregoing discussion discloses, among Christians biblical argument in ethics calls forth a parallel set of arguments about the character of the church. For example, those Christians who deny that Romans 13: 1–7 is the "center of the New Testament witness about the state" also call attention to the political character of Jesus' words and deeds as presented in the gospels, especially in the Sermon on the Mount (Matthew 5–7) and in Luke's Gospel. Such Christians would argue that the political dimension of the gospel was submerged not only within medieval Catholicism's two-level ethic of the clergy and lay people, but also in the Protestant "two-kingdoms ethic," which provides for a state church.

In the midst of the breakup of Christendom, the two-level ethic became the subject of scorn, especially in the context of the Protestant Reformation, but Protestants also contributed new distinctions, such as the "Two Kingdoms ethic" of the Lutheran tradition. Once again, Romans 13: 1–7 was set against the teachings of Jesus in Matthew 5–7. This time, discussion fixed upon the role of the Christian magistrate. Could the magistrate kill in the course of fulfilling the responsibilities of his office? According to the magisterial reformers, this would be permissible because it is appropriate to distinguish between one's personal ethics and the requirements of a public ethic (the individual good versus the good of the political community). Over time, this kind of distinction has led to the assumption that Jesus' ethics are

---

[3] The Quakers, Mennonites, and Brethren traditions are commonly referred to as the "Historic Peace Churches" because of their consistent pacifist witness during and after the Protestant Reformation.

"politically irrelevant," a claim that the Historic Peace Churches resist.

In contrast to the mainstream Protestant traditions, the Mennonites, Brethren, and Quakers have resisted attempts to describe their religious ethic as private or apolitical in comparison with some version of common morality. In fact, one of Hugo Grotius's early legal treatises was occasioned by the protest of a group of Mennonite shareholders in the Dutch East India Company to the company's practice of confiscating Portuguese property during skirmishes (the Portuguese and the Dutch were competitors in maritime trade). Grotius was employed by the Amsterdam Chamber of the Dutch East India Company "to defend the right of the Dutch to capture Portuguese property as lawful prize on account of violations of international law by the Portuguese." Grotius not only argued that it was legal "but expedient and honorable" as well (Dumbauld 1957, viii). Very little is known about the Dutch Mennonites' arguments against the law of prize but clearly such objections point back to the tension between "the law of nature" and "the law of God."

From the Mennonites' perspective, Grotius's argument compromises the authority of Christ's words and deeds while also minimizing the radical significance of the reconciled fellowship of the Church. Indeed the Mennonites might have argued that, biblically speaking, Christians cannot abstract themselves from what they understand as the "the law of God" in living "among the nations" precisely because they are called to live as the peaceable "colony of heaven" (Philippians 3:20) in the midst of a world often at war with itself. According to this perspective, even if there is some kind of "international law" or common morality basis for seizing the goods of the Portuguese, the Mennonites would argue that Christians should not do so because, in Christ, they are a "new humanity" (Ephesians 2:15).

Furthermore, from the perspective of the Historic Peace Churches, Grotius's argument requires that different emphases of the biblical canon be disregarded, in effect to employ what might be called a "flat level reading strategy" (McClendon 1985, 315). These churches claim that the Bible must be read "directionally" (Yoder 1984, 9) from the perspective of the historical event of the incarnation, death, and resurrection of Jesus Christ. This means that not all passages of the Bible are to be treated as equally authoritative: Christ's words and deeds have a moral authority that surpasses the Ten Commandments of Exodus 20, and even Paul's words about being subject to the governing authorities in Romans 13.

One of the passages most commonly cited by peace church writers on international relations is Isaiah's vision of the "peaceable kingdom":

> The wolf shall dwell with the lamb, and the leopard shall lie down with the kid, and the calf and the lion and the fatling together, and a little child shall lead them . . .
>
> They shall not hurt or destroy in all my holy mountain; for the earth shall be full of the knowledge of the Lord as the waters cover the sea. (Isaiah 11: 6, 9)

One of the most famous uses of this passage in the literature of international affairs was William Penn's eloquent depiction of the messianic reign of Christ in his "Essay Towards the Present and Future Peace of Europe" ([1693] 1915, 580):

> [Our Savior] came to save, and not to destroy the lives of men: to give and plant peace among men . . . Of all His titles this seems the most glorious as well as comfortable for us, that He is the Prince of Peace . . . And it is very remarkable that, in all the New Testament He is but once called Lion, but frequently the Lamb of God; to denote to us his gentle, meek, and harmless nature . . .
>
> Nor is it said the lamb shall lie down with the lion, but the lion with the lamb. That is war shall yield to peace and the soldier turn hermit.

The figure referred to in this passage appears first in Isaiah, and is subsequently taken up in the Revelation of St. John where it serves as a powerful symbol of the sacrificial defenselessness of Jesus of Nazareth.

In the writings of early English Quakers such as George Fox, the image of God as a "warrior" (Joshua, Judges) is combined with the suffering-servant imagery of Isaiah, culminating in a striking vision of peace made possible by the Lamb's death, the blood of the cross. In the process, militarist rhetoric is transformed so that the eighteenth-century Quakers dared to describe themselves as soldiers in the Lamb's army fighting in the "Lamb's War" (Revelation 14: 1–20), a war in which the conquest of the earth is pursued. The difference is that this conquest is spiritual and nonviolent: the conquest of the Lamb demonstrates that "the cross and not the sword, suffering and not brute power determines the meaning of history" (Yoder 1972, 238–39).

For American Quakers, the story of Noah's Ark calls to mind the vision of the New Jerusalem of Revelation 21. Thus, Edward Hicks's 1846 painting of "Noah's Ark" is an evocative rendering of the biblical story that parallels Penn's internationalist vision. In Hicks's painting the various animal species wind their way around a rural lane and into the ark, which is positioned with the prow pointing toward the distant shore where the heavenly city peeks out of the shadows, while the storm clouds gather overhead. In this respect, Hicks's "Noah's Ark" is a striking depiction of William Penn's optimistic vision that the whole world would become Quaker. For the early Quakers there was no conception of "prophetic" religion that can be sundered from the gathered community of Christians; there is no alternative or "worldly" route to the *polis* of the New Jerusalem.

Although William Penn's "Essay" has often been regarded as a product of the "perpetual peace" tradition, this identification does not do justice to the evangelical vision of the Society of Friends. For Quakers as well as the other Historic Peace Churches, images of peoplehood cannot easily be severed from the standards of obedience unique to the Christian faith. From their perspective, Christian peace-making in the world is not merely the contemporary equivalent of William Penn's "European Diet" but a *transformed* world order (2 Corinthians 5:17): "If anyone is in Christ, there is a new creation, the old order has passed away, the new has come."

Twentieth-century arguments

The legacies of Judaism, medieval Catholicism, Protestant Reformation, and the Historic Peace Churches have all been challenged by the rise of communism, two world wars, the advent of nuclear power, third-world revolutionary movements and, more recently, the eclipse of communism in Eastern Europe. In the process, a new set of biblical arguments emerged that combine elements of the Jewish and Christian traditions but also advance proposals in relation to political currents in the twentieth century. These twentieth-century arguments also resort to the Bible, particularly as they engage revisionist arguments for realism in the twentieth century (see Chapter 5) and significant challenges raised by the traditions of liberalism (see Chapter 10) and Marxism (see Chapter 11) in international ethics.

Christian internationalism

In the late nineteenth century, religious and political idealism combined to produce many different internationalist movements. For example, John R. Mott's Student Christian Movement grew out of the Protestant foreign-mission efforts. International contacts led first to the international missionary movement convocation in Edinburgh in

1912, and later to the formation of the Faith and Order movement. This movement subsequently became one of the working groups of the World Council of Churches, the organization that has been most involved in international politics over the course of the twentieth century.

Other groups combined a strong if ecumenically broad commitment to Christianity with an equally passionate desire to address the social concerns of the time. One of the peace groups formed during these years reveals the tensions between what might be called idealistic "Christian internationalism" and a more *realistic* conception of the limits of international order. The Church Peace Union (CPU) was organized on the eve of the First World War by Andrew Carnegie, a wealthy industrialist from Pittsburgh. This group was "not a church nor a pacifist organization; it represented no organic or institutional union" (Carnegie Council 1987, 1). However, its members were intent on bringing the Western heritage of moral and religious values into the deliberations of statesmen searching for world peace. The Church Peace Union boldly declared its intention "to end war forever."

Like most such groups prior to the First World War, the CPU "bore the imprimatur of the dominant Protestant culture: righteous, somehow separated from the world and its values, yet still willing to assert a relationship among virtue, hard work and success" (Carnegie Council 1987, 1). The First World War would bring an end to the CPU's optimism about ending war forever. But other groups such as the international Fellowship of Reconciliation would advocate a kind of pacifist Christian internationalism through the Second World War and into the era of nuclear arms and the cold war.

Groups such as these held a distinctly different notion of the authority of the Bible than did their Protestant forebears. Having drunk deeply at the wells of historical critical thinking, these activists and civic leaders combined a "liberal" Protestant theology with a passionate commitment to international peace. Like Lyman Abbott, the author of a famous essay on "Evolutionary Christianity" that translated Christian ideas into a modern form using the idea of evolution as the key, liberal Protestants treated the Bible as a document that had to be interpreted in light of modern science and historical consciousness. Where they did engage in biblical argument, these liberal Protestants usually adopted the arguments of the "Social Gospel" movement. The scope of the Social Gospel was larger than the traditional Protestant concern for individual salvation; it sought to "bring men under repentance for their collective sins and to create a more sensitive and more modern conscience" (Rauschenbusch 1917, 7).

284

Walter Rauschenbusch's manifesto, *Christianity and the Social Crisis* (1907), rallied liberal Protestants to the task of "Christianizing the social order," a slogan which presupposed that certain "progressive" political movements reflected the ethical values of Christianity. Although much of the Social Gospel movement focused on domestic issues, the internationalist impulse was also present. Rauschenbusch called upon the "Christian nations" of the earth to withstand "the flood of barbarism" (1907, 283) by summoning the "moral forces" to overcome the social crisis.

Rauschenbusch's approach to social problems is notable precisely because he simply assumes that the Christian Bible advocated "progressive politics" grounded in the prophetic tradition of the Hebrew Bible. In retrospect we can see that this politics owed much to the liberal theological tradition as well as to the idealist political currents of the late nineteenth century. Rauschenbusch approaches issues of international order from the assumption that there is a "kingdom movement" embodied in history by social institutions and, above all, by "Christian nations" in the world.

Contemporary Christian ethicists have noted that in his books Rauschenbusch appears to have known what was "good for mankind" *apart* from Scripture (Gustafson 1969). In other words, the use of the Bible was not as indispensable in Rauschenbusch's arguments as it initially appeared to the advocates of the Social Gospel. He began not with Christian Scripture but with the identification of specific social and political movements which he believed were congruent with the "kingdom teaching" of Jesus. Then he proceeded to argue for a "social gospel" which in turn supported the social and political movements he had already advocated. Similarly, many other "Christian internationalists" were equally confident that they knew which political movements were aligned with the "kingdom values" of Jesus' teaching.

Christian realism

In the years just prior to the Second World War, no one did more to repudiate the idealism of the liberal internationalist movement than Reinhold Niebuhr; that refutation, in turn, led Niebuhr to reassert what many came to call Christian realism. Although broadly Protestant in its appeal, Christian realism actually rejected many of the cherished tenets of "orthodox" Protestantism. Yet, like Protestants before him, Niebuhr used the Bible in his arguments against both the idealists and the isolationists of his time.

For example, in his early study, *An Interpretation of Christian Ethics*, Niebuhr alludes to the image of Noah's Ark in the context of rebuking the Social Gospel version of internationalism (1935, 212). Niebuhr identifies his transcendent conception of "prophetic religion" as "an ark surviving the flood" of international disorder of an endangered civilization. "At some time or other the waters of the flood will recede and the ark will land . . . It is the life in this ark of prophetic religion, therefore which must generate the spirituality of any culture of any age in which human vitality is brought under a decent discipline" (1935, 212–13). Here, Noah's Ark reminds us of the fragility of all attempts to establish temporary order in the chaos of human history; furthermore, the chaos of the flood is used to depict the necessity of taking a "realist" approach to problems of international order.

Although Niebuhr often challenged the theological pronouncements of mainstream Protestants and Catholics, in matters of international ethics he advocated something close to the common morality advocated by Grotius in the sixteenth century. But, given the prophetic impulse of the Social Gospel movement of the late nineteenth and early twentieth century, Niebuhr needed to show how the liberals had misunderstood the political dimensions of Jesus' teachings.

In a famous essay written in the context of pre-Second World War American isolationism, Niebuhr argued forcefully against the idealist claims that the Christian church should be pacifist, going so far as to boldly claim that "there is not the slightest support in Scripture for this doctrine of non-violence." Interestingly enough, Niebuhr's own argument is based not so much upon Scripture itself as it is upon empirical judgments about human sin (for a discussion of the idea of egoism in Niebuhr's thought, see "Realist premises: human nature and international anarchy," Chapter 5). He contends that pacifists do not know human nature well enough. They do not understand that "sin introduces an element of conflict into the world and that even the most loving relations are not free of it" (1940, 14).

When Niebuhr does refer to Scripture in his argument, he does so within the context of a series of stipulated claims about the status of Jesus' ethic. "The injunction 'resist not evil' is only part and parcel of a total ethic which we violate not only in war-time, but every day of our lives, and that overt conflict is but a final and vivid revelation of the character of human experience" (1940, 12). According to Niebuhr, the ethic of Jesus is thus best summarized in two injunctions, "Be not anxious for your life" and "Love thy neighbor as thyself."

Then, Niebuhr argues that, despite all idealistic efforts, "the fact is that anxiety is an inevitable concomitant of human freedom, and is the root of the inevitable sin which expresses itself in every human activity and creativity" (1940, 12). Secondly, Niebuhr chastises the idealists with the inconsistency of their love ethic, noting the blindness of idealist sentiments proclaiming that war would be "unnecessary 'if only' nations obeyed the law of Christ" while ignoring "the fact" that even the saints contradict this law "in some measure" (1940, 13). By portraying the problem as a conflict between moral idealism and moral realism, Niebuhr is able to put Christian pacifists in the position of having to defend something that they did not want to have to defend – a literalist conception of nonresistance.

Further, Niebuhr uses this confusion between a politically irresponsible nonviolent resistance and the liberal ideal of nonresistant love to clarify what "the gospel" and "New Testament" are about. "The gospel is something more than the law of love. The gospel deals with the fact that men violate the law of love. The gospel presents Christ as the pledge and revelation of God's mercy which finds man in his rebellion and overcomes his sin" (1940, 18). Contrasting the classical Reformation emphasis on the sinfulness of humanity with the "Renaissance faith in man," Niebuhr offers his own sweeping interpretation of the New Testament:

> The New Testament does not . . . envisage a simple triumph of good over evil in history. It sees human history involved in the contradictions of sin to the end. That is why it sees no simple resolution of the problem of history. It believes that the Kingdom of God will finally resolve the contradictions of history; but for it the Kingdom of God is no simple historical possibility. The grace of God for man and the Kingdom of God for history are both divine realities and not human possibilities. (1940, 20–21)

What is interesting about Niebuhr's analysis is the way in which he refocuses the *eschatological* dimensions of Jesus' words and deeds through the use of categorical classifications of selected sayings of Jesus, thereby relocating the kingdom as a transcendent ideal *outside* human history. Thus, Niebuhr's conception of international ethics presumed a sharp separation between the indiscriminate norm of love and the discriminate norm of justice.

The Anabaptist challenge

Of course, some Christians disagree with Niebuhr's assessment. In particular, they wonder why Niebuhr did not discuss the story of Jesus' passion. Like the early Quakers, the Anabaptists regard themselves as fighting the nonviolent Lamb's War described in the fourteenth chapter of the Revelation of St. John. Corollary to the Anabaptist argument is a second claim, namely that Catholics and Protestants have an ahistorical conception of the state. When mainstream Christians talk about obeying the authority of the state in accordance with Romans 13, the state "is assumed to be the same in essence in all times and cultures":

> Any pluralism of historical interpretation, any real development or change from one age to another, is excluded, not on the grounds of observation but by definition. So the question, "should the Christian be an agent of the State?" always has the same shape and, to be consistent, must always have the same answer. (Yoder 1974, 271–72)

In *The Politics of Jesus* (1972), John Howard Yoder challenged Niebuhr's reading of the New Testament as well as Niebuhr's political realism. In the first place, Yoder attempts to situate Jesus' words and deeds within a historical and eschatological context of prophetic fulfillment. Secondly, Yoder attacked Niebuhr's presumption that "'being politically relevant' is itself a univocal option." Yoder claims that to take such a position is "to overestimate the capacity of 'the nature of politics' to dictate its own direction" while underestimating the power of Jesus' words and deeds in historical context (1972, 111). From Yoder's perspective, Niebuhr has allowed modern categories of "political realism" to structure his interpretation of ethical possibilities.

Significantly, Yoder attributes the misreading of the politics of Jesus to the "Constantinian turn" in Christian ethics. "Mainstream ethics" has assumed that Jesus is not relevant to the important questions of social ethics. From this assumption, it is an easy step to the second claim: "Since . . . Jesus himself is not finally normative in ethics, there must be some kind of bridge or transition into another realm or into another mode of thought when we begin to think about ethics" (1972, 19). Finally, the mainstream position assumes that "reconstruction of a social ethic on this side of the transition will derive its guidance from common sense and the nature of things" (1972, 20).

Yoder's rejection of the mainstream conception of common morality stems from his alternative account of the politics of Jesus. In *The Politics of Jesus* Yoder situates Jesus' public ministry within the political alternatives of first-century Palestine: (1) the revolutionary posture of the zealots; (2) the accommodationist posture of the Herodians who cooperated with Roman rule; (3) the withdrawal of the Essenes, and (4) the pietism of the Pharisees. Yoder shows that Jesus' words and deeds do not fit any of these existing models. Rather, Yoder contends that Jesus' message of the kingdom "was borrowed extensively from the prophetic understanding of the jubilee year" (1972, 36). According to Leviticus 25, the year of jubilee (the fiftieth year) was a time when debts were to be forgiven, debtors returned to the land of their patrimony, and slaves released from bondage.

Further, Yoder emphasizes the eschatological character of the kingdom proclamation by linking Jesus' "political platform" in Luke 4:18–21 with the prophetic visions of renewal in Jeremiah 34 and Isaiah 61, which are all based upon the jubilee theme. Jesus' words and deeds are to be understood as taking place in "the fullness of time," as a prophetic enactment of the jubilee vision, except that now the liberation of the captives has been extended to include all the gentile nations as well as Israel.

Yoder concludes by claiming that "the ministry and the claims of Jesus are best understood as presenting . . . but one particular social-political-ethical option" (1972, 33), nonviolent resistance. Thus, the "politics of Jesus" is also the way of discipleship for all Christians, in whatever nation they find themselves. Although some Mennonites have come to accept certain aspects of the Niebuhrian analysis of social responsibility, many find John Howard Yoder's reading of the biblical witness instructive. According to Yoder, the correct model for change at the national and international levels is that of the Israelite Diaspora or exile and, therefore, Christians should see themselves as resident aliens in whatever nation they live. Like the exiles to whom the prophet Jeremiah spoke, Christians should "seek the welfare" of whatever *polis* they find themselves living in. "The complement to the Exodus of the counter-community is not the *coup d'état* by the righteous oppressed, but rather the saving message of the resident minority" (Yoder 1973, 299).

This interpretation of the Bible displays a different understanding of "Christian internationalism" than Rauschenbusch's "Social Gospel" or the Protestant and medieval Catholic versions of Christendom. Viewing the church as a community marked by servanthood, Yoder and contemporary Anabaptist communities place a high degree of importance on the peace and unity of the church. For these reasons, the Anabaptist tradition stresses that it is precisely because of the "politics" of Jesus that the church is called to be "a unique international peoplehood" that forgoes participation in war and thereby rejects "realism" as misplaced. "When Christians of one nation take up arms to fight against or defend themselves from Christians of another nation, both groups deny their confession that Jesus, and not Caesar, is Lord" (Swartley 1983, 132).

Liberation theology

The Anabaptist objections having been noted, it is also clear that the biblical image of "the exodus" of the Hebrew slaves has had an important role in Western political history, particularly in conjunction with revolutionary movements (Walzer 1985, 7). The Exodus narrative has been used to interpret a number of historic political struggles, including Cromwell's "Revolution of the Saints" (Walzer 1965) in seventeenth-century England and the struggle for the emancipation of slaves in the US in the nineteenth century. As Martin Luther King, Jr. eloquently showed in his 1957 sermon "The Birth of a Nation,"[4] the story of Exodus continues to provide the prototypical story of civil-rights struggles and revolutions around the world.

In the late 1960s and early 1970s, a new set of arguments once again took up the exodus theme as a model for liberation. For these interpreters, the authority of the exodus story derives not so much from its status as "Holy Writ" but from its correlation with their experience of oppression.

> The cries of God's people everywhere, the continents of Africa and Asia particularly, as well as those around us here at home, have reached the ears of the Lord when he tells us first of all to go and tell the Pharaohs of this world 'Let my people go.' Exodus must come before Mt. Sinai, liberation of God's people must come before communion with God. (George 1972)[5]

Thus, the exodus story serves to interpret the political realities of oppression, and the Bible itself is read through the lens of oppression, with the events and personages of the Bible describing the political realities of oppression. Somoza becomes Pharaoh, and Nicaragua becomes the Promised Land (Cardinal 1976–1979) which the oppressed will inherit.

Obviously, a central issue for this tradition is the legitimacy of using violent means to achieve the revolution of the people. Some liberation theologians are outspoken pacifists. Others, such as the martyred Salvadoran Archbishop Oscar Romero, have made strategic use of the traditional just-war criteria to call into question political injustice in their countries. Already disposed to sympathize with the plight of the oppressed, liberation theologians decry institutionalized mechanisms

---

[4] Occasioned by the independence of Ghana under the leadership of Kwame Nkrumah, this sermon was preached at the Dexter Avenue Baptist Church, Montgomery, Alabama, in April 1957.

[5] For an apposite example from the American context, see Cone (1986, 29, 47–48).

of violence which are used to subjugate the poor. In particular, liberation theologians point to the hypocrisy of those who call upon Romans 13: 1–7 to keep the poor from taking power.

Liberation theologians tend to express ambivalence about the intervention of one nation-state in the civil strife of another. Archbishop Romero was a notable exception, calling on the president of the United States to intervene in 1978. Other liberation theologians see the United Nations as a forum for expressing their concerns but, in general, liberationists have a radically different estimate of the value of international order from mainstream Protestants and Catholics. The latter presume some specific order in creation that provides for the function of national and international structures of governance. By contrast, liberationists believe the ark of radical religious socialism must be crafted from whatever materials are at hand within the chaos that is human history. Political change cannot be enacted "from above" but must arise "from below," from the actions of the poor and oppressed. The waters of the flood are necessary to wash away all political inequity from the face of the earth before their revolution can create a new order.

Like the Anabaptists, liberationist interpreters dispute the mainstream Protestant distinctions between individual conduct and political conduct at either the national or international levels. Given their affinity with Marxist methods of class analysis, most liberation theologians in the third world dispute the validity of distinctions between principles and consequences. Consequences in foreign affairs are no more important than consequences at the domestic level. Other liberationists, particularly those in North America, have drawn on Niebuhr's "Christian realism" in their struggle against oppression of the poor.

Finally, some liberationists have discussed how the language of "freedom" and "democracy" has been distorted in Western democracies. In particular, they have challenged the unjust structures of domination in the United States. A few have suggested that Christian realism's trust in the values of freedom and democracy has been shortsighted in overlooking the possibility that the "very values that Niebuhr saw as saving us from idolatry are now being transformed into idols" (Shaull 1988, 138). As this chastened perspective shows, liberation theologians are increasingly aware of the need for rhetorical analysis not only of the biblical arguments but also of the ways in which political values become sacralized within Western democracies.

The uses of Scripture in international ethics

Although there can be no doubt that Jews and Christians have addressed the "nations" of the earth with prophetic zeal throughout their history, biblical argument in *international ethics* coincides with the collapse of Christendom. Before the breakup of the Holy Roman Empire, there were no "nations" in the modern sense, nor could questions of "international ethics" be addressed from the perspective of the biblical argument prior to that time. This claim is true in a second sense as well: religious conflict or biblical *argument* about the interpretation of Scripture within "the churches" is itself partly responsible for international conflict in Western history, especially in the era after the Reformation.

In addition, outside the religious communities that regard the Bible as Scripture, the use of the Bible in international ethics has been more illustrative than substantive, more evocative than rigorous. Often employed in the struggles between variant forms of internationalist idealism and political realism in mainstream Western politics, the Bible has been more of a cultural relic to be used pragmatically than a religious authority to be obeyed. Nevertheless the Bible has clearly played a provocative role in the ongoing conversation about international order. Biblical argument in international affairs cannot be abstracted from history, so any attempt to follow the use of the Bible in the ongoing conversation of international affairs requires that we attend to the contexts of argument.

Thus, for those religious and cultural traditions whose formation can be traced to the canons of the Hebrew Bible and the wider Christian canon, the Bible remains an authoritative source for constructing ethical arguments in international relations. But there is no single notion of authority that focuses their use of the Bible, nor is there a single conception of politics that channels their efforts for peace. Nor is there a single philosophical language by which these moral insights are conveyed. Some religious groups subscribe to the notion of common morality while others dispute the validity of that approach to international ethics. Both believe that they find support for their position in the Bible. Not only do such groups ascribe authority to the Bible in different ways, they use it differently than those communities which assign a lesser degree of moral authority to the Bible. As a consequence, there are significant disputes about the ways in which the Bible is used to support particular proposals for international relations.

The debate about how the Bible should be used as a warrant for proposals in international ethics continues because of very different presumptions about the position and role of these religious traditions in relation to world power. For mainstream Protestants and Catholics, Christians have been placed in the world to assist with responsible government. For the Historic Peace Churches, God has dispersed Christians among the nations to proclaim the "new creation" in Christ. For these Christians, to be in diaspora is to take seriously the biblical tradition of the exile as the normal position of religious communities. Here, we see a significant overlap with the Jewish tradition's use of the Bible, although contemporary Jewish moral philosophers like Michael Walzer would sharply dispute the significance of diaspora for international ethics. In the end, there is no consensus about how "prophetic religion" secures the welfare of the "city of man" while pointing toward the "City of God."

The traditions of biblical argument vary greatly in their support for or criticism of the common morality of international order. Not surprisingly, not all of these traditions are equally esteemed by those in positions of political responsibility. During the twentieth century, Reinhold Niebuhr gained great respect from political leaders and religious leaders alike, precisely because his essays in Christian realism invoked a transcendent authority that judged all human efforts inadequate while also invoking the *necessity* of a criterion that would enable political leaders to work toward a "balance of powers" within the limitations of human finitude. By contrast, the Historic Peace Churches are often viewed as "noble, but irrelevant" to the cause of international relations. Of course, they would dispute that characterization of their contribution, and they would proceed by turning first to the Bible.

Suggested reading

There is no book-length study of the use of the Bible in international ethics, but many of the issues are addressed by cultural and religious historians, as well as moral philosophers. Scholarly translations of the canons are readily available, however, often with helpful annotations. The best English translation of the Hebrew Bible is *TANAKH*, published by the Jewish Publication Society of America in 1984. The standard for English-language study of the Christian Canon is *The New Oxford Annotated Bible with the Apocrypha*, New Revised Standard Version (New York: Oxford University Press, 1991).

A good, though incomplete, survey of the history of biblical exegesis is Robert Grant and David Tracy, *A Short History of the Interpretation of the Bible* (1988). Michael Walzer's *Exodus and Revolution* (1985) offers a fascinating, if narrowly focused, account of the role of the exodus narrative in Western political history, particularly in conjunction with revolutions and the rise of nation-states. Michael Goldberg's *Jews and Christians: Getting Our Stories Straight* (1991) offers a very useful discussion of the contrasting narratives of the Hebrew and Christian Bibles.

Because there exist few scholarly studies of biblical argument in international ethics, one has to turn directly to the classic sources of contending biblical arguments. Saint Augustine's *The City of God* offers one of the earliest interpretations of the history of the nations using biblical narratives to provide the framework. The classical biblical argument for natural law can be found in "The Treatise on Law" in St. Thomas Aquinas's *Summa Theologica* I–II. Hugo Grotius's *Prolegomena to the Law of War and Peace* serves as an important exemplar of the use of the Bible in the earliest stages of the tradition of international law.

Among the twentieth-century arguments, Reinhold Niebuhr's essay on "Why the Christian Church is Not Pacifist" in *Christianity and Power Politics* (1940) represents one of the best examples of the use of the Bible from the modern "realist" perspective. In contrast, John Howard Yoder's *The Politics of Jesus* (1972) sharply criticizes the hermeneutic undergirding Niebuhr's realist version of common morality and enunciates the "possibility of a messianic ethic" characterized by pacifism. Finally, Richard Shaull's *Naming the Idols* (1988) provides a good overview of arguments of liberation theologians with respect to the current world order, including the foreign policies of nation-states in the Western hemisphere.

Given the prominence of war and peace in biblical arguments regarding international ethics, some readers may desire further clarification of historical and theological issues. James Turner Johnson's *The Quest for Peace* (1987) provides a good, if somewhat biased, account of the just-war and pacifist traditions, in conjunction with the rise of the tradition of international law. Duane Friesen's *Christian Peacemaking and International Relations* (1986) offers a good discussion of the biblical roots of the position of the Historic Peace Churches (Quakers, Mennonites, Brethren) on international relations, as well as a strong argument for the participation of contemporary Christians in the international relations. The best one-volume discussion of the use of Scripture in Christian ethics is Stephen E. Fowl and L. Gregory Jones, *Reading in Communion: Scripture and Ethics in the Christian Life* (London: SPCK, 1991).

References

Aquinas, Saint Thomas. 1952. "The Treatise on Law." In *Summa Theologica*, I–II. Great Books Series, vol. 20. Chicago: Encyclopedia Britannica.

Augustine, Saint. 1950. *The City of God*. New York: Random House.

Birch, Bruce and Larry L. Rasmussen. 1989. *Bible and Ethics in the Christian Life*. Rev. edn. Minneapolis: Augsburg Press.

Borowitz, Eugene B. 1980. *Contemporary Christologies: A Jewish Response*. New York: Paulist Press.

Cardinal, Ernesto. 1976–1979. *The Gospel in Solentiname*, vols. 1–4. Maryknoll, NY: Orbis Books.

Carnegie Council. 1987. *The Carnegie Council: The First Seventy-Five Years*. New York: Carnegie Council on Ethics and International Affairs.

Cone, James. 1986. *A Black Theology of Liberation*. 2nd edn. Maryknoll, NY: Orbis Books.

Dumbauld, Eduard. 1957. "Editor's Introduction" to *Prolegomenon to the Laws of War and Peace*. Indianapolis, IN: Bobbs-Merrill Company.

Encyclopedia Judaica. 1972. Jerusalem: Keter Publishing House.

Frye, Northrop. 1983. "Typology II: Phases of Revelation." In *The Great Code: The Bible and Literature*, 105–38. New York: Harcourt Brace Jovanovich.

George, Poikail John. 1972. "Whence and Whither World Council Studies?" Unpublished address to the US Conference for the World Council of Churches at Toledo, Ohio (May 1972), cited in John H. Yoder, "Exodus and Exile: The Two Faces of Liberation," *Cross Currents* (Fall 1973): 299.

Goldberg, Michael. 1991. *Jews and Christians: Getting Our Stories Straight*. New York: Trinity Press International.

Grant, Robert and David Tracy. 1984. *A Short History of the Interpretation of the Bible*. 2nd edn. rev. Philadelphia: Fortress Press.

Grotius, Hugo. 1957. *Prolegomena to the Law of War and Peace*. Trans. Francis W. Kelsey. Indianapolis, IN: Bobbs-Merrill Company, Library of Liberal Arts.

Hauerwas, Stanley. 1990. "On the Importance of Being Catholic." *First Things* 1: 23–30.

Johnson, James Turner. 1987. *The Quest for Peace*. Princeton, NJ: Princeton University Press.

Kelsey, David. 1975. *The Uses of Scripture in Recent Protestant Theology*. Philadelphia: Fortress Press.

King, Martin Luther, Jr. 1957. "The Birth of a Nation." Unpublished sermon available at the Martin Luther King, Jr. Archives at the King Center for Non-violent Social Change, Atlanta, GA.

Lohfink, Gerhard. 1984. *Jesus and Community: The Social Dimension of the Gospel*. New York: Paulist Press.

McClendon, James William. 1985. *Ethics: Systematic Theology*, vol. I. Nashville: Abingdon.

New Revised Standard Version of the Bible with the Apocrypha. 1990. New York: Oxford University Press.

Niebuhr, Reinhold. 1935. *An Interpretation of Christian Ethics*. Reprint. New York: Meridian Books, 1956.

— 1940. "Why the Christian Church Is Not Pacifist." *Christianity and Power Politics*, 1–32. New York: Scribner's Sons.

O'Donovan, Oliver. 1986. *Resurrection and Moral Order*. Grand Rapids, MI: Eerdmans.

Penn, William. [1693]. "An Essay Towards the Present and Future Peace of Europe By the Establishment of a European Diet, Parliament, or Estates." Reprinted in *The Peace of Europe: The Fruits of Solitude and Other Writings*. New York: E. P. Dutton, 1915.

Rauschenbusch, Walter. 1907. *Christianity and the Social Crisis*. New York: Macmillan Company.

— 1917. *A Theology for the Social Gospel*. Reprint, Nashville, TN: Abingdon, 1987.

Romero, Archbishop Oscar. 1988. *Voice of the Voiceless: The Four Pastoral Letters and Other Statements*. Introductory essays by Jon Sobrino and Ignacio Martin-Baro. Maryknoll, NY: Orbis Books.

Shaull, Richard. 1987. *Naming the Idols: Biblical Alternatives to U.S. Foreign Policy*. Oak Park, IL: Meyer Stone Books.

Swartley, Willard. 1983. "The Bible and War." In *Slavery, Sabbath, War, and Women: Case Issues in Biblical Interpretation*, 96–149. Scottdale, PA: Herald Press.

TANAKH. 1984. A new translation of the Holy Scriptures according to the traditional Hebrew text. Philadelphia: Jewish Publication Society of America.

Verhey, Allen. 1984. *The Great Reversal: Ethics and the New Testament*. Grand Rapids, MI: Eerdmans.

Walzer, Michael. 1965. *Revolution of the Saints: A Study in the Origins of Radical Politics*. Cambridge, MA: Harvard Univ. Press.

1977. *Just and Unjust Wars: A Moral Argument with Historical Illustrations*. New York: Basic Books.

1985. *Exodus and Revolution*. New York: Basic Books.

1987. *Interpretation and Social Criticism*. Cambridge, MA: Harvard University Press.

Yoder, John H. 1972. *The Politics of Jesus*. Grand Rapids, MI: Eerdmans.

1973. "Exodus and Exile: The Two Faces of Liberation." *Cross Currents* 23: 297–309.

1974. "'Anabaptists and the Sword' Revisited: Systematic Historiography and Undogmatic Nonresistance." *Zeitschrift fur Kirchengeschichte* 85: 270–83.

1984. "The Hermeneutics of Peoplehood." In *The Priestly Kingdom*. Notre Dame, IN: University of Notre Dame Press.

14 CONVERGENCE AND DIVERGENCE IN INTERNATIONAL ETHICS

DAVID R. MAPEL AND TERRY NARDIN

Now that we have considered some ethical traditions of major importance for international relations, what fundamental points of convergence and divergence in international ethics can be identified? The present chapter presents a taxonomy of these traditions, using it to gain a synoptic view of the conversation among them and of the implications of this conversation for international affairs. Any method of classification is bound to ignore much of the internal diversity within each tradition as well as many similarities and differences among the traditions. A taxonomy is like a caricature, which may reveal a face more clearly than a portrait but only by selecting and exaggerating a few prominent features. As we proceed we will explain why these traditions do not always fit neatly into the categories to which they have been assigned, but we also invite the reader to refer back to the fuller discussions of each tradition in earlier chapters, as well as to the larger literature on which those chapters are based.

Arguably, the most fundamental distinction between these traditions is whether they link judgments of right and wrong to consequences or to rules. Political realism, utilitarianism, and Marxism belong to the first class of traditions, which assign primary importance to consequences; international law, natural law, Kantianism, and contractarianism belong to the second class of traditions, which emphasize the interpretation of rules. The traditions of biblical argument and of rights also belong here because of the importance they assign to rules. For the first group, an act, policy, or institution is right or just according to its causal contribution (actual or expected) to bringing about a desired state of affairs; for the second, its rightness depends on the interpretation of rules, the question being whether or not the act or practice in question falls under the rule.

Of course, this broad distinction has its limitations: for example, it is ambiguous for a tradition like liberalism, which embraces both pragmatic and rule-based arguments, and it fails to make room for philosophers like Aristotle who emphasize neither consequences nor rules, but character and motive. And in all the traditions one can find fish swimming against the current: consequentialist natural lawyers, rule utilitarians, rights-based Marxists, and other interesting anomalies. With all its imperfections, however, the distinction between consequence-oriented and rule-oriented traditions does separate two broad types of ethical thinking.

Each of these types can be subdivided. Within the class of traditions that emphasize consequences, the most basic divergence is between realism, which reckons the value of consequences in terms of the survival and well-being of particular communities, and utilitarianism and Marxism, which reckon the value of consequences in terms of the well-being of humanity at large. In the jargon of contemporary moral philosophy, Marxism and utilitarianism not only focus on consequences, but are "consequentialist," that is, they evaluate consequences from an "impersonal" or universal point of view. In adopting a more particularistic perspective, realism differs not only from Marxism and utilitarianism but from all of the other traditions discussed in this book. For this reason, realism is the most insistently state-centric.[1] Given their focus on the welfare of all humanity, utilitarianism and Marxism are – in principle if not always in fact – the most cosmopolitan.

It is hard to identify any comparably fundamental division within the class of rule-oriented traditions, since all of them place principled constraints on conduct and almost all have a fairly complex relation to the political community. We can, however, roughly distinguish between the natural-law, Kantian, and rights traditions, each of which is largely concerned with the duties or rights of human beings as such rather than as members of particular communities, and those traditions – especially contractarianism, international law, and liberalism – that give considerable weight to the claims of particular communities. The biblical traditions themselves divide according to whether they are addressing human beings as such or as members of a community of faith. Another classification can be made according to whether the tradition regards authority as based primarily on revelation, reason, agreement, or custom.

---

[1] International law, though state-centric in presupposing the continued existence of states, is as much concerned with the rules that bind states together as with the interests that divide them. It focusses not only on the state but on the society of states.

The consequence-oriented traditions

Classical and modern realism

Although it can be said that political realism, as an ethical tradition, is distinguished by its recognition of "extremity" or "necessity," this is somewhat misleading. With the exception of those strands of biblical argument that forbid violence under any circumstances, all the traditions discussed in this book acknowledge that normally forbidden measures are sometimes justified or excused by considerations of individual or communal self-defense. Thus, the natural-law tradition seeks to square the use of lethal force with the requirement to respect life through a casuistry of publicly authorized killing, particularly through the just-war doctrine. To take another example, some utilitarians also justify the use of deadly force in self-defense while seeking limits in a doctrine of proportionality and by arguing that rules of war are of general benefit to humanity. More precisely, then, realism maintains that there may be situations that require violating even these sorts of limits. Although a few realists have argued that these violations are necessary in a strictly deterministic sense, most realists have argued that "necessity" in some sense justifies such extreme actions. Thus, making use of a distinction suggested in Chapter 1, we can say that while realism sets itself in opposition to the requirements of "morality," it is still an "ethical" tradition that uses the language of justification.

Realism is internally diverse, however, and offers a variety of justifications. Realist arguments have been based on moral skepticism, an egoistic view of human nature, cultural relativism, the primacy of power in politics, the anarchical character of international society, and the special role of the public official as trustee. Often these arguments are combined with others that also find favor outside the tradition. Machiavelli, for example, agrees with the natural-law tradition (and against Kant) that nature provides the proper standard for ethical judgment, but doubts that the rules of morality are natural. Machiavelli also questions the natural basis of the political community, and concludes that by nature, the political community reflects only a balance of forces between individuals competing for security, power, and glory.[2] One prominent strand of realist thinking is based on a thoroughgoing moral skepticism combined with an egoistic theory of human nature and skepticism about the value of political

---

[2] As Steven Forde indicates in Chapter 4, other interpretations of Machiavelli place his commitment to republicanism in a different light.

community. Another quite different strand views the state itself as the primary source of value.[3] But most realists have been neither so skeptical nor so reverent toward the political community. As Forde and Donnelly observe in Chapters 4 and 5, most realists assume that states are necessary for the realization of independently grounded values, especially in a world of many states lacking any effective central authority.

Realists doubt the power of morality alone to engender self-restraint and reciprocity under conditions of anarchy. Among the traditions discussed in this book, realism is distinctive in its single-minded focus on the conditions that purportedly render morality ineffective. At the same time, this emphasis on the absence of international reciprocity is one of the points at which realism and contractarianism converge. There is also an early modern convergence (in Hobbes, for example) between realism and the traditions of liberalism, rights, and international law on the idea that states have a quite robust liberty or "right" to self-defense.

Given their view of international relations as intrinsically anarchical, realists regard necessity as a more or less permanent condition and therefore tend to regard intervention and war as standard instruments of statecraft. But a concern with long-term insecurity is more characteristic of classical realists like Machiavelli and Hobbes than it is of the modern realists treated by Donnelly in Chapter 5. As Forde notes, this emphasis on insecurity as a permanent condition leads Machiavelli to a sweeping justification of imperialism and destroys any distinction between defensive and aggressive wars. Modern realists are typically reluctant to acknowledge the full force of the Machiavellian logic, arguing rather tamely that a statecraft motivated by a prudent concern for the national interest is generally better for all concerned than a statecraft motivated by more universal values. This, however, cannot be the central justification of realism without transforming it into a kind of universal consequentialism.

Utilitarianism and Marxism

While political realism demands that state leaders act to produce the best consequences for a particular community, utilitarianism and Marxism demand that individuals act to produce the best

[3] To say that the community is a source of value can mean either that community is intrinsically valuable or that our values are ultimately shaped by the communities to which we belong. Here realism converges with the arguments of "communitarian" theorists, though these theorists disagree in many ways with one another and with most realists.

consequences for humanity. Unlike realism, utilitarianism and Marxism are basically cosmopolitan, since our responsibilities as citizens (if any) are derivative, our responsibilities in the world fundamental. Because the state is only a contingent vehicle for maximizing human welfare, it can be either a means or an obstacle in pursuit of that goal. But, while both are fundamentally consequentialist and cosmopolitan, utilitarianism and Marxism differ in two important respects.

First, they differ on the nature of the individual good. Utilitarianism begins from the existing preferences of individuals in seeking to maximize well-being or "utility." Marxism does not aim at utility in this sense at all, but at human autonomy or "liberation," and this involves a radical transformation of existing preferences.

Second, though both utilitarians and Marxists argue that choices should be based primarily on issues of fact and empirical theory, Marxism has a distinctive and, in principle, more critical account of ordinary morality and existing institutions. This second difference has several important ramifications.

Although utilitarianism was closely associated with radical politics in the days of Bentham and Mill, it has no necessary connection with radical politics, for contingent social and political facts may sometimes dictate a conservative policy as the best way of maximizing utility. Nor is there any distinctively utilitarian empirical theory, even though utilitarians are generally "methodological individualists" and the individualist discipline of economics has a historical connection with utilitarianism.[4] While often critical of ordinary morality, utilitarians sometimes argue that general adherence to moral rules maximizes utility (which is why these rules have emerged). This is one reason utilitarians often reach substantive conclusions that resemble those of the rule-oriented ethical traditions, as when they argue that adherence to the rules of war is in the best interests of humanity.

For example, utilitarians have generally held that the state has a duty to protect its citizens. Thus, utilitarians agree with those who claim, on non-consequentialist grounds, that the state has such a duty. Similarly, though utilitarians may differ from natural- and international-law theorists over the precise content of the *jus ad bellum*, they agree that the occasions of war must be severely limited. The biggest disagreement with the rule-oriented traditions concerns their

---

[4] There is no simple relationship between utilitarianism and Marxism at the level of empirical theory. Utilitarians can in principle subscribe to Marxist economic and social theories, and some recent "analytical" Marxists are methodological individualists who employ the tools of rational-choice theory. There is debate among Marxists about whether this latter development puts analytical Marxists outside the tradition.

characteristically sharp distinction between acts and consequences (essential to the natural-law doctrine of the double effect), which utilitarians regard as incoherent or without moral significance. As Chapter 8 illustrates, some utilitarians have reached radical conclusions on substantive international issues like famine relief or nuclear disarmament. But utilitarian arguments can also be used to ground conservative conclusions.

Marxism, in contrast, is necessarily radical. Given their understanding of historical change, Marxists may have tactical reasons for supporting the state. Unlike utilitarians, however, Marxists must in principle reject the state in favor of the worldwide community of the proletariat. In rejecting the state, Marxists also reject the idea of an international community of states as having any positive ethical significance, although some Marxist theorists have argued that imperialism may have progressive consequences by contributing to the final collapse of the capitalist world economy. Also in contrast to utilitarianism, the Marxist theory of social change rejects ordinary morality as an "ideological" expression of class interests. As Chris Brown suggests in Chapter 11, Marxism replaces the idea of an independently justified realm of moral principle with the idea that knowledge generated by theoretically informed practice is self-validating. Marx himself expressed doubt that one could "maximize" heterogeneous and nonquantifiable goods like freedom, self-actualization, and community. Instead, Marxism sides with natural law and some strains of liberalism in holding that all these goods might be realized in a well-ordered society.

These doubts about morality yield a determination within the Marxist tradition to avoid moral argument, as well as a willingness to take extreme measures in pursuit of revolution. In both these respects, the Marxist tradition resembles political realism. For example, there is little interest within Marxism in traditional questions about the just war. Of course, we must again avoid oversimplifying: as Brown notes, Marxists in the Second International tried to introduce neo-Kantian ideas into the tradition, and the tradition is replete with expressions of moral judgment. But, because the ends of a particular class, the proletariat, are always connected to the ends of humanity through a philosophy of history, the Marxist tradition moves beyond the particularism of political realism to the full-blown universalism characteristic of utilitarianism and other cosmopolitan perspectives.

Marxism typically substitutes analyses of the historical process for ethical argumentation. Marxists focus on an end-state, the classless society, and discuss tactics for producing that end-state, not moral obligations. In contrast, utilitarianism sometimes begins with the moral premise that each individual is to count for one and only one. By constructing an explicitly moral argument on this premise, it moves in the direction of those traditions that privilege rules over consequences.

The rule-oriented traditions

The expression "rule-oriented" signals an issue to be discussed as much as a category to be used. As Chapter 1 notes in discussing common morality and international law, "rules" are best thought of as abstractions from or abridgements of more complicated traditions of conduct. But it is an open question whether such abstractions can adequately reflect a living moral tradition, or provide an adequate guide to preserving or reforming it. Using the term "rule-oriented" does not imply that the traditions grouped under this label are necessarily abstract or formal. It does, however, remind us that they conceive ethics as in essence a matter of interpreting the meanings of the rules and other formulations through which moral judgments are expressed.

Roughly speaking, these traditions focus on the permissibility of actions and intentions rather than on the desirability of their consequences. They do not exclude a concern with consequences but they set limits on consequence-oriented reasoning. In particular, they usually reject the idea that such limits can be violated in cases of necessity. But there are also differences among them. For example, whereas the natural law, Kantian, and rights traditions focus primarily on moral duties or rights, the traditions of liberalism, contractarianism, and international law give more attention to political and legal obligations. Natural law and Kantianism can be understood as attempting to articulate, in different ways, the idea of a "common morality" (for the meaning of this term, see "Common morality and international law," Chapter 1 and "Natural law, common morality, and consequentialism," Chapter 6). The idea of common morality is more controversial within the biblical and rights traditions, each of which is marked by tension between communal and universal understandings of morality. And, while connected in various ways to the idea of common morality, liberalism and contractarianism have been more concerned with a distinctive "morality of states," as has international law. The following discussion reflects a distinction between traditions that are cosmopolitan and those that are state-centric. But, as we shall see, this distinction is rough indeed.

As previously mentioned, these traditions can also be distinguished by their views of authority: the biblical traditions emphasize divine authority; the natural-law, Kantian, rights, and liberal traditions emphasize the authority of reason; the contractarian tradition emphasizes the authority of agreement; and international law, the authority of both agreement and custom. Within the broad distinction between cosmopolitan and state-centric traditions, our discussion also follows this fourfold distinction concerning sources of authority.

The biblical traditions

Though the biblical traditions all defer to the authority of Scripture, no single authority determines how the Bible is to be used in reaching moral judgments about the conduct of nations. Rather, as Michael Cartwright shows in Chapter 13, there is a continuing conversation about international relations within and among the traditions that ground their authority in the Hebrew and Christian canons. Mainstream Protestantism and Catholicism, for example, rest on the premise that Christians have a duty to obey and support responsible government. But Jewish tradition, the historic peace churches, and liberation theology suggest that the mission of the religious community is to preserve its identity by adjusting to the realities of diaspora or exile or, alternatively, to challenge established power via radical, prophetic social criticism or active, even armed, resistance to oppression. These traditions also reveal a tension between using the Bible to ground a specifically religious ethic and using it to articulate a common morality or common international law.

Jewish visions of international order, for example, are mainly discussed in terms of the Mosaic and Noachic covenants, the first binding only on Jews, the second universally binding on humanity. This difference explains how the early prophets could appeal to a minimal code of conduct or "international law" when denouncing "the nations," yet reserve their most severe denunications for the nation of Israel. The emphasis of the post-exilic prophets is on reforming the temple, not the political order, and on peaceful coexistence with the inhabitants of the nations to which the Jews have been exiled. With the Holocaust and the subsequent founding of Israel, however, the ethical concept of diaspora becomes less influential among many Jewish interpreters. Some of the most important recent Jewish reflections about international ethics have instead centered on the legitimacy and claims of the state of Israel, with biblical arguments deployed across the political spectrum. But while Jewish tradition has been used to defend a unique mission for the Jews and in some cases to justify Israeli violations of just-war principles, it also supports the idea of a common morality for all nations, including Israel.

Unlike the Jews, Christians view the world as already redeemed, although they disagree about the nature of that redemption. Medieval Christendom filtered the message of the Bible through the traditions of the church, using allegorical interpretations of the Bible to conceptualize a variety of positions on the relations between Christendom and the non-Christian nations and, later, among the Christian nations. In the writings of Aquinas, biblical arguments are combined with the philosophical to provide a new basis for the proposition that both Christian and non-Christian peoples must observe certain minimum moral standards.[5] As Cartwright notes, however, the Crusades of the late middle ages demonstrate that the medieval theory of the just war was understood to apply primarily within Christendom.

Augustine laid the foundations for a view of social order as a symbolic mixture of useful wheat and useless weeds that are best left to grow together until the harvest. Many centuries later, the Protestant Reformation adapted this biblical image of "wheat and tares" to the emerging international system under the principle that each ruler might enforce his own religion within his realm (*cuis regio, eius religio*), which served to rationalize the diversity as well as the multiplicity of European nations. Against the background of the religious wars of the seventeenth century, Protestants like Grotius distinguished "the law of God" from the *jus gentium* or law of nations, but in a way that again illustrates the tension between using the bible to sustain a specifically religious ethic and using it to defend a universal morality and encourage the emergence of a body of international law. Choosing the former path, the Historic Peace Churches have challenged the close relation between church and state favored by Catholics and mainstream Protestants, arguing instead for a spiritual, nonviolent, and critical role for the church and against the kind of realist ethic of responsibility typified by Reinhold Niebuhr. In turn, mainstream Protestants have accused the peace churches of focusing narrowly on the "politics" of Jesus to the exclusion of other aspects of the biblical message.

As Cartwright's discussion indicates, there is tremendous diversity in the biblical traditions, leading at times (as with liberation theology) to criticism of common morality's bedrock distinction between prin-

---

[5] The different readings of Aquinas provided by Joseph Boyle in Chapter 6 and Michael Cartwright in Chapter 13 reflect the continuing dispute over the relation between natural-law and biblical arguments in Aquinas's writings.

ciples and consequences. Different interpretations of various central images – the flood, the ark, the wheat and tares, the exodus story – have emerged, as have different views about whether the church, the individual conscience, or historical study provide the proper method of authoritative interpretation. Drawing on several distinct religious traditions, biblical argument about international affairs is unified largely by a recognition of the primacy of Scripture, though it remains divided about its canonical arrangement, proper interpretation, and implications for world affairs.

The tradition of natural law

The idea of a universal or common morality runs through the biblical traditions, the great syntheses of Aquinas and Kant, and beyond into the contemporary language of rights. In contrast with the biblical traditions, however, these other traditions attempt to ground universal morality in reason rather than revelation. The commandment to love one's neighbor, for example, has been construed by some within these traditions as, alternatively, a requirement to promote basic human goods, to respect persons as ends in themselves, or to respect human rights. Such rational reinterpretations exclude much that is part of any religious view of a full human life. The natural-law, Kantian, and rights traditions are all relatively cosmopolitan in character, yet disagree about connections between individual good, the common good, the state, and the international community.

As Joseph Boyle argues in Chapter 6, the natural-law tradition is a tradition of inquiry. While regarding the writings of Aquinas as an especially authoritative source of insight, natural-law theorists share a common analytical approach and set of questions rather than agreement on particular conclusions. Natural law does, however, begin from principles of practical reason that identify basic human goods and the moral precepts through which they are attained. These principles are said to be knowable by reason and therefore accessible to all who can reason (which is not to say, however, that mistakes are impossible). They include the most basic precepts of common morality, such as those of the decalogue, as well as constructions like St. Paul's principle and the principle of the double effect that operate to ensure consistency in the application of these precepts.

It is important to stress that only the most fundamental precepts and principles are considered natural or self-evident in the tradition. Most natural-law theorists do not consider specific laws and policies to be either self-evident or deducible from the basic principles. Instead, law and policy are connected to these principles through human invention and decision. This human decision in turn requires political authority, which can exist only within the framework of a community. And although communities can be formed with more or less expansive common purposes, the natural-law tradition defines a "complete" community as one in which, as Boyle puts it in the last section of Chapter 6, "all the human goods are in view." But, contrary to what Aristotle, many realists, and even some natural-law philosophers may have thought, this idea of complete community does not refer uniquely to some particular kind of community, like the "polis" or "state." Rather, it refers to any community structured to provide for the realization of all human goods by regulating, if necessary, human interactions of every kind. Like utilitarianism, natural law requires us to take account of contingent possibilities in evaluating the claims of any community to comprehensive – that is, political and legal – authority. According to the natural-law tradition, it is possible that today or in the near future a single world community might provide the best structure for coordinating the achievement of the whole set of human goods, contrary claims for state sovereignty notwithstanding.

This does not mean that the tradition necessarily condemns existing sovereignties and the international system. So long as states exist, however, their interactions are open to moral judgment and regulation. They have duties toward one another even in the absence of superior authority. The natural-law tradition considers international agreements, like individual promises, to be morally binding without enforcement. But, in contrast with the realist and contractarian traditions, natural law does not suppose that international society is based on a merely prudential reciprocity. As Boyle argues, the natural-law understanding of common morality implies that our shared humanity grounds moral duties that are prior to the obligations incurred through particular agreements. While refusing to ground either political or international society on contractual agreement, natural-law theorists do support the view found in international law that the customary law of nations can acquire both legal and moral authority. According to the natural-law tradition, much of international law has such authority even for countries that have not explicitly consented to it. In contrast to legal positivism, however, the natural-law tradition holds that this authority must ultimately be justified in terms of the common good, not simply state practice.

Some additional contrasts should help clarify the natural-law view of politics and international affairs. Unlike political realism, the natural-law tradition does not regard the survival of any particular

307

kind of polity as essential for the continuation of the moral life. The tradition recognizes that public officials may have specific obligations to the citizens of their own communities, but the fulfillment of those obligations is constrained by more fundamental moral duties. Natural law is intrinsically more inclined than either realism or utilitarianism to count obedience to the precepts of common morality as part of the common good of a society. And, like realism, but unlike utilitarianism, the natural-law tradition is unequivocal about the importance of political authority in regulating human activity for the common good. But this authority is limited in many ways: by absolute prohibitions on certain kinds of conduct; by the doctrine that an unjust law is not law (and, recently, by the recognition of the importance of rights in determining the justice of the laws); and by a highly developed casuistry of publicly authorized killing, which includes detailed reflection about the just war.

Still, authority is essential on natural-law grounds, for moral life involves the interpretation of moral principles in ways that go beyond deductive reasoning. Where deductive reasoning is inconclusive, the resulting indeterminacies must be resolved if morality is to provide guidance in such cases. This resolution requires practical wisdom, which rests in turn on character, experience, and a feel for moral subtlety – traits that are desirable in anyone but especially important for political leaders. Thus, in considering the use of force by a state, practical wisdom requires us to examine the legitimacy of that state, its officials, and its claims, the possibility of effective action, the precise character of the action to be taken, its moral permissibility, and the contours of a larger set of considerations that may justify apparent exceptions. The complexity of practical judgments – of ethical judgments in cases requiring decision – generates disagreement within the tradition, which is why the tradition is better identified through its premises and methods of reasoning than through its conclusions. Such disagreement frequently prompts critics to charge that natural-law casuistry can be used to justify anything. Yet the tradition is virtually unanimous in condemning wars of aggression and barbaric practices in any war, and such judgments show that casuistry can, over time, lead to reasoned agreement.

The Kantian-deontological tradition

The world "deontological" is used in contemporary moral and political philosophy to identify an approach to ethics that identifies moral conduct with respect for principle. Deontological systems characteristically stress the importance of the agent's motives and counsel fidelity to moral rules even and perhaps especially where they are opposed by consequential considerations. In Kant, however, these general features are given more precise articulation: for example, Kant's concern for motive is expressed by the distinction he makes between an action done merely "in accordance" with duty and one done for "for the sake of duty." Only the latter has moral worth. According to Kant, we determine our duty by subjecting possible maxims of conduct to a fundamental test, the categorical imperative, which is discovered by reason operating independently of experience. In other words, as Thomas Donaldson suggests in Chapter 7, Kant repudiates naturalism: the way the world ought to be cannot be derived from the way it is. Instead, individuals as rational beings inhabit a "realm of freedom." They *can* and therefore should act for the sake of duty. Because there is no gap between ethical theory and what is required in practice, Kantian thought is at the opposite extreme from realism in emphasizing the motivational efficacy of reason and morality.

Although both natural law and the Kantian tradition stress the demands of practical reason, the latter sharply separates the ideas of right and good and expresses a more radical emphasis on freedom. It also emphasizes more explicitly than does natural law the idea that one should always act to respect human beings as ends in themselves, and the idea that one should act according to maxims that one could will as universal laws of human action (both offered by Kant as effectively equivalent formulations of the categorical imperative). There is debate within the Kantian tradition about the precise interpretation of each of these ideas. But they have also been subject to plain misunderstandings. For example, it has been suggested that the categorical imperative requires us not only to subordinate consequences to moral prohibitions but to ignore them altogether. It has also been suggested that Kant and the deontological tradition are simply unaware of the problem of specifying possible maxims of conduct at the right level of generality. As Donaldson points out, neither of these criticisms is accurate.

The general features of Kant's moral philosophy help explain some of the ways the Kantian-deontological tradition diverges from other traditions in politics and international affairs. In the Kantian tradition, both domestic and international duties rest on the *a priori* demands of reason. In contrast to contractarianism, Kantians hold that contingencies like the achievement of a certain level of material existence or the likelihood of reciprocity are irrelevant to what individuals or states

309

should do. Neither the existence of a single cosmopolitan culture supporting human rights, nor agreements among states of the sort found in the declaratory tradition of modern international law, are required as a basis for international duties. Even if international society were headed toward a complete Hobbesian anarchy, the categorical imperative would require us to ignore this reality. Our fundamental moral duties are universally binding unless it can be shown that fulfilling them is impossible. In emphasizing the importance of noncontingent, universally binding duties, Kantianism is perhaps the most cosmopolitan of the rule-oriented traditions.

Yet Kant himself introduces a strange state-centric twist into his international ethics by also subscribing to a metaphysical view of the state as a moral person. As a moral person, the state exists in a condition of natural freedom while remaining subject to the same constraining duties to which individuals are subject. To be sure, each state is directed to form a social contract with other states and is required to seek peace. But, although the international social contract creates a confederation, this confederation lacks sovereignty. Arguing the view (later picked up by the utilitarian John Austin) that law presupposes effective sanctions, Kant concludes that international society also lacks law in a strict sense. Within the terms of the social contract, war in self-defense remains permissible, and this permission is broad enough to allow preemptive wars under some circumstances.

Despite these limitations of the international social contract, Kant maintains that we have a duty to pursue a stable or "perpetual" peace through international confederation, to further ensure peace by creating republican governments within each state, and to refrain from barbaric actions during war that demean both agent and victim and undermine the faith between individuals and nations required for the establishment of peace after the war is over. The last requirement, which rules out actions of the sort that are proscribed today under the Nuremberg principles as war crimes and crimes against humanity, results in considerable convergence with the judgments of the natural-law and international-law traditions. And, like natural-law theorists, Kantians today are far more disturbed than are consequentialists by the intentional threat to civilians that underlies nuclear deterrence.

As Donaldson suggests, Kantian ethics has affinities with rights-based ethical theories in that both argue for the existence of universal principles that take precedence over consequential considerations. Many moralists who take a broadly deontological approach to international ethics have, in fact, appropriated the language of rights as a vehicle for expressing moral claims, and both the natural-law and

Kantian-deontological traditions are currently embroiled in a debate about whether law and duty (as Aquinas and Kant thought) or rights (as many today believe) are foundational. These seemingly abstruse debates in fact have significant implications for international affairs. For example, it makes a big difference whether obligations to relieve hunger and poverty abroad, or to open national borders to refugees and other migrants, are described using Kant's notion of "imperfect" duties or in the language of rights: the former leaves considerably more room than does the latter for favoring the well-being of fellow nationals over that of foreigners.

As Donaldson also notes, Kant's influence on modern moral and political philosophy is so ubiquitous that a wide variety of thinkers and concerns have come to be called "Kantian." For example, John Rawls understands his own contractarian theory of justice to be an expression of Kant's ethical outlook. Under the influence of Rawls, moral philosophers have become increasingly interested in issues of global distributive justice. Kant himself argues in *Perpetual Peace* that prior to the social contract all persons have a right to communal possession of the earth's surface, and Charles Beitz has compared this view to Rawls's understanding of original possession, which insists on the arbitrariness of entitlements to natural resources. Is this comparison apt? Is Rawls's theory (or Beitz's) "really" Kantian? Although there are sometimes clear answers to such questions, it is often more helpful to answer both "yes" and "no."

The idea of rights

Most of the traditions discussed in this book employ the idea, or at least the language, of rights. Among the classical realists, for example, Spinoza argues that individuals and states have a natural liberty or "right" to acquire what they can. Although Aquinas does not speak of rights, modern natural-law theorists like Maritain and Finnis are quite concerned with them. Rights have been justified both on utilitarian grounds and as correlatives of more basic duties. Both contractarianism and liberalism typically presume the existence of rights. In the history of international law, the rights of states are immensely important, especially the right to proclaim war. And in the declaratory tradition of international law, the rights of individuals are added to the traditional rights of states. The only traditions that remain generally skeptical about the significance of rights are Marxism and modern political realism.

We may doubt whether there is a rights "tradition," given the extent to which reliance on the language of rights has permeated other traditions and the possibility of justifying rights on consequentialist, deontological, or communitarian grounds. Yet this language of rights deserves separate treatment, not only because the idea of rights has emerged as a philosophical starting point in contemporary moral and political theory, but because it shifts the focus of attention from rules to those protected by rules and, in the case of natural or human rights, to their claims as persons.

Rights are important at three levels of world politics: for individuals as members of a society of mankind; for states as members of an international society of states; and for subnational or transnational groups, such as national liberation movements and multinational corporations. In liberalism, individual rights are fundamental. All individuals have rights to life, liberty, and property. These basic rights encompass claims to privacy, claims to security against violence, claims to various forms of public expression, claims to stable possession, and (in some liberal theories) claims to subsistence. In Marxist and various "Southern" or "third world" political doctrines, however, individual rights appear somewhat differently. Marxism regards rights as part of the "superstructure" of society, based on and rationalizing underlying economic relations. Socialism, having transcended liberal individualism, makes the social group itself the subject of rights. The idea of group rights – as well as an emphasis on rights to economic and social well-being – also appears in the third world, where personhood is sometimes not distinguished from membership in a group. Despite this diversity, few nations today challenge the idea of human rights, although there is disagreement about their nature and justification.

Despite the depressing frequency with which governments violate human rights, individuals have rights largely as nationals or citizens of particular states. Indeed, to be deprived of one's citizenship is a grave offense against one's human dignity, to be stateless a catastrophe. The value of statehood, defined by the basic collective rights of political independence and territorial integrity, has repeatedly caused national and other nonstate groups to claim statehood and to fight for it. International law has long distinguished between rebellion, insurgency, and belligerency as expressing different degrees of success in presenting such claims. Groups that have no wish to become states may still want governments to recognize their rights as transnational organizations, such as the right to trade freely in the case of multinational corporations, or to proselytize in the case of churches.

The idea of rights came into its own when rights ceased being considered just another way of expressing claims under existing rules and came to be regarded as morally fundamental. As ethical discourse has come more and more to be cast in the language of rights, an ever more complex set of distinctions has evolved and this has in turn produced an increasingly autonomous tradition of thought about rights. The distinctive moral attitude that drives this emphasis on rights is one of assertive moral egalitarianism, demanding respect for individuals as a matter of course rather than as an occasion for gratitude.

Liberalism and contractarianism

As we have seen, the rights tradition might well be described as state-centric rather than cosmopolitan: it is concerned with the rights of states as well as of individuals, and it recognizes that states are the main locus of individual rights even if not their ultimate source. Liberalism, too, is concerned with rights, but it has been primarily concerned with those rights that protect individual liberty against the state. In international affairs this has led to efforts to reform the international milieu by extending to that plane its domestic victories over arbitrary state power. This liberal desire to reform the state system gives the tradition a cosmopolitan cast. At the same time, liberals have feared the power of a world state and have therefore more often wished to reform the state system than to abolish it.

Like most of the traditions we have discussed, liberalism emphasizes the authority of reason. It has continued an optimistic Enlightenment conception of reason that rejects any sharp distinction between theory and practice or between private and public morality. Unlike Marxists and realists, liberals have confidence in the independence and efficacy of ideas, and refuse to reduce them to class or national interests. In these respects, both Bentham and Kant are liberals – a fact that reveals liberalism to be more inclusive than other traditions. As Michael Smith observes at the end of Chapter 10, the utilitarian, Kantian, and contractarian traditions, the emerging concern with human rights, and the effort to strengthen international law can all be regarded as expressions of a broader liberal tradition.

Given the wide range of perspectives within the tradition, it is not surprising that liberals disagree among themselves about how best to promote freedom and reconcile it with other values like prosperity and peace. For some liberals, the spread of liberal regimes is the inevitable consequence of education and commerce, which are incompatible with the militarist spirit that has historically pervaded international

313

relations. Other liberals are less optimistic, yet regard international reform as a moral duty whatever the prospects for its success may be.

Similar tensions are reflected elsewhere in the liberal tradition. Some liberals have been noninterventionist, arguing that the best way of promoting freedom is by example. Some, like Woodrow Wilson and Arthur Schlesinger, have taken an actively interventionist stance. Still others, like J. S. Mill and Michael Walzer, have attempted to articulate principles for distinguishing permissible and impermissible interventions. Liberals also disagree about the relative importance of domestic and international reform, though typically they favor some kind of reform at both levels: at the domestic level, civil liberties should be strengthened and society made more democratic, while at the international level state sovereignty should be limited and more respect paid to international law. But the tradition embraces many different views about the priority of domestic and international reform. It is also divided about whether international reform should seek to strengthen international law or should aim toward world federation or world government. What makes all these views part of the same liberal tradition is their common emphasis on reason rather than custom, on reform rather than revolution, and on the priority of freedom over other conceptions of the individual or common good.

Like liberalism, contractarianism emphasizes individual freedom. But contractarianism is not concerned merely with reforming the state to protect and expand freedom. Rather, it offers a theory of the state that imagines free and equal individuals who establish a political community to secure and protect their liberty. In addition, the contractarian tradition emphasizes the authority of agreement rather than either reason or revelation. It is therefore even more state-centric than liberalism.

The social contract bridges ethical and political theory by bringing together three considerations: (1) a view of the individual good; (2) a set of moral constraints; and (3) an account of the conditions under which social cooperation is both possible and necessary. Contractarianism converges with other traditions at each of these points.

Contractarians are skeptical about our ability to reach theoretical or practical agreement about final ends. The contractarian tradition therefore leaves individuals (and states) largely free to choose their own ends. Contractarianism agrees with utilitarianism and liberalism on this point, while being opposed to the natural-law tradition, which has a substantive theory of basic individual and common goods. While the natural-law tradition makes room for procedural authority, it ultimately grounds the authority of political leaders in their ability to discern the common good. In the contractarian tradition, skepticism about the possibility of identifying the common good leads to the view that authority is grounded on agreement.

Yet, as many critics have pointed out, the social contract cannot be based solely on agreement, but presupposes rights and duties prior to the contract itself. Hobbes, Locke, and Rousseau, for example, all begin with the idea that individuals have a natural right to liberty. Kant attributes a similar right to states. Most of these theorists also recognize a natural duty to seek peace. Classical contractarianism thus makes use of moral notions drawn from other traditions. As Mapel notes in Chapter 9, there are no "pure" contractarians, since the moral force of the contract partly depends on such extra-contractarian assumptions.

The contractarian tradition comes into its own by combining skepticism about the good and tacit acknowledgment of pre-contractual rights and duties with assumptions about the conditions for social cooperation. These are assumptions about how interdependence, vulnerability, levels of scarcity, capacities for action, and kinds of motivation all affect the possibility of social cooperation. Classical contractarianism and the realist tradition converge strongly on the view that circumstances of international relations make reliable cooperation or mutual self-restraint highly doubtful. Contractarians argue that questions of political or social justice cannot arise unless we have reliable expectations of cooperation or reciprocity, and the classical contractarians therefore accept the realist judgment that moral rules cease to apply when circumstances make them ineffective.

Contemporary contractarians challenge this view in several ways, however. Under the influence of Kant, some argue that moral principles are binding even in the absence of reciprocity. Others argue that it is not actual cooperation but the existence of interdependence, which implies the *possibility* of cooperation, that gives rise to moral obligations. On this view, the highly interdependent character of the current international system makes extensive global cooperation a practicable ideal. These contemporary versions of the contractarian argument are more cosmopolitan than the classical versions, and are capable of supporting demands for a fair distribution of goods for every person on earth, regardless of nationality.

In spite of these similarities, however, contractarianism today is divided in other ways. Contemporary "Hobbesians" and "Kantians," for example, argue over how the contract should be set up and what the contracting parties would choose. They disagree more profoundly about the degree of reciprocity that must exist before principles of social and political justice come into play. This emphasis on existing or potential cooperation as a condition of justice is one of the distinctive ways in which the contractarian tradition converges with political realism and diverges from other ethical traditions. Natural law and Kantianism, for example, place much more emphasis on the idea of the common good or the *a priori* demands of reason than on actual or hypothetical agreement.

The tradition of international law

Agreement on common rules is clearly an important part of the tradition of international law. But many theorists of international law agree with critics of contractarianism that these rules must be grounded in something more fundamental than a contract. In international law, this more fundamental source of authority is customary practice, not moral principle. Treaties between states, for example, would be impossible without prior authoritative procedures for making treaties. And they would be ineffective without prior acknowledgment of the basic principle of *pacta sunt servanda* (agreements are to be observed). The existence of such principles and procedures, which are grounded not just in philosophical reflection but in the actual practice of states, challenges the more extreme claims of political realism.

In this book, "international law" refers to a complex system of practices and rules created in European diplomacy starting at the end of the sixteenth century. Although it is often said that international law developed to curb the excesses of state sovereignty, the idea of sovereignty is in fact central to its development. The medieval "state" lacked the internal unity and external independence characteristic of the modern sovereign state. Implicit in the idea of sovereignty is the idea of the state as a person capable of having rights and duties, which gave rise in turn to the idea of a society of equal states capable of mutually defining and delimiting these rights and duties, and thus establishing rules of international law.

This idea of the state as a *magna persona* resembles the Kantian idea of the state as a moral personality or the view held by some realists that the state is a source of value. Because one can view early international law as confirming the expansion of the rights of sovereign states, the development of international law is also linked to the parallel development of the idea of rights. And, because both Catholic natural-law thinkers and Protestant contractarians like Hobbes and Pufendorf viewed international law as applying natural law to the relations of sovereigns, international law has affinities with both these traditions (for detailed discussion of these points, see "Common morality and international law," Chapter 1 and "The origins of the tradition," Chapter 2).

The idea of sovereignty was originally connected with the right to make war. A lawful state of war could therefore exist only externally, between sovereigns. And because the sovereign is supreme, by definition, each sovereign is also the authoritative judge of the rightness of his cause. To this sort of reasoning, early jurists such as Gentili added the idea that often we cannot know whether a particular cause is just, and therefore that we should focus not on the objective justice of one side or the other, but on rules governing how war is fought on both sides. The resulting development of the *jus in bello* at the expense of the *jus ad bellum* follows as the logical consequence of regarding war as a sovereign prerogative.

Until the middle of the eighteenth century, the "law of nations" was commonly regarded as an application of the "law of nature" to the relations of sovereigns. Toward the end of the eighteenth century, however, jurists began to argue that this law was based on the unique practices of the nations of Christian Europe, not on a universal code. The authority of international law, in other words, was derived from the customs and agreements of particular nations – from "modes of interaction habitually practiced and accepted" within a particular community of nations, as Murray Forsyth puts it in Chapter 2. The result is "legal positivism," the view that the rules of international law are those actually acknowledged by states to be binding.

As non-Christian and non-Western states were brought into the European system, international law gradually reclaimed its status as a universal code. But because it had to bridge much larger cultural differences, international law was forced to sever its ties with the particular religious and moral ideals that had shaped its early history and to develop principles reflecting the moral outlook of a more inclusive and, indeed, nearly universal community of nations.

In the present century, international law has continued to change through the evolution of state practice, but it has also been increasingly shaped by the deliberations and decisions of the United Nations, the World Court, and other international agencies. As Dorothy Jones explains in Chapter 3, current international law is significantly influenced by the efforts of states to articulate its basic principles in general declaratory treaties whose authority is increasingly acknowledged by almost all nations. One consequence of this development is that international law, though still based on state practice, once again applies universally within the society of states. This universality has in turn increased its usefulness as an instrument for making claims against states on behalf of individuals, national minorities, and other groups – a development most visible in the international law of human rights, but active in other areas as well.

The importance of the traditions of international ethics

The taxonomy we have presented is no doubt misleading in a number of ways, perhaps especially in representing these traditions as more systematic than they really are. But our discussion is potentially misleading in another, more specific, way as well. Not only is each of these traditions less unified than it might at first appear, but practical political discourse typically combines elements from several traditions in a rather haphazard way. It requires all the skill of the historian to chart how a set of traditions has been used in political controversy over even a short period of time. Nevertheless, it may be helpful to indicate at least a few of the sources of support for these traditions within international society today.

The languages of rights and liberalism are probably the most frequently used in contemporary international politics. The language of rights, in particular, has become predominant. Virtually all nations now subscribe, at least in principle, to the idea of human rights. International politics today is to a significant degree a great debate about the nature and extent of such rights.

The language of liberalism, a primary resource of Western states-men from Gladstone to Carter, has also recently gained wider cur-rency. Liberalism has traditionally been a language of danger – warning, for example, of the power of the state, the threat of war, or the "statist" bias of international lawyers. But it has also been a language of global cooperation, and nowhere more obviously than in recent demands for freedom in Eastern Europe. Of course, liberalism's current triumph is connected with the crisis of legitimacy that the Marxist tradition now faces almost everywhere. As Chris Brown suggests, the language of Marxism currently seems to have power only where it can be employed to mobilize resistance against a specific threat: it may still have some resonance against US intervention in Latin America. But liberalism too has defined itself, at least in part, in response to specific threats – most recently, the specter of fascist and communist totalitarianism – and liberal idealism has tended to wax and wane in a cycle with realism. With some liberals appropriating the

Hegelian–Marxist vocabulary of the "end of history" to describe the collapse of Soviet communism, the language of realism seems to have fallen on times almost as hard as those facing Marxism. At the same time the rhetoric of realism seems to be finding a new use in debates over the security of Western access to Persian Gulf oil and over the dangers of low-intensity conflict and regional instability. Except in moments of crisis, the language of realism has never had much popular appeal, however, and realists have indeed often congratulated themselves on their unpopularity.

In contrast to realism and Marxism, the languages of biblical argument, natural law, and international law have had more stable constituencies over time. Yet the practical currency of these traditions has undergone various shifts as well. The language of natural law has lost the prestige it had between the sixteenth and eighteenth centuries, yet it has revived remarkably in debates since the Second World War on the morality of war. The languages of the biblical traditions have recently played an important role in Poland and Latin America. And, while the tradition of international law has been compromised, though perhaps not fatally, by twentieth-century efforts (clearly reflected in the League Covenant and the UN Charter) to turn it into an instrument of collective security, it is also, as Dorothy Jones points out, increasingly the language of minority groups, citizen watch organizations, and government agencies concerned with protecting human rights.

Because they are more abstruse, the Kantian-deontological, utilitarian, and contractarian traditions have little self-conscious popular support. But as Anthony Ellis observes, public discussion of the ethics of international affairs is permeated by the notion that the right decisions are those that produce the most welfare, and this pervasive "utilitarianism" is matched by an equally pervasive opposition that draws much of its vocabulary from the Kantian-deontological tradition. Of the three traditions, contractarianism is the most academic. Yet the academy has its own not inconsiderable influence. The contractarian vocabulary – of agreement, reciprocity, contractual obligation, and especially "fairness" – is widely used in popular debate on international issues, particularly when the issues are economic ones. As with utilitarianism and Kantianism, academic scribbling about the social contract will inevitably influence the way the more popular vocabulary is understood and used. In the long run, Rawls may yet have a political impact comparable to that of Bentham or Kant.

Despite the current misfortunes of Marxism, then, all these traditions can be expected to exert a continuing influence on ethical discourse regarding international affairs. One way of accounting for this influence is in terms of the perennial importance of three basic questions the traditions address. The first two questions are fundamental to ethics, for they underlie more particular judgments of right and wrong: "Is it always better to suffer than to do wrong?" and "Is it ever permissible deliberately to sacrifice some for the benefit of others?" The third question is central to both politics and international relations: "Why the state?" We can look back over the ground we have covered in this volume by briefly considering how these questions have been answered.

To the fundamental question, "Is it always better to suffer than to do wrong?" the natural-law and Kantian-deontological traditions answer "yes"; the realist, Marxist, classical contractarian, and utilitarian traditions answer "no." Of course, there are crucial qualifications. The first group of traditions, for example, is marked by differences regarding the interpretation of the precepts of common morality, their ultimate basis, and the extent to which they may be qualified by circumstances – including the circumstances of international anarchy. Various qualifications are perhaps even more critical to the second group of traditions, for none of them licenses gratuitous wrongdoing. Thus, the realist or classical contractarian may argue that it is sometimes better to do than to suffer harm – but only in cases of necessity or radical insecurity in which the claims of justice do not arise or must be overridden. Marxism says that such wrongdoing is permissible only if it advances mankind toward forms of community in which all are emancipated from dehumanizing servitude. Utilitarianism also teaches that conventional wrongdoing is permissible only if justified by the beneficial consequences to humanity. With all these qualifications, however, these traditions clearly do offer different answers to the first question.

To the second question – "Is it permissible to sacrifice some for the benefit of others?" – the answers just given remain the same, with one critical difference. While both the realist and the utilitarian are sometimes prepared to sacrifice the rights or interests of some for the benefit of others, they differ over whether special weight should be given to the interests of a particular community. This difference corresponds to our distinction between traditions that are broadly "consequence-oriented" in the sense that they judge actions to be right or wrong according to their outcomes, and those that are strictly "consequentialist" in the sense that they evaluate such outcomes from an "impersonal" or universal point of view. It also highlights again realism's emphasis on the limitations of morality.

To the question "Why the state?" there are many answers: because it is an indispensable condition of value; because it is currently the best vehicle for achieving the welfare of humanity; because it is the best approximation of a "comprehensive" community; because it is the most effective guarantor of rights; because it expresses the freedom of a self-determining group; because it rests on a contract; because it is part of a system of legal authority; or because it is useful from a tactical viewpoint in securing a world communist society. And, by extension, the traditions generate a comparable range of judgments regarding the international system. This broad summary of the kinds of answers given should remind the reader that these traditions split in different ways with respect to one of the most basic questions of domestic and international politics.

We could compare the traditions in yet other ways. Without taking our discussion too much further, perhaps one final comparison is warranted. One can account for the continuing importance of all the traditions we have considered by understanding each as an attempt to come to terms with three constants in international society: force, order, and justice. Realism and classical contractarianism emphasize that international relations is at bottom of a realm of force: force is the necessary condition of whatever international order exists. In contrast, international law emphasizes that the society of states is not simply a war of all against all, but a particular kind of order. For international law, the society of states is also a realm of justice – as long as it is understood that this is a procedural sort of justice between those who otherwise may disagree about what justice means. Most of the other traditions we have considered insist on the priority of justice over either force or order. Utilitarianism excepted, these other traditions argue that we must act according to the demands of justice, even if the heavens should fall.

It may be objected that this traditional opposition between force, order and justice can be overdrawn: as many commentators have remarked, justice presupposes order and may require force to vindicate it, and force sometimes imposes an order that is itself a minimal but necessary element of justice. Still, different developments in current international society seem to illustrate the primacy of each of these considerations. Moralists can point to powerful aspirations for freedom and common decency that are transforming large parts of the world; jurists and diplomats can point to law and diplomacy as the absolute prerequisites of international civility; and realists can point to war and nuclear deterrence as evidence of what peoples and states have always been prepared to do. Each of the traditions we have considered tries to come to terms with this sort of evidence in its own way. But because force, order, and justice can each appear paramount, it is doubtful whether there will ever be complete agreement about how we should resolve the tensions between them.

INDEX